Lecture Notes in Computer Science 2386

Edited by G. Goos, J. Hartmanis, and J. van Leeuwen

Springer
Berlin
Heidelberg
New York
Barcelona
Hong Kong
London
Milan
Paris
Tokyo

Eerke A. Boiten   Bernhard Möller (Eds.)

Mathematics of Program Construction

6th International Conference, MPC 2002
Dagstuhl Castle, Germany, July 8-10, 2002
Proceedings

Springer

Series Editors

Gerhard Goos, Karlsruhe University, Germany
Juris Hartmanis, Cornell University, NY, USA
Jan van Leeuwen, Utrecht University, The Netherlands

Volume Editors

Eerke A. Boiten
University of Kent at Canterbury, Computing Laboratory
CT2 7NF Canterbury, Kent, United Kingdom
E-mail: e.a.boiten@ukc.ac.uk

Bernhard Möller
Universität Augsburg, Institut für Informatik
Universitätsstr. 14, 86135 Augsburg, Germany
E-mail: bernhard.moeller@informatik.uni-augsburg.de

Cataloging-in-Publication Data applied for

Die Deutsche Bibliothek - CIP-Einheitsaufnahme

Mathematics of program construction : 6th international conference ;
proceedings / MPC 2002, Dagstuhl Castle, Germany, July 8 - 10, 2002. Eerke
A. Boiten ; Bernhard Möller (ed.). - Berlin ; Heidelberg ; New York ;
Barcelona ; Hong Kong ; London ; Milan ; Paris ; Tokyo : Springer, 2002
    (Lecture notes in computer science ; Vol. 2386)
    ISBN 3-540-43857-2

CR Subject Classification (1998): F.3, F.4, D.2, F.1, D.3

ISSN 0302-9743
ISBN 3-540-43857-2 Springer-Verlag Berlin Heidelberg New York

Springer-Verlag Berlin Heidelberg New York
a member of BertelsmannSpringer Science+Business Media GmbH

http://www.springer.de

© Springer-Verlag Berlin Heidelberg 2002
Printed in Germany

Typesetting: Camera-ready by author, data conversion by Christian Grosche, Hamburg
Printed on acid-free paper   SPIN 10870520   06/3142   5 4 3 2 1 0

Preface

This volume contains the proceedings of MPC 2002, the sixth international conference on the Mathematics of Program Construction. This series of conferences aims to promote the development of mathematical principles and techniques that are demonstrably useful and usable in the process of constructing computer programs (whether implemented in hardware or software). The focus is on techniques that combine precision with conciseness, enabling programs to be constructed by formal calculation. Within this theme, the scope of the series is very diverse, including programming methodology, program specification and transformation, programming paradigms, programming calculi, and programming language semantics.

The quality of the papers submitted to the conference was in general very high, and the number of submissions was comparable to that for the previous conference. Each paper was refereed by at least four, and often more, committee members.

In addition to the 11 papers selected for presentation by the program committee, this volume contains three invited talks: *Implementing Algebraic Dynamic Programming in the Functional and the Imperative Programming Paradigm* by Robert Giegerich (Technical University of Bielefeld, Germany), and abstracts of *Some Results in Dynamic Model Theory* by Dexter Kozen (Cornell University, USA) and *Mathematics in Computer Science Curricula* by Jeannette Wing (Carnegie Mellon University, USA).

The conference took place in Dagstuhl, Germany. The previous five conferences were held in 1989 in Twente, The Netherlands, in 1992 in Oxford, United Kingdom, in 1995 in Kloster Irsee, Germany, in 1998 in Marstrand near Göteborg in Sweden, and in 2000 in Ponte de Lima, Portugal. The proceedings of these conferences were published as LNCS 375, 669, 947, 1422, and 1837, respectively.

Three international events were co-located with the conference: the IFIP WG2.1 working conference on *Generic Programming*, the third workshop on *Constructive Methods for Parallel Programming*, and the workshop on *Types in Programming*. We thank the organizers of these events for their interest in sharing the atmosphere of the conference.

May 2002

Eerke Boiten
Bernhard Möller

Acknowledgments

We are very grateful to the members of the program committee and their referees for their care and diligence in reviewing the submitted papers. We are also grateful to the sponsoring institutions.

Program Committee

Roland Backhouse (UK)
Eerke Boiten (co-chair, UK)
Michael Butler (UK)
Ernie Cohen (USA)
Jules Desharnais (Canada)
Jeremy Gibbons (UK)
David Gries (USA)
Lindsay Groves (New Zealand)
Ian Hayes (Australia)
Eric Hehner (Canada)
Zhenjiang Hu (Japan)
John Hughes (Sweden)
Bart Jacobs (The Netherlands)

Johan Jeuring (The Netherlands)
Dick Kieburtz (USA)
Dexter Kozen (USA)
Rustan Leino (USA)
Christian Lengauer (Germany)
Bernhard Möller (co-chair, Germany)
David Naumann (USA)
José N. Oliveira (Portugal)
Alberto Pardo (Uruguay)
Peter Pepper (Germany)
Kaisa Sere (Finland)
Mark Utting (New Zealand)

Sponsoring Institutions

The generous support of the following companies and institutions is gratefully acknowledged:

Deutsche Forschungsgemeinschaft
University of Augsburg, Germany
University of Kent at Canterbury, UK

External Referees

All submitted papers were reviewed by members of the program committee and a number of external referees, who produced extensive review reports and without whose work the conference would lose its quality status. To the best of our knowledge the list below is accurate. We apologize for any omissions or inaccuracies.

Paulo Sérgio Almeida
Juan C. Augusto
Luís Barbosa
José Barros

Rudolf Berghammer
Gustavo Betarte
Orieta Celiku
Jörg Fischer

Daniel Fridlender
Sergei Gorlatch
Stefan Hallerstede
Christoph Herrmann

Petra Hofstedt
Andy King
Ulrike Lechner
Markus Lepper
Andres Löh
Thomas Nitsche

John O'Donnell
Luke Ong
Jorge Sousa Pinto
Michael Poppleton
Rimvydas Ruksenas
Luis Sierra

Gregor Snelting
Baltasar Trancón y
   Widemann
Stephan Weber
Jacob Wieland

Table of Contents

Invited Talks

Contributed Papers

Implementing Algebraic Dynamic Programming in the Functional and the Imperative Programming Paradigm

Robert Giegerich and Peter Steffen

Faculty of Technology, Bielefeld University
33501 Bielefeld, Germany
{robert,psteffen}@techfak.uni-bielefeld.de

Abstract. Algebraic dynamic programming is a new method for developing and reasoning about dynamic programming algorithms. In this approach, so-called yield grammars and evaluation algebras constitute abstract specifications of dynamic programming algorithms. We describe how this theory is put to practice by providing a specification language that can both be embedded in a lazy functional language, and translated into an imperative language. Parts of the analysis required for the latter translation also gives rise to source-to-source transformations that improve the asymptotic efficiency of the functional implementation. The multi-paradigm system resulting from this approach provides increased programming productivity and effective validation.

1 Motivation

1.1 Towards a Discipline of Dynamic Programming

Dynamic Programming (DP)[2] is a well-established and widely used programming technique. In recent years, the advances of molecular biology have created thriving interest in dynamic programming algorithms over strings, since genomic data pose sequence analysis problems in unprecedented complexity and data volume [4]. In this context, it became apparent that there is the lack of a formal method for developing the intricate matrix recurrences that typically constitute a DP algorithm.

1.2 A Short Review of ADP

Algebraic dynamic programming (ADP) is a technique designed to alleviate this situation. Postponing technical definitions to later sections, the ADP approach can be summarised as follows: Any DP algorithm evaluates a search space of candidate solutions under a scoring scheme and an objective function. The classical DP recurrences reflect the three aspects of search space construction, scoring and choice, and efficiency in an indiscriminable fashion. In the new algebraic approach, these concerns are separated. The search space is described by a so-called yield grammar, evaluation and choice by an algebra, and efficiency concerns can

E.A. Boiten and B. Möller (Eds.): MPC 2002, LNCS 2386, pp. 1–20, 2002.

be pursued on a very high level of abstraction. No subscripts, no (subscript) errors.

Based on the abstract concepts of yield grammars and evaluation algebras, ADP is essentially a piece of programming theory. The present paper is concerned with putting this theory into practice.

1.3   Overview of this Contribution

Section 2 reviews the central notion of the ADP approach and introduces a domain-specific notation for describing ADP algorithms. The core of implementing ADP algorithms (in either programming paradigm) is the technique of tabulating yield parsers, introduced in Section 3. An embedding of ADP notation in Haskell is given in Section 4, which allows rapid prototyping, but has some methodical and some practical limitations. Section 5 is dedicated to compilation techniques, which allow to generate either optimised ADP/Haskell notation or C code. Finally, Section 6 describes the overall style of algorithm development that arises from this approach.

1.4   Related Work

The wide use of DP in bioinformatics is documented in [4], but without methodical guidance. The relation between parsing and dynamic programming is discussed as an open problem in [17].

Yield parsing, as introduced here, takes a string as its input, and therefore, although based on a tree grammar, it is more closely related to string than to tree parsing methods. Its closest relatives are methods for parsing ambiguous context free languages, such as Earley's or the CYK algorithm [1].

The ADP approach has evolved in the recent years in the application context of biosequence analysis. An informal description of the method is found in [6], the first rigorous definition is given in [8], while some applications have appeared earlier: The first application developed in the spirit of the yet-to-be-developed ADP method is a program for aligning recombinant DNA [7]. ADP has further been applied to solve the problem of folding saturated RNA secondary structures, posed by Zuker and Sankoff in 1984 [5, 21]. An application to statistical scoring in pattern matching is reported in [14]. The development of the ADP compiler described here is new and based on ongoing research [19].

2   Tree Grammars and Yield Languages

2.1   Basic Terminology

Alphabets. An *alphabet* $\mathcal{A}$ is a finite set of symbols. Sequences of symbols are called strings. ε denotes the empty string, $\mathcal{A}^1 = \mathcal{A}$, $\mathcal{A}^{n+1} = \{aw | a \in \mathcal{A}, w \in \mathcal{A}^n\}$, $\mathcal{A}^+ = \bigcup_{n \geq 1} \mathcal{A}^n$, $\mathcal{A}^* = \mathcal{A}^+ \cup \{\varepsilon\}$. By convention, a denotes a single symbol, w and x a string over $\mathcal{A}^*$.

Signatures and Algebras. A (single-sorted) signature Σ over some alphabet $\mathcal{A}$ consists of a sort symbol S together with a family of operators. Each operator o has a fixed arity $o : s_1...s_{k_o} \to S$, where each s_i is either S or $\mathcal{A}$. A Σ-algebra $\mathcal{I}$ over $\mathcal{A}$, also called an interpretation, is a set $\mathcal{S_I}$ of values together with a function o_I for each operator o. Each o_I has type $o_I : (s_1)_I...(s_{k_o})_I \to S_I$ where $\mathcal{A}_I = \mathcal{A}$.

A *term algebra* T_Σ arises by interpreting the operators in Σ as *constructors*, building bigger terms from smaller ones. When variables from a set V can take the place of arguments to constructors, we speak of a term algebra with variables, $T_\Sigma(V)$, with $V \subset T_\Sigma(V)$.

Trees and Tree Patterns. Terms will be viewed as rooted, ordered, node-labelled trees in the obvious way. Note that only leaf nodes can carry symbols from $\mathcal{A}$. A term/tree with variables is called a *tree pattern*. A tree containing a designated occurrence of a subtree t is denoted $C[...t...]$. We adopt the view that the tree constructors represent some structure that is associated explicitly with the sequence of leaf symbols from $\mathcal{A}^*$. The nullary constructors that may reside at leaf nodes are not considered part of the yield. Hence the yield function y on $T_\Sigma(V)$ is defined by $y(t) = w$, where $w \in (\mathcal{A} \cup V)^*$ is the sequence of leaf symbols from $\mathcal{A}$ and V in left to right order.

2.2   Tree Grammars

A tree language over Σ is a subset of T_Σ. Tree languages are described by tree grammars, which can be defined in analogy to the Chomsky hierarchy of string grammars. Here we use regular tree grammars originally studied in [3], with the algebraic flavour introduced in [9]. Our specialisation so far lies solely with the distinguished role of the alphabet $\mathcal{A}$.

Definition 1. *(Tree Grammar) A regular tree grammar $\mathcal{G}$ over Σ is given by*

  – *a set V of nonterminal symbols,*
  – *a designated nonterminal symbol Ax called the axiom,*
  – *a set P of productions of the form $v \to t$, where $v \in V$ and $t \in T_\Sigma(V)$.*

The derivation relation for tree grammars is $\to^*$, with $C[...v...] \to C[...t...]$ if $v \to t \in P$. The language of $v \in V$ is $\mathcal{L}(v) = \{t \in T_\Sigma | v \to^* t\}$, the language of $\mathcal{G}$ is $\mathcal{L}(\mathcal{G}) = \mathcal{L}(Ax)$. For arbitrary $q \in T_\Sigma(V)$ we define $\mathcal{L}(q) = \{t \in T_\Sigma | q \to^* t\}$. □

2.3   Lexical Level and Conditional Productions

The following two extensions are motivated by the fact that yield grammars are to be used as a programming device. We add a *lexical level* to our grammars. As with context free grammars, this is not necessary from a theoretical point of view, but makes examples less trivial and applications more concise. In the sequel we shall admit strings over $\mathcal{A}^*$ in place of single symbols. By convention, the terminal symbol `char` will denote an arbitrary symbol from $\mathcal{A}$, and the terminal symbol `string` will denote a string from $\mathcal{A}^*$.

Our tree grammars will further be augmented with *conditional productions*. Their meaning is explained as a conditional form of derivation:

Definition 2. *(Conditional Productions) A conditional production has the form $v \xrightarrow{c} t$ where c is a predicate defined on $\mathcal{A}^*$. A derivation using a conditional production, $v \xrightarrow{c} t \rightarrow^* t'$, where $t' \in T_\Sigma$, is well-formed only if $c(y(t'))$ holds. The language of a tree grammar with conditions is the set of trees that can be derived from the axiom by well-formed derivations.* □

Note that the use of a conditional production $v \xrightarrow{c} t$ with c at some point in a derivation affects the complete derivation that continues from the subtree t inserted by this production. Only after the derivation is complete, the condition can be checked. A typical example is a condition that imposes a minimal or maximal length on $y(t')$.

2.4   Examples: Palindromes and Separated Palindromes

Figure 1 shows four simple tree grammars for palindromic languages, depending on the choice of the axiom. They describe separated palindromes (*pal1*) of the form uvu^{-1}, and approximate separated palindromes (*pal3*) under the standard edit distance model of single character (R)eplacements, (D)eletions and (I)nsertions [11]. Operator N marks the middle part v of uvu^{-1}. Choosing axioms *pal2* or *pal4*, we obtain local palindromes, embedded in an arbitrary context string. Note that this example makes use of a syntactic predicate $equal(a_1...a_n) = a_1 \equiv a_n$ and the lexical symbols `char`, `string` as described in Section 2.3. Note that $t \in \mathcal{L}(\mathrm{Pal}_i)$ explicitly describes the internal structure of a palindrome, while the palindromic string by itself is $y(t)$.

Figure 2 shows two examples for the input sequence `panamacanal`, each with term representation and the corresponding tree.

2.5   Yield Languages and the Yield Parsing Problem

We can now define the particular parsing problem we shall have to solve:

Definition 3. *(Yield Grammars and Yield Languages) The pair $(\mathcal{G}, y)$ is called a yield grammar, and its yield language $\mathcal{L}(\mathcal{G}, y) = y(\mathcal{L}(\mathcal{G}))$.* □

Definition 4. *(Yield Parsing) Given a yield grammar $(\mathcal{G}, y)$ over $\mathcal{A}$ and $w \in \mathcal{A}^*$, the yield parsing problem is to construct $P_\mathcal{G}(w) := \{t \in \mathcal{L}(\mathcal{G}) | y(t) = w\}$.* □

Compared to string languages described by context free grammars – such as programming languages – yield languages that arise in practise are often trivial and could be defined by much simpler means. For example, $\mathcal{L}(\mathrm{Pal}_i, y)$ is $\mathcal{A}^*$ for all four example grammars. Here, all our interest lies in determining the trees $P_\mathcal{G}(w)$, which represent various palindromic structures we associate with a given yield string w.

Note that the trees $P_\mathcal{G}(w)$ returned by a yield parser are not derivation trees according to $\mathcal{G}$, but terminal trees derivable by $\mathcal{G}$ with yield w.

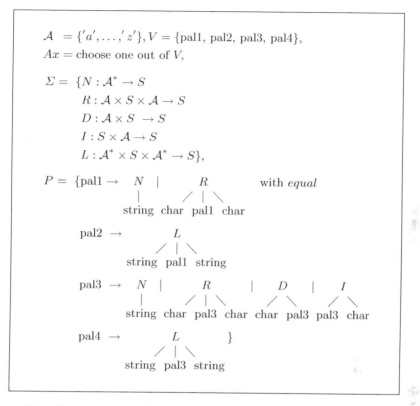

$$\mathcal{A} = \{'a', \dots, 'z'\}, V = \{\text{pal1, pal2, pal3, pal4}\},$$
$$Ax = \text{choose one out of } V,$$

$$\begin{aligned}
\Sigma = \{ &N : \mathcal{A}^* \rightarrow S \\
&R : \mathcal{A} \times S \times \mathcal{A} \rightarrow S \\
&D : \mathcal{A} \times S \rightarrow S \\
&I : S \times \mathcal{A} \rightarrow S \\
&L : \mathcal{A}^* \times S \times \mathcal{A}^* \rightarrow S\},
\end{aligned}$$

Fig. 1. Tree Grammars Pal_1 through Pal_4, depending on the choice of the axiom

2.6   Yield Languages versus Context Free Languages

For the record, we dwell a moment on aspects of formal language theory and show that yield languages are context free languages, and vice versa. This allows to carry over useful (un)decidability results (such as emptiness or ambiguity) from context free languages to yield languages.

Definition 5. *(Flat Grammar) The flat grammar associated with the yield grammar* $(\mathcal{G}, y)$, *where* $\mathcal{G} = (V, Ax, P)$ *is the context free string grammar* $y(\mathcal{G}) = (V, \mathcal{A}, Ax, \{v \quad y(t) | v \rightarrow t \in P\})$. □

Note that several distinct productions of the tree grammar may map to the same production in the flat grammar.

By construction, $\mathcal{L}(y(\mathcal{G})) = \mathcal{L}((\mathcal{G}, y))$ – for each derivation in $\mathcal{G}$ there is one in $y(\mathcal{G})$, and vice versa. So, yield languages are context free languages. The converse is also true. Each string grammar $\mathcal{G}'$ can be turned into a corresponding tree grammar by naming its productions, and using these names with suitable arities as operators of Σ. Each tree derived by this tree grammar is a syntax tree in $\mathcal{G}'$, labelled by explicit production names. We conclude:

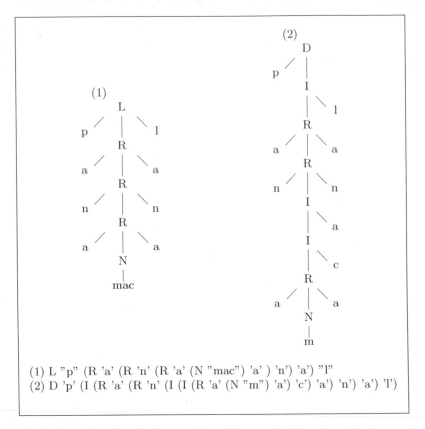

(1) L "p" (R 'a' (R 'n' (R 'a' (N "mac") 'a') 'n') 'a') "l"
(2) D 'p' (I (R 'a' (R 'n' (I (I (R 'a' (N "m") 'a') 'c') 'a') 'n') 'a') 'l')

Fig. 2. A local separated palindrome derived from pal2 (1) and a global approximate palindrome derived from pal3 (2)

Theorem 6. *The class of yield languages is the class of context free languages.*
□

2.7 Evaluation Algebras

Definition 7. *(Evaluation Algebra) Let Σ be a signature with sort symbol Ans. A Σ-evaluation algebra is a Σ-algebra augmented with an objective function $h : [Ans] \to [Ans]$, where $[Ans]$ denotes lists over Ans.* □

In most DP applications, the purpose of the objective function is minimising or maximising over all answers. We take a slightly more general view here. The objective may be to calculate a sample of answers, or all answers within a certain threshold of optimality. It could even be a complete enumeration of answers. We may compute the size of the search space or evaluate it in some statistical fashion, say by averaging over all answers, and so on. This is why in general, the objective function will return a list of answers. If maximisation was the objective, this list would hold the maximum as its only element.

2.8   Algebraic Dynamic Programming and Bellman's Principle

Given that yield parsing traverses the search space, all that is left to do is evaluate candidates in some algebra and apply the objective function.

Definition 8. *(Algebraic Dynamic Programming)*

- *An ADP problem is specified by a signature Σ over $\mathcal{A}$, a yield grammar $(\mathcal{G}, y)$ over Σ, and a Σ-evaluation algebra I with objective function h_I.*
- *An ADP problem instance is posed by a string $w \in \mathcal{A}^*$. The search space it spawns is the set of all its parses, $P_{\mathcal{G}}(w)$.*
- *Solving an ADP problem is computing*

$$h_I\{t_I \mid t \in P_{\mathcal{G}}(w)\}.$$

□

There is one essential ingredient missing: efficiency. Since the size of the search space may be exponential in terms of input size, an ADP problem can be solved in polynomial time and space only under the condition known as Bellman's principle of optimality. In his own words:

> An optimal policy has the property that whatever the initial state and initial decision are, the remaining decisions must constitute an optimal policy with regard to the state resulting from the first decision. [2]

We can now formalise this principle:

Definition 9. *(Algebraic Version of Bellman's Principle)*   For each k-ary operator f in Σ, and all answer lists $z_1, \ldots, z_k$, the objective function h satisfies

$$h(\ [\ f(x_1, \ldots, x_k) \mid x_1 \leftarrow z_1, \ldots, x_k \leftarrow z_k\ ]\ )$$
$$= h(\ [\ f(x_1, \ldots, x_k) \mid x_1 \leftarrow h(z_1), \ldots, x_k \leftarrow h(z_k)\ ]\ )$$

Additionally, the same property holds for the concatenation of answer lists:

$$h(\ z_1 \mathbin{+\!\!+} z_2\ ) = h(\ h(z_1) \mathbin{+\!\!+} h(z_2)\ )$$

□

The practical meaning of the optimality principle is that we may push the application of the objective function inside the computation of subproblems, thus preventing combinatorial explosion. We shall annotate the tree grammar to indicate the cases where h is to be applied.

Compared to the classic description of DP algorithm via matrix recurrences, we have achieved the following:

- An ADP specification is *more abstract* than the traditional recurrences. Separation between search space construction and evaluation is perfect. Tree grammars and evaluation algebras can be combined in a modular way, and the relationships between problem variants can be explained clearly.

- The ADP specification is also *more complete*: DP algorithms in the literature often claim to be parametric with respect to the scoring function, while the initialisation equations are considered part of the search algorithm [4]. In ADP, it becomes clear that initialisation semantically is the evaluation of empty candidates, and is specified within the algebra.
- Our formalisation of Bellman's principle is *more general* than commonly seen. Objectives like complete enumeration or statistical evaluation of the search space now fall under the framework. If maximisation is the objective, our criterion implies Morin's formalisation (strict monotonicity) [15] as a special case.
- The ADP specification is *more reliable*. The absence of subscripts excludes a large class of errors that are traditionally hard to find.

2.9   The ADP Programming Language

Yield Grammars in ASCII Notation. For lack of space, we can only show the core of the ADP language. The declarative semantics of this language is simply that it allows to describe signatures, evaluation algebras and yield grammars. The signature Σ is written as an algebraic data type definition in Haskell. Alike EBNF, the productions of the yield grammar are written as equations. The operator <<< is used to denote the application of a tree constructor to its arguments, which are chained via the ~~~-operator. Operator ||| separates multiple righthand sides of a nonterminal symbol. The axiom symbol is indicated by the keyword axiom, and conditions are attached to productions via the keyword with. Finally, the application of the objective function h is indicated via the ...-operator. Here is one of our example grammars in ADP language:

```
data Palindrome =
   N  (Int, Int)      |  R  Char Palindrome Char |
   D  Char Palindrome |  I        Palindrome Char

grammar_Pal3 x  = axiom pal3    where
   pal3  =  N <<< string                     |||
            R <<< char   ~~~ pal3 ~~~ char    |||
            D <<< char   ~~~ pal3             |||
            I <<<            pal3 ~~~ char    ... h
```

The operational semantics of Section 4 turns this little program into a yield parser for Grammar Pal$_3$.

From Yield Parsing to Algebraic Dynamic Programming. The tree parser becomes a generic dynamic programming algorithm by replacing the signature Σ (Palindrome in our example) by an arbitrary Σ-evaluation algebra, which becomes a parameter to the grammar. Tabulation is controlled via the keywords tabulated and p.[1] -~~ and ~~- are variants of the ~~~-operator, which are equivalent in their declarative semantics (cf. 4.3).

---

[1] The initial binding clauses serve the Haskell embedding and are explained below. All lines preceded by > jointly result in an executable Haskell program.

```
> import Array

> type Palindrome_Algebra answer =
>    ((Int,Int)                      -> answer,   -- evaluation function n
>     Char        -> answer -> Char -> answer,   -- evaluation function r
>     Char        -> answer          -> answer,   -- evaluation function d
>     answer      -> Char            -> answer,   -- evaluation function i
>     [answer]    -> [answer])                    -- objective   function h

> grammar_Pal3 alg x  = axiom (p pal3)    where
>    (n, r, d, i, h)   = alg
>    axiom ax   = ax (0,m)
>    (_, m)     = bounds x
>    tabulated  = table m
>    char (i,j) = [x!j | i+1 == j]

>    pal3 = tabulated(
>             n <<< string                        |||
>             r <<< char  -~~ p pal3 ~~- char      |||
>             d <<< char  -~~ p pal3               |||
>             i <<<           p pal3 ~~- char       ... h)
```

3   Tabulating Yield Parsers

3.1   The Yield Parsing "Paradox"

Yield parsers, to be developed in this section, will serve as the computational engine for implementing ADP algorithms. Our claim is that ADP applies generally to dynamic programming over sequence data. Apparently, there is a contradiction:

On the one hand, there exist DP algorithms of various polynomial complexities, such as diverse $O(n^2)$ algorithms for sequence comparison [4], $O(n^3)$ algorithms for RNA structure prediction [21], or the $O(n^6)$-algorithm of Rivas and Eddy [16] for folding RNA pseudoknots.

On the other hand, we have learned in Section 2.6 that yield languages are context free languages. The trees to be delivered by a yield parser are built from the operators of the underlying signature, but otherwise isomorphic to syntax trees returned by a context free parser for the corresponding flat grammar. We know that languages defined by ambiguous context free string grammars can be parsed in $O(n^3)$ by the CYK algorithm [1] or even slightly faster [18, 20]. Two questions come to mind:

1. Why should we introduce yield languages at all – could we not stick with string grammars and their established parsing methods?
2. Wouldn't this imply that we can solve all dynamic programming problems in the scope of ADP in $O(n^3)$? Or, formulated the other way, does this mean that the scope of ADP is limited to dynamic programming problems within the $O(n^3)$ complexity class?

Let us first note that Question 1 is correct in the sense that there is a simple and general tree grammar transformation that makes the yield parser run in $O(n^3)$. Each tree returned by the parser can be postprocessed in $O(n)$ to correspond to the original grammar. This makes Question 2 even more puzzling.

Well, ADP *is* a general method, not limited to $O(n^3)$ algorithms, so something essential must have been overlooked in Question 1. It is the fact that the yield parser's obligation is not just to determine the parse trees. It must construct them in a special way, in order to provide for amalgamation of recognition and evaluation phase (cf. Section 2.8). Remember that the trees constructed are formulas of T_Σ, to be interpreted in the evaluation algebra I. The parser must construct the trees such that, at any point, a (partial) tree t can be substituted by the (partial) answer value t_I. Only so, the choice function can be applied to partial answers and prevent the combinatorial explosion of their number. This prevents the use of grammar transformations that might speed up the parsing.

3.2   Adopting the CYK Parsing Algorithm

We shall adopt the so-called Cocke-Younger-Kasami (CYK) parsing technique for ambiguous context free grammars [1] to yield parsing. Two problems arise:

- Two tree productions like $v \to N(w), v \to M(w)$ both correspond to the same string production $v \to w$. In order not to loose results, the yield parser must be based directly on $\mathcal{G}$ rather than a string grammar.
- CYK relies on a transformation of the string grammar into Chomsky normal form. Such a transformation is not allowed in our case, as it would imply a change of the signature underlying the tree grammar.

Neither the explicit transformation to Chomsky normal form, nor the implicit transformation of the Graham-Harrison parser [10] can be used. We shall start with a nondeterministic, top-down parser that is subsequently transformed into a CYK-style parser implemented via dynamic programming.

3.3   Top-Down Nondeterministic Yield Parsers

For a given yield string w, the set $P_\mathcal{G}(w)$ of all its parses can be defined recursively using the productions of $\mathcal{G}$. For $v \in V$ and $a \in \mathcal{A}^*$ we define the sets of parses $P_v(w)$ and $P_a(w)$, respectively. Without loss of generality we assume that all productions for a nonterminal v are defined via a single rule with alternative righthand sides, in the form $v \to q_1|...|q_r$. Possibly different conditions c_i can be associated with each alternative q_i, denoted q_i with c_i.

$$P_v(w) = P_{q_1}(w) \cup ... \cup P_{q_r}(w) \quad \text{for} \quad v \in V \tag{1}$$

For the tree patterns on the righthand sides, we define the parse sets $P_q(w)$ via structural recursion over pattern q:

$$P_a(w) = \text{if } w = a \text{ then } \{a\} \text{ else } \emptyset \text{ for } a \in \mathcal{A} \tag{2}$$
$$P_N(w) = \text{if } w = \epsilon \text{ then } \{N\} \text{ else } \emptyset \text{ for } N \in \Sigma \tag{3}$$
$$P_q(w) = \{N(x_1, ..., x_r) | x_i \in P_{q_i}(w_i) \text{ for } q = N(q_1, ..., q_r), \tag{4}$$
$$w = w_1...w_r\}$$
$$P_{q \text{ with } c}(w) = \text{if } c(w) \text{ then } P_q(w) \text{ else } \emptyset \tag{5}$$

Note that in Equation 4, w is split into r subwords in all possible ways. Finally, we define

$$P_\mathcal{G}(w) = \widehat{P_{Ax}(w)} \tag{6}$$

where $\widehat{P_{Ax}(w)}$ is the P_{Ax}-component of the least fixpoint solution to the above equation system.

We now turn the equation system into a top-down, recursive yield parser. Subwords of a string $w = a_1...a_n$ are indicated by index pairs: $w_{(i,j)} = a_{i+1}...a_j$. The length of $w_{(i,j)}$ is $j - i$, and $w_{(i,k)}w_{(k,j)} = w_{(i,j)}$. When w is the string to be parsed, we often write (i,j) instead of $w_{(i,j)}$. Parsers are functions defined on yield strings, returning lists (rather than sets) of trees. A parser $p_v(w)$ computes $P_v(w)$, for each $v \in V$. A parser fails by returning an empty list. We shall use list comprehension notation, in analogy to set notation: $[f(x,y)|x \subset xs, y \subset ys, \phi(x,y)]$ denotes the list of all values $f(x,y)$ such that x is from the list xs, y from the list ys, and the argument pair (x,y) satisfies the predicate ϕ. $[\,]$ denotes the empty list, ++ denotes list concatenation.

$$p_\mathcal{G}(w) = p_{Ax}(0, n) \tag{7}$$
$$p_v(i,j) = p_{q_1}(i,j)++...++p_{q_r}(i,j) \qquad \text{for } v \in V \tag{8}$$
$$p_a(i,j) = \text{if } w_{(i,j)} = a \text{ then } [a] \text{ else } [\,] \quad \text{for } a \in \mathcal{A} \tag{9}$$
$$p_N(i,j) = \text{if } w_{(i,j)} = \epsilon \text{ then } [N] \text{ else } [\,] \quad \text{for } N \in \Sigma \tag{10}$$
$$p_q(i,j) = [t(x_1, ..., x_r) | x_1 \in p_{q_1}(i, k_1), ..., x_r \in p_{q_r}(k_{r-1}, j)] \tag{11}$$
$$\text{for } q = t(q_1, ..., q_r), \ t \in \Sigma, \ i \le k_1... \le k_{r-1} \le j$$
$$p_q(i,j) = [t | t \in p_{q'}(i,j), c(i,j)] \qquad \text{for } q = q' \text{ with } c \tag{12}$$

The partial correctness of the yield parsers is obvious, as they are an operational form of the equations defining the parse sets $P_v(w)$. Termination, however, is a problem. The parser does not terminate if the grammar allows an infinite set of parses, resulting from circular productions chains that produce tree nodes, but an empty contribution to the yield (e.g. $v \rightarrow N(v)$). The parser may also run into futile recursion when $p_v(i,j)$ recalls itself on the same subword (i,j) in the production $v \rightarrow N(v,a), a \in \mathcal{A}$, rather than restricting its efforts to $(i, j - 1)$. And even when termination occurs, the parser will surely enjoy the thrills of combinatorial explosion, because its top-down nature leads it to parsing certain subtrees an exponential number of times. Two more steps are needed to turn the yield parser into an effective and efficient program.

3.4   Tabulating Yield Parsers

We turn the nondeterministic, top-down parser into a bottom-up CYK-style parser in two steps: We add tabulation of parser results, and we provide the necessary bottom-up control structure.

Adding Tabulation. Dynamic programming is recursion combined with tabulation of intermediate results. A DP table is nothing but a function mapping a (finite) index domain to some values. When f is a function of a pair of integers, let us denote by $f!$ a table such that $f!(i,j) = f(i,j)$.[2] Reconsider equations 7 - 12. Replace each occurrence of a parser p_v on either side of the equations by the corresponding table $p_v!$, according to the notation introduced above. E. g., a parser call $p_v(i,j)$ now turns into the table lookup $p_v!(i,j)$, and Equation 8 turns into a table definition $p_v!(i,j) = ...$. There is no need to tabulate parsers $p_\mathcal{G}$ and p_a, as they perform only a constant amount of computation per call. Parsers p_q need not be tabulated either, as they do not perform redundant work once all the p_v are tabulated. In pasting together the trees they construct, the parsers p_q use pointers to subtrees already stored in the tables $p_v!$, rather than copying subtrees.

Adding Control Structure. Unless we assume a data-flow oriented implementation language, we must organise the calculation of table entries in a way such that all entries are computed before they are used. Furthermore, the splitting of subwords in Equation 11 should be restricted to subwords of appropriate size.

Definition 10. *(Yield Size) The yield size of a nonterminal symbol v of grammar $\mathcal{G}$ is the pair $(\inf_{x \in y(\mathcal{L}(v))} |x|, \sup_{x \in y(\mathcal{L}(v))} |x|)$ if $\mathcal{L}(v) \neq \emptyset$, and $(\infty, 0)$ otherwise.* □

Since all parser calls only access parser results on the same or a smaller subword of the input, all the recurrences as derived in the previous paragraph are arranged in a double for-loop, such that shorter subwords are parsed before longer ones. Parsers that do not need tabulation are defined outside these for-loops.
In the loop body, recurrences for all tabulated parsers are arranged in dependency order. The notation $p_{q_i}?(k_{i-1}, k_i)$ denotes $p_v!(k_{i-1}, k_i)$ if q_i is a variable v and hence p_v is tabulated, and otherwise it denotes $p_{q_i}(k_{i-1}, k_i)$. Equation 16 gives rise to inner loops, with subscript ranges determined by yield size analysis. For $q \in T_\Sigma(V)$ this analysis computes $low'(q) = \inf_{t \in \mathcal{L}(q)} |y(t)|$ and $up'(q) = \sup_{t \in \mathcal{L}(q)} |y(t)|$. This is detailed in Section 5.2. Altogether, we obtain the following refined definition for the tabulating yield parser:

---

[2] This notation is borrowed from Haskell, where $(f!)$ actually turns an array into a function.

$$p_{\mathcal{G}}(w) \quad = p_{Ax}(0, n) \tag{13}$$

$$p_a(i, j) \quad = \text{if } w_{(i,j)} = a \text{ then } [a] \text{ else } [\,] \qquad \text{for } a \in \mathcal{A}^* \tag{14}$$

$$p_N(i, j) \quad = \text{if } w_{(i,j)} = \epsilon \text{ then } [N] \text{ else } [\,] \qquad \text{for } N \in \Sigma \tag{15}$$

$$p_q(i, j) \quad = [t(x_1, ..., x_r)|x_1 \in p_{q_1}?(i, k_1), ..., x_r \in p_{q_r}?(k_{r-1}, j)]$$
$$\text{for } q = t(q_1, ..., q_r), t \in \Sigma \tag{16}$$

$$\text{for } k_1, ..., k_{r-1} \quad \text{such that } k_0 = i, \; k_r = j,$$
$$max(k_{i-1} + low'(q_i))(k_{i+1} - up'(q_{i+1})) \le k_i \le$$
$$min(k_{i-1} + up'(q_i))(k_{i+1} - low'(q_{i+1}))$$

$$p_q(i, j) = [t|t \in p_{q'}(i, j), c(i, j)] \qquad \text{for } q = q' \text{ with } c \tag{17}$$
$$\text{for } j = 0 \text{ to } n$$
$$\text{for } i = 0 \text{ to } j$$
$$p_v!(i, j) = p_{q_1}(i, j)\text{++}...\text{++}p_{q_r}(i, j) \qquad \text{for } v \in V \tag{18}$$

3.5   Asymptotic Efficiency of Tabulating Yield Parsers

The number of parses for $w \in \mathcal{A}^*$ can be exponential in $|w|$. An example is the grammar $v \to N(a, v) \mid M(a, v) \mid b$, where the yield string $a^n b$ has 2^n parses. In such a case, the size of the answer dominates the computational cost both in terms of time and space. In the subsequent analysis, we assume that the number of parses computed is bounded by a constant k. This is achieved by application of the objective function. Often only one or the k-best parses are retained, subject to some criterion of optimality.

The space requirements of the yield parser are determined by the table sizes. There are at most $|V|$ tables of size $(n+1) \times (n+1)$, yielding $O(n^2 * |V| * k)$ overall. For the runtime efficiency of a yield parser, the critical issue is the number of moving subword boundaries when w is split into subwords $w_1...w_r$ according to Equation 16. If for all i, $|w_i|$ is proportional to $|w|$, then this splitting introduces an $(r - 1)$-fold nested for-loop in addition to the double for-loop iterating over subwords (i, j). Yield size analysis serves to avoid this worst case where possible.

Definition 11. (*Width of Productions and Grammar*) *Let t be a tree pattern, and let k be the number of nonterminal or lexical symbols in t whose yield size is not bounded from above. We define $width(t) = k - 1$. Let π be a production $v \to q_1| ... |q_r$. $width(\pi) = max\{width(q_1, ..., q_r)\}$, and $width(\mathcal{G}) = max\{width(\pi) \mid \pi \text{ production in } \mathcal{G}\}$.* $\square$

Theorem 12. *The execution time of a tabulating yield parser for tree grammar $\mathcal{G}$ on input w of length n is $O(n^{2+width(\mathcal{G})})$.*

Proof: *The outer for-loops lead to a minimal effort of $O(n^2)$. Inner for-loops generated from the righthand side patterns do not contribute to asymptotic efficiency if their index range is independent of n. The maximum nesting of for-loops with index range proportional to n arising from a given production is equal to the width of the production. Hence, the width of the grammar determines overall asymptotic efficiency as stated.* $\square$

Grammar transformations can greatly improve efficiency, but their feasibility depends on properties of the evaluation algebra. Two such transformations are described with the program development methods in [8].

4   Embedding ADP in Haskell

The ADP notation was designed such that its operational semantics can be defined adapting the technique of parser combinators [13].

4.1   Parser and Combinator Definitions

The input is an array x with bounds $(1, n)$. A subword $x_{i+1}, ..., x_j$ of x is represented by the subscript pair (i,j). Functions char and axiom explicitly depending on input x and $n = length\ x$ are given for documentation here; they must actually be defined within the main function. A parser is a function that given a subword of the input, returns a list of all its parses. The lexical parser char recognises any subword of length 1 and returns it, while string recognises a possibly empty subword.

```
> type Parser b = (Int,Int) -> [b]

  char :: Parser Char
  char (i,j) = [x!j | i+1 == j]

> string :: Parser (Int,Int)
> string (i,j) = [(i,j) | i <= j]
```

The nonterminal symbols are interpreted as parsers, with the productions serving as their mutually recursive definitions. The operators introduced in ADP notation are defined as parser combinators: ||| concatenates result lists of alternative parses, and <<< grabs the results of subsequent parsers connected via ~~~ and successively "pipes" them into the tree constructor. Combinator ... applies the objective function to a list of answers.

```
> infixr 6 |||
> (|||)          :: Parser b -> Parser b -> Parser b
> (|||) r q (i,j) = r (i,j) ++ q (i,j)

> infix  8 <<<
> (<<<)          :: (b -> c) -> Parser b -> Parser c
> (<<<) f q (i,j) =  map f (q (i,j))

> infixl 7 ~~~
> (~~~)          :: Parser (b -> c) -> Parser b -> Parser c
> (~~~) r q (i,j) =  [f y | k <- [i..j], f <- r (i,k), y <- q (k,j)]

> infix  5 ...
> (...)          :: Parser a -> ([a] -> [a]) -> Parser a
> (...) p h (i,j)  = h (p (i,j))
```

The operational meaning of a with-clause can be defined by turning with into a combinator, this time combining a parser with a filter. Finally, the keyword axiom of the grammar is interpreted as a function that returns all parses for the axiom symbol ax and the complete input.

```
> type Filter    =  (Int, Int) -> Bool
> with           :: Parser a -> Filter -> Parser a
> with p c (i,j) =  if c (i,j) then p (i,j)  else []

  axiom          :: Parser a -> [a]
  axiom ax       =  ax (0,n)
```

Although these functions are called parsers, they do not necessarily deliver trees. The answers are solely computed via the functions of the evaluation algebra, whatever their type is.

4.2   Tabulation

As in Section 3, adding tabulation is merely a change of data type. The function table records the results of a parser p for all subwords of an input of size n. The function p is table lookup. Note the invariance p (table n f) = f.

```
> type Parsetable a = Array (Int,Int) [a]

> table       :: Int -> Parser a -> Parsetable a
> table n q =  array ((0,0),(n,n))
>                     [((i,j),q (i,j)) | i<- [0..n], j<- [i..n]]

> p           :: Parsetable a -> Parser a
> p t (i,j) =  if i <= j then t!(i,j) else []
```

4.3   Yield Parser Combinators for Bounded Yields

If the length of the yield of a nonterminal v is restricted to a fixed interval known from yield size analysis, the ~~-combinator may be used to restrict the parsing effort to subwords of appropriate length range. Note the direct correspondence to the calculation of the loop bounds k_i defined in Equation 16.

```
> infixl 7 ~~,-~~ , ~~-
> (~~) :: (Int,Int) -> (Int,Int)
>        -> Parser (b -> c) -> Parser b -> Parser c
> (~~) (l,u) (l',u') r q (i,j)
>        = [x y | k <- [max (i+1) (j-u') .. min (i+u) (j-l')],
>                 x <- r (i,k), y <- q (k,j)]

> (-~~) q r (i,j) = [x y | i<j, x <- q (i,i+1), y <- r (i+1,j)]
> (~~-) q r (i,j) = [x y | i<j, x <- q (i,j-1), y <- r (j-1,j)]
```

The combinators -~~ and ~~- are special cases of the ~~~ combinator in another way: they restrict the lefthand (respectively righthand) parser to a single character. The parser pal3 in Section 2.9 avoids all uses of ~~~ and runs in $O(n^2)$.

5   Compiling and Optimising ADP Algorithms

5.1   Experience with the Haskell Implementation

For about two years, we have been using the Haskell embedding for reformulation and unification of classical DP algorithms, for teaching, and for development of new applications. While this has been a worthwhile effort intellectually, there are two serious shortcomings of this approach from the practical point of view. The first concern is efficiency. Although the Haskell prototype has the same asymptotic efficiency as an imperative implementation, its space requirements prohibit application to large size biosequence data.

The second concern is a methodical one: In sophisticated examples, we strive for best runtime efficiency by using the special combinators for bounded yields wherever possible. This is sometimes nontrivial, and always error-prone. Based on this experience, it appears most beneficial to automate yield size and dependency analysis.

5.2   Yield Size Analysis

Let $\mathbb{N}^\infty = \mathbb{N} \cup \{\infty\}$. The minimal and maximal yield sizes for all nonterminal symbols are described by a pair of functions $low, up : V \to \mathbb{N}^\infty$ and their extensions to arbitrary tree patterns $low', up' : T_\Sigma(V) \to \mathbb{N}^\infty$. They are computed using the following equation system: Let $v \to q_1|...|q_r$ be the production defining v.

$$(low(v),\ up(v)) \quad = (\min_{i=1}^{r} low'(q_i),\ \max_{i=1}^{r} up'(q_i)) \qquad \text{for } v \in V \qquad (19)$$

$$(low'(w),\ up'(w)) = (|w|, |w|) \qquad\qquad\qquad \text{for } w \in \mathcal{A}^* \qquad (20)$$

$$(low'(q),\ up'(q))\ \ = (\sum_{i=1}^{r} low'(q_i),\ \sum_{i=1}^{r} up'(q_i)) \qquad \begin{aligned}&\text{for } q = t(q_1, ..., q_r),\\ &\qquad t \in \Sigma \end{aligned} \qquad (21)$$

$$(low'(q),\ up'(q))\ \ = (\max\ low'(q')\ c_l,\ \min\ up'(q')\ c_u) \quad \text{for } q = q'\ \text{ with } c \quad (22)$$

$$(low'(v),\ up'(v))\ \ = (low(v),\ up(v)) \qquad\qquad\qquad \text{for } v \in V \qquad (23)$$

In Equation 22, the bounds c_l and c_u associated with a syntactic predicate c are defined as $c_l = min\{|x| \mid c(x)\}$ and $c_u = max\{|x| \mid c(x)\}$ if the maximum exists, and $c_u = \infty$ otherwise. In general, they cannot be determined automatically, but must be specified explicitly by the designer of the grammar.

These equations are monotonically decreasing in the first component, and monotonically increasing in the second. The solution can be computed by Kleene fixpoint iteration, starting with the initial value $(low(x), up(x)) = (\infty, 0)$. The low component always converges, since all strictly decreasing chains in $\mathbb{N}^\infty$ are finite. The strictly increasing chains of $up(x)$ are not necessarily finite. In the absence of syntactic conditions one can show that if $up(v)$ is still increasing after $|V|$ iterations, then $up(v) = \infty$ is the least fixpoint solution. The handling of conditions in full generality is an open problem. In any case, $(c_l, c_u) = (0, \infty)$ is a safe approximation.

5.3   Dependency Analysis

The nested for-loops of the parser guarantee that when a word $w_{(i,j)}$ is to be parsed, all of its proper subwords have been parsed already. A problem arises with chain productions: In yield grammars, the analogue to chain productions $u \to v$ found in string grammars is the situation where $u \to C[...v...] \to^* C[...t...]$ such that $y(C[...t...]) = y(t)$. In other words, the tree context generated from u around v does not contribute to the yield. We denote this $u \to_{chain} v$. In this situation, a parser must reduce the input word $w_{(i,j)}$ to v before reducing it to u in the same iteration of the nested loop. The relation $\to_{chain}$ can be determined directly using the results from yield size analysis:

Let $u \to q_1|...|q_r$.

$$u \to_{chain} v \quad \text{iff} \quad \bigvee_{i=1}^{r} d(q_i) \quad \text{where} \tag{24}$$

$$
\begin{aligned}
d(q) &= \bigvee_{i=1}^{r'} (\sum_{j=1}^{i-1} low'(q'_j) \equiv 0 \wedge d(q'_i) \wedge \sum_{j=i+1}^{r'} low'(q'_j) \equiv 0) &&\text{for } q = t(q'_1, ..., q'_{r'}), \\
& && t \in \Sigma \\
d(q) &= d(q') &&\text{for } q = q' \text{ with } c \\
d(q) &= v' \equiv v &&\text{for } q = v' \in V \\
d(q) &= false &&\text{for } q = w \in \mathcal{A}^*
\end{aligned}
$$

low' is the above extension of low. The order of equations in the loop body (cf. Section 3.4) is chosen according to a topological sort with respect to $\to_{chain}$. Should $\to_{chain}$ be circular, a grammar design error is reported (see Section 6.2). The results of yield size and dependency analysis complete the definition of the tabulating yield parser.

Stepping back mentally from these technicalities for a moment, we observe the following: Anyone developing DP recurrences in the traditional way implicitly must solve the problems of yield size and dependency analysis, in order to define the control structure and the subscripts in the table accesses. Moreover, she must do so without the guiding help of a tree grammar. This explains much of the technical difficulty of developing correct recurrences.

5.4   Translation to C

We are developing a compiler translating ADP algorithms to C. Aside from parsing the ADP program and producing C code, the core of the compiler is implementing the grammar analyses described in Section 5. With respect to the evaluation algebra we follow the strategy that simple arithmetic functions are inlined, while others must be provided as native C functions. Compiler options provide a simplified translation in the case where the evaluation algebra computes scalar answers rather than lists. As an example, the code produced for the grammar Pal₃ is shown in Appendix A.

5.5   Haskell Source-to-Source Compilation

Yield size analysis determines the entire information required for minimal index ranges in all loops. We added a *source-to-source option* to the compiler, reproducing ADP input with all ˜˜˜ operators replaced by variants bound to exact yield sizes. Hence, the user is no longer committed to delicate tuning efforts.

6   The ADP Multi-paradigm Programming System

6.1   Working with ADP

As a programming methodology, the ADP approach gives a clear five step guidance for developing a new algorithm [8]. Prior to the work reported here, the ADP program had to be translated into C by hand, following the definitions of Section 3. The C program was then tested systematically against the Haskell prototype, a procedure that guarantees much higher reliability than ad-hoc testing. This has been applied to non-trivial problems in RNA structure prediction [5], DNA sequence comparison [6] and gene prediction (ongoing work).

Still, the main difficulties with this approach were twofold: It proved to be time consuming to produce a C program equivalent to the Haskell prototype. Furthermore, for sake of efficiency developers were tempted to perform ad-hoc yield size analysis and used special combinators in the prototype. This introduced through the backdoor the possibility of subscript errors otherwise banned by the ADP approach. The compiler now developed eliminates both problems.

6.2   Grammar Analysis Support for Improved Prototyping

Grammar analysis further supports the prototyping phase by *reporting design errors* reflected by grammar anomalies. *Infinitely many derivations* of a given yield string are possible iff the relation $\rightarrow_{chain}$ is circular. This is detected during dependency analysis. An error message can be produced instead of a parser that may not terminate on some input. *Useless nonterminals*, which cannot produce a finite terminal tree and hence do not contribute to the language, are recognised by yield size analysis. u is useless, iff $low(u) = \infty$. They indicate oversights in the designer's case-analysis. No parser needs to be generated for nonterminal u, and the designer might appreciate a warning in this situation.

6.3   Future Work

Our prevalent goal is to create a stable elementary ADP programming system that, thanks to the C compilation, can be utilised to speed up program development in large-scale applications. A number of advanced DP techniques have already experimented with, like attributed nonterminals and parsers which use precomputed information. The current formulation of ADP is directed towards string and applies to (single) string analysis and (pairwise) string comparison. Beyond strings, we have first results showing that ADP can be extended to trees [12], while other data domains have not yet been considered.

References

1. A.V. Aho and J.D. Ullman. *The Theory of Parsing, Translation and Compiling.* Prentice-Hall, Englewood Cliffs, NJ, 1973. I and II.
2. R. Bellman. *Dynamic Programming.* Princeton University Press, 1957.
3. W.S. Brainerd. Tree generating regular systems. *Information and Control,* 14:217–231, 1969.
4. R. Durbin, S. Eddy, A. Krogh, and G. Mitchison. *Biological Sequence Analysis.* Cambridge University Press, 1998.
5. D. Evers and R. Giegerich. Reducing the conformation space in RNA structure prediction. In *German Conference on Bioinformatics,* pages 118–124, 2001.
6. R. Giegerich. A systematic approach to dynamic programming in bioinformatics. *Bioinformatics,* 16:665–677, 2000.
7. R. Giegerich, S. Kurtz, and G. F. Weiller. An algebraic dynamic programming approach to the analysis of recombinant DNA sequences. In *Proc. of the First Workshop on Algorithmic Aspects of Advanced Programming Languages,* pages 77–88, 1999.
8. R. Giegerich and C. Meyer. Algebraic dynamic programming. In *Proc. of the 9th International Conference on Algebraic Methodology And Software Technology,* 2002. To appear.
9. R. Giegerich and K. Schmal. Code selection techniques: Pattern matching, tree parsing and inversion of derivors. In *Proc. European Symposium on Programming 1988,* Lecture Notes in Computer Science **300,** Springer Verlag, pages 247–268, 1988.
10. S.L. Graham and M.A. Harrison. An improved context-free recognizer. *ACM Transactions on Programming Languages and Systems,* 2(3):415–462, 1980.
11. D. Gusfield. *Algorithms on Strings, Trees, and Sequences.* Computer Science and Computational Biology. Cambridge University Press, 1997.
12. M. Höchsmann. Tree and Forest Alignments - An Algebraic Dynamic Programming Approach for Aligning Trees and Forests. Master's thesis, Bielefeld University, Mai 2001.
13. G. Hutton. Higher order functions for parsing. *Journal of Functional Programming,* 3(2):323–343, 1992.
14. C. Meyer and R. Giegerich. Matching and Significance Evaluation of Combined Sequence-Structure Motifs in RNA. *Z.Phys.Chem.,* 216:193–216, 2002.
15. T.L. Morin. Monotonicity and the principle of optimality. *Journal of Mathematical Analysis and Applications,* **86:**665–674, 1982.
16. E. Rivas and S. Eddy. A dynamic programming algorithm for RNA structure prediction including pseudoknots. *J. Mol. Biol.,* 285:2053–2068, 1999.
17. D.B. Searls. Linguistic approaches to biological sequences. *CABIOS,* 13(4):333–344, 1997.
18. K. Sikkel and M. Lankhorst. A parallel bottom-up tomita parser. In G. Görz, editor, *1. Konferenz Verarbeitung natürlicher Sprache (KONVENS'92), Nürnberg, Germany,* Informatik Aktuell, pages 238–247. Springer-Verlag, 1992.
19. P. Steffen. Basisfunktionen für die Übersetzung von Programmen der Algebraischen Dynamischen Programmierung. Master's thesis, Bielefeld University, February 2002. In German.
20. M. Tomita. *Efficient Parsing for Natural Language — A Fast Algorithm for Practical Systems.* Int. Series in Engineering and Computer Science. Kluwer, Hingham, MA, 1986.
21. M. Zuker and S. Sankoff. RNA secondary structures and their prediction. *Bull. Math. Biol.,* 46:591–621, 1984.

Appendix A: C-Code for Pal₃ Example

```
void calc_pal3(int i, int j) {
   struct t_result   *v[8];
   if ((j-i) >= 0) { v[0] = allocMem(0); }
      else { v[0] = NULL; };                          /*  n s       = 0 */
   if ((j-i) >= 2) { v[1] = allocMem(pal3[i+1][j-1]
                            + isEqual(x[i+1], x[j])); }
      else { v[1] = NULL; };           /*  r a s b  = s + isEqual(a,b) */
   if ((j-i) >= 1) { v[2] = allocMem(pal3[i+1][j]); }
      else { v[2] = NULL; };                          /*  d _ s    = s */
   if ((j-i) >= 1) { v[3] = allocMem(pal3[i][j-1]); }
      else { v[3] = NULL; };                          /*  i   s _  = s */

   v[4] = append(v[2], v[3]);                                  /* ||| */
   v[5] = append(v[1], v[4]);                                  /* ||| */
   v[6] = append(v[0], v[5]);                                  /* ||| */

   v[7] = maximum_v(v[6]);               /*  h x      = [maximum x] */
   freemem_result(v[6]);
   pal3[i][j] = (*v[7]).value;
   freemem_result(v[7]);
};

void mainloop() {
   int i; int j;
   for (j=0; j<=n; j++)
       for (i=j; i>=0; i--)
          calc_pal3(i, j);
};
```

Some Results in Dynamic Model Theory

Dexter Kozen

Computer Science Department, Cornell University
Ithaca, New York 14853-7501, USA
kozen@cs.cornell.edu

Traditional model theory (Chang and Keisler 1973, Bell and Slomson 1971), like classical predicate logic, is static in nature. Models, valuations of variables, and truth values of predicates are regarded as fixed and immutable. This tradition has surely contributed to the dominance of denotational over operational semantics in programming languages. It is somewhat ironic that first-order predicate logic is in general inadequate for handling even the most elementary and pervasive of logical constructions in computer science, namely induction. For this reason, and for its general lack of programmability, one might argue that the emphasis on first-order predicate logic in the undergraduate computer science curriculum may be detrimental to the development of sound algorithmic reasoning.

Dynamic logic and other logics of programs allow one to study properties of models from a natural computational perspective. Instead of attempting to strip away all traces of dynamics from the objects under study, a programming language and data structures are provided along with a formal semantics that allow one to reason in a natural algorithmic way and still maintain rigor.

In this talk we will show how trace-based and relational Kleene algebras with tests (KAT) built upon first-order (Tarskian) Kripke frames can be used to give a natural semantics for studying the dynamic properties of models. We prove the following results:

Let V be a fixed vocabulary. Given a recursive atomic theory E over V, we exhibit a Kripke frame U whose trace algebra is universal for Tarskian trace algebras over V satisfying E, although U itself is not Tarskian. Using U, we show

1. The following problem is r.e.-complete: given a recursive atomic theory E over V, a scheme S over V, and input values specified by ground terms $t_1, \ldots, t_n$, does S halt on input $t_1, \ldots, t_n$ in all models of E? The traditional halting problem for program schemes (see Manna 1974) is the case where E is empty.
2. The following problem is Π_2^0-complete: given a recursive atomic theory E over V and two schemes S and T over V, are S and T equivalent in all models of E? The classical scheme equivalence problem (see Manna 1974) is the case where E is empty.

Both these problems remain hard for their respective complexity classes even if E is empty and V is restricted to contain only a single constant, a single unary function symbol, and a single monadic predicate.

E.A. Boiten and B. Möller (Eds.): MPC 2002, LNCS 2386, pp. 21–21, 2002.
© Springer-Verlag Berlin Heidelberg 2002

Mathematics in Computer Science Curricula

Jeannette M. Wing

School of Computer Science, Carnegie Mellon University
Pittsburgh, PA 15213, USA
wing@cs.cmu.edu
http://www.cs.cmu.edu/ wing/

Abstract. Mathematics provides the theoretical foundation to computer science. So, it is not surprising that mathematics finds its way into computer science curricula, at both the undergraduate and graduate levels. They come in many guises:

- Mathematics courses, e.g., Logic, Number Theory;
- "Mathematics for Computer Scientists" courses, e.g., Probability and Statistics for Computer Science, Introduction to Feedback Control Systems (for Roboticists);
- Computational X where is a field of mathematics or science, e.g., Computational Geometry, Scientific Computing;
- Theoretical computer science courses, e.g., Algorithms, Semantics.

As the field of computer science evolves, I have seen an increase in the numbers of courses in the second and third categories. In my talk I will comment on how the maturation of computer science as a discipline has affected the role of mathematics in undergraduate and graduate computer science curricula, and on the implications these changes have had on our faculty and students. My views will be based on my experience with the academic programs offered by Carnegie Mellon's School of Computer Science.

E.A. Boiten and B. Möller (Eds.): MPC 2002, LNCS 2386, pp. 22–22, 2002.
© Springer-Verlag Berlin Heidelberg 2002

Logical Relations and Galois Connections

Kevin Backhouse [1] and Roland Backhouse [2]

[1] Computing Laboratory, University of Oxford
Oxford OX1 3QD, England
kevinb@comlab.ox.ac.uk
[2] School of Computer Science and Information Technology
University of Nottingham, Nottingham NG8 1BB, England
rcb@cs.nott.ac.uk

Abstract. Algebraic properties of logical relations on partially ordered sets are studied. It is shown how to construct a logical relation that extends a collection of base Galois connections to a Galois connection of arbitrary higher-order type. "Theorems-for-free" is used to show that the construction ensures safe abstract interpretation of parametrically polymorphic functions.

Logical relations were introduced by Plotkin [Plo80] and Reynolds [Rey83] as a basis for reasoning about possible implementations of the polymorphic lambda calculus and its models. Later, Wadler [Wad89] showed that Reynolds' "abstraction theorem" can be used to derive many useful properties of parametrically polymorphic functions from their types. This paper is about applying the algebraic properties of logical relations to constructing Galois connections of higher-order type.

The paper begins in section 1 with a review of the basic algebraic properties of the arrow operator on relations. Proofs are omitted in this section because most of the results are known. Section 2 contains the main results of the paper. The essential ideas have already been observed by Abramsky [Abr90]; our contribution is to specialise his "uniformisation theorem" to Galois-connected functions. This enables us to give a concise calculational formulation of the construction of a Galois connection of any given type, given a collection of Galois connections on the base types.

The primary application of this work is to the construction of abstract interpretations [CC77,CC79]. The first author has successfully applied the theorems presented here to the construction of a definedness test for attribute grammars [Bac02]. In the literature on abstract interpretations, it would appear that there is incomplete understanding of the relevance of logical relations — Cousot and Cousot [CC94] claim that their guidelines for designing abstract interpretations exhibit "a definite advantage of the Galois connection approach to abstract interpretations over its variant formalisation using logical relations". We show, however, that the construction of Galois connections of higher-order type is entirely equivalent to the construction of a logical relation.

E.A. Boiten and B. Möller (Eds.): MPC 2002, LNCS 2386, pp. 23–39, 2002.
© Springer-Verlag Berlin Heidelberg 2002

1   Preliminaries

This section introduces the basic notions for future reference.

Types. For the purposes of this paper we assume that types are partially ordered sets. Supposing $(A, \sqsubseteq)$ and $(B, \preceq)$ are posets, $(A, \sqsubseteq) \leftarrow (B, \preceq)$ denotes the set of *monotonic* functions with range A and domain B, ordered pointwise.

Relation Algebra. A *binary relation of type* $A \sim B$ is a subset of $A \times B$. Given binary relations $R \in A \sim B$ and $S \in B \sim C$, $R \bullet S$ denotes their composition, the relation of type $A \sim C$ defined by

$$(x, z) \in R \bullet S \quad \equiv \quad \langle \exists y :: (x, y) \in R \wedge (y, z) \in S \rangle \quad . \tag{1}$$

We use $^{\cup}$ as a postfix operator to denote the converse operation on relations. So, if $R \in A \sim B$ then $R^{\cup}$ is the relation of type $B \sim A$ defined by

$$(x, y) \in R^{\cup} \quad \equiv \quad (y, x) \in R \quad . \tag{2}$$

Functions. Functions are considered to be special sorts of relations. For function f of type $A \sim B$ we have, for all x in A and all y in B,

$$(x, y) \in f \equiv x = f.y \quad .$$

Galois Connections and Pair Algebras. Galois connections are most often defined in terms of a pair of functions. A better starting point for a discussion of Galois connections is, arguably, relations — or so-called "pair algebras", as proposed by Hartmanis and Stearns [HS64,HS66]. A binary relation R on the posets $(A, \sqsubseteq)$ and $(B, \preceq)$ is called a *pair algebra* if there are functions $f \in A \leftarrow B$ and $g \in B \leftarrow A$ such that

$$f^{\cup} \bullet \sqsubseteq \quad = \quad R \quad = \quad \preceq \bullet g \quad .$$

If R is a pair algebra, the two functions f and g are said to be the *lower* and *upper adjoints* (respectively) of a *Galois connection* between the posets.

Theorems for Free. Based on Reynolds' abstraction theorem [Rey83], Wadler [Wad89] showed how to derive a theorem about a polymorphic function from its type. The key to such "theorems for free" is, in Wadler's words, "that types may be read as relations". Briefly, the type A is read as the identity relation id_A on A and the function space constructor "$\leftarrow$" is read as a mapping from a pair of relations R and S of types $A \sim B$ and $C \sim D$, respectively, to a binary relation $R \leftarrow S$ on functions f and g of type $A \leftarrow C$ and $B \leftarrow D$, respectively. Formally, suppose R and S are binary relations of type $A \sim B$ and $C \sim D$, respectively. Then $R \leftarrow S$ is the binary relation of type $(A \leftarrow C) \sim (B \leftarrow D)$ defined by, for all functions $f \in A \leftarrow C$ and $g \in B \leftarrow D$,

$$(f, g) \in R \leftarrow S \quad \equiv \quad \langle \forall u, v :: (f.u, g.v) \in R \Leftarrow (u, v) \in S \rangle \quad . \tag{3}$$

In words, f and g construct R-related values from S-related values.

As an example, suppose $(A, \sqsubseteq)$ and $(B, \preceq)$ are partially ordered sets. Then we can instantiate R to $\sqsubseteq$ and S to $\preceq$ getting a relation $\sqsubseteq \leftarrow \preceq$ between functions f and g of type $A \leftarrow B$. In particular, switching to the usual infix notation for membership of an ordering relation,

$$(f, f) \in \sqsubseteq \leftarrow \preceq \quad \equiv \quad \langle \forall u, v :: f.u \sqsubseteq f.v \Leftarrow u \preceq v \rangle \quad .$$

So $(f, f) \in \sqsubseteq \leftarrow \preceq$ is the statement that f is a monotonic function. In Wadler's words, f maps $\preceq$-related values to $\sqsubseteq$-related values.

Particularly relevant to this paper is that, if f and g are both *monotonic* functions of type $A \leftarrow B$ where $(A, \sqsubseteq)$ and $(B, \preceq)$ are posets,

$$(f, g) \in \sqsubseteq \leftarrow \preceq \quad \equiv \quad \langle \forall u :: f.u \sqsubseteq g.u \rangle \quad .$$

(The easy proof is left to the reader.) We thus recognise $\sqsubseteq \leftarrow \preceq$ as the usual pointwise ordering on monotonic functions of type $(A, \sqsubseteq) \leftarrow (B, \preceq)$. Equivalently, in point-free relation algebra,

$$\sqsubseteq \leftarrow \preceq \ = \ \sqsubseteq \leftarrow \mathsf{id}_{\preceq} \tag{4}$$

where $\mathsf{id}_{\preceq}$ denotes the identity relation on the carrier of the poset ordering $\preceq$. See lemma 11 for the generalisation of this property to higher order types.

"Theorems for free" is the property that, if θ is a parametrically polymorphic function of type t, where t is a type expression parameterised by type variables $a, \ldots, c$, and, for each type variable a, R_a is a relation, then $(\theta, \theta) \in t[a, \ldots, c := R_a, \ldots, R_c]$. For numerous examples of "free" theorems, see Wadler's paper [Wad89].

Note that we should distinguish between the different instances of θ. The free theorem is actually that the pair $(\theta(A), \theta(B))$ is an element of relation $t[a, \ldots, c := R_a, \ldots, R_c]$ where A and B indicate how the particular instances of θ are determined (depending on the types of the relations R). We omit these details for the moment but include them later.

An instance of $R \leftarrow S$ that is used extensively in this paper is when R is a function and S is the converse of a function. For all monotonic functions $f \in (A, \sqsubseteq) \leftarrow (C, \trianglelefteq)$ and $g \in (B, \preceq) \leftarrow (D, \leq)$, $f \leftarrow g^{\cup}$ is the monotonic function of type $(A \leftarrow D) \leftarrow (B \leftarrow C)$ defined by

$$(f \leftarrow g^{\cup}).h \ = \ f \bullet h \bullet g \tag{5}$$

(The easy proof is left to the reader.)

Properties. The following *distributivity* properties of the $\leftarrow$ operator are easily derived from its definition. For all relations R and S,

$$(R \leftarrow S)^{\cup} \ = \ R^{\cup} \leftarrow S^{\cup} \quad . \tag{6}$$

For all relations R and S, and all functions f and g,

$$(R \bullet f) \leftarrow (S \bullet g^{\cup}) \ = \ (R \leftarrow S) \bullet (f \leftarrow g^{\cup}) \quad , \text{ and} \tag{7}$$

$$(f^{\cup} \bullet R) \leftarrow (g \bullet S) = (f^{\cup} \leftarrow g) \bullet (R \leftarrow S) \quad . \tag{8}$$

Note carefully that (7) and (8) require f and g to be functions. Using id_X to denote the identity relation on set X, we also have:

$$\mathsf{id}_A \leftarrow \mathsf{id}_B = \mathsf{id}_{A \leftarrow B} \quad . \tag{9}$$

From now on we assume that composition has precedence over the arrow operator (so that the parentheses can be omitted in the lhs of (7) but not in the rhs).

Relators. Another element of "theorems for free" is that type constructors, like disjoint sum $+$, Cartesian product $\times$ and *List* have to be extended to map relations to relations. This led Roland Backhouse to propose the notion of a *relator* as the basis for a relational theory of datatypes [BBH$^+$92,BVW92]. Briefly, a relator is a monotonic functor that commutes with converse. Formally, a relator, F, is a pair of mappings from a source allegory to a target allegory. The first element of the pair is from objects (types) of the source allegory to objects of the target allegory and the second element is from arrows (relations) of the source allegory to arrows of the target allegory. The mappings are required to have the properties that they form a functor from the underlying source category to the underlying target category and, for all arrows R and S,

$$F.R \subseteq F.S \ \Leftarrow \ R \subseteq S \ ,$$

and

$$(F.R)^{\cup} = F.(R^{\cup}) \ .$$

An example of a unary relator is *List*. Suppose R relates values of type A to values of type B. Then *List.R* relates values of type *List.A* to values of type *List.B*. Specifically, the list as is related to the list bs by *List.R* if as and bs have the same length and corresponding elements are related by R. An example of a binary relator is Cartesian product. Suppose R relates values of type A to values of type B and S relates values of type C to values of type D. Then $R \times S$ relates values of type $A \times C$ to values of type $B \times D$. Specifically, the pair (a, c) is related to the pair (b, d) by $R \times S$ if a is related by R to b and c is related by S to d. An example of a zero-ary relator is $\mathbb{N}$; this relates two natural numbers exactly when they are equal. (Any type defines a zero-ary relator in this way.)

By design, it is easy to show that relators preserve functions. That is, if f is a function then $F.f$ is also a function.

Note that the formal definition of a relator encompasses the possibility of relators with different source and target allegories. We will be somewhat informal in our treatment of relators. Typically, we assume that the source allegory is the n-fold product of the target allegory with itself, for some unspecified number n ($n \geq 0$) and will write $F.(u \ldots v)$ for the application of the relator to arguments $u, \ldots, v$.

In this paper, we also require that relators preserve partial orderings (so that if R is reflexive, antisymmetric and transitive then so too is $F.R$). For this we need the additional property that relators distribute through binary intersections. That is, we assume that, for all relations R and S, $F.(R \cap S) = F.R \cap F.S$. This assumption is satisfied by all "regular" datatypes [Hoo97]. Indeed, it is easily verified for disjoint sum and Cartesian product and then a straightforward proof shows that the property is preserved by the usual fixpoint construction of datatypes like $List$. So the assumption is a reasonable one in the context of modern programming languages.

2   Extending Galois Connections

In this section, we give a brief introduction to logical relations (the extension of the arrow operator discussed in section 1 to arbitrary types) and then introduce a *binary* logical-relation operator. (See definitions (14), (15) and (16).) The operator is a key ingredient in the construction of Galois connections of higher-order type. (See lemma 3 and theorem 1.)

2.1   Types and Assignments to Variables

We consider the following (extended BNF) grammar of type expressions:

$$Exp \quad ::= \quad (Relator\ Exp^*) \mid (Exp \leftarrow Exp) \mid Variable$$

where $Variable$ and $Relator$ are (disjoint) finite sets. Variables act as placeholders for types and relations, as explained in detail later. (A common name for them is "polymorphic type variable".) Each element of $Relator$ denotes a relator of a certain arity.

According to the syntax above, the application of a binary relator, say $+$, to types t and u would be denoted by the prefix notation $+t\,u$. We will, however, deviate from the formal syntax in our examples and write $t+u$ instead. Also, the formal syntax stipulates that subtypes are parenthesised (in order to avoid specifying precedence and associativity rules); again we will ignore this requirement when presenting examples. Instead we assume that $\leftarrow$ has the lowest precedence and associates to the left.

An example of a type expression is

$$List.a \;\leftarrow\; (Bool \leftarrow a) \times List.a \;.$$

This uses the the unary relator $List$, binary product relator, $\times$, and the zero-ary relator $Bool$. It describes the type of the (uncurried) *filter* function on lists, which is parametrically polymorphic in the variable a.

A *variable assignment* is a function with domain $Variable$, the set of type variables. We consider two kinds of variable assignments, one with range posets and the other with range (binary) relations on posets. A variable assignment will be denoted by an assignment statement as in, for example,

$$a,b := integer, boolean \;.$$

Given a variable assignment V, its application to type variable a is denoted by V_a.

In the case of variable assignments whose ranges are sets of relations we need to define the converse and composition operators. The definitions are:

$$(V^{\cup})_a = (V_a)^{\cup} \tag{10}$$

and

$$(V \bullet W)_a = V_a \bullet W_a \quad . \tag{11}$$

We extend variable assignments to type expressions in two ways. The simpler of the two extends a variable assignment V inductively to all type expressions t: for all type expressions u, v

$$V_{u \leftarrow v} = V_u \leftarrow V_v \tag{12}$$

and, for all type expressions u, $\ldots$, v,

$$V_{F.(u \ldots v)} = F.(V_u \ldots V_v) \quad . \tag{13}$$

Note that these definitions make sense whenever the range of V is an assignment of posets or relations to the type variables. In the case that V is a poset assignment we define the $\leftarrow$ operator to map posets A and B into the poset of *monotonic* functions mapping values of poset B into values of poset A, ordered pointwise. Correspondingly, in the case that V assigns relations to the type variables, we restrict the arrow operator to relate *monotonic* functions of the appropriate type. The requirement that the arrow operator relates monotonic functions is essential to the main results in this paper although many of its properties do not depend on this requirement.

In the case that V assigns relations to the type variables, the function mapping type expression t to V_t is called a *logical relation*[1].

The more complicated extension uses two assignments, one for the positive and the other for the negative occurrences of type variables. Specifically, suppose V and W are two variable assignments of the same kind. Then the variable assignment $[V,W]$ is defined inductively as follows:

$$[V,W]_a = V_a \quad , \tag{14}$$

$$[V,W]_{u \leftarrow v} = [V,W]_u \leftarrow [W,V]_v \quad , \tag{15}$$

$$[V,W]_{F.(u \ldots v)} = F.([V,W]_u \ldots [V,W]_v) \quad . \tag{16}$$

For example,

$$[(a := R),(a := S)]_{a \leftarrow a \leftarrow (a \leftarrow a \times a) \leftarrow List.a}$$
$$= R \leftarrow S \leftarrow (S \leftarrow R \times R) \leftarrow List.S \quad .$$

---

[1] The standard definition of a logical relation is a bit more general: a logical relation is a family of relations indexed by types such that properties (12) and (13) hold for all types u, $\ldots$, v. Clearly, a logical relation in our sense uniquely defines a logical relation according to the standard definition.

From the above definitions, the following properties are easily proved for all type expressions t by induction on the structure of type expressions.

$$V_t = [V,V]_t \quad , \tag{17}$$

$$(V_t)^\cup = (V^\cup)_t \quad , \tag{18}$$

$$([V,W]_t)^\cup = [V^\cup, W^\cup]_t \quad . \tag{19}$$

Because of (18) we write $V_t^\cup$, omitting the parentheses. We also write $[V,W]_t^\cup$; here the justification is that we define $[V,W]^\cup$ to be $[V^\cup, W^\cup]$.

Note that it is not the case that $(V \bullet W)_t = V_t \bullet W_t$ for all type expressions t. Property (11) is only valid for type variables a.

2.2 Basic Constructions

The following lemma generalises what is known in the literature as the "independent attribute method" [NNH98, page 247]. Specifically, the independent attribute method is the case that the relator F is the product relator. We state and prove the lemma only for a unary relator. The extension to non-unary relators is easy but requires extra apparatus. (Replace posets, relations and functions everywhere by vectors of posets, relations and functions.)

Lemma 1. Let $(A, \leq)$ be a poset. Suppose F is a relator that preserves binary intersections. (That is, for all relations R and S, $F.(R \cap S) = F.R \cap F.S$.) Then $(F.A, F.\leq)$ is a poset.

Proof. It is easy to verify that transitivity and reflexivity of $F.\leq$ follows from transitivity and reflexivity of $\leq$. Antisymmetry of $F.\leq$ is the property that

$$F.\leq \cap (F.\leq)^\cup \subseteq F.\mathrm{id}_A \quad .$$

This follows from the antisymmetry of $\leq$ ($\leq \cap \leq^\cup \subseteq \mathrm{id}_A$) and that F commutes with converse and is monotonic, and the assumption that F preserves binary intersections.
□

We now take the generalisation a step further, to arbitrary higher-order types.

Lemma 2. Let t be a type expression and let $\sqsubseteq$ and $\preceq$ assign partial ordering relations to the type variables in t. Let A and B be the corresponding poset assignments, respectively. (So for each type variable a, $\sqsubseteq_a$ is a partial ordering relation on A_a and $\preceq_a$ is a partial ordering relation on B_a.) Then $[\sqsubseteq, \preceq]_t$ is a partial ordering on $[A,B]_t$. As a corollary, $\sqsubseteq_t$ is a partial ordering relation on A_t.

Proof. Straightforward induction on the structure of type expressions using lemma 1 for the case that t is a relator application. (Reflexivity in the case of

the arrow operator is by definition: it is the requirement mentioned above that if A and B are posets then $A \leftarrow B$ is the set of *monotonic* functions with target A and source B.) Property (17) is then used to derive the special case.
□

We remarked earlier that, if f is a total function of type $A \leftarrow B$ and g is a total function of type $C \leftarrow D$ then $f \leftarrow g^{\cup}$ is a total function of type $(A \leftarrow D) \leftarrow (B \leftarrow C)$. The following lemma generalises this property to arbitrary type expressions.

Lemma 3. Suppose f and g are type assignments such that, for all type variables a, f_a and g_a are total functions of type $A_a \leftarrow B_a$ and $C_a \leftarrow D_a$, respectively. Then, for all type expressions t, $[f,g^{\cup}]_t$ is a total function of type $[A,D]_t \leftarrow [B,C]_t$.

Proof. Straightforward induction on the structure of type expressions using (19) and the fact that relators preserve total functions.
□

The function that maps type assignments f and g and type expression t to $[f,g^{\cup}]_t$ is parametrically polymorphic. The "theorem for free" that this observation yields is the following [Bru95]. (Compare lemma 4 with lemma 3 noting how types are replaced by relations.)

Lemma 4. Suppose that f, g, h and k assign total functions to type variables, and R and S assign relations to type variables. Suppose further that, for all type variables a, $(f_a,h_a) \in R_a \leftarrow S_a$ and $(g_a,k_a) \in T_a \leftarrow U_a$. Then, for all type expressions t,

$$([f,g^{\cup}]_t \, , \, [h,k^{\cup}]_t) \in [R,U]_t \leftarrow [S,T]_t \quad .$$

□

De Bruin [Bru95] shows how lemma 4 is used to derive a so-called "dinaturality" property from the type of a parametrically polymorphic function. Here, the following corollary is fundamental.

Lemma 5. Suppose that f and g assign total functions to type variables, and R and S assign relations to type variables. Suppose further that, for all type variables a, $(f_a,f_a) \in R_a \leftarrow S_a$ and $(g_a,g_a) \in S_a \leftarrow R_a$. Then, for all type expressions t,

$$([f,g^{\cup}]_t \, , \, [f,g^{\cup}]_t) \in R_t \leftarrow S_t \quad , \text{ and}$$

$$([g,f^{\cup}]_t \, , \, [g,f^{\cup}]_t) \in S_t \leftarrow R_t \quad .$$

Thus, if, for each a, R_a and S_a are ordering relations, and f_a and g_a are monotonic functions, then $[f,g^{\cup}]_t$ and $[g,f^{\cup}]_t$ are monotonic functions.

Proof. Make the instantiation $h,k,T,U := f,g,S,R$ in lemma 4 and use (17).
□

Lemma 6. For all assignments f, g, h and k of functions to type variables and for all type expressions t,

$$[f, g^\cup]_t \bullet [h, k^\cup]_t = [f \bullet h, (k \bullet g)^\cup]_t \ .$$

(Note the contravariance in the second argument.)

Proof. Straightforward induction on the structure of type expressions. The basis follows immediately from (14) and the induction step uses (7) and (16).
□

2.3   Main Theorems

Lemma 7. For all partial orderings $\sqsubseteq$ and $\preceq$ and all functions g,

$$\sqsubseteq \leftarrow \preceq \bullet g \ = \ \sqsubseteq \leftarrow g \quad \text{and}$$

$$\sqsubseteq \leftarrow g^\cup \bullet \preceq \ = \ \sqsubseteq \leftarrow g^\cup \ .$$

Proof. We have, for all monotonic functions h and k,

$(h, k) \in \sqsubseteq \leftarrow \preceq \bullet g$

$=$ $\qquad \{ \qquad$ definitions: (3), (1) $\}$

$\langle \forall u, v :: h.u \sqsubseteq k.v \ \Leftarrow \ u \preceq g.v \rangle$

$=$ $\qquad \{ \qquad (\Rightarrow)$ reflexivity of $\preceq$

$\qquad \qquad \ \ (\Leftarrow)$ h is monotonic, transitivity of $\sqsubseteq$ $\}$

$\langle \forall v :: h.(g.v) \sqsubseteq k.v \rangle$

$=$ $\qquad \{ \qquad$ definitions: (3), (1) $\}$

$(h, k) \in \sqsubseteq \leftarrow g$.

The second claim is proved similarly. (This is where monotonicity of k is used.)

□

Lemma 7 is often used in combination with the distributivity properties (7) and (8). Its most immediate application is property (4).

The next lemma can be seen as a special case of Abramsky's "uniformisation theorem" [Abr90, proposition 6.4]. (Abramsky does not assume that the function g has an upper adjoint.)

Lemma 8 (Uniformisation).   If f is a monotonic function with range $(A, \sqsubseteq)$ and the pair $(g, g^\sharp)$ is a Galois connection between the posets $(B, \preceq)$ and $(C, \leq)$ then

$$f^\cup \bullet \sqsubseteq \leftarrow g^\cup \bullet \preceq \ = \ (f^\cup \leftarrow g^\sharp) \bullet (\sqsubseteq \leftarrow \preceq) \ .$$

Also,

$$\sqsubseteq \bullet f \leftarrow \leq \bullet g^\sharp \ = \ (\sqsubseteq \leftarrow \leq) \bullet (f \leftarrow g^\cup) \ .$$

Proof.

$$f^{\cup} \bullet \sqsubseteq \leftarrow g^{\cup} \bullet \preceq$$

$$= \qquad \{ \qquad (g, g^{\sharp}) \text{ is a Galois connection.}$$

$$\text{So, } g^{\cup} \bullet \preceq \ = \ \leq \bullet g^{\sharp}. \quad \}$$

$$f^{\cup} \bullet \sqsubseteq \leftarrow \leq \bullet g^{\sharp}$$

$$= \qquad \{ \qquad \text{distributivity: (8) and lemma 7} \quad \}$$

$$(f^{\cup} \leftarrow id_C) \bullet (\sqsubseteq \leftarrow g^{\sharp})$$

$$= \qquad \{ \qquad \text{distributivity: (8) (applied twice)} \quad \}$$

$$(f^{\cup} \leftarrow g^{\sharp}) \bullet (\sqsubseteq \leftarrow id_B)$$

$$= \qquad \{ \qquad \text{lemma 7} \quad \}$$

$$(f^{\cup} \leftarrow g^{\sharp}) \bullet (\sqsubseteq \leftarrow \preceq) \ .$$

The second property is proved similarly.
□

Lemma 9.   Suppose we are given two assignments of Galois connections (f_a, g_a) between the posets $(A_a, \sqsubseteq_a)$ and $(B_a, \preceq_a)$ and (h_a, k_a) between the posets $(C_a, \trianglelefteq_a)$ and $(D_a, \leq_a)$, for each type variable a. Then, for all type expressions t,

$$[f, k^{\cup}]_t^{\cup} \bullet [\sqsubseteq, \trianglelefteq]_t \ = \ [\preceq, \leq]_t \bullet [g, h^{\cup}]_t \ .$$

In particular, the pair of functions $([f, k^{\cup}]_t, [g, h^{\cup}]_t)$ forms a Galois connection between the partially ordered sets $([A, C]_t, [\sqsubseteq, \trianglelefteq]_t)$ and $([B, D]_t, [\preceq, \leq]_t)$.

Proof. Lemma 3 establishes that $[f, k^{\cup}]_t$ and $[g, h^{\cup}]_t$ are functions (of the right type) and lemma 2 that $[\sqsubseteq, \trianglelefteq]_t$ and $[\preceq, \leq]_t$ are partial ordering relations. So it suffices only to prove the equality. This we do as follows.

The induction hypothesis is the equality stated above, together with the symmetric equality:

$$[h, g^{\cup}]_t^{\cup} \bullet [\trianglelefteq, \sqsubseteq]_t \ = \ [\leq, \preceq]_t \bullet [k, f^{\cup}]_t \ .$$

We are given the equalities: for all type variables a,

$$f_a^{\cup} \bullet \sqsubseteq_a \ = \ \preceq_a \bullet g_a \quad , \text{ and}$$

$$h_a^{\cup} \bullet \trianglelefteq_a \ = \ \leq_a \bullet k_a \ .$$

Combined with (14), these establish the basis of the proof.

For the case $t = u \leftarrow v$ we have:

$$[f, k^\cup]_t^\cup \bullet [\sqsubseteq, \trianglelefteq]_t$$

$=$ { $t = u \leftarrow v$, definition (15)   }

$$([f, k^\cup]_u \leftarrow [k^\cup, f]_v)^\cup \bullet ([\sqsubseteq, \trianglelefteq]_u \leftarrow [\trianglelefteq, \sqsubseteq]_v)$$

$=$ {   converse: (6) and (19)   }

$$([f, k^\cup]_u^\cup \leftarrow [k, f^\cup]_v) \bullet ([\sqsubseteq, \trianglelefteq]_u \leftarrow [\trianglelefteq, \sqsubseteq]_v)$$

$=$ {   uniformisation (lemma 8) and induction hypothesis

$([k, f^\cup]_v$ is the upper adjoint of $[h, g^\cup]_v$)   }

$$[f, k^\cup]_u^\cup \bullet [\sqsubseteq, \trianglelefteq]_u \leftarrow [h, g^\cup]_v^\cup \bullet [\trianglelefteq, \sqsubseteq]_v$$

$=$ {   induction hypothesis   }

$$[\trianglelefteq, \leq]_u \bullet [g, h^\cup]_u \leftarrow [\leq, \trianglelefteq]_v \bullet [k, f^\cup]_v$$

$=$ {   uniformisation (lemma 8) and induction hypothesis

$([k, f^\cup]_v$ is the upper adjoint of $[h, g^\cup]_v$)   }

$$([\trianglelefteq, \leq]_u \leftarrow [\leq, \trianglelefteq]_v) \bullet ([g, h^\cup]_u \leftarrow [h, g^\cup]_v^\cup)$$

$=$ {   converse (19), $t = u \leftarrow v$, definition (15)   }

$$[\trianglelefteq, \leq]_t \bullet [g, h^\cup]_t \quad .$$

The proof of the second equality is completely symmetric.

Finally, the case $t = F.(u \ldots v)$ is a straightforward application of the fact that relators distribute through composition and commute with converse.
□

The pair $(g, g^\sharp)$ is a *perfect* Galois connection between the posets $(B, \preceq)$ and $(C, \leq)$ if $g \bullet g^\sharp$ is the identity relation on B.

Lemma 10.   If the base Galois connections defined in lemma 9 are all perfect then so are the constructed Galois connections.

Proof. That the base connections are perfect means that $f_a \bullet g_a = A_a$ and $h_a \bullet k_a = C_a$. (We are taking the liberty of using A_a and C_a to denote identity relations here.) We have to prove that, for all type expressions t,

$$[f, k^\cup]_t \bullet [g, h^\cup]_t = [A, C]_t \quad .$$

The proof is an application of lemma 6:

$$[f, k^\cup]_t \bullet [g, h^\cup]_t = [A, C]_t$$

$=$ {   lemma 6   }

$$[f \bullet g, (h \bullet k)^\cup]_t = [A, C]_t$$

$\Leftarrow$ {   definition: (14), (15), (16)   }

$$\langle \forall a :: (f \bullet g)_a = A_a \;\; \wedge \;\; (h \bullet k)_a^{\cup} = C_a \rangle$$

$$= \qquad \{ \qquad (11), \text{ assumption}, \; C_a^{\cup} = C_a \qquad \}$$

$$true \;\; .$$

□

In the following theorems we suppose we are given an assignment of Galois connections (abs_a , con_a) between the posets (A_a , $\sqsubseteq_a$) and (B_a , $\preceq_a$) for each type variable a . In other words, we are given six functions A , B , $\sqsubseteq$, $\preceq$, abs and con on the type variables. For each variable a , we define P_a to be the pair algebra corresponding to the given Galois connection. That is,

$$abs_a^{\cup} \bullet \sqsubseteq_a \;=\; P_a \;=\; \preceq_a \bullet con_a \;\; . \tag{20}$$

Theorem 1 (Logical Pair Algebras).   For all type expressions t ,

$$[abs , con^{\cup}]_t^{\cup} \bullet \sqsubseteq_t \;=\; P_t \;=\; \preceq_t \bullet [con , abs^{\cup}]_t \;\; .$$

In words, the logical relation P defines a Galois connection for all type expressions t , namely the pair of functions ($[abs , con^{\cup}]_t$, $[con , abs^{\cup}]_t$) connecting the partially ordered sets (A_t , $\sqsubseteq_t$) and (B_t , $\preceq_t$). Moreover, P_t is a pair algebra for all type expressions t .

Proof   Lemma 9 establishes the equality between the outer terms. (Take f and h to be equal, and g and k also to be equal.) We, therefore, only have to establish the equality between the first two terms.

The proof is by induction on the structure of type expressions. The basis is the assumption (20) combined with (14). For $t = u \leftarrow v$ we have:

$$[abs , con^{\cup}]_t^{\cup} \bullet \sqsubseteq_t$$

$$= \qquad \{ \qquad t = u \leftarrow v , \text{ definition and (15)} \qquad \}$$

$$([abs , con^{\cup}]_u \leftarrow [con^{\cup} , abs]_v)^{\cup} \bullet (\sqsubseteq_u \leftarrow \sqsubseteq_v)$$

$$= \qquad \{ \qquad \text{converse: (6) and (19)} \qquad \}$$

$$([abs , con^{\cup}]_u^{\cup} \leftarrow [con , abs^{\cup}]_v) \bullet (\sqsubseteq_u \leftarrow \sqsubseteq_v)$$

$$= \qquad \{ \qquad \text{uniformisation (lemma 8) and induction hypo} \qquad \}$$

$$[abs , con^{\cup}]_u^{\cup} \bullet \sqsubseteq_u \;\leftarrow\; [abs , con^{\cup}]_v^{\cup} \bullet \sqsubseteq_v$$

$$= \qquad \{ \qquad \text{induction hypothesis}, \; t = u \leftarrow v , \text{ definition (12)} \qquad \}$$

$$P_t \;\; .$$

Finally, the case $t = F.(u \dots v)$ is a straightforward application of the fact that relators distribute through composition and commute with converse.

□

Theorem 1 expresses formally the fact that the extension of a family of Galois connections from a collection of base types to arbitrary higher-order types is precisely defined by a logical relation (the pair algebra P in the theorem), in contradiction of Cousot and Cousot's [CC94] claim of "a definite advantage of the Galois connection approach to abstract interpretations over its variant formalisation using logical relations". An important corollary (already observed by Abramsky [Abr90]) is that the "safety" of this extension is a "free" theorem.

Theorem 2 (Safety for Free).   If θ is a parametrically polymorphic function of type t, where t is a type expression parameterised by type variables $a, \ldots, c$, then

$$[abs, con^{\cup}]_t \,.\theta(B) \ \sqsubseteq_t \ \theta(A) \ .$$

($\theta(X)$ denotes the instance of θ of type X_t.)

   Proof   The assumption that θ has type t and is parametrically polymorphic in all the type variables in t means that

$$(\theta(B), \theta(A)) \in P_t \ .$$

The theorem follows immediately from theorem 1.
□

3   Pointwise Orderings

In this section we specialise the theorems of the previous section in order to demonstrate more clearly their relevance to practical application. For example, we show that the logical relation $\sqsubseteq_t$ in the statement of theorem 2 is just a pointwise ordering relation. We first introduce a novel way of assigning to type variables.

   Suppose V and W are two variable assignments of the same kind. Then the variable assignment $[\![V,W]\!]$ is defined inductively as follows:

$$[\![V,W]\!]_a \ = \ V_a \ , \tag{21}$$

$$[\![V,W]\!]_{u \leftarrow v} \ = \ [\![V,W]\!]_u \leftarrow W_v \ , \tag{22}$$

$$[\![V,W]\!]_{F.(u \ldots v)} \ = \ F.([\![V,W]\!]_u \ldots [\![V,W]\!]_v) \ . \tag{23}$$

The assignment $[\![V,W]\!]$ applies the assignment V to the highest positive occurrences of the variables and applies assignment W to all others. For example,

$$[\![(a,b := \sqsubseteq, \trianglelefteq) , (a,b := I,J)]\!]_{List.((a \leftarrow b) \times b) \ \leftarrow \ a}$$
$$= \ List.((\sqsubseteq \leftarrow J) \times \trianglelefteq) \leftarrow I \ .$$

If I and J are identity relations on posets A and B, respectively, the relation $List.((\sqsubseteq \leftarrow J) \times \trianglelefteq) \leftarrow I$ is the pointwise ordering relation on functions of type $List.((A \leftarrow B) \times B) \leftarrow B$. As the next lemma states, it is equal to the relation $List.((\sqsubseteq \leftarrow \trianglelefteq) \times \trianglelefteq) \leftarrow \sqsubseteq$.

Lemma 11 (Higher Order Pointwise Orderings).   If for each variable a, $\sqsubseteq_a$ is a partial ordering relation on the set A_a and id_a is the identity relation on A_a then, for all type expressions t,

$$[\![\sqsubseteq, id]\!]_t \;=\; \sqsubseteq_t \;.$$

Proof   Straightforward induction on the structure of type expressions with lemma 7 providing the crucial inductive step.
□

In words, lemma 11 states that the pointwise ordering of functions, $[\![\sqsubseteq, id]\!]_t$, is the logical relation $\sqsubseteq_t$ generated by the given base orderings.

Lemma 12.

$$P_t \;=\; [\![abs^{\cup} \bullet \sqsubseteq , [abs, con^{\cup}]^{\cup}]\!]_t \;.$$

Proof. The proof is by induction on the structure of type expressions. The basis is trivial. For $t = u \leftarrow v$ we have:

$$P_t$$

$$= \qquad \{ \qquad t = u \leftarrow v, \text{ definition (12), theorem 1} \quad \}$$

$$P_u \;\leftarrow\; [abs, con^{\cup}]_v^{\cup\,\cup} \bullet \sqsubseteq_v$$

$$= \qquad \{ \qquad \text{distributivity: (7) and lemma 7}$$

$$\text{(noting that } P_u = [abs, con^{\cup}]_u^{\cup\,\cup} \bullet \sqsubseteq_u) \quad \}$$

$$P_u \;\leftarrow\; [abs, con^{\cup}]_v^{\cup\,\cup}$$

$$= \qquad \{ \qquad \text{induction hypothesis} \quad \}$$

$$[\![abs^{\cup} \bullet \sqsubseteq , [abs, con^{\cup}]^{\cup}]\!]_u \;\leftarrow\; [abs, con^{\cup}]_v^{\cup\,\cup}$$

$$= \qquad \{ \qquad \text{definition: (22), } t = u \leftarrow v \quad \}$$

$$[\![abs^{\cup} \bullet \sqsubseteq , [abs, con^{\cup}]^{\cup}]\!]_t \;.$$

□

Corollary 1 (Safety For Free, Special Case).   If θ has type $t = a \leftarrow v$, where a is a type variable and v is a type expression, and is parametrically polymorphic in all the type variables in t then

$$abs_a \bullet \theta(B) \;\;\dot{\sqsubseteq}\;\; \theta(A) \bullet [abs, con^{\cup}]_v$$

where $\dot{\sqsubseteq}$ denotes the pointwise ordering $[\![\sqsubseteq, A]\!]_t$ on functions with range A_a.
Proof The assumption that θ has type t and is parametrically polymorphic in all the type variables in $a \leftarrow v$ means that

$$(\theta(B), \theta(A)) \in P_{a \leftarrow v} \;.$$

Now,

$$P_{a \leftarrow v}$$

$=$ {   lemma 12   }

$$[\![abs^{\cup} \bullet \sqsubseteq \, , \, [abs , con^{\cup}]^{\cup}]\!]_{a \leftarrow v}$$

$=$ {   definitions: (22) and (11)   }

$$abs_a^{\cup} \bullet \sqsubseteq_a \leftarrow [abs , con^{\cup}]_v^{\cup}$$

$=$ {   distributivity: (7) and (8)   }

$$(abs_a^{\cup} \leftarrow A_v) \bullet (\sqsubseteq_a \leftarrow A_v) \bullet (A_a \leftarrow [abs , con^{\cup}]_v^{\cup})$$

$=$ { $\dot{\sqsubseteq} = [\![\sqsubseteq , A]\!]_{a \leftarrow v} = \sqsubseteq_a \leftarrow A_v \, ,$

converse: (6)   }

$$(abs_a \leftarrow A_v)^{\cup} \bullet \dot{\sqsubseteq} \bullet (A_a \leftarrow [abs , con^{\cup}]_v^{\cup}) \, .$$

Hence, using (5) and the definitions of composition and converse,

$$abs_a \bullet \theta(B) \quad \dot{\sqsubseteq} \quad \theta(A) \bullet [abs , con^{\cup}]_v \, .$$

$\square$

We conclude with a simple example. Consider the *fold* function which, given a starting value m of some type a, a binary operator $\oslash$ of type $a \leftarrow a \times a$ and a list $[m_o , \ldots , m_{n-1}]$ of a's, evaluates $((m \oslash m_o) \oslash \ldots) \oslash m_{n-1}$. Suppose that we want to determine whether a product of numbers is divisible by k for some given positive number k. For brevity, define the function dk mapping integers to booleans by

$$dk.m = m / k$$

where m/k is read as "m is divisible by k". The function dk is the lower adjoint in a Galois connection (dk, kd) between $(\, \mathsf{Bool} , \Leftarrow \,)$ and $(\, \mathsf{PosInt} , / \,)$ where $dk \in \mathsf{Bool} \leftarrow \mathsf{PosInt}$, $kd \in \mathsf{PosInt} \leftarrow \mathsf{Bool}$ and $/$ is the is-divisible-by ordering on positive integers. Specifically, kd is defined by, for all booleans b,

$$kd.b = \textbf{if } b \textbf{ then } k \textbf{ else } 1$$

and satisfies, for all positive integers m and all booleans b,

$$dk.m \Leftarrow b \equiv m / kd.b \, .$$

(Read "(m is divisible by k if b) is (m is divisible by $kd.b$)".) The pair algebra corresponding to this Galois connection relates all positive integers to the boolean *false* and the positive integers divisible by k to the boolean *true*.

Theorem 1 predicts that the function

$$dk \leftarrow kd^{\cup} \leftarrow (kd^{\cup} \leftarrow dk \times dk) \leftarrow List.kd^{\cup}$$

is the lower adjoint in a Galois connection between the poset of monotonic functions of type

$$\mathsf{Bool} \leftarrow \mathsf{Bool} \leftarrow (\mathsf{Bool} \leftarrow \mathsf{Bool} \times \mathsf{Bool}) \leftarrow List.\mathsf{Bool}$$

(ordered pointwise by $\Leftarrow$) and monotonic functions of type

$$\mathsf{PosInt} \leftarrow \mathsf{PosInt} \leftarrow (\mathsf{PosInt} \leftarrow \mathsf{PosInt} \times \mathsf{PosInt}) \leftarrow List.\mathsf{PosInt}$$

(ordered pointwise by divisibility). The upper adjoint is the function

$$kd \leftarrow dk^{\cup} \leftarrow (dk^{\cup} \leftarrow kd \times kd) \leftarrow List.dk^{\cup} \ .$$

Theorem 2 says that the Galois connection defines a safe abstract interpretation of the evaluation of the $fold$ function. This is made explicit by "uncurrying" the function and applying corollary 1. To be precise, assuming $fold$ has type

$$a \leftarrow a \times (a \leftarrow a \times a) \times List.a$$

the corollary states that

$$dk.ConcreteValue \ \Leftarrow \ AbstractValue$$

where

$$ConcreteValue \ = \ fold.(m,(\times),ms)$$

and

$$AbstractValue \ = \ fold.(dk.m\,,\,(dk \leftarrow kd^{\cup} \times kd^{\cup}).(\times)\,,\,List.dk.ms)\ .$$

(The argument $(\times)$ to $fold$ is normal arithmetic multiplication and is not to be confused with Cartesian product as used in the type of $fold$.) Note that, for booleans b and c,

$$(dk \leftarrow kd^{\cup} \times kd^{\cup}).(\times).(b,c) \ = \ dk.(kd.b \times kd.c) \ = \ b \vee c \ .$$

So the theorem predicts the (obvious) property that it is safe to evaluate whether the product of a list of numbers is divisible by k by interpreting each number as the boolean value "the number is divisible by k" and interpreting multiplication as logical disjunction. "Safe" means that a $true$ answer can be relied upon.

For a more substantial example involving a definedness test on attribute grammars, see [Bac02].

4   Conclusion

We have shown how to extend a collection of Galois connections to a Galois connection of arbitrary higher-order type. The construction is more general than any that we are aware of in the literature. In addition, we have shown that the construction is defined by a logical relation thus hopefully clarifying misunderstandings about the relationship between higher-order Galois connections, their safety properties and logical relations.

References

Abr90.   Samson Abramsky. Abstract interpretation, logical relations, and Kan extensions. *J. Logic and Computation*, 1(1):5–41, 1990.

Bac02.   K.S. Backhouse. A functional semantics of attribute grammars. In *International Conference on Tools and Algorithms for Construction and Analysis of Systems*, Lecture Notes in Computer Science. Springer-Verlag, 2002. Available from: http://web.comlab.ox.ac.uk/oucl/research/areas/progtools/publications.htm.

BBH + 92. R.C. Backhouse, P. de Bruin, P. Hoogendijk, G. Malcolm, T.S. Voermans, and J. van der Woude. Polynomial relators. In M. Nivat, C.S. Rattray, T. Rus, and G. Scollo, editors, *Proceedings of the 2nd Conference on Algebraic Methodology and Software Technology, AMAST'91*, pages 303–326. Springer-Verlag, Workshops in Computing, 1992.

Bru95.   Peter J. de Bruin. *Inductive Types in Constructive Languages*. PhD thesis, Rijksuniversiteit Groningen, 1995.

BVW92.   R.C. Backhouse, T.S. Voermans, and J. van der Woude. A relational theory of datatypes. Available via World-Wide Web at
           http://www.cs.nott.ac.uk/~rcb/MPC/papers.
           Available via anonymous ftp from ftp://ftp.win.tue.nl in directory pub/math.prog.construction, December 1992.

CC77.   Patrick Cousot and Radhia Cousot. Abstract interpretation: A unifed lattice model for static analysis of programs by construction or approximation of fixpoints. In *Conference Record of the Fourth Annual ACM Symposium on Principles of Programming Languages*, pages 238–252, Los Angeles, California, January 1977.

CC79.   Patrick Cousot and Radhia Cousot. Systematic design of program analysis frameworks. In *Conference Record of the Sixth Annual ACM Symposium on Principles of Programming Languages*, pages 269–282, San Antonio, Texas, January 1979.

CC94.   Patrick Cousot and Radhia Cousot. Higher-order abstract interpretations (and application to comportment analysis generalizing strictness, termination, projection and per analysis of functional languages). In *Procs. ICCL'94, IEEE*, pages 95–112, 1994.

Hoo97.   Paul Hoogendijk. *A Generic Theory of Datatypes*. PhD thesis, Department of Mathematics and Computing Science, Eindhoven University of Technology, 1997.

HS64.   J. Hartmanis and R.E. Stearns. Pair algebras and their application to automata theory. *Information and Control*, 7(4):485–507, 1964.

HS66.   J. Hartmanis and R.E. Stearns. *Algebraic Structure Theory of Sequential Machines*. Prentice-Hall, 1966.

NNH98.   Flemming Nielson, Hanne Riis Nielson, and Chris Hankin. *Principles of Program Analysis*. Springer-Verlag, 1998.

Plo80.   Gordon D. Plotkin. Lambda-definability in the full type hierarchy. In J.P. Seldin and J.R. Hindley, editors, *To H.B. Curry: Essays on Combinatory Logic, Lambda Calculus and Formalism*. Academic Press, London, 1980.

Rey83.   J.C. Reynolds. Types, abstraction and parametric polymorphism. In R.E. Mason, editor, *IFIP'83*, pages 513–523. Elsevier Science Publishers, 1983.

Wad89.   P. Wadler. Theorems for free! In *4'th Symposium on Functional Programming Languages and Computer Architecture, ACM, London*, September 1989.

Transformational Derivation of Greedy Network Algorithms from Descriptive Specifications

Juan Eduardo Durán

FAMAF, Universidad Nacional de Córdoba, Argentina
duran@mate.uncor.edu

Abstract. In this work an approach for the transformational development of efficient imperative network algorithms is presented which is based on Möller's algebra of formal languages. We use a very flexible methodology that contemplates the description of a rather general derivation method, the use of different derivation procedures to support the phases of this method, and the derivation of algorithm schemes based on such procedures. We propose a method that consists of the formulation of a descriptive specification, the development of an abstract recursive algorithm, and the derivation of an efficient imperative algorithm. As an example, we present algorithm schemes and derivation procedures for the development of efficient greedy algorithms, which are illustrated with the derivation of a shortest path arborescence algorithm.

1 Introduction

The presentation of network algorithms in algorithmic books is usually informal because network algorithms habitually contain text in natural language and are informally verified. Furthermore, the transition from abstract network algorithms (i.e. those involving abstract datatypes and using non-algorithmically defined functions) to efficient concrete imperative network algorithms is not formally made. For these reasons, we are motivated to study the formal derivation of network algorithms.

There is little work in the literature about this topic ([3, 1, 17, 7, 5, 6, 4]). With the exception of some shortest path costs algorithm derivations made by Berghammer ([3]), the existing derivation examples either start with a rather concrete problem specification or produce an abstract or inefficient algorithm. In addition, very different approaches are used for all these examples.

The aim of our investigation is the transformational derivation of network algorithms, by starting with descriptive specifications and obtaining a rather efficient imperative algorithm. Besides, we would like to discover which formalism is best suited for this task. Another objective is the derivation of algorithm schemes for classes of network algorithms.

We base our investigation on Möller's algebra of formal languages ([7, 20]) because it is suitable for the development of graph algorithms, includes proper relation algebra, and permits the formulation of concise and elegant optimisation problem specifications.

E.A. Boiten and B. Möller (Eds.): MPC 2002, LNCS 2386, pp. 40–67, 2002.

In this paper, we study the derivation of efficient imperative greedy algorithms that calculate optimal objects together with their costs from descriptive specifications. For the formal construction of such algorithms, we present development procedures and algorithm schemes. They are illustrated with the derivation of an efficient shortest path arborescence algorithm.

This paper is organised as follows: Sect. 2 contains the basic concepts that are useful to specify network problems and that will be used in the rest of the paper. Sects. 3 and 4 explain a method for the development of efficient imperative network algorithms from descriptive optimisation specifications. This method is decomposed into seven phases that can be specialised with the definition of different derivation procedures which sometimes can be used for the derivation of algorithm schemes.

2 Basic Concepts

Total Functions. We shall denote the set of total functions from X to Y by $[X \to Y]$ and the formula $f \in [X \to Y]$ by $f : X \to Y$. The total functions id_X (identity on X), π (first projection) and ρ (second projection) are used in this work. The following operations on total functions are employed in this paper: $f \circ g$ (composition), (f, g) (tupling), $dom(f)$ (domain), $cod(f)$ (codomain) and $f_{|X}$ (restriction). The tupling operation is defined by

$$x \in X \Rightarrow (f, g)(x) \stackrel{\text{def}}{=} (f(x), g(x)) \qquad (f : X \to Y, \ g : X \to Z) \ .$$

A linear ordered finite set is called an *Enumeration*. For instance, $\{x_1, \dots, x_n\}$ with the ordering $x_i \le x_j \Leftrightarrow i \le j$ is an enumeration.
$f : Y_1 \times \dots \times Y_n \to X$ is called a *matrix* if $Y_1, \dots, Y_n$ are enumerations. We write $\mathbf{c}$ for the *constant matrix* with value equal to c (i.e. $cod(\mathbf{c}) = \{c\}$).

Words and Relations. We denote the set of words over an alphabet X by X^*. A word of length 1 is not distinguished from the only letter it contains. We use from [7, 20] ε (empty word), $u \bullet w$ (concatenation), $\| w \|$ (length), $u \bowtie v$ (join) and $u; v$ (composition). Join and composition are defined by

$$\varepsilon \bowtie s \stackrel{\text{def}}{=} \emptyset \ , \qquad s \bowtie \varepsilon \stackrel{\text{def}}{=} \emptyset \ ,$$
$$\varepsilon ; s \stackrel{\text{def}}{=} \emptyset \ , \qquad s ; \varepsilon \stackrel{\text{def}}{=} \emptyset \ ,$$

$$(s \bullet x) \bowtie (y \bullet t) \stackrel{\text{def}}{=} \textbf{if } x = y \textbf{ then } s \bullet x \bullet t \textbf{ else } \emptyset \ ,$$
$$(s \bullet x) ; (y \bullet t) \stackrel{\text{def}}{=} \textbf{if } x = y \textbf{ then } s \bullet t \textbf{ else } \emptyset \ ,$$

where $x, y \in X$ and $s, t \in X^*$.

The operations *reverse* (x^{T}), *head* (hd) and *tail* (tl) can be defined by

$$\varepsilon^{\mathrm{T}} \stackrel{\text{def}}{=} \varepsilon \ , \qquad (x \bullet l)^{\mathrm{T}} \stackrel{\text{def}}{=} l^{\mathrm{T}} \bullet x \ ,$$
$$tl(\varepsilon) \stackrel{\text{def}}{=} \emptyset \ , \qquad tl(x \bullet l) \stackrel{\text{def}}{=} l \ ,$$
$$hd(\varepsilon) \stackrel{\text{def}}{=} \emptyset \ , \qquad hd(x \bullet l) \stackrel{\text{def}}{=} x \ ,$$

where $x \in X$ and $l \in X^*$.

The sets of *words of length 2* and of *non-empty words* over X are defined by

$$X^2 \stackrel{\text{def}}{=} X \bullet X , \qquad X^+ \stackrel{\text{def}}{=} X^* - \{\varepsilon\} .$$

In [7, 20] a *formal language* is a subset of X^* and a *relation* of arity n is a language R over X such that all words of R have length n. We will use the following well-known operation of functional programming

$$foldr(\oplus, a) \stackrel{\text{def}}{=} a ,$$
$$foldr(\oplus, a \bullet u) \stackrel{\text{def}}{=} a \oplus foldr(\oplus, u) ,$$

where $a \in X$, $u \in X^+$, $\oplus : X \times X \to X$.

From now on we shall denote $foldr(\oplus, x_1 \bullet \ldots \bullet x_n)$ by $\oplus_{i=1}^n x_i$.

The *incidence functions* $+$ and $-$ belong to $[X^2 \to X]$, which are defined by

$$(x \bullet y)^+ \stackrel{\text{def}}{=} y , \qquad (x \bullet y)^- \stackrel{\text{def}}{=} x .$$

Pointwise Extension, Assertions, and Filters. We use the notion of *pointwise extension of functions* given in [17]. Let $f : Y_1 \times \ldots \times Y_n \to \wp(X)$. The pointwise extension of f is denoted by the same symbol. It has the functionality $f : \wp(Y_1) \times \ldots \times \wp(Y_n) \to \wp(X)$ and is defined by

$$f(U_1, \ldots, U_n) \stackrel{\text{def}}{=} \bigcup \{f(x_1, \ldots, x_n) : (x_1, \ldots, x_n) \in U_1 \times \ldots \times U_n\} .$$

Using this notion we obtain the usual operations on relations $R;S$ (composition) and R^{T} (transposition).

We call a function $f : X \to \wp(X)$ an *assertion* on X if it can be defined in the form

$$f(x) = \text{ if } \varphi(x) \text{ then } \{x\} \text{ else } \emptyset .$$

In this work, we will use the following assertions on $[X \to \wp(Y)]$

$$DET(f) \stackrel{\text{def}}{=} \text{ if } \forall x \in X.(|f(x)| = 1) \text{ then } \{f\} \text{ else } \emptyset ,$$
$$MDET(f) \stackrel{\text{def}}{=} \text{ if } \forall x \in X.(|f(x)| \leq 1) \text{ then } \{f\} \text{ else } \emptyset ,$$
$$DEF(f) \stackrel{\text{def}}{=} \text{ if } \forall x \in X.(f(x) \neq \emptyset) \text{ then } \{f\} \text{ else } \emptyset .$$

The *filter* corresponding to an assertion P is denoted by $P \lhd$ and defined by

$$P \lhd S \stackrel{\text{def}}{=} \{s \in S : P(s) = \{s\}\} .$$

Graphs and Networks. As in [20] a *1-graph* (graph in short) $G = (V, A)$ consists of a set of *nodes* V and of a relation A of *arcs* such that $A \subseteq V^2$.

We define the sets of subgraphs and of spanning subgraphs of a graph (V, A) by

$$sg((V, A)) \stackrel{\text{def}}{=} \{(U, E) \text{ graph } : U \subseteq V \wedge E \subseteq A\} ,$$
$$ssg((V, A)) \stackrel{\text{def}}{=} \{(U, E) \text{ graph } : (U, E) \in sg((V, A)) \wedge U = V\} .$$

The addition operation of arcs to graphs is defined by

$$AddA((V, A), a) \stackrel{\text{def}}{=} (V \cup \{a^+, a^-\}, A \cup \{a\}) \ .$$

We denote the set of *real numbers extended with infinity* by $\mathbb{R} \cup \{\infty\}$. We use $a + b$ (addition), and the relations $a \le b$ (less or equal) and $a < b$ (less).

A *network* $N = (G, W)$ consists of a graph $G = (V, A)$ and of a *weight function* $W : A \to \mathbb{R} \cup \{\infty\}$.

The projections $\pi : X \times Y \to X$ and $\rho : X \times Y \to Y$ are defined by

$$\pi(x, y) \stackrel{\text{def}}{=} x , \qquad \rho(x, y) \stackrel{\text{def}}{=} y \ .$$

We define the following selectors on networks

$$V_N \stackrel{\text{def}}{=} \pi(\pi(N)) , \quad A_N \stackrel{\text{def}}{=} \rho(\pi(N)) , \quad W_N \stackrel{\text{def}}{=} \rho(N) \ .$$

The operation that given a graph (V, A) and a set of vertices V_1 returns the set of arcs of A leading out of V_1 is defined by

$$ALO((V, A), V_1) \stackrel{\text{def}}{=} (V_1 \bullet (V - V_1)) \cap A \ . \tag{1}$$

A very similar operation can be defined on networks:

$$Alo(N, G) \stackrel{\text{def}}{=} ALO(\pi(N), \pi(G)) \ .$$

Example 1. The next figure shows a network $N = (G, W)$ where

$$G = (\{1, 2, 3, 4\}, \{1\bullet2, 2\bullet4, 1\bullet3\}) \ ,$$

$$W = \{(1\bullet2, 2), (1\bullet3, 7), (2\bullet4, 6)\} \ .$$

The set of spanning subgraphs of G is

$$ssg(G) = \{(\{1, 2, 3, 4\}, T) : T \in \wp(\{1\bullet2, 2\bullet4, 1\bullet3\})\} \ .$$

The addition of the arc $3\bullet5$ to the graph G is the graph

$$AddA(G, 3\bullet5) = (\{1, 2, 3, 4, 5\}, \{1\bullet2, 2\bullet4, 1\bullet3, 3\bullet5\}) \ .$$

The set of arcs of G leading out of $\{1, 2\}$ is

$$ALO(G, \{1, 2\}) = \{2\bullet4, 1\bullet3\} \ .$$

Paths. The set of *paths of length* $n \subset \mathbb{N}$ in a graph G is inductively defined:

$$^0G \stackrel{\text{def}}{=} \varepsilon , \quad ^1G \stackrel{\text{def}}{=} \pi(G) , \quad ^{n+1}G \stackrel{\text{def}}{=} \rho(G) \bowtie {}^nG \quad (n \ge 1) \ .$$

The set of paths on G with length greater or equal than n is defined by

$$^{\ge n}G \stackrel{\text{def}}{=} \bigcup_{i \ge n} {}^iG \ . \tag{2}$$

The set of paths from r to v on G $(r, v \in \pi(G))$ is defined by

$$paths(G, r)(v) \stackrel{\text{def}}{=} r \bowtie {}^{\ge 1}G \bowtie v \ . \tag{3}$$

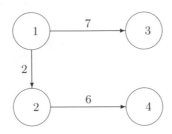

Fig. 1. This is an example of a network

Extrema and Optimization Specifications. The *minlist* operation on X^+ is defined by

$$minlist(f, a) \stackrel{\text{def}}{=} a \ ,$$
$$minlist(f, a \bullet y) \stackrel{\text{def}}{=} bmin(f, (a, minlist(f, y))) \ ,$$
$$bmin(f, (a, b)) \stackrel{\text{def}}{=} \textbf{if } f(a) \leq f(b) \textbf{ then } a \textbf{ else } b \ ,$$

where $a, b \in X$, $y \in X^+$ and $f : X \to \mathbb{R} \cup \{\infty\}$.

Let $R \subseteq X^2$. R is said to be a *quasiordering* if it is transitive $(R \, ; R \subseteq R)$ and reflexive $(id_X \subseteq R)$. Let $R \subseteq X^2$ and $S \subseteq X$ such that R is a quasiordering. The set of *maximal objects* of S wrt R can be defined by

$$maximal(R, S) \stackrel{\text{def}}{=} \{y \in S : (y \bullet S) \cap R \subseteq id_X\} \ .$$

The set of minimum elements of S wrt R can be defined by

$$least(R, S) \stackrel{\text{def}}{=} \{x \in S : x \bullet S \subseteq R\} \quad (R \subseteq X^2, \ S \subseteq X) \ .$$

An equation is said to be an *optimization specification* if it has the form

$$F(y, z) = least(R(y), T(y, z)) \ .$$

$T(y, z)$ is called a *generator of feasible solutions.* Sometimes $R(y) = \leq_{f(y)}$ where $f(y) : X \to \mathbb{R} \cup \{\infty\}$ and $\leq_{f(y)} \stackrel{\text{def}}{=} f(y) \, ; \leq \, ; f(y)^{\text{T}}$.

Descendence. The *descendence* relation on $\wp(A)$ is defined by

$$S \rightsquigarrow T \stackrel{\text{def}}{\Leftrightarrow} T \subseteq S \ \wedge \ (S \neq \emptyset \Rightarrow T \neq \emptyset) \ .$$

$\rightsquigarrow$ is a partial order. The *descendence* relation on $[X \to \wp(Y)]$ is defined by

$$f \rightsquigarrow g \stackrel{\text{def}}{\Leftrightarrow} \forall x \in X.(f(x) \rightsquigarrow g(x)) \ .$$

3   Specification of the Shortest Path Arborescence Problem

Shortest Paths. The cost operation on the paths of a network $N = ((V, A), W)$ can be defined by

$$cost(W)(v) \stackrel{\text{def}}{=} 0 \quad (v \in V) , \qquad cost(W)(a) \stackrel{\text{def}}{=} W(a) \quad (a \in A) , \qquad (4)$$

$$cost(W)(p \bowtie v \bowtie q) \stackrel{\text{def}}{=} cost(W)(p \bowtie v) + cost(W)(v \bowtie q) \quad (p \bowtie v \bowtie q \neq \emptyset) , \quad (5)$$

where $p, q \in {}^{\geq 2}(V, A)$.

The set *of shortest paths* from r to u is defined by

$$shp((G, W), r)(u) \stackrel{\text{def}}{=} least(\leq_{cost(W)}, paths(G, r)(u)) . \qquad (6)$$

The cost of the shortest paths from r to u is defined by

$$cshp((G, W), r)(u) \stackrel{\text{def}}{=} cost(W)(shp((G, W), r)(u)) . \qquad (7)$$

Shortest paths with source r exist on a network $N = ((V, A), W)$ when N does not contain negative length circuits and $DEF(paths((V, A), r)) \neq \emptyset$ ([21]). We have curried the functions *paths*, *shp* and *cshp*, because currying permits shorter specifications, in the sense to avoid the use of universal quantification (see the specifications below).

Arborescences. A graph $G = (V, A)$ is called an *arborescence* with *root* r if r is connected to the other vertices of G by precisely one path in G:

$$r \in V \wedge \quad |.| \circ paths(G, r) = \mathbf{1} , \qquad (8)$$

where $\mathbf{1}$ is the constant matrix associated with 1.

There exist several equivalent definitions for arborescences in the literature, but we have chosen the previous one because it has the a very simple specification in our notation and seems to be the most appropriate definition for the derivation example in this paper.

We define the set of arborescences with nodes in V and root r by

$$arb(r, V) \stackrel{\text{def}}{=} \{(U, T) \text{ arborescence with root r} : U \subseteq V\} .$$

A priori, it is not clear how to specify the set of shortest path arborescences of N with root r with an optimization specification. For this reason we propose to start with a descriptive specification of this set:

$$shpa(N, r) \stackrel{\text{def}}{=} \{G \in sarb(N, r) : paths(G, r) \subseteq shp(N, r)\} , \qquad (9)$$

where $sarb(N, r) \stackrel{\text{def}}{=} \{G \in ssg(\pi(N)) : G \in arb(r, V_N)\}$.

Shortest path arborescences exist on a network $N = ((V, A), W)$ if N does not contain negative length circuits and $DEF(paths((V, A), r)) \neq \emptyset$.

In this paper we will use the following arborescence and path properties.

Proposition 1. *Suppose that $G_1, G_2 \in arb(r, V_1)$, $G_1 = (V_1, A_1)$, $G_2 = (V_2, A_2)$ and $G_2 \in sg(G_1)$. Then the following properties are valid:*
If an arborescence with root r is a spanning subgraph of another arborescence with root r, then both arborescences are equal.

$$ssg(G_1) \cap arb(r, V_1) = \{G_1\} \ . \tag{10}$$

If an arborescence with root r is a subgraph of another arborescence with root r, then the later inherits all the paths from the former.

$$paths(G_2, r) = paths(G_1, r)_{|V_2} \ , \tag{11}$$

Every vertex of V_1 cannot be the end of more than one arc in A_1.

$$+_{|A_1} is\ injective \ . \tag{12}$$

Here $+$ is one of the incidence functions on arcs and not addition.

Proposition 2. *Assume that $G_1 \in sg(G)$, $V = \pi(G)$ and $V_1 = \pi(G_1)$. Then the following two properties are valid:*
A sufficient condition for the existence of an arc of G leading out of V_1 is the existence of a path in G that goes from a vertex in V_1 to a vertex not in V_1.

$$V_1 \bowtie^{\geq 2} G \bowtie (V - V_1) \neq \emptyset \ \Rightarrow \ ALO(G, V_1) \neq \emptyset \ . \tag{13}$$

Each path in G from a vertex of V_1 to a vertex of $V - V_1$ consists of a path in G_1 followed by an arc leading out of G_1 and by a path in G :

$$^{\geq 1} G_1 \bowtie ALO(G, V_1) \bowtie^{\geq 1} G \bowtie (V - V_1) = V_1 \bowtie^{\geq 2} G \bowtie (V - V_1) \ . \tag{14}$$

4   From Specifications to Abstract Algorithms

An abstract optimization algorithm is a recursive definition that uses abstract data types (i.e. it is based on an algebra of formal languages) and calculates a set of optimal solutions. For the transition from specifications to abstract optimization algorithms we consider a method consisting on five tasks: first, an optimization specification is derived from the descriptive specification of the problem, next an optimization recursive definition using some logically defined operations is derived, following a recursive algorithm that calculates optimal objects together with their costs is calculated, next some optimization specifications of this recursive algorithm are transformed into equivalent optimization specifications and finally the obtained recursive algorithm is transformed into an algorithm that only uses algorithmically defined operations.

4.1   Derivation of an Optimization Specification

In our previous work [11, 12] we studied the derivation of recursive network algorithms from optimization specifications. But sometimes, the specification of the problem at hand has not the form of an optimization specification, because it is not clear how to define one. The use of optimization specifications is recommendable, because there are available some design principles and derivation procedures that can be applied to specifications with this form. For that reason, we are motivated to study the derivation of optimization specifications from logical specifications. For such kind of derivations we need results stating the existence of solutions for the logically specified problem.

As an example, we derive an optimization specification from the specification of $shpa(N)$ $(N = (H, W))$. We need the property

$$\left. \begin{array}{l} paths(G, r) \subseteq shp(N, r) \\ DEF(paths(G, r)) \neq \emptyset \end{array} \right\} \Rightarrow paths(G, r); cost(W) = cshp(N, r) \ . \qquad (15)$$

We reason:

$$G \in shpa(N, r)$$
$$\Leftrightarrow \{ \text{ definition } (9) \}$$
$$G \in sarb(N, r) \wedge paths(G, r) \subseteq shp(N, r)$$
$$\Leftrightarrow \{ \text{ by property } (15) \}$$
$$G \in sarb(N, r) \wedge paths(G, r) ; cost(W) = cshp(N, r)$$
$$\Leftrightarrow \{ \text{ definition of shortest paths } \}$$
$$G \in sarb(N, r) \wedge paths(G, r) ; cost(W) = cshp(N, r) \ \wedge$$
$$paths(sarb(N, r), r) ; cost(W) \subseteq cshp(N, r) ; \leq$$
$$\Rightarrow \{ \text{ trivially } \}$$
$$G \subset sarb(N, r) \wedge$$
$$paths(sarb(N, r), r) ; cost(W) \subseteq paths(G, r) ; cost(W) ; \leq$$

Summarizing, we have shown that $shpa(N, r) \subseteq least(S, sarb(N, r))$, where

$$G_1 \, S \, G_2 \stackrel{\text{def}}{\Leftrightarrow} paths(G_2, r) ; cost(W) \subseteq paths(G_1, r) ; cost(W) ; \leq \ .$$

Next, we demonstrate the other inclusion ($\supseteq$). Let $G \in least(S, sarb(N, r))$. Using the existence of shortest path arborescences on N we reason:

$$G_1 \in shpa(N, r)$$
$$\Rightarrow \{ \text{ definition } (9) \}$$
$$paths(G_1, r) \subseteq shp(N, r)$$
$$\Rightarrow \{ \text{ by property } (15) \}$$
$$paths(G_1, r) ; cost(W) = cshp(N, r)$$
$$\Rightarrow \{ \text{ by our assumption } \}$$

48   Juan Eduardo Durán

$$cshp(N,r) \ = \ paths(G_1,r)\,;cost(W) \ \subseteq \ paths(G,r)\,;cost(W)\,;\leq$$
$$\Rightarrow \{ \ \text{trivially} \ \}$$
$$paths(G,r) \subseteq shp(N,r)$$

Hence G is a shortest path arborescence.
Thus the derived optimization specification is

$$shpa(N,r) \ = \ least(S, sarb(N,r)) \ ,$$

where $G_1\,S\,G_2 \stackrel{\text{def}}{\Leftrightarrow} paths(G_2,r)\,;cost(W) \subseteq paths(G_1,r)\,;cost(W)\,;\leq$. Note that
we have used curried functions (*paths*, *shp* and *cshp*) and assertions (*DEF*),
to avoid the use of universal quantification. This makes possible the definition
of more concise properties and the writing of shorter derivations.

4.2   Optimization Algorithms Using Logically Defined Operations

Having an optimization specification, we can attack the problem of deriving a
recursive optimization algorithm from it. Such an algorithm can involve some
logically defined operations. This development task can be done by applying a
design principle (for example, greedy, dynamic programming, etc.) or by using
another derivation procedure (for instance, the procedure in [10, 11] that combines fold, unfold and distributive properties of the *least* operation wrt. algebraic
operations and set operations.) In this section we study how to accomplish this
phase when we apply the greedy design principle.

4.3   A Greedy Theorem

We say that $bases(X)$ is a *set of bases* if

$$bases(X) \ \stackrel{\text{def}}{=} \ maximal(\preceq, pobset(X)) \ , \tag{16}$$

where $\langle pobset(X), \preceq \rangle$ is an ordered set, whose elements are called *partial objects*.
    Next, we present a theorem that can be used for the derivation of greedy
algorithms from a specification of the form

$$obas(X) \ \stackrel{\text{def}}{=} \ least(RB(X), bases(X)) \ , \tag{17}$$

where $RB(X)$ is a relation on $bases(X)$.
    The set of bases containing a partial object t is defined by

$$basc(X,t) \ \stackrel{\text{def}}{=} \ \{t1 \in bases(X) : t \in pobset(X) \land t \preceq t1\} \ . \tag{18}$$

We call t_0 an *initial partial object* if

$$bases(X) = basc(X,t_0) \ . \tag{19}$$

We say that $GS(X,t)$ is a *greedy step* if

$$(basc(X,t) \cap obas(X) \neq \emptyset \wedge t_1 \in GS(X,t)) \Rightarrow (basc(X,t_1) \cap obas(X) \neq \emptyset) \ . \quad (20)$$

In words, if t can be extended to an optimal bases and t_1 is produced after performing a greedy step, then t_1 can be extended to an optimal bases.

Theorem 1 (Greedy Theorem). *Let $GS(X,t)$ be a greedy step and let t_0 be an initial partial object. If the function*

$$h(X,t) \overset{\text{def}}{=} \text{if } t \in bases(X) \text{ then } \{t\} \text{ else } \bigcup \{h(X,t_1) : t_1 \in GS(X,t)\} \quad (21)$$

terminates for t_0, then $obas(X) \rightsquigarrow h(X,t_0)$.

A proof of this theorem is given in the appendix.

4.4   Some Hints for the Application of the Greedy Theorem

The descriptive condition $t \in bases(X)$ is very inefficient and rather complicated. However, it is usually possible to find a more simple or efficient termination condition $cond(X,t)$, which satisfies the formula

$$t \in bases(X) \Leftrightarrow (t \in pobset(X) \wedge cond(X,t)) \ . \quad (22)$$

Usually we can define greedy steps $GS(X,t)$ that have the form

$$GS(X,t) \overset{\text{def}}{=} \{ext(t,a) : a \in selmin(X,t)\} \ .$$

In words, $ext(t,a)$ is used to extend a partial object t with an element a, which is provided by $selmin(X,t)$.

Having a condition $cond(X,t)$ satisfying (22) and the above definition of $GS(X,t)$ the algorithm (21) is trivially equivalent to

$$h(X,t) \overset{\text{def}}{=} \text{if } cond(X,t) \text{ then } \{t\} \text{ else } \bigcup \{h(X,ext(t,a)) : a \in selmin(X,t)\} \ . \quad (23)$$

There is no general rule for the definition of $selmin(X,t)$. In the minimum spanning tree derivation example in [12] $selmin(X,t)$ has the form

$$selmin(X,t) \overset{\text{def}}{=} \bigcup_{C \in sel2(X,t)} least(U(X,t), sel1(X,C)) \ .$$

In the derivation example of this paper $selmin(X,t)$ has the form

$$selmin(X,t) \overset{\text{def}}{=} least(U(X,t), sel(X,t)) \ .$$

We propose to choose/calculate $sel(X,t)$ from the requirement

$$t \in pobset(X) \Rightarrow (cond(X,t) \Leftrightarrow sel(X,t) = \emptyset) \ . \quad (24)$$

To show that h (23) terminates for t_0 it is enough to demonstrate that $pobset(X)$ is finite and

$$a \in sel(X,t) \Rightarrow (t \neq ext(t,a) \wedge t \preceq ext(t,a)) \ . \quad (25)$$

4.5   Derivation of a Shortest Path Arborescences Algorithm

We define the set of partial objects and of bases by

$$pobset(N,r) \overset{\text{def}}{=} \{G \in sg(\pi(N)) : G \in arb(r, V_N)\} \ ,$$
$$bases(N,r) \overset{\text{def}}{=} sarb(N,r) \ .$$

The property (10) and the assumption $DEF(paths(\pi(N),r)) \neq \emptyset$ can be used to show that

$$sarb(N,r) = maximal(SG, pobset(N,r)) \ ,$$

where $G_1 \ SG \ G \overset{\text{def}}{\Leftrightarrow} G_1 \in sg(G)$.

It is trivial that $cond(N,r,G) \overset{\text{def}}{\Leftrightarrow} \pi(G) = V_N$ satisfies (22).
It is also obvious that $G_0 \overset{\text{def}}{=} (\{r\}, \emptyset)$ is an initial partial object.
The extension operation is defined by $ext(G,a) \overset{\text{def}}{=} AddA(G,a)$.
Using (13) it is easy to show that

$$G \in pobset(N,r) \Rightarrow (\pi(G) \neq V_N \ \Leftrightarrow \ Alo(N,G) \neq \emptyset) \ .$$

Thus (24) says that we can define sel by

$$sel(N,r,G) \overset{\text{def}}{=} Alo(N,G) \ .$$

To compare arcs we consider the relation $\leq_{CPA(N,r,G)}$:

$$CPA(N,r,G)(a) \overset{\text{def}}{=} cost(W_N)(p) \ ,$$

where $\{p\} = paths(G,r)(a^-) \bowtie a$.

Thus, our greedy step candidate is

$$GS(N,r,G) \overset{\text{def}}{=} \{AddA(G,a) : a \in selmin(N,r,G)\} \ ,$$

where $selmin(N,r,G) \overset{\text{def}}{=} least(\leq_{CPA(N,r,G)}, Alo(N,G))$.

Next we show that $GS(N,r,G)$ is a greedy step. The proof assumes that the arcs of the network parameter have non negative weights

$$W_N(A_N) \subseteq 0 \, ; \leq \ , \tag{26}$$

Let $a \in least(\leq_{CPA(N,r,G)}, Alo(N,G))$ and let $G_1 = (V_1, A_1)$ be a graph such that $G_1 \in basc(N,r,G) \cap shpa(N,r)$.

We have to show that $basc(N,r,ext(G,a)) \cap shpa(N,r) \neq \emptyset$. We propose to construct an element of $basc(N,r,ext(G,a)) \cap shpa(N,r)$.
If $a \in A_1$ then it is trivial that G_1 is a good candidate.
Now let $a \notin A_1$. Because G_1 spans N there exists an arc $d \in A_1$ such that $d^+ = a^+$. The graph candidate that we would like to construct must contain a and be an arborescence. Therefore, it can not contain d. The following proposition says that a graph that plays the desired role is $(V_1, A_1 \cup \{a\} - \{d\})$.

Proposition 3. *Assume that (26) is valid, $a \in least(\leq_{CPA(N,r,G)}, Alo(N,G))$, $G_1 = (V_1, A_1) \in basc(N, r, G) \cap shpa(N, r)$, $a \notin A_1 \wedge d \in A_1 \wedge d^+ = a^+$. Then*

$$(V_1, A_1 \cup \{a\} - \{d\}) \in basc(N, r, ext(G, a)) \cap shpa(N, r) .$$

A proof of this proposition can be found in the appendix.
Because $pobset(N, r)$ is finite and (25) is valid we have that

$$h(N, r, G) \stackrel{\text{def}}{=} \begin{array}{l} \textbf{if } \pi(G) = V_N \textbf{ then } \{G\} \\ \textbf{else } \bigcup\{h(N, r, AddA(G, a)) : a \in selmin(N, r, G)\} \end{array} ,$$

terminates for G_0.

The result of applying the greedy theorem is $shpa(N, r) \rightsquigarrow h(N, r, (\{r\}, \emptyset))$.

4.6   Computation of the Costs of Optimal Solutions

In [12] and in this work we studied the derivation of greedy algorithms that calculate a set of optimal objects. However, in practice it is sometimes required to compute not only optimal objects but also their costs. For the derivation of a recursive definition that computes a set of optimal objects together with their costs we propose the use of the following derivation procedure

1. First, fuse the cost function with the recursive definition of a set of optimal objects.
2. Finally, if the cost function is not algorithmically specified, we can eliminate the use of it in the previous result by applying the finite differencing strategy.

When we use the above strategy for the case of greedy algorithms of the form (23) we obtain an algorithm schema that calculates optimal objects together with their costs. This schema is presented in the next proposition. We consider the problem of deriving a recursive definition from the specification

$$cobas(X) \stackrel{\text{def}}{=} (id_{pobset(X)}, CPO(X))(obas(X)) ,$$

where $CPO(X)$ is a cost function for partial objects.

Proposition 4. *Suppose the following conditions are satisfied*

1. $(a \in selmin(X, t) \wedge D = CPO(X)(t)) \Rightarrow act(X, t, a, D) = CPO(X)(ext(t, a))$.

2. $D_0 = CPO(X)(t_0)$.

If the function

$$g(X, t, D) \stackrel{\text{def}}{=} \begin{array}{l} \textbf{if } cond(X, t) \textbf{ then } \{(t, D)\} \\ \textbf{else } \bigcup\{g(X, ext(t, a), act(X, t, a, D)) : a \in selmin(X, t)\} \end{array} ,$$

terminates for (X, t_0, D_0) then $cobas(X) \rightsquigarrow g(X, t_0, D_0)$.

To calculate an algorithm for $act(X, t, a, D)$ we propose to use the assumptions $a \in selmin(X, t)$ and $D = CPO(X)(t)$.

4.7   Calculating Shortest Path Arborescences Together with their Costs

The cost function on arborescences can be defined by

$$CPO(N, r)(G)(u) \stackrel{\text{def}}{=} cost(W_N)(paths(G, r)(u)) .$$

The *selective updating* operation on matrices is defined in [14] by

$$x[i \leftarrow e](j) \stackrel{\text{def}}{=} \textbf{if } j = i \textbf{ then } e \textbf{ else } x(j) , \tag{27}$$

where x is a matrix.

It can be trivially shown that the condition 4.2 is satisfied by $D_0 \stackrel{\text{def}}{=} \emptyset[r \leftarrow 0]$. Using $a \in Alo(N, G)$ and $D = CPO(N, r)(G)$ let us calculate $act(N, r, G, a, D)$. We reason:

- $u \in \pi(G)$: By property (11) and our assumption:

$$cost(W_N)(paths(AddA(G, a), r)(u)) = cost(W_N)(paths(G, r)(u)) = D(u)$$

- $u = a^+$:

$$
\begin{aligned}
& cost(W_N)(paths(AddA(G, a), r)(a^+)) & \\
& = cost(W_N)(paths(AddA(G, a), r)(a^-) \bowtie a) & \text{definition } (8) \\
& = cost(W_N)(paths(G, r)(a^-) \bowtie a) & \text{arborescences } (11) \\
& = cost(W_N)(paths(G, r)(a^-)) + cost(W_N)(a) & \text{costs } (5) \\
& = D(a^-) + W_N(a) & \text{assumption, } (4)
\end{aligned}
$$

Hence, by definition (27) we can define

$$act(N, r, G, a, D) \stackrel{\text{def}}{=} D[a^+ \leftarrow D(a^-) + W_N(a)] .$$

It is obvious that the algorithm

$$
\begin{aligned}
g(N, r, G, D) \stackrel{\text{def}}{=} & \textbf{if } \pi(G) = V_N \textbf{ then } \{(G, D)\} \\
& \textbf{else } \bigcup \{g(N, r, AddA(G, a), act(N, r, G, a, D)) : \\
& \quad a \in selmin(N, r, G)\}
\end{aligned}
\tag{28}
$$

terminates for (N, r, G_0, D_0). Thus by the last proposition we have that

$$cobas(N, r) \rightsquigarrow g(N, r, (\{r\}, \emptyset), D_0) .$$

It can be trivially shown that if $D = CPO(N, r)(G)$ and $b \in Alo(N, G)$ then

$$CPA(N, r, G)(b) = D(b^-) + W_N(b) .$$

4.8   Transformation of Optimization Specifications

A tactic for the improvement of an optimization algorithm is the transformation of some of its optimization specifications in such a way that a benefit is obtained. For instance, in [12] an optimization specification involving a generator that cannot be computed by an efficient algorithm is transformed into another equivalent optimization specification which has a generator set that can be computed by a very efficient algorithm. Another example is that sometimes an optimization specification can be transformed into new equivalent optimization specification whose generator is a subset of the generator of the old specification. Such kind of transformations can be captured by transformation rules. For instance, the rule saying that if $C : w \to \mathbb{R} \cup \{\infty\}$ then:

$$(v \subseteq w \ \wedge \ (w - v) \subseteq v \, ; <_C) \Rightarrow least(\leq_C, v) \, = \, least(\leq_C, w) \, . \qquad (29)$$

To illustrate the use of this rule, we give an outline of the proof of the equivalence

$$least(\leq_{CPA(N,r,G)}, Alo(N, G)) = least(\leq_{CPA(N,r,G)}, w) \, , \qquad (30)$$

where $w = \bigcup \{least(\leq_{CPA(N,r,G)}, Alo(N, G) \bowtie x) : x \in V_N\}$.
If $\pi(G) = V_N$ the proof is trivial. Assume that $\pi(G) \neq V_N$. Because

$$least(\leq_{CPA(N,r,G)}, Alo(N, G) \bowtie x) \subseteq Alo(N, G) \, .$$

it is true that $w \subseteq Alo(N, G)$.

Using (13), it is trivial to show that $w \neq \emptyset$. Using that $w \neq \emptyset$ it can be easily shown that $(Alo(N, G) - w) \subseteq w \, ; <_{CPA(N,r,G)}$.

4.9   Derivation of a Recursive Algorithm that only Uses Algorithmically Defined Operations

Suppose that an optimization recursive algorithm, which uses some implicitly defined operations is available. To perform the task of transforming such an algorithm into another one that only uses algorithmically defined operations, the paradigm of finite differencing ([19, 18]) can be used. Next we show for the case of greedy algorithms how this strategy can be applied.

Proposition 5. *Suppose that the definition*

$$h(x) \stackrel{\text{def}}{=} \textbf{if} \ \varphi(x) \ \textbf{then} \ \{H(x)\} \ \textbf{else} \ \bigcup \{h(O(x, a)) : a \in T(x)\} \, ,$$

terminates for x_0, $s(x)$ is an operation such that

$$(a \in T(x) \wedge K = s(x)) \Rightarrow upd(x, a, K) = s(O(x, a)) \, ,$$

and there exists an operation $T1$ such that $T(x) \rightsquigarrow T1(x, s(x))$.
Then $h(x_0) \rightsquigarrow f(x_0, K_0)$, where

$$K_0 \stackrel{\text{def}}{=} s(x_0) \, ,$$
$$f(x, K) \stackrel{\text{def}}{=} \textbf{if} \ \varphi_1(x, K) \ \textbf{then} \ \{H(x)\}$$
$$\textbf{else} \ \bigcup \{f(O(x, a), upd(x, a, K)) : a \in T1(x, K)\} \qquad ,$$
$$\varphi_1(x, K) \stackrel{\text{def}}{=} \varphi(x)[K/s(x)] \, .$$

$t[x/l]$ denotes the expression t with x substituted for each occurrence of l.

This result is more general than the one presented in [12], because we require that $T(x) \rightsquigarrow T1(x, s(x))$ instead of assuming that $T1(x, s(x)) = T(x)$. We will see below that this proposition is necessary for our shortest path arborescence derivation example.

Usually an algorithm for $upd(x, a, K)$ can be calculated by assuming that $a \in T(x)$ and $K = s(x)$.

4.10 Application of Finite Differencing to a Shortest Path Arborescence Algorithm

The obvious choice for s is

$$s(N, r, G, D)(v) = least(\leq_{CPA(N,r,G)}, Alo(N, G) \bowtie v) \ .$$

With this definition $s(N, r, G, D)(v)$ $(v \in V_N)$ can contain more than one element. We noted that this is more than we need, because it is enough to have one element available. Thus, for efficiency reasons, we propose to choose $s(N, r, G, D)(v)$ to be as small as possible. Hence we specify s by

$$U(N, r, G) \rightsquigarrow s(N, r, G, D) \ \land \ MDET(s(N, r, G, D)) \neq \emptyset \ ,$$

where $U(N, r, G)(v) \overset{\text{def}}{=} least(\leq_{CPA(N,r,G)}, Alo(N, G) \bowtie v)$.

Next, we calculate K_0. Using (1) we have:
$$least(\leq_{CPA(N,r,(\{r\},\emptyset))}, Alo(N, \{r\}) \bowtie x)$$
$$= least(\leq_{CPA(N,r,(\{r\},\emptyset))}, \textbf{if } r \bullet x \in A_N \textbf{ then } \{r \bullet x\} \textbf{ else } \emptyset)$$
$$= \textbf{if } r \bullet x \in A_N \textbf{ then } \{r \bullet x\} \textbf{ else } \emptyset$$
Thus the condition $K_0 = s(N, (\{r\}, \emptyset), D_0)$ is satisfied if we define

$$K_0(x) \overset{\text{def}}{=} \textbf{if } r \bullet x \in A_N \textbf{ then } \{r \bullet x\} \textbf{ else } \emptyset \ .$$

Next we calculate $T1$. Armed with (30) and

$$\forall\, i \in I. \begin{pmatrix} least(\leq_f, X_i) \\ \rightsquigarrow \\ least(\leq_f, Y_i) \end{pmatrix} \Rightarrow least(\leq_f, \bigcup_{i \in I} X_i) \rightsquigarrow least(\leq_f, \bigcup_{i \in I} Y_i) \ , \quad (31)$$

we calculate:
$$selmin(N, r, G)$$
$$= least(\leq_{CPA(N,r,G)}, Alo(N, G))$$
$$= least(\leq_{CPA(N,r,G)}, \bigcup \{least(\leq_{CPA(N,r,G)}, Alo(N, G) \bowtie v) : v \in V_N\})$$
$$\rightsquigarrow least(\leq_{CPA(N,r,G)}, \bigcup \{s(N, r, G, D)(v) : v \in V_N\})$$
$$= least(\leq_{CPA(N,r,G)}, s(N, r, G, D)(V_N))$$

Let $\ T1(N, r, G, D, K) \overset{\text{def}}{=} least(\leq_{CPA(N,r,G)}, K(V_N))$. The last proposition is necessary because the result of the reasoning above says that

$$T(N, r, G, D) = selmin(N, r, G) \rightsquigarrow T1(N, r, G, D, s(N, r, G, D)) \ .$$

The following algorithm for $upd(N, r, G, y \bullet v, D, K)$ can be calculated

$$upd(N, r, G, y \bullet v, D, K)(i) = \begin{cases} \emptyset & v = i \\ \sigma(N, r, G, y \bullet v, D, K)(i) & v \bullet i \in A_N \wedge i \notin \pi(G) \wedge v \neq i \\ K(i) & else \end{cases} ,$$

where

$$\sigma(N, r, G, y \bullet v, D, K)(i) \stackrel{\text{def}}{=} \textbf{if } K(i) = \emptyset \textbf{ then } \{v \bullet i\}$$
$$\textbf{else } bmin(CPA(N, r, AddA(G, a)), (K(x), v \bullet i)) \quad .$$

A derivation of this algorithm is presented in the appendix for the interested reader. Thus the result of applying the last proposition is

$$g(N, r, (\{r\}, \emptyset), D_0) \rightsquigarrow f(N, r, (\{r\}, \emptyset), D_0, K_0) \quad ,$$

where

$$
\begin{aligned}
&f(N, r, G, D, K) = \\
&\quad \textbf{if } \pi(G) = V_N \textbf{ then } \{(G, D)\} \\
&\quad \textbf{else } \bigcup \{f(N, AddA(G, a), act(N, r, G, a, D), \\
&\qquad\qquad upd(N, r, G, a, D, K)) : a \in least(\leq_{CPA(N, r, G)}, K(V_N))
\end{aligned}
\qquad (32)
$$

5 From Recursive Definitions to Imperative Algorithms

The transition from a recursive definition computing an optimal set of objects to an imperative algorithm is decomposed into the following three tasks:

1. The optimization recursive algorithm is transformed into another one that calculates only one optimal solution.
2. In addition the abstract datatypes used by the recursive definition are implemented with concrete datatypes.
3. Finally, an imperative algorithm is obtained after the application of recursion elimination rules.

In the derivation example of this paper we follow these stages in order; but in general, there is no obligatory order for the tasks 1. and 2. In [12] we proposed to follow first the stage 2. and then the stage 1. and we presented a minimum spanning tree derivation example.

5.1 Computation of One Optimal Solution

For the derivation of a recursive definition that computes only one optimal solution, we propose the use of the following derivation procedure:

1. First, transform each optimization specifications into an optimization expression denoting only one optimal solution.

2. Finally, apply a transformation rule to go from a recursive definition that calculates a set of solutions to a recursive algorithm that computes only one optimal solution. The verification of such transformation rules usually involves the application of monotonicity rules of the descendence relation wrt. set and algebraic operations; for instance:

$$P \rightsquigarrow Q \;\Rightarrow\; \bigcup\{S(a) : a \in P\} \rightsquigarrow \bigcup\{S(a) : a \in Q\}$$

Sometimes, the first task can be done by applying special transformation rules; for example:

$$least(\leq_f, \bigcup_{i \in I} h(i)) \rightsquigarrow minlist(f, \bullet_{j=1}^{n} h^{\mathcal{E}}(g(j))) \;, \tag{33}$$

where $h : Z \to \wp(X)$, $I \subseteq Z$, $f : X \to \mathbb{R} \cup \{\infty\}$, $MDET(h) = \{h\}$, $g : \{1, ..., n\} \to I$ is a bijection and $h^{\mathcal{E}}(z) \overset{\text{def}}{=}$ if $h(z) = \emptyset$ then ε else $h(z)$.

We perform the last task by applying transformation rules that are valid for specific recursive patterns. As an example, we propose a rule that can be used for the class of greedy algorithms.

Proposition 6. *If f is defined as in (5) and $T_1(x, K) \rightsquigarrow \{T_2(x, K)\}$ then*

$$f(x_0, K_0) \rightsquigarrow \{l(x_0, K_0)\} \;,$$
$$l(x, K) \overset{\text{def}}{=} \; \text{if } \varphi_1(x, K) \text{ then } H(x)$$
$$\text{else } l(O(x, T_2(x, K)), upd(x, T_2(x, K), K)) \;.$$

5.2   Computation of a Shortest Path Tree

Assuming that $V_N = \{1, ..., n\}$ and using (33) we reason:

$$least(\leq_{CPA(N,r,G)}, K(V_N)) = least(\leq_{CPA(N,r,G)}, \bigcup_{i=1}^{n} K(i))$$
$$\rightsquigarrow minlist(CPA(N, r, G), \bullet_{i=1}^{n} K^{\mathcal{E}}(i)) \;.$$

Hence we can define $T_2(N, r, G, D, K)$ by

$$T_2(N, r, G, D, K) \overset{\text{def}}{=} minlist(CPA(N, r, G), \bullet_{i=1}^{n} K^{\mathcal{E}}(i)) \;.$$

Using the last proposition we obtain that

$$f(N, r, (\{r\}, \emptyset), D_0, K_0) \rightsquigarrow \{l(N, r, (\{r\}, \emptyset), D_0, K_0)\} \;,$$

where f is defined in (32) and

$$l(N, r, G, D, K) = \; \text{if } \pi(G) = V_N \text{ then } (G, D) \tag{34}$$
$$\text{else } l(N, r, AddA(G, a), act(N, r, G, a, D),$$
$$upd1(N, r, G, a, D, K))$$
$$\text{where } a = T_2(N, r, G, D, K)$$

5.3   Datatype Representation and Implementation of Functions

Datatypes are modeled by *heterogeneous algebras*. We use the following procedure for the representation of abstract datatypes: First a *concrete domain* T is defined to represent each *abstract domain* T'. We denote the fact that X is represented by Y by $Y' \approx X$. Following, an onto *abstraction function* $' : T \to T'$ is defined for each abstract domain T'. An operation $f^\circ : S_1 \times \ldots \times S_m \to T$ is said to *implement* an *abstract operation* $f : S_1' \times \ldots \times S_m' \to T'$ if $f(x') = (f^\circ(x))'$. Next, for each abstract operation f we calculate an operation f° such that f° implements f. Finally, *concrete implementations* of abstract recursive definitions are calculated with the help of the following proposition.

Proposition 7. *Suppose that f° and g° implement f and g, $X' \times Y'$ is represented by $X \times Y$, and $(x, y)' = (x', y')$ for all $x \in X$, $y \in Y$. Then π implements π, ρ implements ρ, $f^\circ \circ g^\circ$ implements $f \circ g$ and (f°, g°) implements (f, g).*

Next we show some examples of abstract datatype implementations. Due to size limitations, we do not present the derivations of abstract operation implementations.

5.4   Implementation of Graphs and Networks

We represent a graph with a pair of *boolean matrices*

$$GRAPH(Z)' \approx \{(V, A) \text{ graph} : V \subseteq Z\} \ ,$$
$$GRAPH(Z) \stackrel{\text{def}}{=} \{(Y, M) \in B(Z) \times B(Z \times Z) : \phi((Y, M), Z)\} \ ,$$

where

$$B(Z) \stackrel{\text{def}}{=} [Z \to \{0, 1\}] \ ,$$
$$\phi((Y, M), Z) \stackrel{\text{def}}{\Leftrightarrow} \forall (x, y \in Z).(M(x, y) = 1 \to Y(x) - Y(y) = 1) \ .$$

The abstraction function is defined by $(Y, M)' \stackrel{\text{def}}{=} (V, A)$ where

$$x \in V \stackrel{\text{def}}{\Leftrightarrow} Y(x) = 1 \ , \qquad x \bullet y \in A \stackrel{\text{def}}{\Leftrightarrow} M(x, y) = 1 \ .$$

It is easy to verify that $\mathcal{G}_0' = (\{r\}, \emptyset)$, where $\mathcal{G}_0 \stackrel{\text{def}}{=} \mathbf{0}[r \leftarrow 1]$ (remember definition (27)).

We can derive the following implementation of $AddA$:

$$AddA^\circ((Y, M), (x, y)) \stackrel{\text{def}}{=} (Y[x \leftarrow 1][y \leftarrow 1], M[(x, y) \leftarrow 1]) \ .$$

We use matrices of numbers to represent weight functions

$$WF(nodes(E))' \approx [E \to \mathbb{R} \cup \{\infty\}] \ ,$$
$$WF(Z) \stackrel{\text{def}}{=} [Z \times Z \to \mathbb{R} \cup \{\infty\}] \ ,$$
$$P'(x \bullet y) \stackrel{\text{def}}{=} P(x, y) \qquad (x \bullet y \in E) \ .$$

We use the representation of graphs and of weight functions to define the representation of networks.

$$NETWORK(Z)' \approx \{((V,A),W) \text{ network} : V \subseteq Z\} \ ,$$
$$NETWORK(Z) \stackrel{\text{def}}{=} \{(((Y,M),P) \in GRAPH(Z) \times WF(Z) : \varphi(((Y,M),P),Z)\} \ ,$$
$$((Y,M),P)' \stackrel{\text{def}}{=} ((Y,M)',P') \ .$$

where $\varphi(((Y,M),P),Z) \stackrel{\text{def}}{=} \forall\,(x,y \in Z).(M(x,y) = 0 \Rightarrow P(x,y) = \infty).$

5.5   Implementation of Cost Functions

The set of cost functions for arborescences with vertices on V is denoted by $CFA(V)$ and represented by a set of matrices with values on $\mathbb{R} \cup \{\infty\} \cup \{\uparrow\}$.

$$CFA(V)' \approx MDET \lhd [V \rightarrow \wp(\mathbb{R} \cup \{\infty\})] \ ,$$
$$CFA(V) \stackrel{\text{def}}{=} [V \rightarrow \mathbb{R} \cup \{\infty\} \cup \{\uparrow\}] \ ,$$
$$h'(i) \stackrel{\text{def}}{=} \textbf{if } h(i) = \uparrow \textbf{ then } \emptyset \textbf{ else } \{h(i)\} \ .$$

The value $\uparrow$ is used to denote undefinition (i.e. $h(i) = \uparrow$ means that $h(i)$ is undefined).

It is easy to verify that $\mathcal{D}_0' = \mathcal{D}_0$, where $\mathcal{D}_0 \stackrel{\text{def}}{=} \uparrow[r \leftarrow 0]$.

We can derive the following implementation of act:

$$act^{\circ}(\mathcal{N}, r, \mathcal{G}, (x,y), \mathcal{D}) \stackrel{\text{def}}{=} \mathcal{D}[y \leftarrow \mathcal{D}(x) + \rho(\mathcal{N})(x,y)] \ .$$

Now we implement a domain for the length functions $CPA(N,r,G)$.

$$(CF(Y))' \approx DET \lhd [Y' \rightarrow \wp(\mathbb{R} \cup \{\infty\})] \ ,$$
$$CF(Y) \stackrel{\text{def}}{=} [Y \rightarrow \mathbb{R} \cup \{\infty\}] \ ,$$
$$h'(x \bullet y) \stackrel{\text{def}}{=} \{h(x,y)\} \ ,$$

where $Y' = \{y' : y \in Y\}$ and Y is a binary relation.

One can derive the following solution to the equation $(\mathcal{CPA}(\mathcal{N},r,\mathcal{G}))' = CPA(\mathcal{N}',r,\mathcal{G}')$

$$\mathcal{CPA}(\mathcal{N}, r, \mathcal{G})(x,y) \stackrel{\text{def}}{=} \mathcal{D}(x) + \rho(\mathcal{N})(x,y) \ .$$

Note that we have used filters and assertions to obtain a very concise definition of the abstract domains above.

5.6   Implementation of a Shortest Path Tree Algorithm

Next we implement a domain for the K argument of (34).

$$DK' \approx MDET \lhd [V \rightarrow \wp(V^2)] \ ,$$
$$DK \stackrel{\text{def}}{=} [V \rightarrow (V \times V) \cup \{\uparrow\}] \ ,$$
$$h'(i) \stackrel{\text{def}}{=} \textbf{if } h(i) = \uparrow \textbf{ then } \emptyset \textbf{ else } \{h(i)\} \ .$$

The value $\uparrow$ is used to denote undefinition.

One can derive the following solution to $\mathcal{K}_0' = \mathcal{K}_0$:

$$\mathcal{K}_0(i) \stackrel{\text{def}}{=} (r, i) ,$$

where $i \in V$.

One can calculate the following solution to the equation

$$(upd^{\circ}(\mathcal{N}, r, \mathcal{G}, (v, y), \mathcal{D}, \mathcal{K})' = upd(\mathcal{N}', r, \mathcal{G}', v \bullet y, \mathcal{D}', \mathcal{K}') ,$$

$$upd^{\circ}((\mathcal{H}, \mathcal{W}), r, \mathcal{G}, (y, v), \mathcal{D}, \mathcal{K})(i) =$$
$$\begin{cases} \uparrow & v = i \\ \sigma^{\circ}((\mathcal{H}, \mathcal{W}), r, \mathcal{G}, (y, v), \mathcal{D}, \mathcal{K})(i) & v \neq i \wedge \rho(\mathcal{H})(v, i) = 1 \wedge \pi(\mathcal{H})(i) = 0 \\ \mathcal{K}(i) & else \end{cases} ,$$

where

$$\sigma^{\circ}(\mathcal{N}, r, \mathcal{G}, (y, v), \mathcal{D}, \mathcal{K})(i)$$
$$\stackrel{\text{def}}{=} \textbf{if } \mathcal{K}(i) = \uparrow \textbf{ then } (v, i)$$
$$\textbf{else } bmin(\mathcal{CPA}(\mathcal{N}, r, AddA(\mathcal{G}, (y, v))), (\mathcal{K}(i), (v, i))) .$$

Following, we implement T_2. We can derive the following solution to the equation
$(T_2^{\circ}(\mathcal{N}, r, \mathcal{G}, \mathcal{D}, \mathcal{K})' = T_2(\mathcal{N}', r, \mathcal{G}', \mathcal{D}', \mathcal{K}')$

$$T_2^{\circ}(\mathcal{N}, r, \mathcal{G}, \mathcal{D}, \mathcal{K}) \stackrel{\text{def}}{=} minlist^{\circ}(\mathcal{CPA}(\mathcal{N}, r, \mathcal{G}), \bullet_{i=1}^{n} \mathcal{K}^{\varepsilon^{\circ}}(i)) ,$$

where $\mathcal{K}^{\varepsilon^{\circ}}(i) \stackrel{\text{def}}{=} \textbf{if } \mathcal{K}(i) = \uparrow \textbf{ then } \varepsilon \textbf{ else } \mathcal{K}(i)$.

It can be trivially shown that the implementation of the abstract recursive shortest path tree algorithm (34) is $l^{\circ}(\mathcal{N}, r, \mathcal{G}_0, \mathcal{D}_0, \mathcal{K}_0)$, where

$$l^{\circ}(\mathcal{N}, r, \mathcal{G}, \mathcal{D}, \mathcal{K}) = \textbf{if } \pi(\mathcal{G}) = \pi(\pi(\mathcal{N})) \textbf{ then } (\mathcal{G}, \mathcal{D}) \qquad (35)$$
$$\textbf{else } l^{\circ}(\mathcal{N}, r, AddA^{\circ}(\mathcal{G}, b), act^{\circ}(\mathcal{N}, r, \mathcal{G}, b, \mathcal{D}),$$
$$upd^{\circ}(\mathcal{N}, r, \mathcal{G}, b, \mathcal{D}, \mathcal{K}))$$
$$\textbf{where } b = T_2^{\circ}(\mathcal{N}, r, \mathcal{G}, \mathcal{D}, \mathcal{K})$$

5.7 Derivation of Imperative Algorithms

To go from recursive definitions using concrete datatypes to an imperative algorithm, we use rules that eliminate recursion and rules that remove some non recursive functional definitions by cases. To improve the resulting imperative algorithms we consider the transformation of imperative algorithms.

Language. We consider a subset of the language Modula-2 [22] consisting of the statements assignment, sequential composition, the conditional statement, while loop and for repetition. In addition, we use functional procedures whose parameters are only passed by value. An expression is called a functional procedure if it has the syntax

$$\textbf{FUN } f(x_1 : T_1; \ldots; x_n : T_n) : T; d \textbf{ BEGIN } S \textbf{ RETURN } E \textbf{ END } f , \quad (36)$$

where $x_1, \ldots, x_n$ are the formal parameters, $T_1, \ldots, T_n, T$ are types, d is a local declaration of variables, S is a sentence and E is the result expression. In addition we require that the identifier f does not appear in S and E.

An expression is said to be a functional procedure call if it has syntax $f(e_1, \ldots, e_n)$ where $e_1, \ldots, e_n$ are actual parameter expressions.

We base our study on Hoare formulas and their semantics. For the verification of Hoare formulas the Hoare calculus can be used.

The semantics of the functional procedure (36) for the domain $\{x : \varphi(x)\}$ is a function g such that $\{\varphi(x)\}\ S; y := E\ \{y = g(x)\}$ is correct. (We require that y does not appear on S.)

Using definition (27) we define the assignment of a value to an index of a matrix as in [14] by

$$x(i_1, \ldots, i_m) := e \quad \stackrel{\text{def}}{=} \quad x := x[(i_1, \ldots, i_m) \leftarrow e] \ . \tag{37}$$

Transformation Rules. The *transformation rule* $\dfrac{[\,C\,]\quad def.g}{deffp.f}$ where C is a formula, $def.g$ is a recursive definition that defines a function h and $deffp.f$ is a functional procedure is correct iff: The condition C implies that the semantics of $deffp.f$ coincides with h on $dom(h)$.

The transformation rule $\dfrac{[\,C\,]\ S}{T}$, where S and T are imperative programs and C is a formula, is correct iff $\forall\, \phi.\forall\, \varphi.(C \Rightarrow (\{\phi\}\ S\ \{\varphi\} \Rightarrow \{\phi\}\ T\ \{\varphi\}))$ (This definition can be found in [2]). To show such a property the Hoare calculus can be used.

5.8   Derivation of a Shortest Path Tree Imperative Algorithm

The sets $REG(V)$ and $ARCS(V)$ are defined by

$$REG(V) \stackrel{\text{def}}{=} GRAPH(V) \times CFA(V) \ ,$$
$$ARCS(V) \stackrel{\text{def}}{=} V \times V \ .$$

Applying the rule of tail recursion elimination to $def.l°$ (35) and using the fact that $x, y, z := b, c, d$ is equivalent to $z := d;\ y := c;\ x := b$ if z does not appear in c and b, and y does not appear on b , we obtain:

FUN $l°((\mathcal{H}, \mathcal{W}) : NETWORK(V), r : V, (\mathcal{U}, \mathcal{T}) : GRAPH(V),$
$\qquad\qquad \mathcal{K} : DK) : REG(V);$

$VAR\ a : ARCS(V)$
BEGIN
WHILE not $(\mathcal{U} = \pi(\mathcal{H}))$ **DO**
$\quad a := T_2°((\mathcal{H}, \mathcal{W}), r, (\mathcal{U}, \mathcal{T}), \mathcal{D}, \mathcal{K});\quad \mathcal{K} := upd1°((\mathcal{H}, \mathcal{W}), r, (\mathcal{U}, \mathcal{T}), a, \mathcal{D}, \mathcal{K});$
$\quad \mathcal{D} := act°((\mathcal{H}, \mathcal{W}), r, (\mathcal{U}, \mathcal{T}), a, \mathcal{D});\quad (\mathcal{U}, \mathcal{T}) := AddA°((\mathcal{U}, \mathcal{T}), a)$
END
RETURN $((\mathcal{U}, \mathcal{T}), \mathcal{D})$
END $l°$

Using definition (37) and applying to the second assignment of the iteration step a well known rule to eliminate matrix assignments we obtain:

FUN $l°((\mathcal{H}, \mathcal{W}) : NETWORK(V), r : V, (\mathcal{U}, \mathcal{T}) : GRAPH(V),$
$\qquad\qquad\qquad \mathcal{D} : CFA(V), \mathcal{K} : DK) : REG(V);$
$VAR\ a : ARCS(V)$
$VAR\ R : [V \rightarrow LIST(V)]$
BEGIN
WHILE not $(\mathcal{U} = \pi(\mathcal{H}))$ **DO**
FOR $i := 1$ **TO** n **DO**
IF $\mathcal{K}(i) = \uparrow$ **THEN** $R(i) := \varepsilon$ **ELSE** $R(i) := \mathcal{K}(i)$ **END**
END
$\quad a := minlist°(\mathcal{CPA}((\mathcal{H}, \mathcal{W}), r, (\mathcal{U}, \mathcal{T})), \bullet_{i=1}^{n} R(i));$
FOR $i := 1$ **TO** n **DO**
IF $i = \pi(a)$
THEN $\mathcal{K}(i) := \uparrow$
ELSIF $\rho(\mathcal{H})(\pi(a), i) = 1 \wedge \mathcal{U}(i) = 0 \wedge i \neq \pi(a)$
THEN $\mathcal{K}(i) := \sigma°((\mathcal{H}, \mathcal{W}), r, (\mathcal{U}, \mathcal{T}), (y, v), \mathcal{D}, \mathcal{K})(i)$
ELSE $\mathcal{K}(i) := \mathcal{K}(i)$
END
END
$\mathcal{D}(\rho(a)) := \mathcal{D}(\pi(a)) + \mathcal{W}(a);$
$\mathcal{U}(\pi(a)) := 1; \mathcal{U}(\rho(a)) := 1; \mathcal{T}(a) := 1;$
END
RETURN $((\mathcal{U}, \mathcal{T}), \mathcal{D})$
END $l°$

The algorithm for $l°$ is $O(n^2)$ because the iteration condition can be computed in $O(n)$ and each iteration step is $O(n)$.

6 Discussion

We propose a flexible methodology for the derivation of network algorithms because, whenever an algorithm scheme for a derivation phase is difficult to be found, we can search for a derivation procedure to complete the phase.

In contrast with the previous work in the literature ([5, 9]), where the generator part of optimisation specification is an algorithm, we propose to specify feasible sets logically. This helps avoiding the presentation of incorrect feasible set algorithms.

Our greedy theorem is rather general, because it can be used to derive algorithms for all the problems in [9, 10] and the minimum spanning tree algorithms of Prim and Kruskal. Furthermore, our greedy algorithm schema (23) uses a more efficient greedy step than the greedy step of the greedy algorithm in [9], which takes a minimum element from a set of partial object extensions. Moreover, our greedy theorem assumes a logical definition of bases instead of considering algorithms that generate bases like in [5, 9]. Our greedy algorithm schema (23) is similar to one of the algorithm schemas of Sect. 6 of [8]. But in [8] the author says that the problem of finding conditions that guarantee the correctness of the algorithm schemas of Sect. 6 is open and we have improved upon this situation. In addition, our greedy theorem is applicable to obtain the well-known best-in greedy algorithms for set systems like matroids, greedoids and matroid embeddings ([13, 16, 15]).

Another characteristic of our derivation method is that the fourth phase for the derivation of an abstract optimisation algorithm (i.e the phase involving finite differencing) is necessary. This phase was not needed previously in the literature, because optimisation algorithms were derived from algorithms that calculate feasible object sets.

The proposed derivation method is rather general in the sense that it can be used for the derivation of several network algorithms and of other kind of optimisation problems.

In [12] we show that the phase for the derivation of an algorithm that computes only one optimal solution can be done after the datatype implementation phase to allow a very efficient implementation of optimization expressions. The reason is that we are not obligated to use the word notation.

We hope that after the development of some new network algorithms, new derivation phases could be discovered. As a consequence, new derivation procedures could be proposed.

We originally based our research on relation algebras and we found that the use of Möller's algebra of formal languages permits more concision and a simpler transition from recursive definitions to imperative algorithms than our previous work using relations ([10]). This happens because we now use a more concise notation and a translation phase from relational into functional notation is unnecessary. In addition, in this paper we suggest a direct derivation of an optimisation algorithm from a descriptive specification instead of having an intermediate step consisting of the derivation of a recursive algorithm that generates a set of objects that are feasible to be optimal ([10, 11]). This results in shorter and simpler derivations.

References

[1] R. C. Backhouse, van den Eijnde, and A.J.M. van Gasteren. Calculating path algorithms. *Science of Computer Programming*, 22:3–19, 1994.

[2] R. Behnke. *Transformationelle Programmentwicklung im Rahmen relationaler und sequentieller Algebren*. PhD thesis, Christian Albrecht Universität zu Kiel, 1998.

[3] R. Berghammer. *Zur formalen Entwicklung von graphentheoretischen Algorithmen durch Transformationen*. PhD thesis, Technische Universität München, Februar 1984. TUM-I8403.

[4] R. Berghammer, B. von Karger, and A. Wolf. Relation-algebraic derivation of spanning tree algorithms. In Johan Jeuring, editor, *Mathematics of Program Construction*, volume 1422 of *Lecture Notes in Computer Science*, pages 167–189, Marstrand, Sweden, June 1998. Springer Verlag.

[5] R. Bird and O. de Moor. *Algebra of Programming*. C.A.R. Hoare series editor. Prentice Hall, 1997.

[6] R.S. Bird, O. De Moor, and J.C.P. Woodcock. Solving optimization problems with catamorphisms. In *Mathematics of Program Construction*, volume 669 of *Lecture Notes in Computer Science*, pages 45–66. Springer Verlag, 1993.

[7] T. Brunn, B.Möller, and Russling M. Layered graph traversals and hamiltonian path problems - an algebraic approach. In Jeuring, editor, *Mathematics of Program Construction*, volume 1422 of *Lecture Notes in Computer Science*, pages 96–121. Springer Verlag, June 1998.

[8] B. Charlier. The greedy algorithms class: Formalization, syntesis and generalization. Technical Report B-1348, Université Catholique de Louvain, 1995.

[9] S. Curtis. *A Relational Approach to Optimization Problems*. PhD thesis, Somerville College, Oxford, 1996.

[10] J.E. Durán. *Desenvolvimento transformacional de algoritmos em redes baseado em álgebras relacionais*. PhD thesis, Departamento de Informática da Pontifícia Universidade Católica do Rio de Janeiro, October 1999.

[11] J.E. Durán. Transformational derivation of network algorithms based on an algebra of formal languages. In *WAIT 2000 Proceedings (Argentine Workshop on Theoretical Computer Science)*, pages 1–12, 2000.

[12] J.E. Durán. Derivation of efficient imperative network algorithms from descriptive optimisation specifications. In *WAIT'2001 Proceedings (Argentine Workshop on Theoretical Computer Science)*, pages 71–90, 2001.

[13] J. Edmonds. Matroids and the greedy algorithm. *Math. Programming*, 1:127–136, 1971.

[14] D. Gries. *The Science of Programming*. Springer-Verlag, 1981.

[15] P. Helman, B. M. E. Moret, and H. D. Shapiro. An exact characterization of greedy structures. *SIAM Journal of Discrete Mathematics*, 6(2):274–283, May 1993.

[16] B. Korte and L. Lovasz. Mathematical structures underlying greedy algorithms. In *Fundamentals of Computation Theory*, volume 177 of *Lecture Notes in Computer Science*, pages 205–209. Springer, Berlin, 1981.

[17] B. Möller and Russling M. Shorter paths to graph algorithms. *Science of Computer Programming*, 22:157–180, 1994.

[18] R. Paige and S. Koenig. Finite differencing of computable expressions. *ACM TOPLAS*, 4(3):402–454, July 1982.

[19] H. A. Partsch. *Specification and Transformation of Programs – A Formal Approach to Software Development*. Texts and Monographs in Computer Science. Springer-Verlag, 1990.

[20] M. Russling. *Deriving General Schemes for Classes of Graph Algorithms*. PhD thesis, Universität Augsburg, 1996.

[21] R.E. Tarjan. *Data Structures and Network Algorithms*. CBMS-NFS Regional Conference Series in Applied Mathematics. Society for Industrial and Applied Mathematics, 1983.

[22] N. Wirth. *Programming in Modula-2*. Springer-Verlag, 1982.

A   Appendix: Proofs

A.1   Proof of the Greedy Theorem

Theorem 2. *Let $GS(X,t)$ be a greedy step and let t_0 be an initial partial object. If the function*

$$h(X,t) \overset{\text{def}}{=} \text{if } t \in bases(X) \text{ then } \{t\} \text{ else } \bigcup \{h(X,t_1) : t_1 \in GS(X,t)\} \quad (38)$$

terminates for t_0, then $obas(X) \leadsto h(X,t_0)$.

Proof. It is trivial to show by induction that:

$$(38) \text{ terminates for } t \Rightarrow h(X,t) \neq \emptyset . \quad (39)$$

We define the sets $GS^n(X,t)$ $(n \geq 0)$ by induction:

$$GS^0(X,t) \overset{\text{def}}{=} \{t\}, \qquad GS^{k+1}(X,t) \overset{\text{def}}{=} \bigcup \left\{ GS(X,t') : t' \in GS^k(X,t) \right\} . \quad (40)$$

The following two properties can be easily shown by induction:

$$h(X,t) \subseteq \bigcup_{k \geq 0} GS^k(X,t) , \quad (41)$$

$$t_1 \in h(X,t) \Rightarrow t_1 \in bases(X) . \quad (42)$$

Next, we show by induction on the positive natural numbers that

$$t_1 \in GS^k(X,t_0) \Rightarrow basc(X,t_1) \cap obas(X) \neq \emptyset . \quad (43)$$

– Assume that $k = 1$: Suppose that $t_1 \in GS(X,t_0)$. Using (17) and (19) we obtain that
$$obas(X) \subseteq basc(X,t_0) = bases(X) .$$

Because $GS(X,t_0)$ is a greedy step and the requirements of (20) are valid for $t = t_0$ we have
$$basc(X,t_1) \cap obas(X) \neq \emptyset .$$

– Assume that the desired result holds for $k = j$.
– Assume that $k = j + 1$. By definition (40) we have that

$$GS^{j+1}(X,t_0) = GS(GS^j(X,t_0)) = \bigcup \left\{ GS(X,t') : t' \in GS^j(X,t_0) \right\} .$$

$$
\begin{array}{ll}
t_1 \in GS^{j+1}(X,t_0) & \\
\Rightarrow t_1 \in \bigcup \left\{ GS(X,t') : t' \in GS^j(X,t_0) \right\} & \text{by the equation above} \\
\Rightarrow (\exists t'). \begin{cases} t_1 \in GS(X,t') \\ t' \in GS^j(X,t_0). \end{cases} & \text{indexed union} \\
\Rightarrow (\exists t'). \begin{cases} t_1 \in GS(X,t') \\ basc(X,t') \cap obas(X) \neq \emptyset. \end{cases} & \text{inductive hypothesis} \\
\Rightarrow basc(X,t_1) \cap obas(X) \neq \emptyset & \text{by (20)}
\end{array}
$$

Next, we show that $h(X, t_0) \subseteq obas(X)$:

$t_1 \in h(X, t_0)$

$\Rightarrow \begin{cases} t_1 \in bases(X) \\ (\exists k > 0).(t_1 \in GS^k(X, t_0)). \end{cases}$ 　　　　　　properties (41) and (42)

$\Rightarrow \begin{cases} t_1 \in bases(X) \\ basc(X, t_1) \cap obas(X) \neq \emptyset. \end{cases}$ 　　　　　　property (43)

$\Rightarrow \begin{cases} \{t_1\} = basc(X, t_1) \\ basc(X, t_1) \cap obas(X) \neq \emptyset. \end{cases}$ 　　　　　　by (18) and (16)

$\Rightarrow t_1 \in obas(X)$

$\square$

A.2   Proof of Proposition 3

The proof of this proposition makes use of the following

Lemma 1. *If* $G_1 = (V_1, A_1) \in sarb(N, r)$, $a \notin A_1$, $d \in A_1$, $d^+ = a^1$ *and* $H = (V_1, A_1 \cup \{a\} - \{d\})$ *then*

$$H \in sarb(N, r) \ . \tag{44}$$

If in addition to the above assumptions $u \neq a^+$ *is valid, then*

$$paths(G_1, a^+)(u) = \emptyset \Rightarrow (paths(G_1, r)(u) = paths(H, r)(u)) \ , \tag{45}$$

$$paths(G_1, a^+)(u) \neq \emptyset \Rightarrow (paths(G_1, a^+)(u) = paths(H, a^+)(u)) \ . \tag{46}$$

We ommit the proof of this lemma by space reasons.

Proposition 8. *Assume that (26) is valid,* $a \in least(\leq_{CPA(N,r,G)}, Alo(N, G))$, $G_1 = (V_1, A_1) \in basc(N, r, G) \cap shpa(N, r)$, $a \notin A_1 \wedge d \in A_1 \wedge d^+ = a^+$. *Then*

$$(V_1, A_1 \cup \{a\} - \{d\}) \in basc(N, r, ext(G, a)) \cap shpa(N, r) \ .$$

Proof. Assume that the hypothesis of this proposition are valid. Let $v = a^+$ and let $H \stackrel{\text{def}}{=} (V_1, A_1 \cup \{a\} - \{d\})$. By (44) of the last lemma $H \in sarb(N, r)$. Because $d \in \rho(G)$ and $G \in sg(G_1)$ it is trivial that $ext(G, a) \in sg(H)$. Next we show that $H \, S \, G_1$. If $u \in V_N$ then we have to consider two cases:

- Let $u = v$. We reason:

$cost(W_N)(paths(G_1, r)(v))$
$= cost(W_N)(r \bowtie^{\geq 2} G_1 \bowtie v)$ 　　　　　definition (3)
$= cost(W_N)(r \bowtie^{\geq 1} G \bowtie ALO(G_1, G) \bowtie^{\geq 1} G_1 \bowtie v)$ 　　　　　(8) and (14)
$\subseteq cost(W_N)(r \bowtie^{\geq 1} G \bowtie ALO(G_1, G))$; $\leq$ 　　　　　(26), costs (5)
$\subseteq cost(W_N)(r \bowtie^{\geq 1} G \bowtie a)$; $\leq$; $\leq$ 　　　　　property of a
$= cost(W_N)(r \bowtie^{\geq 1} H \bowtie a)$; $\leq$ 　　　　　arborescences (11)
$= cost(W_N)(r \bowtie^{\geq 1} H \bowtie \rho(H) \bowtie v)$; $\leq$ 　　　　　arborescences (12)
$= cost(W_N)(paths(H, r)(v))$; $\leq$ 　　　　　definitions (3) and (2)

- Let $u \neq v$. We have to consider the following two cases:

- $paths(G_1, v)(u) = \emptyset$:
  Due to the property (45) it follows that $paths(G_1, r)(u) = paths(H, r)(u)$.
- $paths(G_1, v)(u) \neq \emptyset$: We reason:

$$
\begin{aligned}
&cost(W_N)(paths(G_1, r)(u)) \\
&= cost(W_N)(paths(G_1, r)(v) \bowtie paths(G_1, v)(u)) && (8) \\
&\subseteq cost(W_N)(paths(H, r)(v) \bowtie paths(G_1, v)(u)) \, ; \leq && \text{case } u = v, \ (5) \\
&= cost(W_N)(paths(H, r)(v) \bowtie paths(H, v)(u)) \, ; \leq && \text{by (46)} \\
&= cost(W_N)(paths(H, r)(u)) \, ; \leq && (8)
\end{aligned}
$$

$\square$

A.3   Derivation of an Algorithm for upd(N,G,a,D,K)

We assume that $a \in selmin(N, r, G)$ and $K = s(N, r, G, D)$. From now on, we shall denote $upd(N, r, G, a, D, K))$ by K_1 and a^+ by v. Our derivation makes use of the following

Proposition 9. *Assume that $a \in selmin(N, r, G)$ and $v \overset{\text{def}}{=} a^+$. Then*

1. *If $x \neq v \wedge x \notin \pi(G) \wedge v \bullet x \in A_N$ then*

$$
Alo(N, AddA(G, a)) \bowtie x = \{v \bullet x\} \cup Alo(N, G) \bowtie x \ .
$$

2.
$$
\frac{least(\leq_{CPA(N,r,G)}, Alo(N, G) \bowtie x) =}{least(\leq_{CPA(N,r,AddA(G,a))}, Alo(N, G) \bowtie x)} \ .
$$

The proof of this proposition is omitted due to space reasons.
Next, we start with our derivation.
Let $x \in \pi(G) \cup \{v\}$. We have that

$$
least(\leq_{CPA(N,r,AddA(G,a))}, Alo(N, AddA(G, a)) \bowtie x) = \emptyset \ .
$$

Thus we can take $K_1(x) = \emptyset$.
Let $x \notin \pi(G) \wedge x \neq v$. We have to consider the following two cases:

- Let $v \bullet x \notin A_N$. We reason:
  $$
  \begin{aligned}
  &least(\leq_{CPA(N,r,AddA(G,a))}, Alo(N, AddA(G, a)) \bowtie x) \\
  &= least(\leq_{CPA(N,r,AddA(G,a))}, Alo(N, G) \bowtie x) \\
  &= least(\leq_{CPA(N,r,G)}, Alo(N, G) \bowtie x) && \text{By 9.2} \\
  &\rightsquigarrow s(N, r, G, D)(x) \\
  &= K(x)
  \end{aligned}
  $$
  Thus we can take $K_1(x) = K(x)$.
- Let $v \bullet x \in A_N$. We have to consider the following two cases:
  - Let $least(\leq_{CPA(N,r,G)}, Alo(N, G) \bowtie x) = \emptyset$.
    Using this assumption we obtain that

    $$
    least(\leq_{CPA(N,r,AddA(G,a))}, Alo(N, AddA(G, a)) \bowtie x) = \{v \bullet x\} \ .
    $$

    Thus we can choose $K_1(x) = \{v \bullet x\}$.

- Let $least(\leq_{CPA(N,r,G)}, Alo(N,G) \bowtie x) \neq \emptyset$.
  Using the proposition 9, (31) and the properties

$$least(R, P \cup Q) = least(R, least(R, P) \cup Q) \ ,$$

$$least(\leq_f, \{p\} \cup \{q\}) \rightsquigarrow bmin(f, (p,q)) \quad (p, q \in dom(f)) \ , \qquad (47)$$

we have:

$$\begin{aligned}
&least(\leq_{CPA(N,r,AddA(G,a))}, Alo(N, AddA(G,a)) \bowtie x) \\
&= least(\leq_{CPA(N,r,AddA(G,a))}, \{v \bullet x\} \cup Alo(N,G) \bowtie x) \\
&= least(CPA(N,r,AddA(G,a)), \{v \bullet x\} \cup \\
&\qquad\qquad least(\leq_{CPA(N,r,G)}, Alo(N,G) \bowtie x)) \\
&\rightsquigarrow least(\leq_{CPA(N,r,AddA(G,a))}, \{v \bullet x\} \cup K(x)) \\
&\rightsquigarrow bmin(CPA(N,r,AddA(G,a)), (K(x), v \bullet x))
\end{aligned}$$

Thus we can define

$$K_1(x) = bmin(CPA(N,r,AddA(G,a)), (K(x), v \bullet x)) \ .$$

Due to the facts that $least(\leq_{CPA(N,r,G)}, Alo(N,G) \bowtie v) = \emptyset \Leftrightarrow K(x) = \emptyset$ and that $x \in \pi(G) \Rightarrow K(x) = \emptyset$ we can define:

$$upd(N,r,G,y\bullet v, D, K)(i) = \\
\begin{cases}
\emptyset & v = i \\
\sigma(N, G, y \bullet v, D, K)(i) & v \bullet i \in A_N \wedge i \notin \pi(G) \wedge v \neq i \ , \\
K(i) & else
\end{cases}$$

where

$$\sigma(N, G, y \bullet v, D, K)(i) \overset{def}{=} \quad \begin{aligned} &\textbf{if } K(i) = \emptyset \textbf{ then } \{v \bullet i\} \\ &\textbf{else } bmin(CPA(N,r,AddA(G,a)), (K(x), v\bullet i)) \end{aligned} \ .$$

Fine Control of Demand in Haskell*

William Harrison, Tim Sheard, and James Hook

Pacific Software Research Center
OGI School of Science & Engineering
Oregon Health & Science University
{wlh,sheard,hook}@cse.ogi.edu

Abstract. Functional languages have the λ-calculus at their core, but then depart from this firm foundation by including features that alter their default evaluation order. The resulting *mixed* evaluation—partly lazy and partly strict—complicates the formal semantics of these languages. The functional language Haskell is such a language, with features such as pattern-matching, case expressions with guards, etc., introducing a modicum of strictness into the otherwise lazy language. But just how does Haskell differ from the lazy λ-calculus? We answer this question by introducing a calculational semantics for Haskell that exposes the interaction of its strict features with its default laziness.

1 Introduction

"Real" functional programming languages are neither completely lazy nor completely strict—rather, they are a mixture of the two. Functional languages commonly contain constructs which alter the default evaluation strategy to make programs more efficient or useful in some respect. So-called strict languages like ML[9] and Scheme[1,3] both contain a lazy *if-then-else*, without which programming in them would be much more difficult. Haskell[13] is rife with features perturbing its default lazy evaluation to allow control of demand (primarily for reasons of efficiency). Now at the heart of real functional languages lie various flavors of the λ-calculus (i.e., strict and lazy), and the semantics of these have been well-understood[5,19] for some time. But just how do the semantics of real languages with messy, mixed evaluation relate to these textbook examples? In this paper, we answer this question for a large fragment of Haskell[13].

The contributions of the present work are three-fold. We demonstrate techniques for rigorously specifying "mixed" languages. Many of these techniques—particularly the development of nested patterns—apply to the semantics of functional languages in general. We provide a large case study of the development of a formal language specification from an informal one. The Haskell98 report[13] describes Haskell in a semi-formal manner, and in many instances, these descriptions guided the development of the formal specification. Finally, this work

---

* The work described here was supported in part by National Science Foundation Grant CDA-9703218 and the M.J. Murdock Charitable Trust.

E.A. Boiten and B. Möller (Eds.): MPC 2002, LNCS 2386, pp. 68–93, 2002.

presents a dynamic semantics for a larger fragment of Haskell (including essentially everything but overloading[6,7]) than has ever been gathered together in one place before.

Haskell contains a large number of constructs allowing some control over evaluation and, thus, departing from its standard lazy evaluation. We say that such constructs introduce "fine control of demand," because they all make subtle changes to the default lazy evaluation strategy of Haskell, and all for compelling reasons. The Haskell features with fine control of demand are: nested patterns, `case` expressions and `let` declarations, guards and `where` clauses on equations, strict constructor functions, the `newtype` datatype definition facility, and the `seq` operator. This paper presents a model for all of these features.

In this paper we present a *calculational* semantics which provides a unified model of these constructs and their interactions with Haskell's other features. By *calculational* semantics, we mean a meta-circular interpreter[1] for Haskell, written in Haskell. We distinguish the *calculational* approach to language definition taken in the present work from a denotational one, although the two are similar in form and spirit. The semantics presented here is a Haskell program, but it has been designed using standard techniques and structures from programming language semantics.

The challenge we confronted immediately in writing this language specification arose from the fact that these evaluation control constructs interact with one another in ways that were difficult to understand. Because of this interaction, it was very easy to write a language definition that was either too lazy or too strict. Automated support (in the form of type-checking and unit testing of specifications) was very helpful in eliminating bugs and establishing confidence in the correctness of the definition.

An alternative to the calculational approach to defining languages advocated here would be to provide a purely formal mathematical specification (i.e., a set of equations on paper). But writing the semantics as a functional program has a number of advantages over this approach. The language specification presented here is both type-checked and executable. Subtle errors may be caught and more easily corrected in a type-checked environment. The interpreter presented here has been tested on a large number of examples. Unit testing was invaluable in identifying problems in earlier versions of this semantics, and such problems may well have been overlooked in a purely mathematical specification. Indeed, several earlier, purely formal mathematical specifications for nested pattern matching proved either too lazy or too strict, and having an executable version helped us to expose and isolate the subtleties involved.

1.1   Rationale

As part of the *Programatica*[18] project at the Pacific Software Research Center, we are attempting to develop both a formal basis for reasoning about Haskell programs, and automated tools for mechanizing such reasoning. An important part of our work is to develop a logic with which to manipulate Haskell terms, and a standard model is required to establish the soundness of this logic. This led us to the literature, which to our surprise, was lacking in formal descriptions of the *big picture* of Haskell. There are plenty of papers about particular features of Haskell, (its laziness[12], its class system[7], etc.) but very little work which unifies the *essence of Haskell* with all the fine-control mechanisms that have been added and refined over the years.

```
type Name = String
data Op = Plus | Mult | IntEq | IntLess
data LS = Lazy | Strict deriving Eq

data P --- Nested, Linear (i.e., no repetition of variables) Patterns
    = Pconst Integer          -- { 5 }
    | Pvar Name               -- { x }
    | Ptuple [P]              -- { (p1,p2) }
    | Pcondata Name [P]       -- data T1 = C1 t1 t2; {C1 p1 p1} = e
    | Pnewdata Name P         -- newtype T2 = C2 t1;  {C2 p1} = e
    | Ptilde P                -- { ~p }
    | Pwildcard               -- { _ }

data E --- Haskell Expressions
    = Var Name                -- { x }
    | Const Integer           -- { 5 }
    | Undefined               -- { undefined }
    | App E E                 -- { f x }
    | Abs [P] E               -- { \ p1 p2 -> e }
    | TupleExp [E]            -- { (e1,e2) }
    | ConApp Name [(E,LS)]    -- data T1 = C1 t1 t2; p = {C1 e1 e2}
    | NewApp Name E           -- newtype T2 = C2 t1; p = {C2 e1}
    | Seq E E                 -- { seq e1 e2 }
    | Bin Op E E              -- { e1 + e2 }
    | Cond E E E              -- { if e1 then e2 else e3 }
    | Let [D] E               -- { let x=e1; y=e2 in e3 }
    | Case E [Match]          -- { case e of p -> b where ds ; ... }

type Match  = (P,B,[D])       -- case e of { pat -> body where decs }
type Clause = ([P],B,[D])     -- f { p1 p2 = body where decs }

data D --- Declarations
    = Fun Name [Clause]       -- f p1 p2 = b where ds
    | Val P B [D]             -- p = b where ds

data B -- Bodies
    = Guarded [(E,E)]         -- f p { | e1 = e2 | e3 = e4 } where ds
    | Normal E                -- f p = { e } where ds
```

Fig. 1. Abstract Syntax of Haskell Sublanguage

The Haskell98 report[13] uses a strategy of translating many complex constructs into a simpler core language[14], that is really just a slightly extended lambda-calculus. However, the translation-based approach, while useful and intuitive, is problematic as a semantic definition (we expand on these issues in Appendix A). Some of these translations are semantically harmless, amounting to nothing more than the removal of so-called "syntactic sugar." However, many of the translation schemas in the Haskell Report rely on the generation of new source-level variables. The semantics of languages with variable binding mechanisms are very complex, and when one defines a language feature by a translation that introduces new variables, one leaves the well-understood semantic setting of domains and continuous functions, and moves into a much more complicated world. Recent work on languages with binding mechanisms suggests that these kinds of transformations are by no means trivial to model correctly[10,16]. Another serious defect with the translation-based approach is that it fails to be compositional. For this reason we eschew such techniques when there are relatively simple alternatives we can adapt from denotational semantics. However, many of the specifications presented here are inspired by the translations given in the Haskell98 report, and we compare our definitions with those of the report when appropriate.

Although the semantic metalanguage here *is* Haskell, care has been taken to use notation which will be recognizable by any functional programmer. However unlike the languages ML[9], Miranda[11], Scheme[1,3], and Clean[17], Haskell does have built-in monads, and so we give an overview here of Haskell's monad syntax[1]. The semantics relies on an error monad[8], which is built-in to Haskell as the Maybe monad. The structure of the Maybe monad, its unit return, and its bind (>>=) are given as:

```
data Maybe a = Just a | Nothing   (>>=) :: Maybe a -> (a->Maybe b)->Maybe b
return :: a -> Maybe a            (Nothing >>= f) = Nothing
return = Just                     (Just x >>= f)  = f x
                                     do { y <- x ; f } = (x >>= (\y->f))
```

Haskell has an alternative syntax for bind (>>=) called "do notation" which is defined above.

2   The Abstract Syntax

Haskell is a rich language with many features, and the sublanguage presented here identifies 9 different syntactic categories. These categories include names, operators, strictness annotations, matches, clauses, bodies, expressions, declarations, and patterns. In Figure 1 we display the **data** definitions in Haskell that represent our abstract syntax. Our definitions are conventional and we have used comments to relate the abstract syntax to the concrete syntax of Haskell. The missing syntax, necessary to complete a Haskell definition, has mostly to do with the module system, classes, list comprehensions, and the do notation.

---

[1] We assume the reader has some familiarity with monads [8,20].

```
-- Scalar, function, and structured data values
   data V = Z Integer  | FV (V -> V) | Tagged Name [V]
-- Environments bind names to values
   type Env = Name -> V
-- Meanings for expressions, patterns, bodies, and declarations
   mE  :: E -> Env -> V                 mB  :: B -> Env -> Maybe V
   mP  :: P -> V -> Maybe [V]           mD  :: D -> Env -> V
```

Fig. 2. Calculational Semantics of Haskell

3   A Model for Haskell

This section presents a calculational model of Haskell as a compositional meta-circular interpreter, and Figure 2 presents the definitions of the semantic values V, environments Env, and the types of the semantic functions for expressions (mE), patterns (mP), bodies (mB), and declarations (mD). Semantic values are constructed in a standard way, corresponding to a universal domain construction[5] in denotational semantics. Environments map names to values. All of the semantic functions are *compositional*: the meaning of any term from the syntactic categories E, P, B, and D depends solely on the meaning of its subterms.

We model laziness in Haskell using the laziness of the metalanguage (i.e., Haskell) and to some degree this limits the generality of the semantics presented here. An alternative we have explored is a *Reynolds-style* monadic interpreter[2] which models laziness explicitly. The advantage of this Reynolds-style approach is that the resulting semantics could be executed in any functional language—even strict languages like ML and Scheme. But the disadvantage is the unavoidable loss of precision in the typing of the semantics. In a Reynolds-style monadic interpreter, all semantic functions are monadically-typed, and it is difficult in such a setting to distinguish clearly between the "pure" value world of expressions and declarations (i.e., mE and mD) and the computational world of patterns and bodies (i.e., mP and mB) as we do here.

3.1   Modeling Failure

In Haskell, there are several distinct kinds of failure, only one of which is explicitly modeled by the Maybe monad.

1. The first kind of failure arises from run-time errors, such as division by zero, and non-exhaustive pattern match coverage. Taking the head of the empty list is an example of this kind of failure.
2. The second kind of failure stems from non-termination. This kind of failure is captured by the interpreter itself not terminating.
3. The third kind of failure stems from an unsuccessful pattern match in a context where the failure may be trapped and controlled by proceeding to the next match of a case expression or the next clause of a multi-line function definition. We model this failure as a computation in the Maybe monad. Such

a trappable failure can become a failure of the first kind, if it occurs in a context with no next match or clause.

In our semantics, a failure of the first kind is not reported—it causes the interpreter to terminate unsuccessfully. We assert that programs which fail in the manner of (1.) and (2.) above denote bottom (where bottom is the semantic value usually written "⊥"—see Figure 3 below).

3.2   Semantic Operators

Rather than give an explicitly categorical or domain-theoretic treatment here, we summarize our assumptions as the existence of certain basic semantic operators (shown in Figure 3). The first three operations, function composition >>>, function application app, and currying sharp, are basic operations in denotational descriptions of functional programming languages. A call to the currying operation (sharp n [] beta) converts an uncurried function value beta of the form $(\backslash[v_1, \ldots, v_n]\text{->} body)$ into an equivalent curried form $(\backslash v_1\text{->} \ldots \backslash v_n\text{->} body)$. We also assume that each semantic domain corresponding to a Haskell type contains a bottom element bottom—that is, that each domain is *pointed*. This is necessary for the existence of least fixed points, which are themselves necessary for modeling recursion. We define a least fixed point operator, fix, in the standard way.

The semseq operation requires some explanation. The operation semseq is meant to specify the Haskell operation seq, and it is named accordingly (for "*semantic seq*"). The purpose of seq is to allow Haskell programmers to force evaluation to occur, and the benefit of seq is only evident in a call-by-need semantics with its attendant sharing. In such a model, one uses (seq x y) to force computation of the first operand, so that subsequent evaluations of x will use its shared value.

In the Haskell98 report[13] (cf. Section 6.2, page 75), (seq :: a->b->b) is defined by the following equations:

$$\text{seq } \perp y = \perp \text{ and } \text{seq } x \, y = y, \text{ if } x \neq \perp$$

The operator (semseq x y) is defined similarly, although with a subtlety arising from our model of failure. (semseq x y) evaluates its first operand x sufficiently to match it to a value in V and, in doing so, may produce a failure of either forms (1) or (2) listed above in Section 3.1 (and thus ultimately producing bottom).

The last three operations, Kleisli composition (<>), alternation (fatbar), and purification (purify) are all integral to modeling Haskell constructs involving fine control of demand such as case expressions, patterns, guards, and multi-line declarations. The Kleisli composition (<>) is used as the control operator for pattern matching. Given (f :: a -> Maybe b) and (g :: b -> Maybe c), (f <> g) is the function which, applied to an input x, performs (f x) first. If (f x) produces (Just v), then the value of ((f <> g) x) is (g v). Otherwise if (f x) produces Nothing, then ((f <> g) x) is Nothing. If f is the meaning of a pattern, then this has similar behavior to pattern matching, because the failure of the

```
-- Function composition (diagrammatic) & application
(>>>) :: (a -> b) -> (b -> c) -> a -> c
f >>> g = g . f
app :: V -> V -> V
app (FV f) x = f x


-- Currying
sharp :: Int -> [V] -> (V -> V) -> V
sharp 0 vs beta = beta (tuple vs)
sharp n vs beta = FV $ \ v -> sharp (n-1) (vs++[v]) beta
    where tuple :: [V] -> V
          tuple [v] = v
          tuple vs = Tagged "tuple" vs


-- Domains are pointed & Least fixed points exist
bottom :: a
bottom = undefined
fix :: (a -> a) -> a
fix f = f (fix f)


-- Purification: the "run" of Maybe monad
purify :: Maybe a -> a
purify (Just x) =  x
purify Nothing  = bottom


-- Kleisli composition (diagrammatic)
(<>) :: (a->Maybe b)->(b->Maybe c)-> a->Maybe c
f <> g = \ x -> f x >>= g


-- Semantic "seq"
semseq :: V -> V -> V
semseq x y = case x of
                  (Z _)        -> y ;
                  (FV _)       -> y ;
                  (Tagged _ _) -> y


-- Alternation
fatbar :: (a -> Maybe b) -> (a -> Maybe b) -> (a -> Maybe b)
f 'fatbar' g = \ x -> (f x) 'fb' (g x)
       where fb :: Maybe a -> Maybe a -> Maybe a
             Nothing 'fb' y = y
             (Just v) 'fb' y = (Just v)
```

Fig. 3. Semantic Operators

match (i.e., signified by Nothing) is propagated. This will be expanded upon in Section 5.2.

The fatbar operation[2] is integral to the specification of case expressions. In ((fatbar m1 m2) v), if (m1 v) is Nothing (indicating a pattern match failure), then the result is the same as (m2 v); otherwise, (m1 v) is returned. This sequencing behavior is very close to the meaning of the Haskell case expression (case v of { m1 ; m2 }).

In the semantics, purification distinguishes the computational aspects of the language from its pure, value aspects, and the operator purify signifies a return from the computational world to the value world. While fine control of demand may occur within Haskell expressions based upon pattern-matching, the meaning of such expressions will be a value in V rather than a computation in (Maybe V), and the "run" of the Maybe monad, purify, converts a computation into a value. Note that a match failure (Nothing) is recast as a bottom by purify, and this reflects unrecoverable errors such as exhausting all the branches of a case.

4 The Meaning of Patterns

Pattern matching of nested patterns is a challenging problem when describing the semantics of any functional programming language, and we consider our treatment of nested patterns to be one of the major contributions of this paper. In Haskell, patterns can occur within several different syntactic contexts: lambda expressions (\ p1 p2 -> e), let expressions (let p = e1 in e2), matches (case e1 of p -> e2), and clauses in multi-line function definitions (f p1 p2 = e). Patterns may also appear as sub-patterns within other patterns—these are the so-called *nested patterns*.

With one important exception, Haskell patterns behave very much like patterns found in other functional languages such as ML [9], Clean [17], and Miranda [11]. Haskell contains a pattern operator (represented with a tilde ~) which can be used to alter the default order of evaluation in a pattern match. Patterns of the form ~p are known in the Haskell literature[13] as *irrefutable* patterns, although we shall see that this term is something of a misnomer because matches against irrefutable patterns can indeed fail. Haskell patterns without ~ are evaluated strictly (as in ML and Miranda, etc.). That is, matching a ~-free pattern p against a value v performs the entire pattern match at the binding-time of variables within p. By contrast in a pattern-match of ~p against v, any matching of p is delayed until a variable within p is evaluated. In that sense, the pattern ~p is lazier than p. The ~ operator in Haskell splits the evaluation of a pattern match between the binding and evaluation times of pattern variables.

Several examples will help clarify how the pattern operator ~ splits up the evaluation of a pattern match. The Haskell function applications (ex0-ex4) from Figure 4 demonstrate some of the evaluation subtleties arising from the use of irrefutable patterns. They all involve variations on the pattern (T (S x) (R y))

---

[2] The name comes from Peyton-Jones[11] where this same function was represented by a fat bar ∥—hence the name "fatbar."

```
data Tree = T Tree Tree | S Tree | R Tree | L
ex0 = (\  (T (S x)  (R y)) -> L) (T L (R L))        --->    match failure
ex1 = (\ ~(T (S x)  (R y)) -> L) (T L (R L))        --->    L
ex2 = (\ ~(T (S x)  (R y)) -> x) (T L (R L))        --->    match failure
ex3 = (\ ~(T ~(S x) (R y)) -> y) (T L (R L))        --->    L
ex4 = (\ ~(T (S x) ~(R y)) -> y) (T L (R L))        --->    match failure
```

Fig. 4. Shifting matching from binding to evaluation with ~

applied to a value (T L (R L)) (call it v). Distinguish each pattern in ex0-ex4 as p affixed with the expression number (e.g., p1 is "~(T (S x) (R y))"). Note also that the lambda expressions of ex0 and ex1 have the constant body L, while those of ex2-ex4 have the variable bodies x and y. Patterns p1-p4 include ~, and this, in combination with the different bodies results in the (different) evaluation behavior as is noted on the right-hand side of the figure.

Because it contains no ~, the pattern match of p0 against v in ex0 is performed entirely at the binding time of variables x and y, which results in a pattern match failure, although neither x nor y are evaluated in the body of ex0. ex1 is identical to ex0 except that p1 has a ~ affixed. Evaluating ex1 succeeds because the irrefutable pattern p1 has shifted the entire pattern match to the evaluation times of its variables x and y, and because neither variable is evaluated in the body of ex1, the failure-producing pattern match is never performed. However, if we were to evaluate one of these variables (as in ex2), a match failure would be produced as before with ex0. In ex3, the evaluation of y in the body forces the match of part of p3 under the outermost ~ (i.e., in "~(T ...)"), but the second ~ (in "~(S x)") allows the whole match to succeed. The variable y is evaluated in the body of ex4 and causes a match failure, despite the fact that the subpattern ~(R y) matches the (R L) in argument v. Interestingly in this case, evaluating y forces the match of (S x) against L as in previous failure cases.

4.1   How Do We Model Patterns?

A pattern p may be modeled as a function taking a value (the object being matched against) which produces either bindings for the variables in p or an error signifying match failure. We will refer to the variables of a pattern as its *fringe*. Specifying potentially error-producing functions is usually accomplished with an error monad[8]; in Haskell, we use the built-in Maybe monad for this purpose. We view a pattern p as a function which takes a value and returns a tuple of values containing bindings for the fringe of p. Because we model arbitrary tuples as lists, the type of the semantic function mP is P -> V -> Maybe [V]. If (mP p v) is (Just vs), then the list of values vs are the bindings for the fringe of p. Pattern match failure occurs if (mP p v) returns Nothing.

We define a special function fringe for calculating the fringe of a pattern, such that (fringe p) returns the fringe of p in order of occurrence from left to right:

```
fringe :: P -> [Name]          fringe (Pcondata n ps) =
fringe (Pconst i) = []                    foldr (++) [] (map fringe ps)
fringe (Pvar x)   = [x]        fringe (Ptuple ps) =
fringe Pwildcard  = []                    foldr (++) [] (map fringe ps)
fringe (Ptilde p) = fringe p
```

Matching a variable never forces any further matching and always succeeds, so the variable x should be bound to the value v. This is signified by returning (Just [v]). To match a pattern constant, the argument i must be compared against the constant k in the pattern. If not equal, return Nothing, signifying pattern match failure. Otherwise, return (Just []). Observe that because no additional bindings were found, that the empty list is returned. The simplest pattern is the wildcard pattern, which always succeeds, returning (Just []).

```
mP  :: P -> V -> Maybe [V]
mP (Pvar x) v                       = Just [v]
mP (Pconst k) (Z i)                 = if i==k then Just [] else Nothing
mP Pwildcard v                      = Just []
mP (Ptuple ps) (Tagged "tuple" vs)  = stuple (map mP ps) vs
mP (Pcondata n ps) (Tagged t vs)    = if n==t then
                                            stuple (map mP ps) vs
                                        else Nothing
mP (Pnewdata n p) v                 = mP p v
mP (Ptilde p) v                     = Just(purifyN (arity p) (mP p v))
   where purifyN n x = project 0 (map purify (replicate n x))
         project i (x:xs) = (x !! i) : (project (i+1) xs)
         project i []     = []
         arity = length . fringe

stuple :: [V -> Maybe [V]] -> [V] -> Maybe [V]
stuple [] []            = Just []
stuple (q:qs) (v:vs)    = do v' <- q v ;
                            vs' <- stuple qs vs ;
                            Just (v'++vs')
replicate 0 x           = []
replicate n x           = x : (replicate (n-1) x)
```

Fig. 5. Semantics of patterns

Tuples and structured data have much in common so we discuss both these cases together. They both use the auxiliary function stuple which performs sufficient evaluation to match against the pattern, and no more. Matching a Haskell pattern (p1,...,pn) against a tuple value (v1,...,vn) succeeds only when each match of pi against vi succeeds. In that sense, matching tuple patterns in Haskell is somewhat strict. The function stuple (for *strict tuple*) takes a list qs of pattern meanings (i.e., functions of type (V -> Maybe [V])) and a corresponding list of values vs, applies each pattern meaning qi to the corresponding vi. If all of these matches succeed, then the bindings collected from each match are returned. However, if one of the matches fails, then `Nothing` is returned.

Structured data is similar. When pattern (`Pcondata n ps`) is matched against (`Tagged t vs`), first the tags `n` and `t` are compared. If the tags are equal, then `ps` are matched against `vs` as in the `Ptuple` case. Otherwise, `Nothing` is returned.

The constructor function introduced by a `newtype` declaration acts like the identity function. Thus to match a `Pnewdata` pattern against an argument, just match its sub-pattern against the argument. A similar rule is found in the evaluation of `newtype` constructor functions in the function `mE`.

The most semantically interesting pattern is the irrefutable pattern `~p`, whose semantics is shown in Figure 5. Laziness of the match of (`Ptilde p`) against `v` is achieved by wrapping any actual matching by the `Just` constructor.

$$
\text{purifyN n (mP p v)} = \begin{cases} [v_1, ..., v_n], & \text{if (mP p v)} = \text{Just}[v_1, ..., v_n] \\ [\text{bottom}, ..., \text{bottom}], & \text{if (mP p v)} = \text{Nothing} \end{cases}
$$

where `n` is (`arity p`). Notice that this is almost identical to (`purify (mP p v)`), except that the `Nothing` branch returns a list of `bottom` values—one for every variable in (`fringe p`). Generally, the effect of deferring pattern match failure is characterized by the following equivalence:

$$
\text{(mP ~p v)} = \text{Just[bottom,...,bottom]} \iff \text{(mP p v)} = \text{Nothing}
$$

Given this view of patterns, it is now possible to describe formally how the two varieties of pattern match failure—binding and evaluation time failure— are manifested in the semantics. The binding time failure for a match (`mP p v`) of pattern `p` against value `v` is manifested by a `Nothing` *computation*. If Haskell did not include irrefutable patterns, that would be the whole story. If the match (`mP p v`) is `Nothing`, then the match (`mP ~p v`) will return (`Just [bottom,...,bottom]`), and each variable in the fringe of `~p` will be bound to `bottom`. This is precisely how the pattern match is deferred until evaluation time. Instead of failing at binding time, each variable in (`fringe p`) is bound to `bottom`, and so the match failure will be reported at the evaluation times of (`fringe p`) (if at all).

5 The Meaning of Expressions

In our semantics, the meaning of a Haskell program is an environment to value function. This section contains a detailed explanation of the semantic function for expressions `mE`. Each of the following subsections describes a few related clauses making up the definition of `mE` along with the auxiliary functions necessary for those clauses. These auxiliary functions supply meaning for the other syntactic categories of Haskell. The semantics of Haskell's mutually recursive `let` expressions is deferred until the discussion of declarations in Section 6.1.

For pedagogical reasons, the text of the paper breaks the definitions into a few clauses at a time. An actual implementation would need to collect them all together in a single place. Because this paper is intended for a general audience,

```
mE :: E -> Env -> V                     ifV :: V -> a -> a -> a
mE (Var n) rho        = rho n           ifV (Tagged "True" []) x y = x
mE (Const i) rho      = (Z i)           ifV (Tagged "False" []) x y = y
mE (TupleExp es) rho  =
 tuple $ map (\e-> mE e rho) es         tuple :: [V] -> V
mE (Cond e0 e1 e2) rho =                tuple [v] = v
 ifV (mE e0 rho) (mE e1 rho) (mE e2 rho)  tuple vs = Tagged "tuple" vs
mE Undefined rho      = bottom
```

Fig. 6. Semantics of simple expressions

constructs which are unique to Haskell are described operationally first when appropriate.

5.1 Simple Expressions

The meaning of a variable is obtained by extracting its binding from the current environment (rho) by applying it to the variables name. Constants are simply turned into values. In the case for tuples, the laziness of Haskell first becomes apparent. The evaluation of each of the subexpressions (the es) must be suspended, and this is accomplished with the lazy list constructor []. Conditional expressions, are easily translated using the control operator ifV. The meaning of the Undefined expression is simply bottom.

5.2 Application and Abstraction

```
mE :: E -> Env -> V
mE (App e1 e2) rho = app (mE e1 rho) (mE e2 rho)
mE (Abs [p] e) rho = FV $ lam p e rho
mE (Abs ps e) rho  = sharp (length ps) [] (lam (ptuple ps) e rho)

lam :: P -> E -> Env -> V -> V
lam p e rho =
        (mP p <> ((\vs -> mE e (extend rho xs vs)) >>> Just)) >>> purify
            where xs = fringe p
ptuple :: [P] -> P
ptuple [p] = p
ptuple ps = Pcondata "tuple" ps
```

Fig. 7. Semantics of application and abstraction

Function application and abstraction are the essence of any functional language. Because nested patterns are λ-bound in Haskell (as in most functional languages), care must be taken to implement Haskell's laziness correctly.

To compute the meaning of an application `App`, use `app` to apply the meaning of `e1` to the meaning of `e2`. The meaning of Haskell abstraction is defined in terms of an auxiliary operation called `lam`, which we describe in detail below. The meaning of an abstraction with a single pattern (`Abs [p] e`) in environment `rho` is simply (`lam p e rho`), injected into V by `FV`. Haskell abstractions may have more than one pattern bound in a lambda; in the abstract syntax, this is: (`Abs [p1,...,pn] e`). We note that this construct is *not* reducible to the previous case as: (`Abs [p1] (... Abs [pn] e)`). It is, in fact, lazier than this translation (cf. [13], section 3.3), because (`Abs [p1,...,pn] e`) waits for all n arguments before matching any of the patterns, while (`Abs [p1] (... Abs [pn] e)`) matches the arguments as each is applied. Laziness for (`Abs [p1,...,pn] e`) is achieved by currying (with `sharp`) n times.

What of `lam`? Evaluating the Haskell expression (`\p-> e`) applied to value v in environment `rho` follows this sequence of steps. First, match p against v. Secondly, if this is (`Just vs`), then evaluate e in the extended environment (`extend rho xs vs`) where xs is the fringe of p; if the match produces `Nothing`, then the whole application should fail. As observed in Section 3.2, this kind of sequencing suggests using Kleisli composition (`<>`). These two steps can be neatly characterized as:

    (mP p <> ((\vs -> mE e (extend rho xs vs)) >>> Just)) :: V -> Maybe V

where xs is the fringe of p. Because function values are functions from V to V, we define (`lam p e rho`) as the above expression composed on the right by `purify`:

    (mP p <> ((\vs -> mE e (extend rho xs vs)) >>> Just)) >>> purify   :: V->V

This is an example of how purification delimits the computational aspects of Haskell. Although an abstraction (`\p -> e`) has effects arising from pattern matching, these impurities are eliminated by post-composing with `purify`.

5.3   The Meaning of Guarded Expressions

A body is a form of guarded Haskell expression occurring only within the scope of a `case` expression, function declaration, or pattern binding. For example in the following `case` expression:

    case e of { p | g1 -> e1 ; ... | gn -> en where { decls } ; <rest> }

the "`| g1 -> e1 ;...; | gn -> en`" is a body, where the guards g1, ..., gn are boolean-valued expressions. This body would be represented in the abstract syntax as (`Guarded [(g1,e1),...,(gn,en)]`). A body may also be unguarded (i.e., represented as (`Normal e`) where e is just an expression in E).

Operationally, bodies with guards behave like nested *if-then-else* expressions. The body "`| g1 -> e1 ;...; | gn -> en`" within the aforementioned `case` expression would evaluate as follows:

1. If the pattern match of p against the value of e fails, then continue with `<rest>`.

· 2. Otherwise if the pattern match succeeds, evaluate g1, ..., gn in ascending order until either a true guard gi is found, or the list is exhausted. If gi is the first true guard, then continue evaluating ei. If all the guards are false, then continue with <rest>.

Guarded bodies restrict when branches of a case expressions are taken. In particular, two identities hold:

```
(1) case v of { p | True -> e ; ... } = case v of { p -> e ; ... }
(2) case v of { p | False -> e ; ... } = case v of { ... }
```

The first identity shows that having a constant True guard is identical to having no guard at all, while in case (2), having a constant False guard on the first branch is equivalent to always ignoring the branch altogether.

```
mB :: B -> Env -> Maybe V
mB (Normal e) rho          = Just (mE e rho)
mB (Guarded gl) rho        = ite gl rho
  where ite [] rho          = Nothing
        ite ((g,e):gs) rho = ifV (mE g rho) (Just (mE e rho)) (ite gs rho)
```

Fig. 8. Semantics of guarded expressions B (bodies)

Because bodies occur within the branches of case statements, they are Maybe-valued. Figure 8 displays the semantics of bodies, mB :: B -> Env -> Maybe V. The meaning of an unguarded body (Normal e) is just the meaning of the expression e injected into the Maybe monad. The meaning of a body (Guarded [(g1,e1),...,(gn,en)]) is:

```
ifV (mE g1 rho) (Just (mE e1 rho))
                    ...
(ifV (mE gn rho) (Just (mE en rho)) Nothing)
```

which behaves as a sequence of nested *if-then-else* where the last "else" clause is a Nothing. In this context, the Nothing signifies that the falsity of the guards has forced an otherwise successful branch in a case to fail, and that the next branch in the case should be attempted.

5.4 Case Expressions

We next consider the semantics of case expressions. All of the definitions discussed in this section are summarized in Figure 9. The meaning of a case expression is defined in terms of two main auxiliary functions, match and mcase. The function match gives the meaning of a Match, which is really just a branch in a case expression. The function mcase uses the fatbar semantic control operator to construct the meaning of a case statement.

A match is a tuple, ((p,b,ds) :: Match), whose semantic specification is similar to that of lam (discussed in Section 5.2), although because it occurs within a

```
mE :: E -> Env -> V
mE (Case e ml) rho = mcase rho ml (mE e rho)

mcase :: Env -> [Match] -> V -> V
mcase rho ml = (fatbarL $ map (match rho) ml) >>> purify
      where fatbarL :: [V -> Maybe V] -> V -> Maybe V
            fatbarL ms = foldr fatbar (\ _ -> Nothing) ms

- The function match is used to construct the meaning of a Match
match :: Env -> (P, B, [D]) -> V -> Maybe V
match rho (p,b,ds) = mP p <> (\vs -> mwhere (extend rho xs vs) b ds)
      where xs = fringe p

- (mwhere rho b ds) is the meaning of body b in where-clause "b where ds"
mwhere ::  Env -> B -> [D] -> Maybe V
```

Fig. 9. Case expressions. Note that `mwhere` is defined in Figure 12

case expression, it is `Maybe`-valued. An additional consideration is that the declarations in `ds` are visible within the body `b`. Such declarations would appear in Haskell concrete syntax as a "where" clause (i.e., "`b where ds`"). We have a third auxiliary function, `mwhere`, which models the mutually recursive `where` clauses of Haskell, but we defer discussion of it until Section 6.1 where such declarations are handled. It suffices to say that (`mwhere rho b ds :: Maybe V`) is the meaning of body `b` within the scope of `rho` extended to contain the bindings from `ds`. And, if `ds` is empty, then (`mwhere rho b ds`) is simply (`mB b rho`).

Function (`match rho p b ds`) is defined as:

```
mP p <> (\vs -> mwhere (extend rho xs vs) b ds)
```

where `xs` is the fringe of `p`. We see the same pattern as in `lam`, where the bindings for the fringe of `p` are extracted by the Kleisli composition: (`mP p <> (\vs -> ...)`). The extended environment is then passed on to a call to (`mwhere (extend rho xs vs) b ds`).

The function `mcase` takes the current environment, `rho`, and a list of `Matchs`, [`m1,...,mn`], and returns a function from `V` to `V`. Unfolding the definitions of `fatbarL` in the definition of `mcase`, the value of (`mcase rho [m1,...,mn]`) can be seen to have the form:

```
( (match rho m1) `fatbar`
                      ...
      (match rho mn) `fatbar` (\ _ -> Nothing)) ) >>> purify
```

Here we use infix notation `fatbar`.

Recall from Section 3.2 that, when the above term is applied to a value `x`, the control operator `fatbar` will sequence through the ((`match rho mi`) `x`) from left to right, until coming to the leftmost computation of the form (`Just v`) (if it exists). The value of the above expression would be in that case (`purify (Just v`)) or simply `v`. If all the ((`match rho mi`) `x`) are `Nothing`, then the value of the

above term is (purify Nothing) or simply bottom. This last eventuality occurs
when all of the branches of a case expression have been exhausted.

Given the function mcase, it is a simple matter to define case expressions as in
Figure 9. This is another example of how purification delimits the computational
aspects of Haskell. Failure in the computational world (i.e., a Nothing) resulting
from the interaction of patterns, cases, and guards is transmuted into value-level
failure (i.e., bottom) by post-composing with purify.

5.5   Constructor Application

Constructor applications are evaluated in a manner much like tuples. The key
difference is the possibility that constructors can have some of their arguments
annotated as strict arguments. For example in Haskell, we might write (data T =
C String !Int), where the ! signifies that the evaluation of second argument to
C should be strict. We represent this in our abstract syntax by annotating each
sub-argument to a constructor application ConApp with a strictness annotation
of type LS.

```
mE :: E -> Env -> V
-- Strict and Lazy Constructor Applications
mE (ConApp n el) rho  = evalL el rho n []
    where
        evalL :: [(E,LS)] -> Env -> Name -> [V] -> V
        evalL [] rho n vs              = Tagged n vs
        evalL ((e,Strict):es) rho n vs =
                    semseq (mE e rho) (evalL es rho n (vs ++ [mE e rho]))
        evalL ((e,Lazy):es) rho n vs   = evalL es rho n (vs ++ [mE e rho])


-- New type constructor applications
mE (NewApp n e) rho   = mE e rho


-- Miscellaneous Functions
mE (Seq e1 e2) rho     = semseq (mE e1 rho) (mE e2 rho)
mE (Bin op e1 e2) rho = binOp op (mE e1 rho) (mE e2 rho)
      where binOp Plus (Z i) (Z j)    = Z $ i+j
            binOp Mult (Z i) (Z j)    = Z $ i*j
            binOp IntEq (Z i) (Z j)   = Tagged (equal i j) []
            binOp IntLess (Z i) (Z j) = Tagged (less i j) []
            equal i j = if i==j then "True" else "False"
            less i j  = if i<j then "True" else "False"
```

Fig. 10. Semantics of constructor applications, seq, and arithmetic operations

To force evaluation of a strict constructor argument, we make use of the
semseq semantic operator defined in Figure 3. If expression e is an argument
to a strictly-annotated constructor, then the correct value for e in the resulting

`Tagged` value should be (`semseq` (`mE e rho`) (`mE e rho`)) for current environment
`rho`. This may seem odd at first, but this expression is not identical to (`mE`
`e rho`), because they have different termination behavior. That is, `semseq` will
force evaluation of (`mE e rho`), and this may fail, causing the entire (`semseq` (`mE`
`e rho`) (`mE e rho`)) to fail.

Sequencing through the arguments of constructor application (`ConApp n el`)
is performed with the auxiliary function `evalL`. `evalL` tests each strictly-annotated
argument in `el` with `semseq` as outlined above, and then constructs and returns
the corresponding `Tagged` value.

Below is a sample Hugs session showing the application of `mE` to two constructor applications, which we represent for readability in Haskell's concrete
syntax. Both are applications of constructors `L` and `S` to the `Undefined` expression, but it is assumed that the `S` constructor has been declared with a
strictness annotation (i.e., with "`!`"). Evaluating (`mE` (`L Undefined`) `rho0`) (for
some environment `rho0`) just results in the `Tagged` value (`L ?`) being returned (in
pretty-printed form) as one would expect of a lazy constructor. Evaluating (`mE`
`Undefined rho0`) produces a failure, because `semseq` forces the evaluation of the
argument `Undefined`.

```
Semantics> mE (L Undefined) rho0
           (L ?)
Semantics> mE (S Undefined) rho0
           Program error: {undefined}
```

5.6   Newtype Constructor Application

A `newtype` constructor acts like the identity function, thus it is easy to define the
clause of `mE` for `newtype` constructors.

5.7   Miscellaneous Expressions

Finally, we come to the last few miscellaneous expression forms for the `Seq`
operation and the primitive binary operators. We assume that the primitive
operators are strict in their operands.

```
mD :: D -> Env -> V
mD (Fun f cs) rho  = sharp k [] body
     where
           body = mcase rho (map (\(ps,b,ds) -> (ptuple ps, b,ds)) cs)
           k  = length ((\(pl,_,_)->pl) (head cs))

mD (Val p b ds) rho = purify (mwhere rho b ds)
```

Fig. 11. Semantics of declarations D

6   The Meaning of Declarations

In this section, we consider how declarations are processed within Haskell. There are two declaration forms, function and pattern, represented in the abstract syntax as (Fun f cs) and (Val p b ds), respectively. Here, cs is a list of Clauses; that is, (cs :: [([P],B,[D])]). The semantics for declarations D, discussed below, is presented in Figure 11.

The Fun declaration corresponds to a multi-line function declaration, such as:

```
nth :: Int -> [a] -> a
nth 0 (x:xs) = x
nth i (x:xs) = nth (i-1) xs
```

Observe that each clause necessarily has the same number of pattern arguments from the assumed well-typedness of terms.

The Haskell98 report[cf. Section 4.4.3, page 54] defines multi-line function declarations through translation into a case expression

> *The general binding form for functions is semantically equivalent to the equation (i.e. simple pattern binding):*

$$x = \backslash x_1 \ldots x_k \text{-> case } (x_1, \ldots, x_k) \text{ of } (p_{11}, \ldots, p_{1k}) \ match_1$$
$$\vdots$$
$$(p_{m1}, \ldots, p_{mk}) \ match_m$$

> *where the "x_i" are new identifiers.*

Let us now consider how to model (Fun f cs) in environment rho. We reuse mcase here to model the case expression behavior, and following the Haskell98 report quoted above, we make each Clause in the cs into a branch of the case:

```
mcase rho (map (\(ps,b,ds) -> (ptuple ps, b,ds)) cs) :: V -> V
```

This term is a function from V to V, but we can say a little more about the V argument. In general, it will expect a tuple value (Tagged "tuple" vs) as input because each branch of the case is made into a tuple pattern by ptuple (defined in Figure 7). But f is a function in curried form, whose arity, k, is the number of arguments to f. So we must apply currying k times using the sharp semantic operator. The full definition of (mD (Fun f cs)) appears in Figure 11. Interestingly, using the currying operator sharp dispenses with the condition "*where the "x_i" are new identifiers*" from the quote above by using variables which are fresh in the metalanguage.

The Haskell98 report[cf. Section 4.4.3, page 54] defines pattern declarations through translation into a let expression. It begins by giving the general form of pattern bindings:

> *[I]n other words, a pattern binding is:*

$$p \mid g_1 = e_1$$
$$\mid g_2 = e_2$$
$$\ldots$$
$$\mid g_m = e_m$$
$$\text{where } \{decls\}$$

Translation: *The pattern binding above is semantically equivalent to this simple pattern binding:*

$p = $ let *decls* in
      if g_1 then e_1 else
      if g_2 then e_2 else
      ...
      if g_m then e_m else error *"Unmatched pattern"*

This translation means that a pattern binding may be reduced to a related `let` expression. In Section 5.4, we made use of the function (`mwhere :: Env -> B -> [D] -> Maybe V`) which models Haskell's `where` clauses, and we make use of that function again here to specify the let-binding (`let decls in...`) above as: `mD (Val p b ds) rho = purify (mwhere rho b ds)`. Observe that the "(`mwhere rho b ds :: Maybe V`)" is a computation and must be brought into the value world using `purify`.

6.1   Mutual Recursion and Let-Binding

Our technique for modeling mutually recursive declarations in Haskell adapts a standard technique from denotational semantics for specifying mutual recursion and recursive let expressions. However, this technique applies only to the lazy λ-calculus in which only variable and tuple patterns are λ-bound, and so care must be taken when generalizing it to Haskell (where nested patterns are also λ-bound). In this section, we overview the standard technique, compare it with the definition in the Haskell98 report, and describe our specification of mutual recursion in Haskell.

To overview how mutual recursion is typically specified denotationally, we consider adding various let-binding constructs to the lazy λ-calculus. Let us say that we have a semantics for the non-recursive lazy λ-calculus, $[\![-]\!] : Lazy \to env \to Value$, where *env* and *Value* are defined similarly to `Env` and `V`, respectively. Non-recursive let expressions are frequently introduced as syntactic sugar for an application:

$$[\![\text{let } x = e \text{ in } e']\!] =_{def} [\![(\lambda x.e')e]\!] \tag{1}$$

The non-recursive let-binding of variable x to e in e' is accomplished merely by function application (which is already handled by $[\![-]\!]$). Handling recursive let-binding follows a similar pattern, although in this case, an explicit use of the least fix point operator fix becomes necessary:

$$[\![\text{letrec } x = e \text{ in } e']\!]\rho =_{def} [\![(\lambda x.e')]\!]\rho \, (fix([\![\lambda x.e]\!]\rho)) \tag{2}$$

Because e may contain references to the recursively defined x, one must apply fix to resolve the recursion.

This last definition handles only one recursive binding ($x = e$). There is a standard technique in denotational semantics for extending Equation 2 to sets of mutually recursive bindings using tuples. In the case of mutually recursive bindings, we are given a set of mutually recursive bindings, $\{x_1 = e_1, \ldots, x_n = e_n\}$, that we refactor into a single tuple pattern $(x_1, \ldots, x_n)$ and tuple expression $(e_1, \ldots, e_n)$. Now, this pattern and expression play the same rôle as x and e did in Equation 2:

$$\llbracket \text{letrec } \{x_1 = e_1 \ldots x_n = e_n\} \text{ in } e' \rrbracket =_{def} \tag{3}$$
$$\llbracket (\lambda \langle x_1, \ldots, x_n \rangle . e') \rrbracket \rho \; (fix(\llbracket \lambda \langle x_1, \ldots, x_n \rangle . \langle e_1, \ldots, e_n \rangle \rrbracket \rho))$$

Now returning to mutually recursive bindings in Haskell, something very similar to the standard technique occurs. The only complications arise in that, in Haskell, nested patterns are λ-bound and not just variables or tuples. Comparing Equation 3 to the relevant equations from the Haskell98 report[cf. Section 3.12, page 22], we can see that something very similar is going on:

(a)   `let` $\{ p_1 = e_1 ; \ldots; p_n = e_n \}$ `in` $e_0 =$
          `let` $(\tilde{\ } p_1, \ldots, \tilde{\ } p_n) = (e_1, \ldots, e_n)$ `in` e_0

(b)   `let` $p = e_1$ `in` $e_0 =$ `case` e_1 `of` $\{ \tilde{\ } p -> e_0 \}$
          where no variable in p appears free in e_0.

(c)   `let` $p = e_1$ `in` $e_0 =$ `let` $p = $ `fix` $(\backslash \tilde{\ } p -> e_1)$ `in` e_0

Definition (b) shows how to convert a simple `let` into a `case` expression in a manner similar to that of Equation 1. Definitions (a) refactors mutually recursive bindings into a single tuple pattern and tuple expression, and (c) resolves the recursion with an explicit fix point. It is worth pointing out that the use of `fix` in (c) is really hypothetical and is meant to direct the reader to the implicit intentions of Haskell's designers; Haskell does not contain a `fix` operator and one must define it as we have in Figure 3.

One semantic subtlety in (a)-(c) arises from the fact that pattern matching perturbs Haskell's default lazy evaluation. A Haskell abstraction (`\p -> e`) may be partially strict in that an argument to the abstraction will be evaluated against `p` to get the bindings for (`fringe p`). Because arguments to `fix` must be lazy, care must be taken to annotate certain patterns with the irrefutable pattern operator $\tilde{\ }$, and this is why $\tilde{\ }$ pops up somewhat mysteriously in definitions (a)-(c). Our specification of mutual recursion will make similar $\tilde{\ }$ annotations where necessary. We condense (a)-(c) into the following schemas, which guides our specification of mutually recursive let-binding in Haskell:

$$\text{let } \{ p_1 = e_1 ; \ldots; p_n = e_n \} \text{ in } e = \tag{4}$$
$$(\backslash \; \tilde{\ } (\tilde{\ } p_1, \ldots, \tilde{\ } p_n) -> e) \, (\text{fix} \, (\backslash \; \tilde{\ } (\tilde{\ } p_1, \ldots, \tilde{\ } p_n) -> (e_1, \ldots, e_n)))$$

To be concrete, let us consider what must be done to specify (`Let ds e`) in the manner discussed above. First, we must gather all of the patterns in the left-hand sides of the declarations in `ds` (call them `p1`, ..., `pn`) and form the necessary tuple pattern: $\tilde{\ }$(`~p1,...,~pn`). This is accomplished chiefly with two auxiliary functions, `tildefy` and `declared` (both shown below). `tildefy` adds a $\tilde{\ }$

```
mE :: E -> Env -> V
mE (Let ds e) rho      = letbind rho ds e

letbind ::  Env -> [D] -> E -> V
letbind rho [] e = mE e rho
letbind rho ds e = (lam dp e rho) v
 where
  dp = tildefy (declared ds)
  xs = frD ds
  decls env = tuple (map (\d -> mD d env) ds)
  v = fix  (((mP dp) <>
                 ((\vs -> decls (extend rho xs vs)) >>> Just)) >>> purify)

mwhere ::  Env -> B -> [D] -> Maybe V
mwhere rho b [] = mB b rho
mwhere rho b ds = (wherecls dp b rho) v
 where
  dp = tildefy (declared ds)
  xs = frD ds
  decls env = tuple (map (\d -> mD d env) ds)
  v = fix (((mP dp) <>
                 ((\vs -> decls (extend rho xs vs)) >>> Just)) >>> purify)
  wherecls p b rho = (mP p <> (\vs -> mB b (extend rho xs vs)))
                         where xs = fringe p

-- the fringe of a declaration D
frD ::  [D] -> [Name]
frD [] = []
frD ((Fun f _):ds) = f : (frD ds)
frD ((Val p _ _):ds) = fringe p ++ (frD ds)
```

Fig. 12. Semantics of mutually recursive bindings

to a pattern if necessary. Note that a variable pattern (Pvar x) needs no ˜ and a no redundant ˜s need be added, either. (declared ds) returns a tuple pattern in which all component patterns have been tildefy'd.

```
declared :: [D] -> P
declared ds = ptuple $ map getbinder ds
    where  getbinder (Fun f _)   = Pvar f
           getbinder (Val p _ _) = tildefy p

tildefy :: P -> P
tildefy p = case p of  (Ptilde p') -> p
                       (Pvar x)    -> p
                       _           -> (Ptilde p)
```

The next step in specifying (Let ds e) is to form a tuple value out of the right-hand sides of its declarations ds. This corresponds to the $(e_1, \ldots, e_n)$ tuple in (a) above. This is accomplished mainly by mapping the semantics of declarations, mD, onto the declaration list `ds`, and then converting the list into a tuple value. Recall `tuple` is defined in Figure 6.

Now we can put all of these pieces together into the auxiliary function `letbind`. (`letbind rho ds e`) takes the current environment `rho`, extends it with the mutually recursive bindings from `ds`, and evaluates `e` in this extended environment. In other words, (`letbind rho ds e`) is precisely (`mE (Let ds e) rho`). (`letbind rho ds e`) implements the scheme given in Equation 4 above, and we define the meaning of Haskell `let` with it in Figure 12.

Defined in an analogous manner to `letbind` is the auxiliary function `mwhere`. This has been used to describe `where` clauses around bodies in B. `letbind` and `mwhere` handle mutual recursive bindings identically, and the principal difference between them is that `mwhere` applies to bodies B, and hence has a computational type.

7   Testing the Interpreter

```
e1 = seq ((\ (Just x) y -> x) Nothing) 3
e2 = seq ((\ (Just x) -> (\ y -> x)) Nothing) 3
e3 = (\ ~(x, Just y) -> x) (0, Nothing)
e4 = case 1 of
        x | x==z -> (case 1 of w | False -> 33)
               where z = 1
        y -> 101
e5 = case 1 of
        x | x==z -> (case 1 of w | True -> 33)
               where z = 2
        y -> 101
e6 = let  fac 0 = 1
          fac n = n * (fac (n-1))
      in fac 3
```

```
Semantics> mE e1 rho0          Hugs> e1
  3                              3
Semantics> mE e2 rho0          Hugs> e2
  Program error: {undefined}      Program error: {e2_v2550 Maybe_Nothing}
Semantics> mE e3 rho0          Hugs> e3
  Program error: {undefined}      Program error: {e3_v2558 (Num_fromInt instNum_v35 0,...)}
Semantics> mE e4 rho0          Hugs> e4
  Program error: {undefined}      Program error: {e4_v2562 (Num_fromInt instNum_v35 1)}
Semantics> mE e5 rho0          Hugs> e5
  101                            101
Semantics> mE e6 rho0          Hugs> e6
  6                              6
Semantics>                     Hugs>
```

Fig. 13. Comparing the semantics to Hugs

Figure 13 presents a number of examples, and compares the output of the semantics (executing in Hugs) against that of the Hugs Haskell interpreter. In the figure, rho0 is the empty environment, and, for the sake of readability, we have not shown the abstract syntax translations of e1 through e6. Two interesting cases are e1 and e2. As we observed in Section 5.2, the lambda expression (\p1 p2 -> e) is lazier than the explicitly curried expression (\p1 -> \p2 -> e), and the semantics mE agrees with the Hugs interpreter on this point.

The semantics mE explains this somewhat surprising distinction nicely. Consider the following Haskell terms:

```
t1 = (\ (Just x) y -> x) Nothing
t2 = ((\ (Just x) -> (\ y -> x)) Nothing
```

(mE t1 rho0) is the function value FV(λ_-.bottom)—that is, a function that, if applied, will fail. According to mE, the meaning of the application t2 is bottom, because the pattern matching of (Just x) against Nothing is performed. mE also distinguishes between $\perp_{a \to b}$ and $(\lambda_-. \perp: a \to b)$ as required by the Haskell98 report[13] (cf. Section 6.2, page 75): (semseq (mE t1 rho0) 3) is simply 3, while (semseq (mE t2 rho0) 3) is bottom.

8   Future Work and Conclusions

The Haskell98 report contains a number of translation schemas which describe the interactions between Haskell features, and by doing so, provide a semi-formal language definition to be used by programmers and language implementors alike. In Section 6.1, we included several such schemas to motivate our formal view of mutual recursion. These schemas may also be viewed as a set of axioms for Haskell which must be satisfied by any candidate semantics (including this one) for it to be considered a *bona fide* Haskell semantics in some sense. An example validation occurs below in Figure 14. We have validated a number of the translation schemas from in the Haskell98 report having to do with pattern-matching, but a number of schemas remain unchecked. A follow-on to this work would collect all of these Haskell "axioms" together with the proofs of their validation with respect to this semantics.

Haskell is commonly referred to as a lazy functional language, but it is more properly understood as a non-eager language because it contains features (patterns, the seq operator, etc.) which introduce strict perturbations of the default lazy evaluation mechanism. These perturbations are important for practical reasons: expert Haskell programmers may use strictness sparingly in their programs to avoid some of the computational overhead associated with laziness without giving it up entirely.

However, this mixed evaluation order complicates Haskell from a semantic point of view. We have modeled Haskell's control of demand by writing a calculational semantics in Haskell, relying on certain built-in aspects of Haskell (laziness, etc.) to model Haskell itself. An alternative would have modeled Haskell's fine control of demand by monadic interpreter[2,8], which can model the full range, from fully strict to fully lazy languages.

The present work is the first formal treatment of the fine control of demand in Haskell, but we believe that many of the techniques presented here apply equally

```
mE (case v of { _ -> e ; _ -> e' }) rho
   = mcase rho { _ -> e ; _ -> e' }) (mE v rho)
   = (((match rho (_) e) 'fatbar'
                    (match rho (_) e')) >>> purify) (mE v rho)
   = ((((mP (_)) <> ((\ _ -> mE e rho) >>> Just) 'fatbar'
                             ...)) >>> purify) (mE v rho)
            where ... = (mP (_)) <> ((\ _ -> mE e' rho) >>> Just)
   = (((((\_ -> Just []) <> ((\ _ -> mE e rho) >>> Just)
                      'fatbar' ...)) >>> purify) (mE v rho)
   = (((((\ _ -> mE e rho) >>> Just)
                      'fatbar' ...)) >>> purify) (mE v rho)
   = (((\ _ -> mE e rho) >>> Just) >>> purify) (mE v rho)
   = purify (Just (mE e rho))
   = mE e rho
```

Fig. 14. Validating the semantics w.r.t. translation "`case` v `of {` $\_{->}e;\_{->}e'$ `}` $=$ e"

well to the semantics of functional languages in general. The patterns considered were nested patterns, and we did not resort to pattern-match compilation to simplify the task. The work clearly defines the interaction between `data` (with and without strictness annotations) and `newtype` data constructors with Haskell's other features.

The code presented in this paper is available online at: http://www.cse.ogi.edu/~wlh.

Acknowledgments

The authors would like to thank John Launchbury, Dick Kieburtz, and Mark Jones for their insights into Haskell and constructive criticism of earlier versions of this work. Both the anonymous referees and the Pacsoft research group at OGI offered many helpful suggestions that led to significant improvements in the presentation.

References

1. Harold Abelson, Gerald Jay Sussman, and Julie Sussman. *Structure and Interpretation of Computer Programs*. McGraw Hill, Cambridge, Mass., second edition, 1996.
2. Olivier Danvy, Jürgen Koslowski, and Karoline Malmkjær. Compiling monads. Technical Report CIS-92-3, Kansas State University, Manhattan, Kansas, December 1991.
3. Daniel P. Friedman, Mitchell Wand, and Christopher T. Haynes. *Essentials of Programming Languages*. McGraw-Hill Book Co., New York, N.Y., second edition, 2001.

4. Murdoch Gabbay and Andrew Pitts. A new approach to abstract syntax involving binders. In G. Longo, editor, *Proceedings of the 14th Annual Symposium on Logic in Computer Science (LICS'99)*, pages 214–224, Trento, Italy, July 1999. IEEE Computer Society Press.

5. Carl A. Gunter. *Semantics of Programming Languages: Programming Techniques*. The MIT Press, Cambridge, Massachusetts, 1992.

6. Cordelia Hall, Kevin Hammond, Simon Peyton Jones, and Phillip Wadler. Type classes in haskell. In *Proceedings of the European Symposium on Programming*, volume 788 of *Lecture Notes in Computer Science*, pages 241–256. Springer Verlag, April 1994.

7. Mark P. Jones. A system of constructor classes: Overloading and implicit higher-order polymorphism. In *FPCA'93: Conference on Functional Programming and Computer Architecture, Copenhagen, Denmark*, pages 52–61, New York, N.Y., June 1993. ACM Press.

8. Sheng Liang, Paul Hudak, and Mark Jones. Monad transformers and modular interpreters. In *Conference record of POPL'95, 22nd ACM SIGPLAN-SIGACT Symposium on Principles of Programming Languages.*, pages 333–343. ACM Press, January 1995.

9. Robin Milner, Mads Tofte, Robert Harper, and David MacQueen. *The Definition of Standard ML (Revised)*. The MIT Press, 1997.

10. Eugenio Moggi. Functor categories and two-level languages. In *Proceedings of the First International Conference on Foundations of Software Science and Computation Structure (FoSSaCS'98)*, volume 1378 of *Lecture Notes in Computer Science*, pages 211–223. Springer Verlag, 1998.

11. Simon Peyton Jones. *The Implementation of Functional Programming Languages*. Computer Science. Prentice-Hall, 1987.

12. Simon Peyton Jones. Implementing lazy functional languages on stock hardware: The spineless tagless G-machine. *Journal of Functional Programming*, 2(2):127–202, July 1992.

13. Simon Peyton Jones and John Hughes (editors). Report on the programming language Haskell 98. February 1999.

14. Simon Peyton Jones and Simon Marlowe. Secrets of the glasgow haskell compiler inliner. In *Proceedings of the Workshop on Implementing Declarative Languages (IDL'99)*, September 1999.

15. Simon Peyton Jones and André L. M. Santos. A transformation-based optimiser for Haskell. *Science of Computer Programming*, 32(1–3):3–47, September 1998.

16. Andrew Pitts and Murdoch Gabbay. A metalanguage for programming with bound names modulo renaming. In *Mathematics of Program Construction*, volume 1837 of *Lecture Notes in Computer Science*, pages 230–255. Springer Verlag, 2000.

17. Rinus Plasmeijer and Marko van Eekelen. Functional programming: Keep it CLEAN: A unique approach to functional programming. *ACM SIGPLAN Notices*, 34(6):23–31, June 1999.

18. Programatica Home Page. http://www.cse.ogi.edu/PacSoft/projects/programatica. James Hook, Principal Investigator.

19. Joseph E. Stoy. *Denotational Semantics: The Scott-Strachey Approach to Programming Language Semantics*. MIT Press, Cambridge, Massachusetts, 1977.

20. Phillip Wadler. The essence of functional programming. *19th POPL*, pages 1–14, January 1992.

A   Pattern-Matching Compilation Is not Just Desugaring

If a pattern p is (C $t_1 \ldots t_n$) where t_i are variables, and C is a constructor function, then p is a *simple* pattern. However, if one or more of the t_i are not variable patterns, then p is a *nested* pattern. Pattern-matching compilation[11,15] is typically performed as part of the front-end (as it is in GHC and Hugs), because it yields more efficient programs (see Chapter 5 by Wadler in [11] for further details). Figure 15 shows an example of pattern-match compilation in which the definition of a Haskell function nodups with nested patterns is transformed into a similar definition without nested patterns. One feature of this transformation was the necessity of generating new variables x, x', xs, and xs' along the way.

```
nodups1 l =      -- Original with nested patterns:
   case l of
      [] -> []
      [x] -> [x]
      (y:(x:xs)) -> if x==y then (nodups1 (x:xs))
                            else (y:(nodups1 (x:xs)))

nodups2 xs'' =    -- After pattern-match compilation:
   case xs'' of
      [] -> []
      x':xs' -> case xs' of
              [] -> [x']
              x:xs -> if x'==x then (nodups2 (x:xs))
                               else (x':(nodups2 (x:xs)))
```

Fig. 15. Pattern-match compilation is syntactic saccharin

Previous attempts[12,15] to define a denotational semantics for the core of Haskell concentrate on the fragment of the language without nested patterns (the kind of programs produced by pattern-match compilation). This semantics for "unnested" Haskell could be extended simply to the full language by defining the meaning of a term with nested patterns to be the meaning of its compilation. For example, the meaning of nodups1 would be identified with that of nodups2. Observe that this extended semantics relies on the ability to generate fresh names *within the semantics*. The implicit assumption in this approach that pattern-match compilation is just a semantically irrelevant elimination of syntactic sugar.

One defect of this extended semantics is that it is no longer compositional. A much more serious flaw, however, derives from the reliance on fresh name generation within the pattern-matching compilation. Recent developments[10,4] in the semantics of staged languages reveal that the structural consequences of including name generation within a denotational semantics are considerable. This would have serious consequences for developing a simple logic for Haskell programs.

Reasoning about Timeouts

Ian J. Hayes

School of Information Technology and Electrical Engineering
The University of Queensland, Brisbane, 4072, Australia
ianh@itee.uq.edu.au

Abstract. In real-time programming a timeout mechanism allows exceptional behaviour, such as a lack of response, to be handled effectively, while not overly affecting the programming for the normal case. For example, in a pump controller if the water level has gone below the minimum level and the pump is on and hence pumping in more water, then the water level should rise above the minimum level within a specified time. If not, there is a fault in the system and it should be shut down and an alarm raised. Such a situation can be handled by normal case code that determines when the level has risen above the minimum, plus a timeout case handling the situation when the specified time to reach the minimum has passed.

In this paper we introduce a timeout mechanism, give it a formal definition in terms of more basic real-time commands, develop a refinement law for introducing a timeout clause to implement a specification, and give an example of using the law to introduce a timeout. The framework used is a machine-independent real-time programming language, which makes use of a deadline command to represent timing constraints in a machine-independent fashion. This allows a more abstract approach to handling timeouts.

1   Introduction

Our overall goal is to provide a method for the formal development of real-time programs. One problem with real-time programs is that the timing characteristics of a program are not known until it is compiled for a particular machine, whereas we would prefer a machine-independent program development method. The approach we have taken is to extend a real-time programming language with a *deadline* command [2] that allows timing constraints to be incorporated into a real-time program. The deadline command has a simple semantics: it takes no time to execute and guarantees to complete by a given time. In isolation a deadline command cannot be implemented, but if it can be shown that all execution paths leading to a deadline command reach it before its deadline, then it can be removed. We consider such checking to be part of an extended compilation phase for the program, rather than part of the program development phase. Unfortunately, there is the possibility that the compiled code may not meet all the deadlines. In this case the program is not suitable and either we

need to redevelop (parts of) the program, or alternatively find a faster machine
or a compiler that generates better code.

The deadline command allows *machine-independent* real-time programs to be
expressed. To date we have developed a sequential real-time refinement calculus
[8, 9] that can be viewed as an extension [4] of the standard sequential refinement
calculus [15]. In this paper we define a timeout construct of the form

$$\lVert \textbf{ timeout } C_1 \textbf{ after } T \textbf{ then } C_2 \rVert$$

which executes the normal case C_1 until it terminates and exits the timeout
block, or the normal case executes until after time T, in which case a timeout
may occur and C_2 is then executed.

Related Work. Process algebras, such as Timed CSP [18, 19], support a limited
form of timeout. A Timed CSP timeout choice allows a choice between two
processes P and Q, $P \overset{t}{\rhd} Q$, with the understanding that if P partakes in any
event before the timeout time t, P will be completed (and Q ignored), but if P
has been inactive up until the timeout time, Q will be executed instead. TAM
[20, 21] has a similar timeout mechanism, but the choice of whether to timeout
or not is based on whether a shunt (communication channel) has been written
to. Hooman [13] introduces an Occam-like real-time language that has a choice
construct in which each branch is guarded by an input communication and there
is an additional timeout alternative; the timeout branch is taken only if none of
the other guards is satisfied by the timeout time.

The main difference is that in our work the timeout mechanism is not limited to situations just waiting for input; the first branch of a timeout may be
partially executed before the timeout occurs. A timeout restricted to waiting for
input is useful for a discrete (event) input, but it is inadequate for situations
in which an analog input is being monitored to detect a certain property of the
signal occuring within a given time limit. For example, software for a heart pace-
maker may have a normal case that analyses the shape of the input pulses, but
if no pulse arrives at all the timeout case can be invoked to handle this critical
situation. For this example, the program cannot just wait, but must actively
monitor the input. Without a timeout mechanism the program must regularly
check on the elapsed time while monitoring the input. This has two disadvan-
tages with respect to a timeout. Firstly, the check needs to be placed within
the code so that the elapsed time is checked frequently enough—depending on
the complexity and structure of the program this may be problematic—and secondly, a hardware timeout mechanism can give a quicker response to a critical
situation.

Section 2 outlines the real-time refinement calculus. Section 3 defines a timeout construct. Section 4 develops refinement laws for introducing timeouts. Section 5 gives examples of the application of the laws, and Section 6 discusses
timing constraint analysis for this example. Section 7 gives a proof of the refinement law.

2   Real-Time Refinement Calculus

The real-time refinement calculus makes use of a special real-valued variable, τ, for the current time. To allow for nonterminating programs, we allow τ to take on the value infinity (∞):

$$Time_\infty \cong \{r : real_\infty \mid 0 \leq r\} \; ,$$

where $real_\infty$ is the set of real numbers including infinity, and operators on the reals are extended to allow infinite arguments. We also define the set $Time$ as the set of finite times.

In real-time programs we distinguish four kinds of variables:

- inputs, which are under the control of the environment of the program;
- outputs, which are under the control of the program;
- local variables, which are under the control of the program, but unlike outputs are not externally visible; and
- auxiliary variables, which are similar to local variables, but are only used for reasoning about the program and do not appear in the machine code generated by a compiler; assignments to auxiliary variables take no time.

Inputs and outputs are modelled as total functions from $Time$ to the declared type of the variable. Note that it is not meaningful to talk about the value of a variable at time infinity. Only the (special) current time variable, τ, may take on the value infinity. Within the semantics of a command, local and auxiliary variables are modelled by their before and after values (rather than as traces). The before value of a variable z is referenced by the zero-subscripting name, z_0, and the after value is referenced by the unsubscripted name, z. We sometimes need to refer to the set of all variables in scope. We call this ρ. It is partitioned into $\rho.in$, $\rho.out$, $\rho.local$ and $\rho.aux$. We use the term *state* to refer to the combined local and auxiliary variables, the abbreviation $\rho.v$ to stand for the state variables, and decorations of $\rho.v$, such as $\rho.v_0$, to stand for decorated state variables.

We represent the semantics of a command by a predicate [6] in a form similar to that of Hehner [11, 10] and Hoare and He [12]. The predicate relates the start time of a command, τ_0, and the initial values of the state variables to its finish time, τ, (which may be infinity) and the final values of the state variables, as well as constraining the traces of the outputs over time. All our commands insist that time does not go backwards: $\tau_0 \leq \tau$.

The meaning function, $\mathcal{M}$, takes the variables in scope ρ, and a command C, and returns the corresponding predicate $\mathcal{M}_\rho(C)$. Refinement of commands is defined as reverse entailment:

$$C \sqsubseteq_\rho D \cong \mathcal{M}_\rho(C) \Longleftarrow \mathcal{M}_\rho(D) \; ,$$

where the reverse entailment holds for all possible values of the variables, including τ_0 and τ. When the environment ρ is clear from the context, it is omitted.

2.1   Real-Time Specification Command

We define a possibly nonterminating real-time *specification command* with a syntax similar to that of Morgan [15]:

$$\infty x \colon \begin{bmatrix} P, & Q \end{bmatrix} \ ,$$

where x is a set of variables called the *frame*, P is the assumption made by the specification, and Q is its effect. The '∞' at the beginning is just part of the syntax; it indicates that the command might not terminate.

P is assumed to hold at the start time of the command. P is a *single-state predicate*, that is, it contains no references to τ_0 or zero-subscripted state (local and auxiliary) variables. P may contain references to the input and output variable traces, but only to value of an output before the start time of the command. The effect Q is a predicate that constrains the output traces and relates the start time τ_0 as well as the initial (zero-subscripted) state variables, and the finish time τ as well as the final state variables. We use the term *relation* to refer to such effect predicates but emphasise that these predicates are more complex than standard binary relations.

The frame, x, of a specification command lists those outputs and state variables that may be modified by the command. All other outputs in scope, i.e., in $\rho.out$ but not x, are defined to be stable for the duration of the command. The predicate $stable(z, S)$ states that the input/output variable z has the same value over all the times in the set S:

$$stable(z, S) \mathrel{\widehat{=}} S \neq \{\} \Rightarrow (\exists\, y \bullet z (\!| \, S \, |\!) = \{y\}) \ ,$$

where $z (\!| \, S \, |\!)$ is the image of the set S through the function z. We allow the first argument of stable to be a set of variables, in which case all variables in the set are stable. The notation $[s \dots t]$ stands for the closed interval of times from s to t, and $(s \dots t)$ stands for the open interval. We also allow half-open, half-closed intervals.

Any state variables which are not in the frame of a specification command are unchanged. We introduce the predicate $eq(out, t_0, t, z_0, z)$ to capture the fact that the outputs out are stable from t_0 until t and that the pre-state, z_0, equals the post-state, z. In the case of the states, if the final time t is infinity, then the state variables do not have any counterpart in reality. Hence the equality between z_0 and z is not required if t is infinity.

$$eq(out, t_0, t, z_0, z) \mathrel{\widehat{=}} stable(out, [t_0 \dots t]) \wedge (t \neq \infty \Rightarrow z_0 = z)$$

Following Hehner [11] and Hoare and He [12] we introduce a special boolean variable ok that tracks whether or not a command is successful. In our case success can allow nontermination. If the time at which a command is executed is infinity ($\tau_0 = \infty$), i.e., the previous command did not terminate, then success of the previous command is preserved because the current command will never be executed ($ok_0 \wedge \tau_0 = \infty \Rightarrow ok$). Otherwise (i.e., $\tau_0 < \infty$) the specification command preserves success provided the assumption, P, of the specification holds initially. The special variable ok is only used in our semantic definitions, and cannot be directly referred to within the predicates P and Q in the specification command.

In the definition below $\rho.v$, $\rho.v_0$, $\rho.out$, x and x_0 are meta-variables standing for sets of variables. The notation $\rho.out \setminus x$ stands for the set of output variables ($\rho.out$) minus the set of variables in x. The parameter to eq is the values of those variables.

Definition 1 (Real-Time Specification). *Given variables, ρ, a frame, x, contained in $\rho.out \cup \rho.local \cup \rho.aux$, a single-state predicate, P, and a relation, Q, the meaning of a possibly nonterminating real-time specification command is defined by the following.*

$$\mathcal{M}_\rho\left(\infty x\colon \begin{bmatrix} P, & Q \end{bmatrix}\right) \;\widehat{=}\; \tau_0 \leq \tau \wedge (ok_0 \wedge \tau_0 = \infty \Rightarrow ok) \wedge$$
$$(ok_0 \wedge \tau_0 < \infty \wedge P\left[\tfrac{\tau_0,\rho.v_0}{\tau,\rho.v}\right] \Rightarrow$$
$$(ok \wedge Q \wedge eq(\rho.out \setminus x, \tau_0, \tau, \rho.v_0 \setminus x_0, \rho.v \setminus x)))\;.$$

As abbreviations, if the assumption, P, is omitted, then it is taken to be *true*, and if the frame is empty the ':' is omitted. Note that if assumption P does not hold initially the command still guarantees that time does not go backwards.

Definition 2 (Real-Time Commands). *Given a vector of noninput variables, x; a single-state predicate P; a relation Q; an idle-stable, time-valued expression T; a vector of idle-stable expressions, E, of the same length as x and assignment compatible with x; a vector of auxiliary variables, y; a vector of expressions, F, of the same length as y and assignment compatible with y; a program variable, z; an input i that is assignment compatible with z; a noninput variable t of type time; and a time-valued expression D; the real-time commands are defined as follows.*

$$x\colon\begin{bmatrix} P, & Q \end{bmatrix} \;\widehat{=}\; \infty x\colon\begin{bmatrix} P, & Q \wedge \tau < \infty \end{bmatrix} \tag{1}$$

$$\mathbf{skip} \;\widehat{=}\; \begin{bmatrix} \tau_0 = \tau \end{bmatrix} \tag{2}$$

$$\mathbf{idle} \;\widehat{=}\; \begin{bmatrix} true \end{bmatrix} \tag{3}$$

$$\mathbf{delay\ until}\ T \;\widehat{=}\; \begin{bmatrix} T \leq \tau \end{bmatrix} \tag{4}$$

$$x := E \;\widehat{=}\; x\colon\begin{bmatrix} x @ \tau = E\left[\tfrac{\rho.v_0}{\rho.v}\right] @ \tau_0 \end{bmatrix} \tag{5}$$

$$y := F \;\widehat{=}\; y\colon\begin{bmatrix} y = F\left[\tfrac{\rho.v_0}{\rho.v}\right] @ \tau_0 \wedge \tau = \tau_0 \end{bmatrix} \tag{6}$$

$$z : \mathbf{read}(i) \;\widehat{=}\; z\colon\begin{bmatrix} z @ \tau \in i(\!\lfloor \tau_0 \dots \tau \rfloor\!) \end{bmatrix} \tag{7}$$

$$t : \mathbf{gettime} \;\widehat{=}\; t\colon\begin{bmatrix} \tau_0 \leq t \leq \tau \end{bmatrix} \tag{8}$$

$$\mathbf{deadline}\ D \;\widehat{=}\; \begin{bmatrix} \tau_0 = \tau \leq D @ \tau \end{bmatrix} \tag{9}$$

$$\mathbf{magic} \;\widehat{=}\; \begin{bmatrix} false \end{bmatrix} \tag{10}$$

Fig. 1. Definition of commands

2.2   Real-Time Commands

Basic real-time commands are defined in Fig. 1 in terms of equivalent specification commands. In the syntax, the frame of each command preceeds a ':'. We define: a terminating (no '∞' prefix) specification command, $x\colon [P, \quad Q]$; the null command, **skip**, that does nothing and takes no time; a command, **idle**, that does nothing but may take time; an absolute delay command; a multiple assignment; an assignment for auxiliary variables that takes no time; a command, **read**, to sample a value from an external input; a command, **gettime**, that returns an approximation to the current time; the deadline command; and the (unimplementable) command, **magic**, that refines all other commands.

As in real-time programming languages, outputs may be modified using assignments, and expressions used in assignments and guards may refer to the value of an output variable. Such references are to the current value of the output. Hence for an expression, E, we use the notation $E \,@\, s$ to stand for E with all free occurrences of τ replaced by s, and all occurrences of any output, o, replaced by $o(s)$.

We require that the value of an expression, that is used in an assignment or a guard, does not change while the expression is being evaluated: This can happen if the expression refers to the current time variable, τ, or to the value of an external input (which is not under the control of the program). Hence, we require that these expressions are *idle-stable*, that is, their value does not change over time provided all output variables are stable and the state does not change. In practice this means that an idle-stable expression cannot refer to the special time variable, τ, or to the value of external inputs.

Definition 3 (Idle-Stable). *Given variables, ρ, an expression E is* idle-stable *provided* $\tau_0 \leq \tau < \infty \land stable(\rho.out, [\tau_0 \,...\, \tau]) \Rightarrow E \,@\, \tau_0 = E \,@\, \tau$.

For example, the expression, o, where o is an integer-valued output, is idle-stable because

$$\tau_0 \leq \tau < \infty \land stable(o, [\tau_0 \,...\, \tau]) \Rightarrow o(\tau_0) = o(\tau) \ .$$

However, the boolean-valued expression, $(\tau \leq D)$, where D is a constant, is not idle-stable because

$$\tau_0 \leq \tau < \infty \land stable(o, [\tau_0 \,...\, \tau]) \Rightarrow (\tau_0 \leq D) = (\tau < D)$$

is not valid.

In the definition of **skip** and **idle** we make use of a terminating specification (no '∞') with an empty frame and a default assumption of *true*. Note that τ is implicitly in the frame of such a specification, and hence in the case of **idle** it may take time.

The **deadline** command is novel. It takes no time and guarantees to complete by the given deadline. It is not possible to implement a deadline command by generating code. Instead we need to check that the code generated for a program that contains a deadline command will always reach the deadline command by

its deadline [3]. We have included the infeasible command **magic** because it
is useful to discuss miraculous behaviour, in particular the possibly miraculous
behaviour of the deadline command and the relationship between magic and
nondeterministic choice.

Given two commands C_1 and C_2, and a nonempty set of commands SC, the compound
commands are defined as follows.

Command – C	Meaning – $\mathcal{M}_\rho(C)$	
$C_1 \sqcap C_2$	$\mathcal{M}_\rho(C_1) \vee \mathcal{M}_\rho(C_2)$	(11)
$C_1 \sqcup C_2$	$\mathcal{M}_\rho(C_1) \wedge \mathcal{M}_\rho(C_2)$	(12)
$C_1;\ C_2$	$\mathcal{M}_\rho(C_1) \,\S\, \mathcal{M}_\rho(C_2)$	(13)
$\bigsqcap SC$	$(\exists C : SC \bullet \mathcal{M}_\rho(C))$	(14)

Fig. 2. Compound commands

2.3   Compound Commands

The meanings of compound commands are given in Fig. 2. The (demonic) nondeterministic choice between two commands, written $C_1 \sqcap C_2$, may behave as
either of the two commands. It is the greatest lower bound (or meet) of the
commands with respect to the refinement ordering. A command is refined by a
choice between two commands if and only if it is refined by each of the commands, and a choice is refined by either of its alternatives. Note that **magic** is
the identity of nondeterministic choice:

magic $\sqcap C = C = C \sqcap$ **magic** .

Hence when there is a choice between miraculous behaviour and nonmiraculous
behaviour, the nonmiraculous behaviour is always chosen.

Nondeterministic choice may be generalised to a choice over a set of commands. A command is refined by a generalised choice over a set of commands
SC if and only if it is refined by every command in SC, and a general choice is
refined by each of its alternatives.

In order to define the timeout mechanism we make use of a join operator
between commands, $C_1 \sqcup C_2$. The behaviours of a join must be behaviours of
both its components. The join operator is introduced purely to let us define the
timeout mechanism; it is not an operator available in the programming language.
The join is the least upper bound of the commands with respect to the refinement
ordering. A join is refined by a command, C, if and only if both components of
the join are refined by C, and a join refines both of its components.

Because we allow nonterminating commands, we need to be careful with
our definition of sequential composition. If the first command of the sequential

composition does not terminate, then we want the effect of the sequential composition on the values of the outputs over time to be the same as the effect of the first command. This is achieved by ensuring that for any command in our language, if it is 'executed' at $\tau_0 = \infty$, it has no effect. For the specification command this is achieved by the assumption $\tau_0 < \infty$ in Definition 1 (real-time specification). The definition of sequential composition combines the effects of the two commands via a hidden intermediate state. The sequential composition of commands is defined in terms of the relational composition operator, '$\mathring{,}$'.

Definition 4 (Relational Composition). *Given an environment with variables ρ (which includes the state variables $\rho.v$ of type S_v), and two relations R_1 and R_2 the relational composition of R_1 and R_2 is defined as follows.*

$$R_1 \mathbin{\mathring{,}} R_2 \mathrel{\widehat{=}} \exists \tau' : Time_\infty;\ \rho.v' : S_v \bullet R_1 \left[\frac{\tau', \rho.v'}{\tau, \rho.v} \right] \wedge R_2 \left[\frac{\tau', \rho.v'}{\tau_0, \rho.v_0} \right].$$

Sequential composition has a higher precedence than both join and nondeterministic choice.

The following law is a generalisation of the standard law for refining a specification to a sequential composition of specifications. For the termination case both commands must terminate. The first establishes the intermediate single-state predicate I as well as the relation R_1 between the start and finish states of the first command. The second command assumes I initially and establishes the single-state predicate S as well as the relation R_2 between its initial and final states. Hence the sequential composition establishes S as well as the relational composition of R_1 and R_2 between its initial and final states.

For the nontermination case either the first command does not terminate and establishes Q_1, or the first command terminates establishing I and R_1 and the second command does not terminate and establishes Q_2. The overall effect is thus either Q_1 or the composition of R_1 and Q_2.

Law 5 (Sequential Composition). *Given single-state predicates P, I and S, and relations R_1, R_2, Q_1 and Q_2,*

$$\infty x \colon \left[P, \quad (\tau < \infty \wedge S \wedge (R_1 \mathbin{\mathring{,}} R_2)) \vee (\tau = \infty \wedge (Q_1 \vee (R_1 \mathbin{\mathring{,}} Q_2))) \right]$$
$$\sqsubseteq$$
$$\infty x \colon \left[P, \quad (\tau < \infty \wedge I \wedge R_1) \vee (\tau = \infty \wedge Q_1) \right];$$
$$\infty x \colon \left[I, \quad (\tau < \infty \wedge S \wedge R_2) \vee (\tau = \infty \wedge Q_2) \right]$$

Taking Q_1 and Q_2 as *false* reduces the law to the standard law of Jones [14] for terminating commands.

The semantics of conditionals, repetitions and variable blocks are given in earlier papers [6, 7]. As their details are not essential for defining timeouts, we refer the reader to these other sources.

3   Definition of a Timeout Command

The timeout construct is of the form $\|[\ \textbf{timeout}\ C_1\ \textbf{after}\ T\ \textbf{then}\ C_2\ ]\|$. At the heart of the definition of the timeout is a nondeterministic choice between the normal case and the timeout case. Let w stand for all the output variables plus all the state variables in the environment: $\rho.out \cup \rho.v$. Our initial approximation to the definition of a timeout command is

$$((C_1 \sqcup w\colon [\tau \leq T + timeout\_response])$$
$$\sqcap (partial(C_1);\ [\tau_0 = \tau \land T \leq \tau]\ ;\ C_2))$$

We explain this approximation in detail first, and then give the complete definition. In the timeout case C_1 is partially executed, represented by $partial(C_1)$ (which is defined below), then a timeout occurs at a time after the value of T, and then C_2 is executed. The normal case is never executed past some $timeout\_response$ beyond the timeout time T. Because C_1 may be a nonterminating command, in order to be able to limit the execution time of the first branch, we make use of the join operator $\sqcup$ to conjoin a specification command that provides the termination requirement. For example, with w as above

$$\infty x\colon [P,\quad Q] \sqcup w\colon [\tau \leq D] = x\colon [P,\quad Q \land \tau \leq D]\ .$$

The nondeterministic choice would appear to allow the timeout construct to (arbitrarily) choose between the normal and timeout cases. However, if the time required by the normal case extends past $T + timeout\_response$, that branch becomes miraculous and the timeout alternative must be taken. Without any further constraint our definition allows the timeout alternative to always be taken. However, the timeout construct is typically followed by a deadline. For the example in Sect. 5, the normal case is required to detect some event occuring at time $ev2$ and then terminate within a timing error bound of err. The timeout alternative should only be taken if the event is not detected before the timeout T and terminate within the timing error bound. The timeout can thus be followed by a deadline of the form

deadline(**if** $ev2 + err < T$ **then** $ev2 + err$ **else** $T + err$)

(where we assume that the value of T has not been modified by the timeout construct). With the deadline in place after the timeout construct, the timeout alternative is only feasible if

$$\exists \tau : Time \bullet T \leq \tau \land \tau \leq \textbf{if}\ ev2 + err < T\ \textbf{then}\ ev2 + err\ \textbf{else}\ T + err$$
$$\equiv \textbf{if}\ ev2 + err < T\ \textbf{then}\ T \leq ev2 + err\ \textbf{else}\ T \leq T + err$$
$$\equiv (ev2 + err < T \land T \leq ev2 + err) \lor (T \leq ev2 + err \land T \leq T + err)$$
$$\equiv \text{as } err \text{ is positive}$$
$$T \leq ev2 + err$$

That is, if the timeout T is after $ev2 + err$, then the timeout alternative is infeasible, and only the normal case can possibly be executed. This issue is discussed further in Sect. 6.

We now give the complete corrected definition of a timeout. The timeout response ultimately depends on the implementation, but for the purposes of our definition a nondeterministic choice over all positive values suffices. Any implementation will meet a particular response time; whether that response time is fast enough is determined by the timing path analysis (see Sect. 6).

In general, the value of the timeout expression T may depend on variables modified by C_1. Hence in the definition below, its initial value is captured in a fresh auxiliary variable, T_{init}. The timeout command initially executes C_1. However, there may be a delay before C_1 actually starts execution to allow for the time to set up the timeout mechanism. In the definition below this delay is represented by the first **idle** command; the actual time taken depends on the particular implementation. Similar **idle** commands are used to represent the time to reset the timeout mechanism on completion of C_1, the time to actually take the timeout before C_2 is executed, and the time to exit the timeout block after C_2 is executed. The notation $\{x : S \mid P(x) \bullet E(x)\}$ stands for the set of values of the expression $E(x)$ for x ranging over the elements of the set S such that $P(x)$ holds. Its use below gives a set of commands, over which a nondeterministic choice is made.

Definition 6 (Timeout). *Given variables ρ, a time-valued, idle-stable expression T, commands C_1 and C_2, and fresh names T_{init} and timeout_response that do not occur in ρ,*

$$
\begin{aligned}
&\lVert \textbf{ timeout } C_1 \textbf{ after } T \textbf{ then } C_2 \rVert \mathrel{\widehat{=}} \\
&\sqcap \{ \mathit{timeout\_response} : \mathit{Time} \mid 0 < \mathit{timeout\_response} \bullet \\
&\quad \lVert \textbf{ aux } T_{init} : \mathit{Time} \bullet T_{init} := T; \textbf{ idle}; \\
&\qquad ((C_1; \textbf{ idle} \quad \sqcup \quad (\rho.\mathit{out}, \rho.v) \colon [\tau \le T_{init} + \mathit{timeout\_response}]) \\
&\qquad \sqcap (\mathit{partial}(C_1); [\tau_0 = \tau \wedge T_{init} \le \tau]; \textbf{ idle}; C_2; \textbf{ idle})) \\
&\quad \rVert \}
\end{aligned}
$$

3.1 Partial Execution of Commands Due to Timeout

The first branch of a timeout construct may be interrupted before it completes. Hence to formally define the behaviour of the timeout construct we need to define the partial behaviours of commands, as given in Fig. 3. If an assignment is partially executed then the final value of the frame of the assignment is arbitrary. Hence the partial execution of an assignment is equivalent to a specification command with the same frame as the assignment but a postcondition of *true*. The **gettime** and **read** commands are treated similarly. The **skip** and **deadline** commands take no execution time and hence their partial executions are unchanged. Both **idle** and **delay until** have partial executions that just consume time. A sequential composition can either partially execute its first command, or it may complete its first command and then partially execute its second command. A **notimeout** block temporarily disables timeouts. Hence its execution will always complete the body of the block unless the timeout occurs before the timeout has been disabled, in which case its behaviour is equivalent to **idle**. To allow for the time taken to disable and reenable timeouts, additional **idle** commands are used before and after C.

Command – C	Partial execution – $partial(C)$
$x := e$	$x\colon [true]$
$x : \mathbf{gettime}$	$x\colon [true]$
$x : \mathbf{read}(i)$	$x\colon [true]$
$\mathbf{skip}$	$\mathbf{skip}$
$\mathbf{deadline}\ D$	$\mathbf{deadline}\ D$
$\mathbf{idle}$	$\mathbf{idle}$
$\mathbf{delay\ until}\ D$	$\mathbf{idle}$
$C_1;\ C_2$	$partial(C_1) \sqcap (C_1;\ partial(C_2))$
$[\![\ \mathbf{notimeout}\ C\ ]\!]$	$(\mathbf{idle};\ C;\ \mathbf{idle}) \sqcap \mathbf{idle}$
$\infty x\colon [P, \quad Q]$	$(\rho.out,\ \rho.v)\colon \left[P,\ \begin{array}{c} (\exists\, \rho.out', \rho.v', \tau' \bullet \tau \le \tau' \wedge Q\left[\frac{\rho.out', \rho.v', \tau'}{\rho.out, \rho.v, \tau}\right] \wedge \\ eq(\rho.out' \setminus x', \tau_0, \tau', \rho.v_0 \setminus x_0, \rho.v' \setminus x') \wedge \\ (\forall\, o : \rho.out \bullet (o' = o)\ \mathbf{over}\ [0 \dots \tau])) \end{array} \right]$

Fig. 3. Partial behaviour of commands

A partial execution of a specification command will be on the way to establishing its postcondition Q at some time τ' in the future. Because the partial execution will not reach the final state, we introduce τ', $\rho.out'$ and $\rho.v'$ to stand for the values that would have been established by Q. These are hidden within the postcondition of the equivalent specification. To be a valid partial execution, the value of an output variable, o, must match a possible output of the complete execution, o', up until the termination time of the partial execution, τ. (Note that the trace variable o' is an element of $\rho.out'$ and hence it is existentially quantified within the postcondition.) The notation $(o' = o)\ \mathbf{over}\ [0 \dots \tau]$ states that the predicate $o' = o$ holds for all times in the set $[0 \dots \tau]$; i.e., it is the same as $\forall\, t : [0 \dots \tau] \bullet o'(t) = o(t)$. Note that the partial execution of a specification command always terminates.

Given the definition of *partial* for the specification command, we have the property that if a specification command, $\infty x\colon [P, \quad Q]$, is refined by a command C, then $partial(\infty x\colon [P, \quad Q])$ is refined by $partial(C)$. This property is necessary in order to allow the first branch of a timeout to be replaced by a refinement, and maintain the refinement ordering between the overall timeout blocks. However, for primitive commands, such as assignment, the property does not hold. For example, we have $x := 1 \sqsubseteq x, y := 1, y$ where x and y are local variables, but their partial executions are not refinements:

$$partial(x := 1) = x\colon [true] \not\sqsubseteq x, y\colon [true] = partial(x, y := 1, y) \ .$$

One approach to maintaining monotonicity for partial execution behaviour is to use a stronger notion of refinement that does not allow a frame to be expanded

[1]. However, this is not necessary in general; we return to this issue when we discuss discharging timeout invariants in Sect. 4.

4   Timeout Introduction Law

Our first timeout law either establishes R in the normal (first) branch, or establishes Q and of course $T \leq \tau$ in the timeout branch. We give the law first and explain it below.

Law 7 (Simple-Timeout). *Given a time-valued constant T; single-state, idle-invariant predicates P and Q, and a pre- and post-idle-invariant relation R*

$$x \colon \left[P, \quad R \vee (Q \wedge T \leq \tau) \right]$$
$$\sqsubseteq \|[\; \mathbf{timeout} \, \infty x \colon \left[P, \quad R \right] \, \mathbf{after} \, T \, \mathbf{then} \, x \colon \left[T \leq \tau, \quad Q \right] \;]\|$$

For the timeout branch, Q is only a single-state predicate (rather than a relation) because the initial state of the timeout clause (i.e., the state after the normal branch is interrupted) is not the same as the initial state of the overall specification.

The timeout construct may take some time to set up the timeout mechanism initially. During this time the precondition P, if it refers to the current time variable τ or to inputs (which may change with the passage of time), may be invalidated. Hence for our law we require that the precondition P is impervious to the delay caused by setting up the timeout: we require P to be *idle-invariant*.

Definition 8 (Idle-Invariant). *For an environment with variables ρ, a single-state predicate P is* idle-invariant *provided*

$$\tau_0 \leq \tau < \infty \wedge stable(\rho.out, [\tau_0 \dots \tau]) \wedge P\left[\tfrac{\tau_0}{\tau}\right] \Rightarrow P \; .$$

The conditions idle-stable and idle-invariant differ in that idle-stable applies to expressions of any type (including boolean), whereas idle-invariant only applies to predicates. For booleans idle-stable is a stronger requirement than idle-invariant: for the former the value does not change over the execution of an idle command, whereas for the latter, if the value holds before, then it holds after. The latter differs from the former in that for idle-invariance, if the predicate is false beforehand, then it may become true during the execution of the idle.

The assumption that P is idle-invariant places restrictions on how P can refer to the current time variable, τ, because τ increases on execution of an idle command, and on how P refers to external inputs, because these may change over the execution of an idle command. For example, predicates of the form $T \leq \tau$, (where T is an idle-stable expression) are idle-invariant, but predicates of the form $\tau \leq T$ are not because the passage of time may cause τ to exceed T. If P can be expressed in a form that does not refer to the current time, τ, and all references to each external input, i, are of the form $i(E)$, where E is an idle-stable expression, then P is idle-invariant.

The specification makes use of a relation R. As with the precondition, we need to be careful about the time intervals corresponding to setting up and resetting the timeout mechanism. Hence we require that the relation used is impervious to these idle periods. We use the terms *pre-idle-invariant* and *post-idle-invariant* to refer to relations that are impervious to pre and post, respectively, idle periods.

A relation R is pre-idle-invariant if whenever it holds over an interval from τ_0 to τ, then for any u less than or equal to τ_0 it holds over the interval from u to τ, provided the variables under the control of the program are not modified over the interval from u to τ_0.

Definition 9 (Pre-Idle-Invariant). *A relation R is* pre-idle-invariant *provided, for fresh u,*

$$\tau_0 < \infty \wedge u \leq \tau_0 \leq \tau \wedge stable(\rho.out, [u \ldots \tau_0]) \wedge R \Rightarrow R\left[\frac{u}{\tau_0}\right]$$

The interval from u to τ_0 corresponds to the idle period before executing the command with effect R. For example, assuming D is a time-valued idle-stable expression, the predicate $D \leq \tau_0$ is not pre-idle-invariant.

A predicate R is post-idle-invariant if, for any u greater than or equal to τ, whenever R holds over an interval from τ_0 to τ, it also holds over the interval from τ_0 to u, provided the variables under the control of the program are not modified between τ and u.

Definition 10 (Post-Idle-Invariant). *A predicate R is* post-idle-invariant *provided, for fresh u,*

$$\tau_0 \leq \tau \leq u < \infty \wedge stable(\rho.out, [\tau \ldots u]) \wedge R \Rightarrow R\left[\frac{u}{\tau}\right]$$

The interval from τ to u corresponds to the idle period after executing the command with effect R. For example, the predicate $\tau \leq D$ is not post-idle-invariant. As a further example, the predicate $\tau - \tau_0 \leq D$ is neither pre- nor post-idle-invariant. Note that we rule out τ and u being infinity; if τ is infinity the command does not terminate and nothing can follow it. If the only references to τ_0 and τ are as indices of outputs, the relation is both pre- and post-idle-invariant.

There are two short comings to Law 7 (simple-timeout): the timeout value T is restricted to be a constant, and the only assumption that the timeout branch makes is $T \leq \tau$ whereas it can validly assume the partial execution behaviour of the first branch has taken place before the timeout. We address these two issues in sequence.

We allow T to be an idle-stable, time-valued expression. Because variables used in the expression T may be modified in the first branch, in order to refer to the initial value of T in the precondition of the timeout branch, we introduce a fresh auxiliary variable, T_{init}, which is initially assigned the value of T. It is an auxiliary variable, rather than a local variable, because it is only used to express an assumption in the precondition of the timeout branch.

Next we would like to strengthen the precondition of the timeout branch to allow assumptions about the partial behaviour of the first branch to be included.

An idle-invariant predicate, I, that holds initially (i.e., $P \Rightarrow I$), and does not refer to any variables modified in the first branch, will still hold when the time-out branch is executed. Unfortunately, when the first branch is a specification command (rather than final code), it is not possible to determine the set of variables that may be modified by the code that implements the specification, because the frame of a specification may be expanded to include an additional local variable, z, provided its postcondition is strengthened to require that the final value of z is the same as its initial value: $z = z_0$.

To overcome this problem we introduce a timeout-invariant block of the form, $\|[\textbf{ tinv } I \bullet C]\|$, similar to the invariant block, $\|[\textbf{ inv } I \bullet C]\|$, of Morgan and Vickers [17]. Regardless of whether C maintains the invariant I, the block $\|[\textbf{ tinv } I \bullet C]\|$, is guaranteed to maintain I. The semantics of the timeout block are given by

$$\|[\textbf{ tinv } I \bullet C]\| \mathrel{\widehat{=}} \{I\};\ (C \sqcup \infty(\rho.out, \rho.v)\colon [I])$$

where the assertion $\{I\}$ reflects the fact that the invariant block assumes that I holds initially, and the joined constraint $\infty(\rho.out, \rho.v)\colon [I]$ ensures the block re-establishes I (even if C does not).

In addition, we have the stronger condition that I is guaranteed to be an invariant of $partial(\|[\textbf{ tinv } I \bullet C]\|)$. Hence the partial execution semantics of an invariant block is given by the following.

$$partial(\|[\textbf{ tinv } I \bullet C]\|) \mathrel{\widehat{=}} \|[\textbf{ tinv } I \bullet partial(C)]\|$$

In a state in which the invariant holds initially, a timeout-invariant block may be introduced.

$$\{I\};\ C \sqsubseteq \|[\textbf{ tinv } I \bullet C]\|$$

If C is final code then the timeout invariant needs to be discharged. For constructs that do not modify variables used in I, this is trivial. However, we return to the issue raised in Sect. 3.1 about monotonicity with respect to partial execution behaviour. Consider a timeout invariant block $\|[\textbf{ tinv } y = 0 \bullet x := 1]\|$. By our definitions $y = 0$ is an invariant of both $x := 1$ and $partial(x := 1)$, i.e., $x\colon [true]$. However, as discussed earlier $x := 1 \sqsubseteq x, y := 1, y$ but, while $y = 0$ is an invariant of $x, y := 1, y$, it is not an invariant of $partial(x, y := 1, y)$, i.e., $x, y\colon [true]$. Hence once we have discharged the timeout invariant we forbid further refinements of the code within the first branch of a timeout block (unless we can show refinement of the partial executions as well). Note that any compiler implementing the language has to respect both the normal and partial execution behaviour.

To allow commands within C to modify variables used in I, we need to make use of a block that temporarily disables timeouts while it executes:

$$\|[\textbf{ notimeout } C]\|$$

Provided C reestablishes I when executed in a state satisfying I then I is a timeout invariant of the notimeout block. In practice, notimeout blocks should be of as short a scope as possible so as to avoid unnecessary delay in invoking the timeout.

We combine the above discussion into a more general law. In the timeout branch, Q may refer to the auxiliary variable T_{init}, which contains the initial value of T. In the specification being refined, because T_{init} is not in scope, any occurrences of T_{init} within Q are replaced by the initial value of T, T_0.

Law 11 (Timeout). *Given an idle-stable, time-valued expression T; single-state, idle-invariant predicates P, I and Q, such that $P \Rightarrow I$; a pre- and post-idle invariant relation R; and an auxiliary variable T_{init} not in the environment ρ and that does not occur free in P, I, R or T (but may occur free in Q); then*

$$x \colon \left[P, \quad R \vee \left(Q \left[\tfrac{T_0}{T_{init}} \right] \wedge T_0 \leq \tau \right) \right]$$
$$\sqsubseteq \| [\textbf{ aux } T_{init} : Time \bullet T_{init} := T;$$
$$\| [\textbf{ timeout}$$
$$\| [\textbf{ tinv } I \bullet \infty x \colon [P, \quad R] \,] \|$$
$$\textbf{ after } T \textbf{ then}$$
$$x \colon [I \wedge T_{init} \leq \tau, \quad Q]$$
$$] \|$$
$$] \|$$

where T_0 is an abbreviation for $(T @ \tau_0) \left[\tfrac{\rho . v_0}{\rho . v} \right]$.

5   Example

Before giving a proof of the general law in Section 7, to illustrate our approach we present the example of a water pump feeding a boiler. We restrict ourselves to the situation in which the water level has gone below some minimum level and the pump has been switched on. The program is required to monitor the water level until it exceeds the minimum level and then terminate (before moving on to the next phase). However, if the water level does not exceed the minimum by a given time T, the pump should be switched off (and in the next phase the boiler will be shut down). The auxiliary variable u represents the time at which the pump was turned on. We let ev stand for the time at which the water level next exceeds the minimum level. It is a derived value satisfying the following property.

$$u \leq ev \wedge min \leq water(ev) \wedge (water < min) \textbf{ over } [\tau \ldots ev)$$

Unfortunately, the water level may exceed *min* for an interval of time that is too short to be detected before the level goes below *min* again. Hence we introduce a second derived time *ev2* that stands for the starting time of the earliest time interval which is at least *err* seconds long and over which the water level exceeds *min.*

$$u \leq ev2 \land (min \leq water) \textbf{ over } [ev2 \ldots ev2 + err] \land$$
$$(\forall ev3 : Time \bullet u \leq ev3 \land (min \leq water) \textbf{ over } [ev3 \ldots ev3 + err] \Rightarrow$$
$$ev2 \leq ev3)$$

Obviously, ev is less than or equal to $ev2$ (and normally they are the same).

The pump is assumed to have been on since time u. The postcondition of the specification has two alternatives. The first corresponds to the normal case in which the water level goes above the minimum level. The finish time in this case is after the earliest time (ev) at which the level goes above min. The second alternative corresponds to the case in which the time exceeds the time limit T without the water level being detected above the minimum. The choice between alternatives is affected by the deadline following it, which adds a constraint on the finish time as discussed in Sect. 3.

$$\mathrm{A} :: \left\{ u \leq \tau \leq ev \land \tau \leq T \right\};$$

$$pump: \begin{bmatrix} pump \textbf{ over } [u \ldots \tau] \land \\ u \leq \tau \end{bmatrix}, \quad \begin{matrix} (pump \textbf{ over } [u \ldots \tau] \land ev \leq \tau) \lor \\ (pump \textbf{ over } [u \ldots T] \land \neg\, pump \land \\ T \leq \tau) \end{matrix} \end{bmatrix}; \quad (15)$$

$$\mathrm{D} :: \textbf{deadline}(\textbf{if } ev2 + err < T \textbf{ then } ev2 + err \textbf{ else } T + err)$$

The above can be refined to the code given in Fig. 4. In addition to the expected standard code there are deadline commands and a number of uses of the auxiliary variable, *before*. These are used to ensure that the operation of the program takes place in a timely fashion. No code needs to be generated for these constructs. Their purpose is to facilitate reasoning and to allow the specification of timing constraints via deadline commands. The assertion immediately after the deadline labelled (C) is an invariant of the repetition [5, 7].

5.1 Refinement to Use a Timeout

The specification command (15) is in a form suitable for the application of Law 11 (timeout). For the law application we choose the timeout invariant I to be $pump \textbf{ over } [u \ldots \tau]$.

$|[\, \textbf{aux } T_{init} : Time;\ T_{init} := T;$

$|[\, \textbf{timeout}$

$\quad |[\, \textbf{tinv } pump \textbf{ over } [u \ldots \tau] \bullet$

$$\infty pump: \begin{bmatrix} pump \textbf{ over } [u \ldots \tau] \land \\ u \leq \tau \end{bmatrix}, \quad \begin{matrix} pump \textbf{ over } [u \ldots \tau] \land \\ ev \leq \tau \end{matrix} \end{bmatrix} \quad (16)$$

$\quad]|$

$\textbf{after } T \textbf{ then}$

$$pump: \begin{bmatrix} pump \textbf{ over } [u \ldots \tau] \land \\ T_{init} \leq \tau \end{bmatrix}, \quad \begin{matrix} pump \textbf{ over } [u \ldots T_{init}] \land \\ \neg\, pump \end{matrix} \end{bmatrix} \quad (17)$$

$]|\ ]|$

$A :: \{u \leq \tau \leq ev \wedge \tau \leq T\};$
  $[\![$ **timeout**
      $[\![$ **tinv** $pump$ **over** $[u \dots \tau] \bullet$
            var $level : \mathbb{N};$
            aux $before : Time;$
            repeat
              $B :: before := \tau;$
                  $level : \mathbf{read}(water);$
              $C :: \mathbf{deadline}\ ev2 + err;$
                  $\{(level < min \Rightarrow before \leq ev2) \wedge (min \leq level \Rightarrow ev \leq \tau)\}$
            until $min \leq level;$
            $\{ev \leq \tau\}$
      $]\!]$
    after T **then**
        $pump := false$
  $]\!]$
$D :: \mathbf{deadline}(\mathbf{if}\ ev2 + err < T\ \mathbf{then}\ ev2 + err\ \mathbf{else}\ T + err)$

Fig. 4. Timeout program

For the timeout branch (17), because $pump$ holds up until τ and $T_{init} \leq \tau$, $pump$ holds until T_{init}, and hence the first part of the postcondition has already been established. The precondition can then be dropped.

$$(17) \sqsubseteq pump: [\neg\ pump] \sqsubseteq pump := false$$

For the normal case, as the pump is on, keeping it on can be achieved by not changing $pump$.

$$(16) \sqsubseteq [\![\ \mathbf{tinv}\ pump\ \mathbf{over}\ [u \dots \tau] \bullet \infty\ [ev \leq \tau]\ ]\!] \tag{18}$$

Note that the specification in the first branch is a possibly nonterminating specification. This is to allow for the fact that the event being waited for may never occur, i.e., $ev = \infty$, in which case the timeout branch will have to be taken. Because the specification in (18) allows nontermination, a possible refinement is a never terminating repetition. However, the timeout branch does not guarantee to meet the deadline if $ev2$ preceeds T by more than err. The body of the normal case can be refined to the repetition shown in Fig. 4. That refinement process does not make use of any further timeouts and hence we do not show the refinement here. The process is similar to that illustrated in [5, 7, 6].

The timeout invariant in the program in Fig. 4 can easily be discharged because, if $pump$ **over** $[u \dots \tau]$ and $u \leq \tau$ hold initially, then as $pump$ and u are not modified within the block, $pump$ **over** $[u \dots \tau]$ holds over any partial execution of the block, as required.

6   Timing Constraint Analysis

In order for compiled machine code to implement a machine-independent program it must guarantee to meet all the deadlines. Determining the timing constraints for an arbitrary program is an uncomputable problem, because it encodes the halting problem, but for programs of a restricted form such analysis is possible.

For the example program in Fig. 4 there are two deadlines: one within the repetition within the first branch (C) and the other at the end of the program (D). The first deadline can be reached either on the initial entry into the first branch of the timeout block (and the first entry into the repetition), or on successive iterations from the previous iteration. These paths are similar to those treated in earlier work [5, 7, 6], and hence we do not consider them here. The final deadline can be reached either by exiting the repetition in the first branch, or by timing out and executing the timeout branch.

B :: *before* := τ;
    level : **read**(*water*);
C :: **deadline** $ev2 + err$;
    $\{(level < min \Rightarrow before \leq ev2) \wedge (min \leq level \Rightarrow ev \leq \tau)\}$;
    $[\neg\ min \leq level]$;
B :: *before* := τ;
    level : **read**(*water*);
C :: **deadline** $ev2 + err$;
    $\{(level < min \Rightarrow before \leq ev2) \wedge (min \leq level \Rightarrow ev \leq \tau)\}$;
    $[min \leq level]$;
    -- timeout normal end;
    $\left[\tau \leq T + timeout\_response\right]$;
D :: **deadline**(**if** $ev2 + err < T$ **then** $ev2 + err$ **else** $T + err$)

Fig. 5. Exit path

For the normal exit from a timeout we consider the path shown in Fig. 5. The path starts at the assignment to *before* (B), reads the value of *water* into *level*, passes through the deadline (C), restarts the body of the repetition because *level* is less than *min*, performs the assignment to *before* (B), reads the value of *water*, passes through the deadline (C), exits the repetition because $min \leq level$, and exits the timeout, before reaching the final deadline (D).

The first guard evaluation is represented by $[\neg\ min \leq level]$, which indicates that in order for the path to be followed, *level* must be less than *min* at that point in the path. The initial time assigned to *before*, i.e., the time at which the path begins execution, must be before time $ev2$ because the value of *level* was less than *min*. The normal exit from the timeout block adds a constraint that in order that the normal exit be taken the exit time must be before a maximum *timeout_response* past the specified timeout, T. For the final deadline there are two cases to consider based on the cases of the conditional. If $ev2 + err < T$ then the deadline is $ev2 + err$, and hence because the starting time of the path is before $ev2$, the timing constraint on the path is err. If $T \leq ev2 + err$ then the deadline is $T + err$. The timeout construct guarantees that if the normal exit is taken, it will exit before $T + timeout\_response$. This can be used to show that the deadline of $T + err$ is reached, provided $timeout\_response \leq err$. As expected, whether this holds depends on the *timeout_response* of the implementation.

A :: $\{u \leq \tau \leq ev \wedge \tau \leq T\}$;
    -- **timeout**;
    partial(*first branch*);
    -- **after** T **then**;
    $[T \leq \tau]$;
    pump := *false*;
    -- **end timeout**;
D :: **deadline**(**if** $ev2 + err < T$ **then** $ev2 + err$ **else** $T + err$)

Fig. 6. Timeout path

For the timeout case the path (Fig. 6) starts before the timeout block, enters the timeout block and partially executes the first branch (the first branch is not shown in detail here; it is the same as in Fig. 4) before it takes the timeout at a time after T, sets *pump* to *false*, and exits the timeout block before reaching the final deadline. As discussed in Sect. 3 this path is only feasible if $T \leq ev2 + err$, in which case the final deadline becomes $T + err$. The initial time on this path is before T, and the final deadline is $T + err$. Hence provided the time taken by the mechanism for setting up and performing the timeout, plus the assignment to *pump* and exiting the timeout block is less than err the deadline will always be met.

If the first branch of a timeout construct contains a notimeout block, the timing path analysis needs to take into account the additional delay introduced by the notimeout block before a timeout can take place. If the timing analysis is done assuming that the timeout is delayed by the maximum time required for any of the notimeout blocks in the first branch, then the deadlines will be met.

7   Proof of General Timeout Law

In this section we give a proof of Law 11 (timeout). We begin with the specification in the law and refine it to the definition of the timeout construct in the law (according to Definition 6 (timeout)). The first step introduces the nonde-terministic choice over *timeout_response*. Because the body of the choice is the same as the specification being refined, the refinement holds trivially.

$$x\colon \left[P, \quad R \vee (Q \left[\tfrac{T_0}{T_{init}} \right] \wedge T_0 \leq \tau) \right]$$

$\sqsubseteq$ by general choice

$$\prod \{ timeout\_response : Time \mid 0 < timeout\_response \bullet$$
$$\qquad x\colon \left[P, \quad R \vee (Q \left[\tfrac{T_0}{T_{init}} \right] \wedge T_0 \leq \tau) \right] \tag{19}$$
$$\}$$

Next the auxiliary variable, T_{init}, for the timeout value is introduced. Because T_{init} is equal to the initial value of T, the renaming of T_{init} within Q can be removed. In addition, the **idle** corresponding to the timeout setup delay in Definition 6 (timeout) is introduced.

(19) $\sqsubseteq$ as P idle-invariant; Q and R pre-idle-invariant

$$\lfloor\ \textbf{aux}\ T_{init} : Time \bullet T_{init} := T;\ \textbf{idle};$$
$$\qquad x\colon \left[P, \quad R \vee (Q \wedge T_{init} \leq \tau) \right] \tag{20}$$
$$\rfloor$$

The specification can be refined by a choice in which each alternative establishes one of the disjuncts in the postcondition.

(20) $\sqsubseteq$ as choice idempotent; strengthen postcondition twice

$$x\colon \left[P, \quad R \right] \tag{21}$$
$$\sqcap x\colon \left[P, \quad Q \wedge T_{init} \leq \tau \right] \tag{22}$$

For the normal case (21) a timeout-invariant block can be introduced because the precondition P is stronger than the invariant I.

(21) $\sqsubseteq$ introduce timeout invariant; given $P \Rightarrow I$

$$\lfloor\ \textbf{tinv}\ I \bullet$$
$$\qquad x\colon \left[P, \quad R \right] \tag{23}$$
$$\rfloor$$

The specification (23) can then be refined by strengthening its postcondition with $\tau \leq T_{init} + timeout\_response$ but then factoring this out into a join of commands in which the first is not required to terminate. An additional **idle** is also introduced corresponding to the delay on normal exit from the timeout mechanism.

(23) $\sqsubseteq$ by definition of join; R post-idle-invariant

$$\infty x\colon \left[P, \quad R \right];\ \textbf{idle}\ \ \sqcup\ \ (\rho.out, \rho.v)\colon \left[\tau \leq T_{init} + timeout\_response \right]$$

The timeout branch (22) can be straightforwardly refined to a sequence of commands, which together establish $Q \wedge T_{init} \leq \tau$.

(22) $\sqsubseteq$ sequential composition

$\quad (\rho.out, \rho.v)\colon \begin{bmatrix} I, & I \end{bmatrix}$;

$\quad \begin{bmatrix} I, & I \wedge \tau_0 = \tau \wedge T_{init} \le \tau \end{bmatrix}$;

$\quad x\colon \begin{bmatrix} I \wedge T_{init} \le \tau, & Q \end{bmatrix}$

$\sqsubseteq$ as I, $T_{init} \le \tau$ and Q are idle-invariant

$\quad partial(\lVert \ \mathbf{tinv}\ I \bullet \infty x\colon \begin{bmatrix} P, & R \end{bmatrix} \rVert)$;

$\quad \begin{bmatrix} \tau_0 = \tau \wedge T_{init} \le \tau \end{bmatrix}$;

$\quad \mathbf{idle};\ x\colon \begin{bmatrix} I \wedge T_{init} \le \tau, & Q \end{bmatrix}$; $\mathbf{idle}$

Combining the above refinement steps together the result is

$$x\colon \begin{bmatrix} P, & R \vee (Q\left[\tfrac{T_0}{T_{init}}\right] \wedge T_0 \le \tau) \end{bmatrix}$$

$\sqsubseteq$

$\quad \bigsqcap\{timeout\_response : Time \mid 0 < timeout\_response \bullet$

$\qquad \lVert\ \mathbf{aux}\ T_{init} : Time \bullet T_{init} := T;\ \mathbf{idle};$

$\qquad\quad ((\lVert\ \mathbf{tinv}\ I \bullet \infty x\colon \begin{bmatrix} P, & R \end{bmatrix} \rVert);\ \mathbf{idle}$

$\qquad\qquad \sqcup (\rho.out, \rho.v)\colon \begin{bmatrix} \tau \le T_{init} + timeout\_response \end{bmatrix})$

$\qquad\qquad \sqcap (partial(\lVert\ \mathbf{tinv}\ I \bullet \infty x\colon \begin{bmatrix} P, & R \end{bmatrix} \rVert);\ \begin{bmatrix} \tau_0 = \tau \wedge T_{init} \le \tau \end{bmatrix}$;

$\qquad\qquad\quad \mathbf{idle};\ x\colon \begin{bmatrix} I \wedge T_{init} \le \tau, & Q \end{bmatrix}$; $\mathbf{idle})$

$\qquad\quad)$

$\qquad \rVert$

$\quad \}$

$\sqsubseteq$ Definition 6 (timeout)

$\quad \lVert\ \mathbf{aux}\ T_{init} : Time \bullet T_{init} := T;$

$\qquad \lVert\ \mathbf{timeout}$

$\qquad\qquad \lVert\ \mathbf{tinv}\ I \bullet \infty x\colon \begin{bmatrix} P, & R \end{bmatrix} \rVert$

$\qquad \mathbf{after}\ T\ \mathbf{then}$

$\qquad\qquad x\colon \begin{bmatrix} I \wedge T_{init} \le \tau, & Q \end{bmatrix}$

$\qquad \rVert$

$\quad \rVert$

8   Conclusions

Timeouts are commonly required in real-time applications. Hence a real-time
program development method needs to support their use. The primary advantage of the approach taken in this paper is that we develop code for a *machine-
independent* real-time programming language, and hence do not need to consider
the detailed execution times of language constructs as part of the development
process. This is achieved through the simple mechanism of adding a deadline

command to our programming language. The approach allows the real-time calculus to appear to be a straightforward extension of the standard refinement calculus. Of course, the compilation process now has the added burden of checking that the deadlines are met [3].

In order to define a timeout block, we needed to define the meaning of a partial execution of a command, and introduce a join operator between commands to allow the timeout response constraint to be conjoined to the normal branch.

The timeout law decomposes a specification with two alternative postconditions into a timeout construct in which each branch establishes one of the alternatives. To allow the timeout branch to be able to assume properties of the partial execution of the first branch of the timeout block, we added a timeout-invariant block that is guaranteed to maintain an invariant over any partial execution of the block. To allow variables referred to in the invariant to be changed, a notimeout block was also introduced.

The timing path analysis for timeout blocks requires the two alternative paths through the block to be analysed. For the normal branch we can also assume that the exit from the block occurs before the timeout response limit. The timeout alternative may have to take into account any delay in taking the timeout due to notimeout blocks within the first branch.

Acknowledgements

This research was supported by Australian Research Council (ARC) Large Grant A49937045 *Effective Real-Time Program Analysis*. I would like to thank Karl Lermer and Sibylle Peuker for feedback on earlier drafts of this paper, and the members of IFIP Working Group 2.3 on Programming Methodology for feedback on this topic.

References

[1] S. Dunne. Abstract commands: A uniform notation for specification and implementation. In C.J. Fidge, editor, *Computing: The Australian Theory Symposium (CATS 2001)*, volume 42 of *Electronic Notes in Theoretical Computer Science*, pages 104–123. Elsevier, 2001.

[2] C.J. Fidge, I.J. Hayes, and G. Watson. The deadline command. *IEE Proceedings—Software*, 146(2):104–111, April 1999.

[3] S. Grundon, I.J. Hayes, and C.J. Fidge. Timing constraint analysis. In C. McDonald, editor, *Computer Science'98: Proc. 21st Australasian Computer Sci. Conf. (ACSC'98)*, Perth, 4–6 Feb., pages 575–586. Springer, 1998.

[4] I.J. Hayes. Separating timing and calculation in real-time refinement. In J. Grundy, M. Schwenke, and T. Vickers, editors, *Int. Refinement Workshop and Formal Methods Pacific 1998*, pages 1–16. Springer, 1998.

[5] I.J. Hayes. Reasoning about non-terminating loops using deadline commands. In R. Backhouse and J.N. Oliveira, editors, *Proc. Mathematics of Program Construction*, volume 1837 of *Lecture Notes in Computer Science*, pages 60–79. Springer, 2000.

[6] I.J. Hayes. A predicative semantics for real-time refinement. In A. McIver and C.C. Morgan, editors, *Essays in Programming Methodology*. Springer, 2002.

[7] I.J. Hayes. Reasoning about real-time repetitions: Terminating and nonterminating. *Science of Computer Programming*, 43(2–3):161–192, April 2002.

[8] I.J. Hayes and M. Utting. Coercing real-time refinement: A transmitter. In D.J. Duke and A.S. Evans, editors, *BCS-FACS Northern Formal Methods Workshop (NFMW'96)*. Springer, 1997.

[9] I.J. Hayes and M. Utting. A sequential real-time refinement calculus. *Acta Informatica*, 37(6):385–448, 2001.

[10] E.C.R. Hehner. Termination is timing. In J.L.A. van de Snepscheut, editor, *Mathematics of Program Construction*, volume 375 of *Lecture Notes in Computer Science*, pages 36–47. Springer, June 1989.

[11] E.C.R. Hehner. *A Practical Theory of Programming*. Springer, 1993.

[12] C.A.R. Hoare and He Jifeng. *Unifying Theories of Programming*. Prentice Hall, 1998.

[13] J. Hooman. *Specification and Compositional Verification of Real-Time Systems*, volume 558 of *Lecture Notes in Computer Science*. Springer-Verlag, 1991.

[14] C.B. Jones. Program specification and verification in VDM. Technical Report UMCS-86-10-5, Department of Computer Science, University of Manchester, 1986.

[15] C.C. Morgan. *Programming from Specifications*. Prentice Hall, second edition, 1994.

[16] C.C. Morgan and T.N. Vickers. Types and invariants in the refinement calculus. *Science of Computer Programming*, 14:281–304, 1990.

[17] C.C. Morgan and T.N. Vickers. Types and invariants in the refinement calculus. In C.C. Morgan and T.N. Vickers, editors, *On the Refinement Calculus*, pages 127–154. Springer-Verlag, 1994. Originally published as [16].

[18] S. Schneider. Specification and verification in timed CSP. In M. Joseph, editor, *Real-time Systems: Specification, Verification and Analysis*, chapter 6, pages 147–181. Prentice Hall, 1996.

[19] S. Schneider. *Concurrent and Real-time Systems: The CSP Approach*. Wiley, 2000.

[20] D.J. Scholefield. *A Refinement Calculus for Real-Time Systems*. PhD thesis, Department of Computer Science, University of York, U.K., 1992.

[21] D.J. Scholefield, H. Zedan, and He Jifeng. A specification-oriented semantics for the refinement of real-time systems. *Theoretical Computer Science*, 131:219–241, 1994.

Eternity Variables to Simulate Specifications

Wim H. Hesselink

Dept. of Mathematics and Computing Science University of Groningen
P.O.Box 800, 9700 AV Groningen, The Netherlands
wim@cs.rug.nl, http://www.cs.rug.nl/~wim

Abstract. Simulation of specifications is introduced as a unification and generalisation of refinement mappings, history variables, forward simulations, prophecy variables, and backward simulations.

Eternity variables are introduced as a more powerful alternative for prophecy variables and backward simulations. This formalism is semantically complete: every simulation is a composition of a forward simulation, an extension with eternity variables, and a refinement mapping. The finiteness and continuity conditions of the Abadi-Lamport Theorem are unnecessary for this result.

1 Introduction

In the theory of Abadi and Lamport [1] on the existence of refinement mappings, a specification is a state machine with a supplementary property. Behaviours of a specification are infinite sequences of states. Behaviours become visible by means of an observation function. A specification implements another one when all visible behaviours of the first one are visible behaviours of the second one.

Under some technical assumptions (finite invisible nondeterminism and internal continuity of L, machine-closedness of K), Abadi and Lamport [1] proved that, when a specification K implements a specification L, there exists an extension M of K with history variables and prophecy variables together with a refinement mapping from M to L. Such a result is described as semantic completeness.

Lamport [8] draws from it the following conclusion: "We have learned that to be complete, assertional methods for reasoning about specifications must allow dummy variables (or their equivalent) – not only history variables for recording past behaviour, but prophecy variables for predicting future behaviour." Lamport's argument is not completely convincing, however, since adding these dummy variables is not enough for completeness when the technical assumptions are not met.

One may argue that imposing finiteness should be acceptable since computer storage is always finite. Yet, it is often useful to prove algorithms about integers or strings that can only be correct on idealised computers with infinite storage. A good proof methodology should be applicable to such algorithms. We therefore prefer proof methods without finiteness assumptions.

E.A. Boiten and B. Möller (Eds.): MPC 2002, LNCS 2386, pp. 117–130, 2002.
© Springer-Verlag Berlin Heidelberg 2002

In this paper we remove these technical conditions of [1] by introducing eternity variables as an alternative for prophecy variables. We first extend the conceptual framework by unifying the ideas of refinement mapping and extension with history variables or prophecy variables to the concepts of simulation. Actually, the term "simulation" has been introduced by Milner [12] in 1971. He used it for a kind of relation, which was later called downward or forward simulation to distinguish it from so-called upward or backward simulation [4,11]. It seems natural and justified to reintroduce the term "simulation" for the common generalisation.

We then introduce eternity variables, which turn out to be simpler and more powerful than prophecy variables and backward simulations. We prove semantic completeness: every simulation is a composition of a forward simulation, an extension with an eternity variable and a refinement mapping. This result has no technical proviso.

1.1   Stuttering Specifications

Although they can change roles, let us call the implementing specification the concrete one and the implemented specification the abstract one. Since the concrete specification may have to perform computation steps that are not needed for the abstract specification, we allow all specifications to stutter: a behaviour remains a behaviour when a state in it is duplicated.

At this point we deviate from [1] where it is allowed that the concrete specification is faster than the abstract one: a concrete behaviour may have to be slowed down by adding stutterings in order to match the abstract behaviour. In our view, this hides an important aspect of the idea of implementation. When the concrete specification needs less steps than the abstract one, perhaps the abstract one is not abstract enough.

In this paper, we therefore present a stricter theory than [1]. This results in a finer hierarchy of implementations. In [5], we treat both hierarchies and provide some more proofs.

1.2   Simulations of Specifications

A refinement mapping is a function between the states that, roughly speaking, preserves the initial states, the next-state relation and the supplementary property. Adding history or prophecy variables to the state gives rise to relations, called downward and upward simulations in [4], forward and backward simulations in [11]. We unify these concepts by introducing simulations.

Our simulations are certain binary relations. For the sake of simplicity, we treat binary relations as sets of pairs, with some notational conventions. Since we use $X \to Y$ for functions from X to Y, and $P \Rightarrow Q$ for implication between predicates P and Q, we write $F : K \twoheadrightarrow L$ to denote that relation F is a simulation of specifications from K to L. We hope the reader is not confused by the totally unrelated arrows $\twoheadrightarrow$ used in [2].

Our first main result is a completeness theorem: a specification implements another one if and only if there is a certain simulation between them. This shows that our concept of simulation is general enough to capture the relevant phenomena.

1.3   Eternity Variables and Completeness

We introduce eternity variables as an alternative for backward simulations or prophecy variables, with a similar kind of "prescient behaviour". An eternity variable is a kind of logical variable with a value constrained by the current execution.

Technically, an eternity variable is an auxiliary variable m, which is initialised nondeterministically and is never modified. The value of m is constrained by a relation with the state. A behaviour that would violate such a constraint, is discarded. The verifier of a program has to prove that the totality of constraints is not contradictory. In our current examples, we do this by taking m to be an infinite array and to ensure that the conditions constrain different elements of array m.

Our Abadi-Lamport theory goes as follows. Every specification K has a so-called unfolding $K^{\#}$ [11] with a forward simulation $K \dashrightarrow K^{\#}$. Given a simulation $F : K \dashrightarrow L$, we construct an intermediate specification W as an extension of $K^{\#}$ with an eternity variable, together with a refinement mapping $W \dashrightarrow L$, such that the composition of the simulations $K \dashrightarrow K^{\#}$ and $K^{\#} \dashrightarrow W$ and $W \dashrightarrow L$ is a subset of F.

1.4   Overview

In Sect. 1.5, we briefly discuss related work. Sect. 1.6 contains technical material on relations and lists. In Sect. 1.7, we treat stuttering and temporal operators. We introduce specifications and simulations, and prove the characterising theorem for them in Sect. 2. In Sect. 3, we present the theory of forward and backward simulations in our setting. Eternity variables are introduced in Sect. 4, where we also prove semantic completeness. Conclusions are drawn in Sect. 5.

New results in this paper are the completeness theorem in Sect. 2, and the eternity variables with their soundness and completeness in Sect. 4.

1.5   Related Work

Our primary inspiration was [1] of Abadi and Lamport. Lynch and Vaandrager [11] and Jonsson [6] present forward and backward simulations and the associated results on semantic completeness in the closely related settings of untimed automata and fair labelled transition systems. Our investigation was triggered by the paper [3] of Cohen and Lamport on Lipton's Theorem [10] about refining atomicity. Jonsson, Pnueli, and Rump [7] present another way of proving refinement that avoids the finiteness assumptions of backward simulations. They use a very flexible concept of refinement based on so-called pomsets, but have no claim of semantic completeness.

1.6 Relations and Lists

We treat a binary relation as a set of pairs. So, a binary relation between sets X and Y is a subset of the Cartesian product $X \times Y$. We use the functions fst and snd given by $fst(x,y) = x$ and $snd(x,y) = y$. A binary relation on X is a subset of $X \times X$. The identity relation 1_X on X consists of all pairs (x,x) with $x \in X$. Recall that a binary relation A on X is called *reflexive* iff $1_X \subseteq A$. The *converse* $cv(A)$ of a binary relation A is defined by $cv(A) = \{(x,y) \mid (y,x) \in A\}$.

For a state x and a binary relation A between sets of states, we define the set $(x; A) = \{y \mid (x,y) \in A\}$. For binary relations A and B, the composition $(A; B)$ is defined to consist of all pairs (x,z) such that there exists y with $(x,y) \in A$ and $(y,z) \in B$. A function $f : X \to Y$ is identified with its graph $\{(x, f(x)) \mid x \in X\}$ which is a binary relation between X and Y. We thus have $(x; f) = \{f(x)\}$ for every $x \in X$. The composition of functions $f : X \to Y$ and $g : Y \to Z$ is a function $g \circ f : X \to Z$, which equals the relational composition $(f; g)$.

We use lists to represent consecutive values during computations. If X is a set, we write X^* for the set of the finite lists, X^+ for the set of the nonempty finite lists, and X^ω for the set of infinite lists over X.

We write $\ell(xs)$ for the length of list xs. The elements of xs are xs_i for $0 \leq i < \ell(xs)$. If xs is a list of length $\ell(xs) \geq n$, we define $(xs|n)$ to be its prefix of length n. We define $last : X^+ \to X$ to be the function that returns the last element of a nonempty finite list, and $init : X^+ \to X^*$ to be the function that removes the last element from such a list.

A function $f : X \to Y$ induces a function $f^\omega : X^\omega \to Y^\omega$. For a binary relation $F \subseteq X \times Y$, we have induced binary relations $F^* \subseteq X^* \times Y^*$ and $F^\omega \subseteq X^\omega \times Y^\omega$ given by

$$(xs, ys) \in F^* \quad \equiv \quad \ell(xs) = \ell(ys) \ \wedge \ (\forall i : i < \ell(xs) : (xs_i, ys_i) \in F) ,$$

and similarly for F^ω.

1.7 Stuttering and Properties

We define a list xs to be an *unstuttering* of a list ys, notation $xs \preceq ys$, iff xs is obtained from ys by replacing some finite nonempty subsequences ss of consecutive equal elements of ys with their first elements ss_0. The number of such subsequences that are replaced may be infinite. For example, $(abb)^\omega$ is an unstuttering of $(aaabbb)^\omega$. It can be proved that relation $\preceq$ is a partial order. We write $\succeq$ for the converse of $\preceq$.

A finite list xs is called *stutterfree* iff every pair of consecutive elements differ. An infinite list xs is called *stutterfree* iff it stutters only after reaching its final state, i.e., iff $xs_i = xs_{i+1}$ implies $xs_{i+1} = xs_{i+2}$ for all i. In either case, xs is stutterfree iff xs is minimal (in X^* or X^ω) for the order relation $\preceq$.

A subset P of X^ω is called a *property over* X iff $xs \preceq ys \in P$ implies $xs \in P$ and $xs \succeq ys \in P$ implies $xs \in P$. This definition is equivalent to the one of [1].

We write $\neg P$ to denote the complement (negation) of a property P. We write $Suf(xs)$ to denote the set of infinite suffixes of an infinite list xs. We define $\Box P$ (always P), and $\Diamond P$ (sometime P) as the properties given by

$$xs \in \Box P \quad \equiv \quad Suf(xs) \subseteq P \ ,$$
$$\Diamond P \quad = \quad \neg\Box\neg P \ .$$

For $U \subseteq X$ and $A \subseteq X \times X$, the subsets $[\![U]\!]$ and $[\![A]\!]$ of X^{ω} are defined by

$$xs \in [\![U]\!] \quad \equiv \quad xs_0 \in U \ ,$$
$$xs \in [\![A]\!] \quad \equiv \quad (xs_0, xs_1) \in A \ ;$$

$[\![U]\!]$ is always a property; $\Box[\![A]\!]$ is a property when A is reflexive.

2   Specifications and Simulations

In this section we introduce the central concepts of the theory. Following [1], we define specifications in Sect. 2.1. In 2.2, we define simulations and refinement mappings. Sect. 2.3 contains an example of them. In Sect. 2.4, we define visible specifications and their implementation relations, and we prove that simulations characterise the implementations between visible specifications.

2.1   Specifications

A *specification* is defined to be a tuple $K = (X, Y, N, P)$ where X is a set, Y is a subset of X, N a reflexive binary relation on X, and P is a property over X. The set X is called the *state space*, its elements are called *states*, the elements of Y are called *initial states*. Relation N is called the *next-state* relation. The set P is called the *supplementary* property.

We define an *execution* of K to be a nonempty list xs over X for which every pair of consecutive elements belongs to N. An execution of K is called *initial* iff $xs_0 \in Y$. We define a *behaviour* of K to be an infinite and initial execution xs of K with $xs \in P$. We write $Beh(K)$ to denote the set of behaviours of K.

It is easy to see that $Beh(K) = [\![Y]\!] \cap \Box[\![N]\!] \cap P$. It follows that $Beh(K)$ is a property. The requirement that relation N is reflexive is imposed to allow stuttering: if xs is a behaviour of K, any list ys obtained from xs by repeating elements of xs or by removing subsequent duplicates is also a behaviour of K.

The components of specification $K = (X, Y, N, P)$ are denoted $states(K) = X$, $start(K) = Y$, $step(K) = N$ and $prop(K) = P$. A state is called *reachable* iff it occurs in an initial execution of K. A subset of $states(K)$ is called an *invariant* iff it contains all reachable states.

Specification K is defined to be *machine closed* [1] iff every finite initial execution of K can be extended to a behaviour of K. Concrete specifications are often machine closed.

2.2   Simulations and Refinement Mappings

Let K and L be specifications. Recall that a relation F between $states(K)$ and $states(L)$ induces a relation F^{ω} between the sets $(states(K))^{\omega}$ and $(states(L))^{\omega}$. Relation F is called a *simulation* $K \dashrightarrow L$ iff, for every behaviour $xs \in Beh(K)$, there exists a behaviour $ys \in Beh(L)$ with $(xs, ys) \in F^{\omega}$.

It is easy to verify that simulations can be composed: if F is a simulation $K \twoheadrightarrow L$ and G is a simulation $L \twoheadrightarrow M$, the composed relation $(F; G)$ is a simulation $K \twoheadrightarrow M$.

It should be noted that the mere existence of a simulation $F : K \twoheadrightarrow L$ does not imply much. If $F : K \twoheadrightarrow L$ and G is a relation with $F \subseteq G$, then $G : K \twoheadrightarrow L$. Therefore, the smaller the simulation, the more information it carries.

A function $f : states(K) \to states(L)$ is called a *refinement mapping* [1] from K to L iff $f(x) \in start(L)$ for every $x \in start(K)$, and $(f(x), f(x')) \in step(L)$ for every pair $(x, x') \in step(K)$, and $f^\omega(xs) \in prop(L)$ for every $xs \in Beh(K)$. It is easy to verify that a refinement mapping $f : states(K) \to states(L)$, when regarded as a relation as in Sect. 1.6, is a simulation $K \twoheadrightarrow L$.

We often encounter the following situation. A specification L is regarded as an extension of specification K with a variable of a type M iff $states(L)$ is (a subset of) the Cartesian product $states(K) \times M$ and the function $fst : states(L) \to states(K)$ is a refinement mapping. The second component of the states of L is then regarded as the variable added. The extension may be called a refinement extension iff the converse $cvf = cv(fst)$ is a simulation $K \twoheadrightarrow L$.

2.3   Example

We give an example to show how specifications correspond to programs with supplementary properties and we give a simple case of a refinement mapping and a simulation.

The first specification $K0$ is based on guarded commands with a fairness assumption. We need only one integer variable.

```
var j: Nat := 0 ;
do   true    -> j := j + 1 ;
[]   j > 0   -> j := 0 ;
od .
```

The first line declares and initialises the variable. Type `Nat` stands for the natural numbers. We impose the fairness assumption that the second alternative is chosen infinitely often. This program corresponds to the specification $K0$ with $states(K0) = \mathbb{N}$ and $start(K0) = \{0\}$ and relation $step(K0)$ given by

$$(i, j) \in step(K0) \quad \equiv \quad j = i + 1 \quad \lor \quad j = 0 \quad \lor \quad j = i .$$

The third alternative in $step(K0)$ serves to allow stuttering. We take the supplementary property to be $prop(K0) = \Box\Diamond[\![>]\!]$, which expresses that the value of j infinitely often decreases.

In our second specification, $K1$, we use two integer variables k and m in the guarded commands program (with demonic choices):

```
var k: Nat := 0, m: Nat := 0 ;
do   k < m   -> k := k + 1 ;
[]   k = m   -> m := 0 ; k := 0 ;
[]   k = 0   -> k := 1 ; choose m > 0 ;
od .
```

We assume that each of the alternatives is executed atomically. The program is formalised by taking $states(K1) = \mathbb{N} \times \mathbb{N}$ with k as the first component and m as the second. The initial state has $k = m = 0$. So $start(K1) = \{(0,0)\}$. The next-state relation $step(K1)$ is given by

$$
\begin{aligned}
((k,m)\,,\,(k',m')) \in step(K1) &\equiv \\
(k < m \ \wedge \ k' = k+1 \ \wedge \ m' = m) & \\
\vee \ (k = m \ \wedge \ k' = m' = 0) & \\
\vee \ (k = 0 \ \wedge \ k' = 1 \le m') & \\
\vee \ (k' = k \ \wedge \ m' = m) \ . &
\end{aligned}
$$

The last alternative serves to allow stuttering. The supplementary property only has to ensure that behaviours do not stutter indefinitely. We thus take $prop(K1) = \Box \Diamond [\![\neq]\!]$.

The function $f_{1,0} : states(K1) \rightarrow states(K0)$ given by $f_{1,0}(k,m) = k$ is easily seen to be a refinement mapping $K1 \dashrightarrow K0$.

More interesting is the converse relation $F_{0,1} = cv(f_{1,0})$. It is not difficult to show by ad-hoc methods that $F_{0,1}$ is a simulation $K0 \dashrightarrow K1$. Every behaviour of $K0$ can be mimicked by $K1$ by choosing adequate values of m. In Sect. 4.2 we show how an eternity variable can be used to prove this more systematically.

2.4 Visibility and Completeness of Simulation

We are usually not interested in all details of the states, but only in certain aspects of them. This means that there is a function from $states(K)$ to some other set that we regard as an observation function. A *visible specification* is therefore defined to be a pair (K, f) where K is a specification and f is some function defined on $states(K)$. Deviating from [1], we define the set of observations by

$$
Obs(K, f) \quad = \quad \{f^\omega(xs) \mid xs \in Beh(K)\} \ .
$$

Note that $Obs(K, f)$ need not be a property. If xs is an observation and $ys \preceq xs$, then ys need not be an observation.

Let (K, f) and (L, g) be visible specifications with the functions f and g mapping to the same set. Then (K, f) is said to *implement* (L, g) iff $Obs(K, f)$ is contained in $Obs(L, g)$. This concept of implementation is stronger than that of [1]: we do not allow that an observation of (K, f) can only be mimicked by (L, g) after inserting additional stutterings.

Our concept of simulation is motivated by the following completeness theorem, the proof of which is rather straightforward.

Theorem 0. Consider visible specifications (K, f) and (L, g) where f and g are functions to the same set. We have that (K, f) implements (L, g) if and only if there is a simulation $F : K \dashrightarrow L$ with $(F; g) \subseteq f$.

Proof. The proof is by mutual implication.

First, assume the existence of a simulation $F : K \dashrightarrow L$ with $(F; g) \subseteq f$. Let $zs \in Obs(K, f)$. We have to prove that $zs \in Obs(L, g)$. By the definition of Obs, there exists $xs \in Beh(K)$ with $zs = f^{\omega}(xs)$. Since F is a simulation, there exists $ys \in Beh(L)$ with $(xs, ys) \in F^{\omega}$. For every number n, we have $(xs_n, ys_n) \in F$ and, hence, $(xs_n, g(ys_n)) \in (F; g) \subseteq f$ and, hence, $g(ys_n) = f(xs_n) = zs_n$. This implies that $zs = g^{\omega}(ys) \in Obs(L, g)$.

Next, assume that (K, f) implements (L, g). We define relation F between $states(K)$ and $states(L)$ by $F = \{(x, y) \mid f(x) = g(y)\}$. For every pair $(x, z) \in (F; g)$ there exists y with $(x, y) \in F$ and $(y, z) \in g$; we then have $f(x) = g(y) = z$. This proves $(F; g) \subseteq f$. It remains to prove that F is a simulation $K \dashrightarrow L$. Let $xs \in Beh(K)$. Since $Obs(K, f) \subseteq Obs(L, g)$, there is $ys \in Beh(L)$ with $f^{\omega}(xs) = g^{\omega}(ys)$. We thus have $(xs, ys) \in F^{\omega}$. This proves that F is a simulation $K \dashrightarrow L$. $\square$

3   Special Simulations

In this section we introduce forward and backward simulations as special kinds of simulations. Forward simulations are introduced in 3.1. They correspond to refinement mappings and to the well-known addition of history variables. We give an example of a forward simulation in Sect. 3.2. In Sect. 3.3, we introduce the unfolding [11] of a specification, which plays a key role in several proofs of semantic completeness. Backward simulations are introduced in Sect. 3.4.

3.1   Forward Simulations

The easiest way to prove that one specification simulates (the behaviour of) another is by starting at the beginning and constructing the corresponding behaviour in the other specification inductively. This requires a condition embodied in so-called forward or downward simulations [4,11], which go back at least to [12]. They are defined as follows.

A relation F between $states(K)$ and $states(L)$ is defined to be a *forward simulation* from specification K to specification L iff

(H0)   For every $x \in start(K)$, there is $y \in start(L)$ with $(x, y) \in F$.

(H1)   For every pair $(x, y) \in F$ and every x' with $(x, x') \in step(K)$, there is y' with $(y, y') \in step(L)$ and $(x', y') \in F$.

(H2)   Every infinite initial execution ys of L with $(xs, ys) \in F^{\omega}$ for some $xs \in Beh(K)$ satisfies $ys \in prop(L)$.

It is easy to verify that a composition of forward simulations is a forward simulation. Every refinement mapping, when regarded as a relation, is a forward simulation. An auxiliary variable added to the state space via a forward simulation is called a history variable [1]; in such cases, the relation is called a history relation in [11]. The definition of forward simulations is justified by the following well-known result:

Lemma. Every forward simulation F from K to L is a simulation $K \dashrightarrow L$. $\square$

3.2   An Example of a Forward Simulation

We extend specification $K0$ of Sect. 2.3 with two history variables n and q. Variable n counts the number of backjumps of j, while q is an array that records the values from where j jumped.

```
var j: Nat := 0, n: Nat := 0,
    q: array Nat of Nat := ([Nat] 0) ;
do  true    -> j := j + 1 ; q[n] := q[n] + 1 ;
[]  j > 0   -> j := 0 ; n := n + 1 ;
od .
```

This yields a specification $K2$ with the supplementary property $\Box\Diamond[\![\,j > j'\,]\!]$ where j' stands for the value of j in the next state. Its next-state relation $step(K2)$ is given by

$$
\begin{aligned}
((j,n,q)\,,\,(j',n',q')) \in step(K2) \quad &\equiv \\
(j' = j + 1 \wedge q'[n] = q[n] + 1 \wedge n' &= n \wedge (\forall\, i : i \neq n : q'[i] = q[i])) \\
\vee \quad (j' = 0 \,\wedge\, q' = q \,\wedge\, n' &= n + 1) \\
\vee \quad (j' = j \,\wedge\, q' = q \,\wedge\, n' &= n)\,.
\end{aligned}
$$

It is easy to verify that the function $f_{2,0} : states(K2) \rightarrow states(K0)$ given by $f_{2,0}(j, n, q) = j$ is a refinement mapping. Its converse $F_{0,2} = cv(f_{2,0})$ is a forward simulation $K0 \dashrightarrow K2$. Indeed, the conditions (H0) and (H2) hold almost trivially. As for (H1), if we have related states in $K0$ and $K2$, and the state in $K0$ makes a step, it is clear that $K2$ can take a step such that the states remain related. The variables n and q are called history variables since they record the history of the execution.

3.3   The Unfolding

The *unfolding* $K^{\#}$ of a specification K plays a key role in the proofs of semantic completeness in [1,11] as well as in our semantic completeness result below.

It is defined as follows: $states(K^{\#})$ consists of the stutterfree finite initial executions of K. The initial set $start(K^{\#})$ consists of the elements $xs \in states(K^{\#})$ with $\ell(xs) = 1$. The next-state relation $step(K^{\#})$ and the property $prop(K^{\#}) \subseteq (states(K^{\#}))^{\omega}$ are defined by

$$
\begin{aligned}
(xs, xt) \in step(K^{\#}) \quad &\equiv \quad xs = xt \quad \vee \quad xs = init(xt)\,, \\
vss \in prop(K^{\#}) \quad &\equiv \quad last^{\omega}(vss) \in prop(K)\,.
\end{aligned}
$$

It is easy to prove that $K^{\#}$ is a specification. The function $last : states(K^{\#}) \rightarrow states(K)$ is a refinement mapping and, hence, a forward simulation $K^{\#} \dashrightarrow K$. We are more interested, however, in the other direction. The following result of [1] is not difficult to prove.

Lemma (0). Relation $cvl = cv(last)$ is a forward simulation $K \dashrightarrow K^{\#}$. $\square$

In Sect. 4.3 below, we shall need the following result.

Lemma (1). Let vss be a stutterfree behaviour of $K^{\#}$. Then $xs = last^{\omega}(vss)$ is a stutterfree behaviour of K such that vss_i is a prefix of xs for all indices i and that $vss_i \preceq (xs|i+1)$ for all i.

Proof. Firstly, xs is a behaviour of K since vss is a behaviour of $K^{\#}$. Since vss is stutterfree, there is r with $0 \leq r \leq \infty$ such that $vss_i = init(vss_{i+1})$ for all i with $0 \leq i < r$ and $vss_i = vss_{i+1}$ for all i with $r \leq i < \infty$. It follows that $vss_i = (xs|i+1)$ for all i with $0 \leq i \leq r$ and $vss_i = (xs|r+1)$ for all i with $r \leq i < \infty$. Since each vss_i is stutterfree, list $(xs|r+1)$ is stutterfree. All remaining elements of xs are equal to xs_r. Therefore, xs is a stutterfree infinite list. It also follows that $vss_i \preceq (xs|i+1)$ for all i. □

3.4   Backward Simulations

It is also possible to prove that one specification simulates (the behaviour of) another by starting arbitrarily far in the future and constructing a corresponding execution by working backwards. An infinite behaviour is then obtained by a variation of König's Lemma. These so-called backward simulations [11] form a relational version of the prophecy variables of [1] and are related to the upward simulations of [4]. We give a variation of Jonnson's version [6], but we give no example since we prefer the eternity extensions introduced in the next section.

Relation F between $states(K)$ and $states(L)$ is defined to be a *backward simulation* from K to L iff

(P0)   Every state y of L with $(x, y) \in F$ and $x \in start(K)$ satisfies $y \in start(L)$.
(P1)   For every pair $(x', y') \in F$ and every x with $(x, x') \in step(K)$, there is y with $(x, y) \in F$ and $(y, y') \in step(L)$.
(P2)   For every behaviour xs of K there are infinitely many indices n for which the set $(xs_n; F)$ is nonempty and finite.
(P3)   Every infinite initial execution ys of L with $(xs, ys) \in F^{\omega}$ for some $xs \in Beh(K)$ satisfies $ys \in prop(L)$.

An auxiliary variable added to the state space via a backward simulation is called a prophecy variable [1] since it seems to show "prescient" behaviour. In such a case, the relation is called a prophecy relation in [11]. Note that condition (P3) just equals (H2). The term backward simulations is justified by the following soundness result, the proof of which is a easy adaptation of the proof in [6].

Lemma. Every backward simulation F from K to L is a simulation $K \dashrightarrow L$. □

A composition of backward simulations need not be a backward simulation. As shown by Jonsson [6], this can be used to construct more general simulations.

4   An Eternity Variable for a Refinement Mapping

We now develop an alternative for prophecy variables or backward simulations that is both simpler and more powerful. Extending the metaphor of history and prophecy variables, they are named eternity variables, since they do not change during execution.

They are simpler than prophecy variables in the sense that, below, both the proof of soundness in Lemma (3) and the proof of completeness in Theorem 1 are simpler than the corresponding proofs for prophecy variables. They are more powerful in the sense that their completeness does not require additional finiteness assumptions. Whether they are simpler to use than prophecy variables is a matter of future research.

The idea is that an eternity variable has an indeterminate constant value, but that the states impose restrictions on this value. A behaviour in which the eternity variable ever has a wrong value is simply discarded. Therefore, in every behaviour, the eternity variable always has a value that satisfies all restrictions of the behaviour.

The specification obtained by adding an eternity variable is called an eternity extension. We introduce eternity extensions and prove their soundness in Sect. 4.1. Section 4.2 contains an example. Completeness of eternity extension is proved in Sect. 4.3.

4.1   Formal Definition of Eternity Extensions

Let K be a specification. Let M be a set of values for an eternity variable m. A binary relation R between $states(K)$ and M is called a *behaviour restriction* of K iff, for every behaviour xs of K, there exists an $m \in M$ with $(xs_i, m) \in R$ for all indices i :

$$(2) \qquad xs \in Beh(K) \quad \Rightarrow \quad (\exists\, m :: (\forall\, i :: (xs_i, m) \in R)) .$$

If R is a behaviour restriction of K, we define the corresponding *eternity extension* as the specification W given by

$$
\begin{aligned}
states(W) \;&=\; R \;, \\
start(W) \;&=\; \{(x, m) \in R \,|\, x \in start(K)\} \;, \\
((x, m), (x', m')) \in step(W) \;&\equiv\; (x, x') \in step(K) \quad \wedge \quad m = m' \;, \\
ys \in prop(W) \;&\equiv\; fst^{\omega}(ys) \in prop(K) \;.
\end{aligned}
$$

It is clear that $step(W)$ is reflexive and that $prop(W)$ is a property. Therefore W is a specification. It is easy to verify that $fst : states(W) \rightarrow states(K)$ is a refinement mapping. The soundness of eternity extensions is expressed by

Lemma (3). Let R be a behaviour restriction. The relation $cvf = cv(fst)$ is a simulation $cvf : K \rightarrow W$.

Proof. Let $xs \in Beh(K)$. We have to construct $ys \in Beh(W)$ with $(xs, ys) \in cvf^{\omega}$. By (2), we can choose m with $(xs_i, m) \in R$ for all i. Then we define $ys_i = (xs_i, m)$. A trivial verification shows that the list ys constructed in this way is a behaviour of W with $(xs, ys) \in cvf^{\omega}$. $\square$

In this construction, we fully exploit the ability to consider specifications that are not machine closed. Initial executions of W that cannot be extended to behaviours of W are simply discarded.

4.2   An Example of an Eternity Extension

We use an eternity extension to show that specification $K0$ implements $K1$ in 2.3. The starting point is the forward simulation $F_{0,2} : K0 \to K2$ of Sect. 3.2. One easily verifies that specification $K2$ preserves the invariant $\Box[\![\, j = q[n] \,]\!]$.

We now extend $K2$ with an eternity variable m, which is an infinite array of natural numbers with the behaviour restriction

$$R: \quad j \leq m[n] \quad \wedge \quad (\forall\, i : 0 \leq i < n : m[i] = q[i]) \ .$$

We have to verify that every execution of $K2$ allows a value for m that satisfies condition R. So, let xs be an arbitrary execution of $K2$. Since j jumps back infinitely often in xs, the value of n tends to infinity. This implies that $q[i]$ is eventually constant for every index i. We can therefore define function $m : \mathbb{N} \to \mathbb{N}$ by $\Diamond\Box[\![\, m(i) = q[i] \,]\!]$ for all $i \in \mathbb{N}$. It follows that $\Box[\![\, i < n \Rightarrow m(i) = q[i] \,]\!]$ for all i. Since $q[i]$ is incremented only, it also follows that $\Box[\![\, q[i] \leq m(i) \,]\!]$ for all i. This implies $\Box[\![\, j \leq m(n) \,]\!]$ because of the invariant $\Box[\![\, j = q[n] \,]\!]$. This proves that m is a value for m that satisfies R.

Let $K3$ be the resulting eternity extension and $F_{2,3} : K2 \to K3$ be the simulation induced by Lemma (3). The next-state relation $step(K3)$ satisfies

$$((j, n, q, m)\,,\,(j', n', q', m')) \in step(K3) \quad \equiv$$
$$m = m' \ \wedge \ ((j, n, q)\,,\,(j', n', q')) \in step(K2) \ .$$

Let function $f_{3,1} : states(K3) \to states(K1)$ be defined by

$$f_{3,1}(j, n, q, m) \quad = \quad (j, (j = 0\,?\,0 : m[n])) \ ,$$

where $(\_\,?\,\_ : \_)$ stands for a conditional expression as in the language C. We verify that $f_{3,1}$ is a refinement mapping. Since $f_{3,1}(0, 0, 0, m) = (0, 0)$, we have $f_{3,1}(start(K3)) \subseteq start(K1)$. We now show that a step of $K3$ is mapped to a step of $K1$. By convention, this holds for a stuttering step. A nonstuttering step that starts with $j = 0$ increments j to 1. The $f_{3,1}$-images make a step from $(0, 0)$ to $(1, r)$ for some positive r. This is in accordance with $K1$. A step of $K3$ that increments a positive j has the precondition $j < m[n]$ because of R; therefore, the $f_{3,1}$-images make a $K1$-step. A backjumping step of $K3$ increments n and has therefore precondition $j = q[n] = m[n]$. Again, the $f_{3,1}$-images make a $K1$-step. This proves $f_{3,1}(step(K3)) \subseteq step(K1)$. It is easy to that $f_{3,1}^{\omega}(prop(K3)) \subseteq prop(K1)$. This shows that $f_{3,1}$ is a refinement mapping from $K3$ to $K1$.

We thus have a composed simulation $G = (F_{0,2}; F_{2,3}; f_{3,1}) : K0 \to K1$. One verifies that $(j, (k, m)) \in G$ implies $j = k$. It follows that relation $F_{0,1}$ of Sect. 2.3 satisfies $G \subseteq F_{0,1}$. Therefore, $F_{0,1}$ is a simulation $K0 \to K1$. This shows that an eternity extension can be used to prove that $F_{0,1}$ is a simulation $K0 \to K1$.

Remark. Once R is chosen, the problem is to find a value for m in (2). Above we constructed m by means of a history variable (q) that approximates m. Since condition (2) is equivalent to the property that $\bigcap_i (xs_i; R)$ is nonempty for every behaviour xs of K, one can always approximate m by a set-valued history variable with values of the form $\bigcap_{i<r} (xs_i; R)$ for a state with a history xs of length r. We leave the investigation of this idea to future research.

4.3 Completeness of Eternity Extensions

The combination of unfoldings, eternity extensions and refinement mappings is semantically complete in the following sense.

Theorem 1. Consider an arbitrary simulation $F : K \rightarrow L$. The unfolding $cvl : K \rightarrow K^\#$ has an eternity extension $cvf : K^\# \rightarrow W$ and a refinement mapping $g : W \rightarrow L$ such that $(cvl; cvf; g) \subseteq F$.

Proof. Firstly, we have a simulation $cvl : K \rightarrow K^\#$ by Lemma (0).

We use an eternity variable in the set $Beh(L)$ and the relation R between $states(K^\#)$ and $Beh(L)$ given by

$$(xs, ys) \in R \quad \equiv \quad (xs, (ys|\ell(xs))) \in F^* .$$

We show that R is a behaviour restriction by verifying condition (2). Let vss be a behaviour of $K^\#$. In order to verify (2), we may assume that vss is stutterfree. By Lemma (1), $xs = last^\omega(vss)$ is a behaviour of K such that vss_i is a prefix of xs for all indices i. Since F is a simulation $K \rightarrow L$, specification L has a behaviour ys with $(xs, ys) \in F^\omega$. For every i, list vss_i is a prefix of xs. This implies that $(vss_i, ys) \in R$ for all $i \in \mathbb{N}$. Taking $\mathbf{m} = ys$, this proves that R satisfies condition (2) and is therefore a behaviour restriction.

Let W be the R-eternity extension of $K^\#$. By Lemma (3), we have a simulation $cvf : K^\# \rightarrow W$. Define $g : R \rightarrow states(L)$ by

$$g(xs, ys) = last(ys|\ell(xs)) .$$

We show that g is a refinement mapping $states(W) \rightarrow states(L)$. Firstly, let $w \in start(W)$. Then w is of the form $w = (xs, ys)$ with $\ell(xs) = 1$ and ys_0 is initial in L. This shows $g(w) \in start(L)$. In every nonstuttering step in W, the length of xs is incremented with 1 and then we have $(ys_n, ys_{n+1}) \in step(L)$. Therefore, function g maps steps of W to steps of L. If ws is in $prop(W)$, it has a constant second component $ys \in Beh(L)$ and we have $g^\omega(ws) \succeq ys$. Therefore $g^\omega(ws)$ is in $prop(L)$. This proves that g is a refinement mapping.

It remains to prove $(cvl; cvf; g) \subseteq F$. Let (x, y) be in the lefthand relation. By the definition of $(cvl; cvf; g)$, there exist $xs \in states(K^\#)$ and $w \in states(W)$ with $x = last(xs)$ and $xs = fst(w)$ and $g(w) = y$. By the definition of W, we can choose $ys \in Beh(L)$ with $w = (xs, ys)$. Let $n = \ell(xs)$. Since $(xs, ys) \in R$, we have $(xs, ys|n) \in F^*$. It follows that $y = g(w) = ys_{n-1}$ and hence $(x, y) = (xs_{n-1}, ys_{n-1}) \in F$. This proves the inclusion. $\square$

5 Concluding Remarks

We have introduced simulations of specifications to unify all cases where an implementation relation can be established. This unifies refinement mappings, history variables or forward simulations, and prophecy variables or backward simulations, and refinement of atomicity as in Lipton's Theorem [3,10].

We have introduced eternity extensions as variations of prophecy variables and backward simulations. We have proved semantic completeness: every simulation of specifications can be factored as an extension with history variables and eternity variables followed by a refinement mapping. The restrictive assumptions machine-closedness, finite invisible nondeterminism, and internal continuity as needed for completeness of prophecy variables or forward-backward simulations in [1,11] are superfluous when eternity variables are allowed.

The theory has two versions. In the strict version described here, we allow the concrete behaviours to take more but not less computation steps than the abstract behaviours. This is done by allowing additional stutterings to the abstract specifications. The strict theory is also the simpler one. It results in a finer hierarchy of specifications. The stuttering version of the theory [5] is completely in accordance with the setting of [1]. Here, the eternity extension needs an additional counter to regulate the stutterings of the concrete specification.

Acknowledgements

I would like to thank H.W. de Haan, G.R. Renardel, and the MPC referees for their helpful suggestions and comments that have led to significant improvements in the presentation.

References

1. Abadi, M., Lamport, L.: The existence of refinement mappings. Theoretical Computer Science **82** (1991) 253–284
2. Abadi, M., Lamport, L.: Conjoining specifications. ACM Transactions on Programming Languages and Systems **17** (1995) 507–534.
3. Cohen, E., Lamport, L.: Reduction in TLA. In: Sangiorgi, D., Simone, R. de (eds.): CONCUR '98. Springer V. 1998 (LNCS 1466), pp. 317–331.
4. He, J., Hoare, C.A.R., Sanders, J.W.: Data refinement refined. In: Robinet, B., Wilhelm, R. (eds.): *ESOP'86* pp. 187–196. Springer Verlag, 1986 (LNCS 213).
5. Hesselink, W.H.: Eternity variables to prove simulation of specifications (draft). http://www.cs.rug.nl/~wim/pub/whh261.pdf
6. Jonsson, B.: Simulations between specifications of distributed systems. In: Baeten, J.C.M., Groote, J.F. (eds.): CONCUR'91. Springer V. 1991 (LNCS 527), pp. 346–360.
7. Jonsson, B., Pnueli, A., Rump, C.: Proving refinement using transduction. Distributed Computing **12** (1999) 129–149.
8. Lamport, L.: Critique of the Lake Arrowhead three. Distributed Computing **6** (1992) 65–71.
9. Lamport, L.: The temporal logic of actions. ACM Trans. on Programming Languages and Systems **16** (1994) 872–923.
10. Lipton, R.J.: Reduction: A method of proving properties of parallel programs. Communications of the ACM **18** (1975) 717-721.
11. Lynch, N., Vaandrager, F.: Forward and backward simulations, Part I: Untimed systems. Information and Computation **121** (1995) 214–233.
12. Milner, R.: An algebraic definition of simulation between programs. In: Proc. 2nd Int. Joint Conf. on Artificial Intelligence. British Comp. Soc. 1971. Pages 481–489.

Constructing Tournament Representations: An Exercise in Pointwise Relational Programming

Ralf Hinze

Institut für Informatik III, Universität Bonn
Römerstraße 164, 53117 Bonn, Germany
`ralf@informatik.uni-bonn.de`
`http://www.informatik.uni-bonn.de/~ralf/`

Abstract. List or set comprehensions are a wonderful means to define nondeterministic or relational programs. Despite their beauty, comprehensions are somewhat underused in program calculation. The purpose of this paper is to remind the program-calculation community that comprehensions provide a convenient language for specifying and deriving nondeterministic programs in a pointwise manner. We illustrate the style of reasoning by re-solving the well-known problem of constructing *tournament representations*: Given a sequence x of integers, construct a heap whose inorder traversal is x itself.

1 Introduction

One attractive feature of pure functional languages such as Haskell [19] is that they are close to the language of reasoning. The programmer can use the programming language she is familiar with also for proving properties of programs or for calculating programs. When deriving a program from a specification she can check some or all of the intermediate steps simply by executing them (at least in principle).

In program calculation, however, there is often a need to go beyond the world of functions: nondeterministic problems, for instance, are most easily specified in terms of *relations*. Even deterministic problems that enjoy deterministic solutions sometimes benefit from a relational setting. The problem of constructing tournament representations, which we consider in this paper, falls into this category.

At first sight, the generalisation from functions to relations does away with the aforementioned benefits of pure functional languages, but not quite. Using *monads* [16,17] (in particular, the set monad) and *monad comprehensions* [27] (in particular, set comprehensions) one can easily embed relations into a pure functional language. As a simple example, consider the converse of list catenation ('[]' and ':' are Haskell's list constructors).

$$
\begin{aligned}
split \quad &:: \quad \forall a . [a] \to Set\,([a],[a]) \\
split\ z \quad &= \quad \{([\,],z)\} \\
&\quad \cup \quad \{(a:x,y) \mid a:z' \leftarrow \{z\}, (x,y) \leftarrow split\ z'\}
\end{aligned}
$$

E.A. Boiten and B. Möller (Eds.): MPC 2002, LNCS 2386, pp. 131–147, 2002.

The call *split z* yields all pairs of lists whose catenation is the list z itself. Here, a relation is defined as a *set-valued function*. In what follows we will use the term relation as a synonym for set-valued function. The set comprehension in the second line nicely describes the behaviour of *split* when the first result list is non-empty. In general, a set comprehension consists of a head and a body, which in turn is a sequence of *generators* of the form $p \leftarrow e$. The left arrow can be read as set membership (pronounced: is drawn from) and the comma separating the generators can be seen as a conjunction (commas are also used for pairs). It is important to note, however, that a generator binds the variables that appear to the left of the arrow, see Sec. 2.

Now, the point of this paper is that set comprehension syntax not only provides a succinct notation for defining nondeterministic functions but that it is also suitable for specifying and deriving relational programs. We will support this claim by re-solving the well-known problem of constructing tournament representations [26], which has been repeatedly considered in the literature [9,5,15,1,20,7]. The derivation, which constitutes the major part of the paper, is structured into four successive steps, each of which yields an executable Haskell program with a decreasing amount of nondeterminism. Though we use Haskell as a target language, we will work in the world of sets and total functions. In particular, lists and trees are always finite and fully defined. All the derivations with the notable exception of the second step are conducted in a pointwise style. The calculations are quite detailed as no intermediate steps are omitted.

2   Notation

Let us introduce the notation by means of a simple derivation: we calculate the inverse of list catenation. Formally, we are seeking a set-valued function *split* that satisfies

$$(x, y) \leftarrow split\ z \quad \equiv \quad x \mathbin{+\!\!+} y = z.$$

The derivation, which is based on fold-unfold transformations [6], proceeds as follows.

$$
\begin{aligned}
&(x, y) \leftarrow split\ z \\
\equiv\quad &\{\text{ specification of } split \,\} \\
&x \mathbin{+\!\!+} y = z \\
\equiv\quad &\{\ x \text{ has type } [a] \,\} \\
&([\,] \mathbin{+\!\!+} y = z,\ x = [\,]) \vee ((a : x') \mathbin{+\!\!+} y = z,\ x = a : x') \\
\equiv\quad &\{\text{ definition of `}\mathbin{+\!\!+}\text{' }\} \\
&(y = z,\ x = [\,]) \vee (a : (x' \mathbin{+\!\!+} y) = z,\ x = a : x') \\
\equiv\quad &\{\text{ introduce } z' \,\} \\
&(y = z,\ x = [\,]) \vee (a : z' = z,\ x' \mathbin{+\!\!+} y = z',\ x = a : x') \\
\equiv\quad &\{\text{ specification of } split \,\} \\
&(y = z,\ x = [\,]) \vee (a : z' = z,\ (x', y) \leftarrow split\ z',\ x = a : x')
\end{aligned}
$$

We can turn this equivalence into an equation by applying the following *comprehension principle*.

$$e_1 \leftarrow e_2 \equiv q \quad \equiv \quad e_2 = \{\, e_1 \mid q \,\} \tag{1}$$

The derived programs (if they are set-valued) will usually take the form on the right side. The left side is, however, more convenient for conducting calculations.

Applying the comprehension principle we obtain the following equation.

$$split\ z \;=\; \{\,(x,y) \mid (y = z,\ x = [\,]) \vee (a : z' = z,\ (x',y) \leftarrow split\ z',\ x = a : x')\,\}$$

The set comprehension on the right is slightly more general than what is currently available in Haskell as it involves a disjunction and equations. However, we can easily eliminate the disjunction using the following law.

$$\{\, e \mid q \vee r \,\} \;=\; \{\, e \mid q \,\} \cup \{\, e \mid r \,\} \tag{2}$$

Furthermore, an equation of the form $p = e$ where p is a pattern can be replaced by a generator:

$$p = e \quad \equiv \quad p \leftarrow \{\, e \,\}. \tag{3}$$

If we additionally inline simple generators of the form $x \leftarrow \{\, e \,\}$ where x is a variable, we obtain the program listed in Sec. 1.

Before we proceed, let us briefly explain why we can use the derived equation as a definition. In principle, we have to show that the equation has a least (or maybe a unique) solution and that this solution satisfies the original specification. The first part is easy to establish by appealing to the Knaster-Tarski theorem [14,24] (using the pointwise ordering on functions and the inclusion ordering on sets). In the sequel, we will take the existence of least fixed points for granted. For the second part, we can reorder the derivation above so that it constitutes an inductive proof (inductive on the result list x) showing that an *arbitrary* solution of the equation is equal to $split$. Note that this implies that the equation has, in fact, a *unique* solution.

Set comprehensions need not be a primitive concept. They can be given a precise semantics via the following identities:

$$\begin{aligned}
\{\, e \mid \epsilon \,\} &= return\ e \\
\{\, e \mid b, q \,\} &= \textbf{if}\ b\ \textbf{then}\ \{\, e \mid q \,\}\ \textbf{else}\ \varnothing \\
\{\, e \mid p \leftarrow s, q \,\} &= s \triangleright \lambda x \rightarrow \textbf{case}\ x\ \textbf{of}\ p \rightarrow \{\, e \mid q \,\}; \_ \; \triangleright \varnothing,
\end{aligned}$$

where *return* and '$\triangleright$' are unit and bind of the set monad:

$$\begin{aligned}
return\ a &= \{\, a \,\} \\
s \triangleright f &= \bigcup \{\, f\ a \mid a \leftarrow s \,\}.
\end{aligned}$$

Like λ- and **case**-expressions, generators are binding constructs: the generator $p \leftarrow e$ *binds* the variables that appear in p.[1] Consequently, equations that appear

---

[1] By contrast, in Zermelo type theory [25] the set comprehension itself constitutes the binding construct.

in comprehensions must also be binding constructs. In line with rule 3 we agree upon that an equation binds the variables of the left (the variables on the right must be bound at an outer level).

It remains to give a semantics to general equations of the form $e_1 = e_2$, which appear, for instance, in the specification of *split* and along the derivation. The idea is simply that the variables on the left are bound to all combinations of values which satisfy the equation. Formally, let $\{x_1, \ldots, x_n\}$ be the free variables of e_1, then $e_1 = e_2$ serves as an abbreviation for

$$x_1 \leftarrow T_1, \ldots, x_n \leftarrow T_n, e_1 \mathbin{==} e_2 \ ,$$

where T_i is the type of x_i and '==' is the test for equality. Since we are working in the world of sets, we view a type simply as a set, possibly given by an inductive definition. Of course, the goal of our program calculations is to eliminate general equations in favour of generators, so the above is 'merely' a precise semantics for the initial specification and the intermediate steps.

3   Tournament Representations

Here is the problem: Given a sequence x of integers, construct a heap whose inorder traversal is x itself. This heap is a so-called *tournament representation* of x [26]. Note that the tournament representation is unique if the given integers are distinct. If the sequence contains duplicates, then there are several heaps that satisfy the condition above. We do not, however, make any additional assumptions and allow ties to be broken in arbitrary ways.

In order to specify the problem formally we require the notions of binary tree, heap and inorder traversal.

We represent *binary trees* (trees for short) by the following data type.

$$\textbf{data } \textit{Tree } a \ = \ E \mid N \ (\textit{Tree } a) \ a \ (\textit{Tree } a)$$

Note that the type of trees is parametric in the type of labels.

A tree is said to be a *heap* if the label of each node is at most the labels of its descendants. To check the heap property it suffices to compare each label to its immediate descendants.

$$
\begin{array}{lcl}
\textit{heap} & :: & \textit{Tree Int} \rightarrow \textit{Bool} \\
\textit{heap E} & = & \textit{True} \\
\textit{heap (N l a r)} & = & \textit{heap l} \wedge \textit{top l} \geqslant a \leqslant \textit{top r} \wedge \textit{heap r}
\end{array}
$$

The helper function *top* returns the topmost element of a tree.

$$
\begin{array}{lcl}
\textit{top} & :: & \textit{Tree Int} \rightarrow \textit{Int} \\
\textit{top E} & = & \infty \\
\textit{top (N l a r)} & = & a
\end{array}
$$

Here and in what follows it is convenient to assume the existence of extremal elements ($-\infty$ and ∞), which must not appear in the given integer sequence. The final Haskell program will do without, however.

The function *list* yields the inorder traversal of a given tree.

$$
\begin{aligned}
list &\quad :: \quad \forall a \,.\, Tree\ a \to [a] \\
list\ E &\quad = \quad [\,] \\
list\ (N\ l\ a\ r) &\quad = \quad list\ l +\!\!+ [a] +\!\!+ list\ r
\end{aligned}
$$

Returning to our problem, we are seeking a function that is the right-inverse of *list* and whose results satisfy the heap property. As we have mentioned before, even though the final program will be deterministic the derivation requires or at least benefits from a relational setting. Consequently, we specify the desired program as a set-valued function *tournament* :: $[Int] \to Set\ (Tree\ Int)$ that satisfies

$$t \leftarrow tournament\ x \quad \equiv \quad list\ t = x,\ heap\ t.$$

Before we proceed, let us slightly generalise the problem. The task of constructing tournament representations is closely related to precedence parsing. Both problems differ only in the relations '$\geqslant$' and '$\leqslant$', on which the *heap* predicate is based. Thus, in order to keep the derivation sufficiently general, we abstract away from the type of integers and from the integer orderings.

$$
\begin{aligned}
heap &\quad :: \quad Tree\ Elem \to Bool \\
heap\ E &\quad = \quad True \\
heap\ (N\ l\ a\ r) &\quad = \quad heap\ l \,\wedge\, top\ l > a < top\ r \,\wedge\, heap\ r
\end{aligned}
$$

Here, *Elem* is some type of elements and '$>$' and '$<$' are some predicates on integers. The predicates must satisfy certain properties, which we will infer in the course of the derivation. The properties are signalled by the hint '**assumption**'.

4   Step 1: Tupling

Most likely, *tournament* (or rather, one of its helper functions) will be defined recursively. Furthermore, the recursive invocations will work on (contiguous) subparts of the original sequence. So, as a first step, we generalise *tournament* to a function *build* :: $[Elem] \to Set\ (Tree\ Elem, [Elem])$ that satisfies

$$(t, y) \leftarrow build\ x \quad \equiv \quad list\ t +\!\!+ y = x,\ heap\ t.$$

This generalisation is an instance of a well-known technique of program optimisation called *tupling* [3] and constitutes the main inventive step of the derivation. Before tackling *build* let us first express *tournament* in terms of *build*.

$$
\begin{aligned}
&\quad t \leftarrow tournament\ x \\
\equiv &\quad \{\ \text{specification of } tournament\ \} \\
&\quad list\ t = x,\ heap\ t \\
\equiv &\quad \{\ \text{`}[\,]\text{' is the unit of `}+\!\!+\text{' }\} \\
&\quad list\ t +\!\!+ [\,] = x,\ heap\ t \\
\equiv &\quad \{\ \text{specification of } build\ \} \\
&\quad (t, [\,]) \leftarrow build\ x
\end{aligned}
$$

Thus, *tournament* can be defined as follows.

$$tournament \; x \;\; = \;\; \{\, t \mid (t, [\,]) \leftarrow build \; x \,\}$$

The derivation of *build* proceeds almost mechanically.

$(t, y) \leftarrow build \; x$

$\equiv$ { specification of *build* }

$list \; t \mathbin{+\!\!+} y = x, \; heap \; t$

$\equiv$ { t has type *Tree Elem* }

$(list \; E \mathbin{+\!\!+} y = x, \; heap \; E, \; t = E)$

$\qquad \vee \; (list \; (N \; l \; a \; r) \mathbin{+\!\!+} y = x, \; heap \; (N \; l \; a \; r), \; t = N \; l \; a \; r)$

To avoid writing a long disjunction we conduct two subproofs. **Case** $t = E$:

$list \; E \mathbin{+\!\!+} y = x, \; heap \; E$

$\equiv$ { definition of *list* and *heap* }

$[\,] \mathbin{+\!\!+} y = x$

$\equiv$ { definition of '$\mathbin{+\!\!+}$' }

$y = x.$

Case $t = N \; l \; a \; r$:

$list \; (N \; l \; a \; r) \mathbin{+\!\!+} y = x, \; heap \; (N \; l \; a \; r)$

$\equiv$ { definition of *list* and *heap* }

$list \; l \mathbin{+\!\!+} [a] \mathbin{+\!\!+} list \; r \mathbin{+\!\!+} y = x, \; heap \; l, \; top \; l > a < top \; r, \; heap \; r$

$\equiv$ { introduce x_1 and rearrange }

$list \; l \mathbin{+\!\!+} x_1 = x, \; heap \; l, \; [a] \mathbin{+\!\!+} list \; r \mathbin{+\!\!+} y = x_1, \; top \; l > a < top \; r, \; heap \; r$

$\equiv$ { specification of *build* }

$(l, x_1) \leftarrow build \; x, \; [a] \mathbin{+\!\!+} list \; r \mathbin{+\!\!+} y = x_1, \; top \; l > a < top \; r, \; heap \; r$

$\equiv$ { introduce x_2 and rearrange }

$(l, x_1) \leftarrow build \; x, \; [a] \mathbin{+\!\!+} x_2 = x_1, \; list \; r \mathbin{+\!\!+} y = x_2, \; heap \; r, \; top \; l > a < top \; r$

$\equiv$ { specification of *build* }

$(l, x_1) \leftarrow build \; x, \; [a] \mathbin{+\!\!+} x_2 = x_1, \; (r, y) \leftarrow build \; x_2, \; top \; l > a < top \; r$

$\equiv$ { definition of '$\mathbin{+\!\!+}$' }

$(l, x_1) \leftarrow build \; x, \; a : x_2 = x_1, \; (r, y) \leftarrow build \; x_2, \; top \; l > a < top \; r.$

To summarise, we have shown that the specification satisfies the following equation.

$$
\begin{aligned}
build \quad &:: \quad [Elem] \rightarrow Set \; (Tree \; Elem, [Elem]) \\
build \; x \quad &= \quad \{(E, x)\} \\
&\cup \quad \{(N \; l \; a \; r, y) \mid (l, x_1) \leftarrow build \; x, \\
&\qquad\qquad\qquad a : x_2 = x_1, \\
&\qquad\qquad\qquad (r, y) \leftarrow build \; x_2, \\
&\qquad\qquad\qquad top \; l > a < top \; r\}
\end{aligned}
$$

In fact, the equation even has a *unique* solution. Again, this can be demonstrated by reordering the steps, so that the derivation above becomes an inductive proof (inductive on the constructed tree t) showing that an arbitrary solution of the equation satisfies the specification (which, by its form, has a unique solution).

Furthermore, if we replace sets by lists and set comprehensions by list comprehensions, then this equation constitutes an executable Haskell program. (Additionally, we must replace the equation $a : x_2 = x_1$ by the generator $a : x_2 \leftarrow [x_1]$.) Of course, there is little point in doing so as the program is hopelessly inefficient. Note in this respect that the construction of the left subtree is 'pure guesswork' as *build* passes its argument list x unchanged to the first recursive call. Clearly, further massage is necessary.

5 Step 2: Turning Top-Down into Bottom-Up

An obvious idea for improving *build* is to promote the tests, that is, $top\ l > a < top\ r$, into the generation of the trees. This step can be simplified considerably if we first eliminate the left-recursive call to *build*, which is what we will do next.

At this point, it is preferable to switch temporarily to a point-free style—left-recursion elimination is purely structural and the program structure is obscured by data variables. Now, using the identities of Sec. 2 *build* can be put into the form

$$build\ x\ \ =\ \ a\ x\ \cup\ build\ x \triangleright b$$

for suitable functions a and b. To obtain a point-free definition we eliminate the data variable x by lifting '$\cup$' to the function level—$(f \cup g)\ n = f\ n \cup g\ n$—and by replacing monadic application by monadic composition—$(f \diamond g)\ n = f\ n \triangleright g$. We obtain the recursion equation:

$$build\ \ =\ \ a\ \cup\ build \diamond b,$$

which has the unique[2] solution $a \diamond b^*$, where $(-)^*$ denotes the reflexive, transitive closure of a relation. Now, the closure operator $(-)^*$ can be defined either as the least fixed point of a left-recursive or of a right-recursive equation:

$$e^*\ \ =\ \ return\ \cup\ e^* \diamond e$$
$$e^*\ \ =\ \ return\ \cup\ e \diamond e^*.$$

Consequently, an equivalent definition of *build* is

$$build\ \ =\ \ a \diamond loop$$
$$loop\ \ =\ \ return\ \cup\ b \diamond loop$$

---

[2] We can show uniqueness in this more general setting using the *unique extension property* [2]: $f = a \cup f \diamond b$ has a unique solution if the relation b is well-founded. In our case, this condition is satisfied as the length of the element list is strictly decreasing.

or reverting back to pointwise style:

$$
\begin{aligned}
build\ x \quad &= \quad loop\ (E, x) \\
loop\ (l, x_1) \quad &= \quad \{(l, x_1)\} \\
&\cup \quad \{(t, z) \mid a : x_2 = x_1, \\
&\qquad\qquad (r, y) \leftarrow loop\ (E, x_2), \\
&\qquad\qquad top\ l > a < top\ r, \\
&\qquad\qquad (t, z) \leftarrow loop\ (N\ l\ a\ r, y)\}.
\end{aligned}
$$

Additionally, we have replaced $build\ x_2$ by $loop\ (E, x_2)$.

The above transformation has, in effect, turned a top-down program into a bottom-up one. The original definition of $build$ constructed a tournament representation from the root to the leaves whereas the helper function $loop$ starts at the leftmost leaf and works its way up to the root.

6   Step 3: Promoting the Tests

We are now in a position that we can easily promote the tests $top\ l > a < top\ r$ into the generation of the trees. In fact, the first half of the condition, that is, $top\ l > a$ can be readily applied since $loop$ receives the left subtree l as an argument and a is the first element of its list argument. It remains to propagate $a < top\ r$ motivating the following specification.

$$
p < top\ l,\ (t, y) \leftarrow loop\text{-}to\ p\ (l, x) \quad \equiv \quad (t, y) \leftarrow loop\ (l, x),\ p < top\ t
$$

Note that the specified function $loop\text{-}to$ maintains an *invariant*: if the topmost label of its tree argument is at least a given bound, then this property also holds for the tree returned by $loop\text{-}to$. Thus, using guards we can nicely express pre- and postconditions and invariants. Furthermore, it is important to note that the specification cannot be satisfied for arbitrary relations '$>$' and '$<$'. Consider the case where $p < top\ l$ is false but the expression on the right has a solution. Rather pleasantly, the derivation below will produce suitable conditions on '$>$' and '$<$'.

The derivation of a program for $loop\text{-}to$ proceeds as follows.

$$
\begin{aligned}
&p < top\ l,\ (t, z) \leftarrow loop\text{-}to\ p\ (l, x_1) \\
\equiv \quad &\{\ \text{specification of } loop\text{-}to\ \} \\
&(t, z) \leftarrow loop\ (l, x_1),\ p < top\ t \\
\equiv \quad &\{\ \text{definition of } loop\ \} \\
&((t, z) \leftarrow \{(l, x_1)\},\ p < top\ t) \\
&\qquad \vee\ (a : x_2 = x_1,\ (r, y) \leftarrow loop\ (E, x_2),\ top\ l > a < top\ r, \\
&\qquad\qquad (t, z) \leftarrow loop\ (N\ l\ a\ r, y),\ p < top\ t)
\end{aligned}
$$

Again, we split the proof into two two subproofs. First disjunction:

$$
\begin{aligned}
&(t, z) \leftarrow \{(l, x_1)\},\ p < top\ t \\
\equiv \quad &\{\ \text{sets}\ \} \\
&p < top\ l,\ (t, z) = (l, x_1).
\end{aligned}
$$

Second disjunction:

$$a : x_2 = x_1,\ (r, y) \leftarrow loop\ (E, x_2),\ top\ l \gtrdot a \lessdot top\ r,$$
$$(t, z) \leftarrow loop\ (N\ l\ a\ r, y),\ p \lessdot top\ t$$

$\equiv$ { specification of *loop-to* }

$$a : x_2 = x_1,\ (r, y) \leftarrow loop\ (E, x_2),\ top\ l \gtrdot a \lessdot top\ r,$$
$$p \lessdot top\ (N\ l\ a\ r),\ (t, z) \leftarrow loop\text{-}to\ p\ (N\ l\ a\ r, y)$$

$\equiv$ { definition of *top* and rearranging }

$$a : x_2 = x_1,\ top\ l \gtrdot a,\ p \lessdot a,\ (r, y) \leftarrow loop\ (E, x_2),\ a \lessdot top\ r,$$
$$(t, z) \leftarrow loop\text{-}to\ p\ (N\ l\ a\ r, y)$$

$\equiv$ { specification of *loop-to* }

$$a : x_2 = x_1,\ top\ l \gtrdot a,\ p \lessdot a,\ a \lessdot top\ E,\ (r, y) \leftarrow loop\text{-}to\ a\ (E, x_2),$$
$$(t, z) \leftarrow loop\text{-}to\ p\ (N\ l\ a\ r, y)$$

$\equiv$ { definition of *top* and **assumption** $e \lessdot \infty$ }

$$a : x_2 = x_1,\ top\ l \gtrdot a,\ p \lessdot a,\ (r, y) \leftarrow loop\text{-}to\ a\ (E, x_2),$$
$$(t, z) \leftarrow loop\text{-}to\ p\ (N\ l\ a\ r, y)$$

$\equiv$ { **assumption** $i \lessdot j\ \wedge\ k \gtrdot j\ \implies\ i \lessdot k$ }

$$p \lessdot top\ l,\ a : x_2 = x_1,\ top\ l \gtrdot a,\ p \lessdot a,\ (r, y) \leftarrow loop\text{-}to\ a\ (E, x_2),$$
$$(t, z) \leftarrow loop\text{-}to\ p\ (N\ l\ a\ r, y).$$

The last step requires that the relations '$\gtrdot$' and '$\lessdot$' are related by a *zig-zag transitivity* law. Loosely speaking, the law expresses that the left subtree of the right subtree is also a legal immediate right subtree.

It remains to express *build* in terms of *loop-to*.

$$(t, y) \leftarrow build\ x$$

$\equiv$ { definition of *build* }

$$(t, y) \leftarrow loop\ (E, x)$$

$\equiv$ { **assumption** $-\infty \lessdot e$ }

$$(t, y) \leftarrow loop\ (E, x),\ -\infty \lessdot top\ t$$

$\equiv$ { specification of *loop-to* }

$$-\infty \lessdot top\ E, (t, y) \leftarrow loop\text{-}to\ (-\infty)\ (E, x)$$

$=$ { **assumption** $\infty \lessdot c$ }

$$(t, y) \leftarrow loop\text{-}to\ (-\infty)\ (E, x)$$

To summarise, we have calculated the following recursion equation.

$$
\begin{aligned}
build\ x \quad &= \quad loop\text{-}to\ (-\infty)\ (E, x) \\
loop\text{-}to\ p\ (l, x_1) \quad &= \quad \{(l, x_1)\} \\
&\cup\ \{(t, z)\ |\ a : x_2 - x_1, \\
&\qquad top\ l \gtrdot a,\ p \lessdot a, \\
&\qquad (r, y) \leftarrow loop\text{-}to\ a\ (E, x_2), \\
&\qquad (t, z) \leftarrow loop\text{-}to\ p\ (N\ l\ a\ r, y)\}
\end{aligned}
$$

As usual, we can reorder the derivation to obtain an inductive proof showing that each solution of the equation satisfies the specification. This time we induct on the length of the list argument (note that this requires showing that the output list is always a suffix of the input list). The recursion equation can be easily turned into a respectable Haskell program. However, there is still ample room for improvement.

7   Step 4: Strengthening

Recall that *build* considers all prefixes of its argument list. Thus, it produces many (intermediate) results which are eventually discarded by *tournament*. The purpose of this section is to calculate a variant of *loop-to* which consumes as many elements as possible building maximal subtrees. It is convenient to introduce a function

$$
\begin{aligned}
hd & :: \ [Elem] \rightarrow Elem \\
hd \ [] & = \ -\infty \\
hd \ (a:x) & = \ a,
\end{aligned}
$$

which returns the first element of a list. Assuming that $p < top \ l$ the desired function (called *loop-to'*) can be specified as follows.

$$top \ l > hd \ x, \ (t, y) \leftarrow loop\text{-}to' \ p \ (l, x) \ \equiv \ (t, y) \leftarrow loop\text{-}to \ p \ (l, x), \ p > hd \ y$$

The precondition guarantees that the first element of the argument list is a legal predecessor of l. Likewise, the postcondition ensures that the first element of the remaining list is a legal predecessor of the tree labelled with p. If the relation '$>$' is the converse of '$<$', then these conditions imply that the constructed trees are maximal. However, even if the relations are not converses of each other, we know at least that the initial call to *loop-to'* with $p = -\infty$ (see below) consumes the complete input sequence as $-\infty > hd \ y$ implies $y = []$ (assuming that $-\infty$ is the least element).

The calculation proceeds as follows.

$$top \ l > hd \ x, \ (t, z) \leftarrow loop\text{-}to' \ p \ (l, x)$$
$\equiv$ { specification of *loop-to'* }
$$(t, z) \leftarrow loop\text{-}to \ p \ (l, x), \ p > hd \ z$$
$\equiv$ { x has type $[Elem]$ }
$$([] = x, (t, z) \leftarrow loop\text{-}to \ p \ (l, []), \ p > hd \ z)$$
$$\lor (a : x_2 = x, (t, z) \leftarrow loop\text{-}to \ p \ (l, a : x_2), \ p > hd \ z)$$

As we are working towards a program we conduct a case analysis on the input list. **Case** $x = []$:

$$(t, z) \leftarrow loop\text{-}to \ p \ (l, []), \ p > hd \ z$$
$\equiv$ { definition of *loop-to* }
$$(t, z) \leftarrow \{(l, [])\}, \ p > hd \ z$$
$\equiv$ { definition of *hd* and **assumption** $e > -\infty$ }
$$top \ l > hd \ x, (t, z) = (l, [])$$

Case $x = a : x_2$:

$$(t, z) \leftarrow loop\text{-}to \ p \ (l, a : x_2), \ p \gg hd \ z$$
$$\equiv \quad \{ \text{ definition of } loop\text{-}to \ \}$$
$$((t, z) \leftarrow \{(l, a : x_2)\}, \ p \gg hd \ z)$$
$$\vee \ (top \ l \gg a, \ p < a, \ (r, y) \leftarrow loop\text{-}to \ a \ (E, x_2),$$
$$(t, z) \leftarrow loop\text{-}to \ p \ (N \ l \ a \ r, y), \ p \gg hd \ z)$$

As usual, we split the proof into two subproofs. First disjunction:

$$(t, z) \leftarrow \{(l, a : x_2)\}, \ p \gg hd \ z$$
$$\equiv \quad \{ \text{ definition of } hd \ \}$$
$$(t, z) = (l, a : x_2), \ p \gg a$$
$$\equiv \quad \{ \ p < top \ l \text{ and } \mathbf{assumption} \ i < j \wedge i \gg k \implies j \gg k \ \}$$
$$top \ l \gg a, (t, z) = (l, a : x_2), \ p \gg a$$
$$\equiv \quad \{ \text{ definition of } hd \ \}$$
$$top \ l \gg hd \ x, (t, z) = (l, a : x_2), \ p \gg a$$

The *zig-zag transitivity* law that is required in the second but last step is dual to the one of the previous section: it expresses that the right subtree of the left subtree is also a legal immediate left subtree.

Second disjunction:

$$top \ l \gg a, \ p < a, \ (r, y) \leftarrow loop\text{-}to \ a \ (E, x_2),$$
$$(t, z) \leftarrow loop\text{-}to \ p \ (N \ l \ a \ r, y), \ p \gg hd \ z$$
$$\equiv \quad \{ \text{ specification of } loop\text{-}to' \ \}$$
$$top \ l \gg a, \ p < a, \ (r, y) \leftarrow loop\text{-}to \ a \ (E, x_2),$$
$$top \ (N \ l \ a \ r) \gg hd \ y, \ (t, z) \leftarrow loop\text{-}to' \ p \ (N \ l \ a \ r, y)$$
$$\equiv \quad \{ \text{ definition of } top \ \}$$
$$top \ l \gg a, \ p < a, \ (r, y) \leftarrow loop\text{-}to \ a \ (E, x_2),$$
$$a \gg hd \ y, \ (t, z) \leftarrow loop\text{-}to' \ p \ (N \ l \ a \ r, y)$$
$$\equiv \quad \{ \text{ specification of } loop\text{-}to' \ \}$$
$$top \ l \gg a, \ p < a, \ top \ E \gg hd \ x_2, \ (r, y) \leftarrow loop\text{-}to' \ a \ (E, x_2),$$
$$(t, z) \leftarrow loop\text{-}to' \ p \ (N \ l \ a \ r, y)$$
$$\equiv \quad \{ \text{ definition of } top \text{ and } \mathbf{assumption} \ \infty \gg e \ \}$$
$$top \ l \gg a, \ p < a, \ (r, y) \leftarrow loop\text{-}to' \ a \ (E, x_2),$$
$$(t, z) \leftarrow loop\text{-}to' \ p \ (N \ l \ a \ r, y)$$
$$\equiv \quad \{ \text{ definition of } hd \ \}$$
$$top \ l \gg hd \ x, \ p < a, \ (r, y) \leftarrow loop\text{-}to' \ a \ (E, x_2),$$
$$(t, z) \leftarrow loop\text{-}to' \ p \ (N \ l \ a \ r, y)$$

We can now define *tournament* directly in terms of *loop-to'*.

$$t \leftarrow tournament\ x$$
$$\equiv \quad \{ \text{ definition of } tournament \}$$
$$(t, [\,]) \leftarrow build\ x$$
$$\equiv \quad \{ \text{ definition of } build \}$$
$$(t, [\,]) \leftarrow loop\text{-}to\ (-\infty)\ (E, x)$$
$$\equiv \quad \{ \text{ definition of } hd \text{ and } \textbf{assumption } -\infty > e \equiv e = -\infty \}$$
$$(t, y) \leftarrow loop\text{-}to\ (-\infty)\ (E, x),\ -\infty > hd\ y$$
$$\equiv \quad \{ \text{ specification of } loop\text{-}to' \}$$
$$top\ E > hd\ x, (t, y) \leftarrow loop\text{-}to'\ (-\infty)\ (E, x)$$
$$\equiv \quad \{ \text{ definition of } top \text{ and } \textbf{assumption } \infty > e \}$$
$$(t, y) \leftarrow loop\text{-}to'\ (-\infty)\ (E, x)$$

As an aside, note that $hd\ y = -\infty \equiv y = [\,]$, which is implicitly used in the third step, holds because the input does not contain $-\infty$ as an element.

To summarise, we have calculated the following program for constructing tournament representations (the proof that *loop-to'* satisfies the specification uses the same induction scheme as in the previous section).

$$
\begin{aligned}
tournament\ x \quad &= \quad \{ t \mid (t, y) \leftarrow loop\text{-}to'\ (-\infty)\ (E, x) \} \\
loop\text{-}to'\ p\ (l, [\,]) \quad &= \quad \{ (l, [\,]) \} \\
loop\text{-}to'\ p\ (l, a : x_2) \quad &= \quad \{ (l, a : x_2) \mid p > a \} \\
&\quad \cup \quad \{ (t, z) \mid p < a, \\
&\qquad\qquad (r, y) \leftarrow loop\text{-}to'\ a\ (E, x_2), \\
&\qquad\qquad (t, z) \leftarrow loop\text{-}to'\ p\ (N\ l\ a\ r, y) \}
\end{aligned}
$$

This program satisfies the original specification under the proviso that $-\infty$ is the least element (∞ is no longer needed),

$$-\infty < e > -\infty,$$

$$-\infty > e \equiv e = -\infty,$$

and that the orderings satisfy the zig-zag transitivity laws,

$$i < j \wedge k > j \implies i < k,$$

$$i < j \wedge i > k \implies j > k.$$

8   A Haskell Program

The derived program is still nondeterministic but the final step to a deterministic Haskell program is a small one. To start with, we instantiate the abstract relations '$>$' and '$<$' setting $(\gtrdot) = (\geqslant)$ and $(\lessdot) = (<)$:

$$
\begin{aligned}
\textit{loop-to}'\ p\ (l, [])\quad &=\quad \{(l, [])\} \\
\textit{loop-to}'\ p\ (l, a : x_2)\quad &=\quad \{(l, a : x_2) \mid p \geqslant a\} \\
&\cup\quad \{(t, z) \mid p \lessdot a, \\
&\qquad\qquad (r, y) \leftarrow \textit{loop-to}'\ a\ (E, x_2), \\
&\qquad\qquad (t, z) \leftarrow \textit{loop-to}'\ p\ (N\ l\ a\ r, y)\}.
\end{aligned}
$$

Since the relations are exclusive, we can now replace the disjoint union in the second equation by a conditional as justified by the following calculation.

$$
\begin{aligned}
&\{ e_1 \mid p,\ q_1 \} \cup \{ e_2 \mid \neg\, p,\ q_2 \} \\
\equiv\quad &\{\ \text{set comprehensions}\ \} \\
&(\textbf{if}\ p\ \textbf{then}\ \{ e_1 \mid q_1 \}\ \textbf{else}\ \varnothing) \cup (\textbf{if}\ \neg\, p\ \textbf{then}\ \{ e_2 \mid q_2 \}\ \textbf{else}\ \varnothing) \\
\equiv\quad &\{\ \textbf{if}\ \neg\, c\ \textbf{then}\ a\ \textbf{else}\ b = \textbf{if}\ c\ \textbf{then}\ b\ \textbf{else}\ a\ \} \\
&(\textbf{if}\ p\ \textbf{then}\ \{ e_1 \mid q_1 \}\ \textbf{else}\ \varnothing) \cup (\textbf{if}\ p\ \textbf{then}\ \varnothing\ \textbf{else}\ \{ e_2 \mid q_2 \}) \\
\equiv\quad &\{\ \text{union distributes over conditionals}\ \} \\
&\textbf{if}\ p\ \textbf{then}\ \{ e_1 \mid q_1 \} \cup \varnothing\ \textbf{else}\ \varnothing \cup \{ e_2 \mid q_2 \} \\
\equiv\quad &\{\ s \cup \varnothing = s = \varnothing \cup s\ \} \\
&\textbf{if}\ p\ \textbf{then}\ \{ e_1 \mid q_1 \}\ \textbf{else}\ \{ e_2 \mid q_2 \}
\end{aligned}
$$

Applying this transformation we get

$$
\begin{aligned}
\textit{loop-to}'\ p\ (l, [])\quad &=\quad \{(l, [])\} \\
\textit{loop-to}'\ p\ (l, a : x_2)\quad & \\
\mid p \geqslant a\quad &=\quad \{(l, a : x_2)\} \\
\mid \textit{otherwise}\quad &=\quad \{(t, z) \mid (r, y) \leftarrow \textit{loop-to}'\ a\ (E, x_2), \\
&\qquad\qquad (t, z) \leftarrow \textit{loop-to}'\ p\ (N\ l\ a\ r, y)\}.
\end{aligned}
$$

Note that we have saved half of the comparisons as compared to the program of Sec. 6. Furthermore, note that $\textit{loop-to}'$ has exactly one solution for each combination of arguments. Thus, to obtain a deterministic program we simply switch from the set monad to the identity monad effectively replacing set comprehensions by **let**-bindings.

$$
\begin{aligned}
\textit{tournament}\ x\quad &=\quad \textbf{let}\ (t, y) = \textit{loop-to}'\ (-\infty)\ E\ x\ \textbf{in}\ t \\
\textit{loop-to}'\ p\ (l, [])\quad &=\quad (l, []) \\
\textit{loop-to}'\ p\ (l, a : x)\quad & \\
\mid p \geqslant a\quad &=\quad (l, a : x) \\
\mid \textit{otherwise}\quad &=\quad \textbf{let}\ (r, y) = \textit{loop-to}'\ a\ (E, x)\ \textbf{in}\ \textit{loop-to}'\ p\ (N\ l\ a\ r, y).
\end{aligned}
$$

It is not hard to see that the derived Haskell program takes linear time and space, which is optimal for the given problem.

We have assumed throughout that we are working with an abstract type *Elem* of elements. Using Haskell's type classes [10] we can nicely capture this abstraction generalising the type of integers to an arbitrary instance of the classes *Ord*

$$
\begin{array}{lll}
tournament & :: & \forall a\,.\,(Ord\ a) \Rightarrow [a] \to Tree\ a \\
tournament\ x & = & loop\ E\ x \\[4pt]
loop & :: & \forall a\,.\,(Ord\ a) \Rightarrow Tree\ a \to [a] \to Tree\ a \\
loop\ l\ [\,] & = & l \\
loop\ l\ (a:x) & = & \textbf{let}\ (r,y) = loop\text{-}to\ a\ E\ x\ \textbf{in}\ loop\ (N\ l\ a\ r)\ y \\[4pt]
loop\text{-}to & :: & \forall a\,.\,(Ord\ a) \Rightarrow a \to Tree\ a \to [a] \to (Tree\ a, [a]) \\
loop\text{-}to\ p\ l\ [\,] & = & (l, [\,]) \\
loop\text{-}to\ p\ l\ as@(a:x) & & \\
\quad |\ p \geqslant a & = & (l, as) \\
\quad |\ otherwise & = & \textbf{let}\ (r,y) = loop\text{-}to\ a\ E\ x\ \textbf{in}\ loop\text{-}to\ p\ (N\ l\ a\ r)\ y
\end{array}
$$

Fig. 1. A Haskell program for constructing tournament representations

and *Bounded*: the first class provides the ordering relation; the second provides the extremal element $-\infty$. Actually, if we are willing to accept some duplication of code, we can even remove the dependence on *Bound* by specialising $loop\text{-}to'\ p$ for $p = -\infty$:

$$
loop'\ (l, x) \quad = \quad fst\ (loop\text{-}to'\ (-\infty)\ (l, x)).
$$

The final program that incorporates this generalisation is displayed in Fig. 1. (Additionally, we have renamed and curried $loop'$ and $loop\text{-}to'$.)

Before we review related work, let us consider two variations of the problem.

Strict heaps A minor twist is to require the heap to be *strict*: the label of each node must be strictly smaller than the labels of its descendants. For this variant we simply instantiate the abstract relations to strict orderings: $(\geqslant) = (>)$ and $(\leqslant) = (<)$. In this case, *tournament* has *at most* one solution. Therefore, we cannot refine *Set* to the identity monad but must use the *Maybe* monad instead. The details of rewriting the program of Sec. 7 are left to the reader.

Precedence parsing The problem of constructing tournament representations closely corresponds to the problem of precedence parsing. In fact, a solution to both problems was first given in the context of parsing by Floyd [8].

In Haskell, an operator can be assigned a *precedence* and an *associativity*. The higher the precedence the more tightly binds the operator. Conflicts between operators of equal precedence are resolved using associativity: left associativity causes grouping to the left, right associativity accordingly to the right. Sequences of non-associative operators of equal precedence are not allowed.

If we represent operators by the data types

$$
\begin{array}{lll}
\textbf{data}\ Assoc & = & L \mid N \mid R \\
\textbf{data}\ Op & = & Op\ Assoc\ Int,
\end{array}
$$

we can define the relations '$>$' and '$<$' as follows:

$$
\begin{array}{rcl}
Op\ a\ p > Op\ L\ p' & = & p \geqslant p' \\
Op\ a\ p > Op\ N\ p' & = & p > p' \\
Op\ a\ p > Op\ R\ p' & = & p > p' \\
Op\ L\ p < Op\ a'\ p' & = & p < p' \\
Op\ N\ p < Op\ a'\ p' & = & p < p' \\
Op\ R\ p < Op\ a'\ p' & = & p \leqslant p'.
\end{array}
$$

The minimal element is given by $Op\ L\ (-\infty)$.

Since there may be still several expression trees for a given sequence of operators, we must refine *Set* to the *List* monad. The details are again left to the reader.

The program of Sec. 7 does not consider the operands of operators. However, since expression trees are *full* binary trees—each node has either no or two subtrees—operands can be easily added at a later stage. Alternatively, operands can be defined as elements of highest precedence.

9   Related Work

Tournament representations were introduced by Vuillemin [26] as a special case of *Cartesian trees*. (A Cartesian tree consists of points in the plane such that the x-part is a binary search tree and the y-part is a binary heap. This data structure is also known as a *treap*.) Both data structures have a number of applications in computational geometry and adaptive sorting [9,15].

The first derivation of a heap construction function is due to Bird [5]; several authors have subsequently presented alternative approaches [1,20,7]. The main idea of most solutions is to represent the tournament tree by its *left spine*, the sequence of pennants (topped binary trees) on the path from the leftmost leaf to the root. This representation change turns a top-down *data structure* into a bottom-up one and nicely corresponds to the second step of our derivation, where we converted a top-down *algorithm* into a bottom-up one.

The derivation that is closest in spirit to ours is the one by Augusteijn [1]. He conducts similar steps but misses the optimisation introduced in Sec. 7. Interestingly, Augusteijn employs a pointwise style for left-recursion elimination, which is based on a rather specific theorem. We feel that the point-free argument of Sec. 5 is more elegant.

We have mentioned before that the problem of constructing tournament representations is closely related to precedence parsing. Though the work in this area [8] predates the papers above, this relationship is hardly recognised. Precedence parsing as an instance of bottom-up parsing uses a stack, which contains the recognised prefix of a sentential form. In the case of an expression grammar this stack corresponds to the right spine representation of a tree. Our algorithm can be seen as a stack-free implementation of the parsing algorithm, where the stack is implicitly represented by the recursion stack, see also [21,13].

List comprehensions, which are due to Burstall and Darlington, were incorporated in several non-strict functional languages such as KRC, Miranda, and Haskell. Wadler generalised list comprehensions to monad comprehensions [27]. List and set comprehensions also appear in several textbooks on program derivation, most notably [4,18], but they seem to play only a minor rôle in actual derivations.

An alternative approach to pointwise relational programming was recently put forward by de Moor and Gibbons [7]. They propose to use a nondeterministic functional language that includes relational combinators such as converse and choice. The use of choice allows for a much tighter integration of the relational and the functional world at the cost of weakening β- and η-conversion to inequalities. In a sense, our approach is closer to pure functional languages such as Haskell, which require an embedding of the relational part, whereas de Moor's and Gibbons's calculus is closer to functional logic languages such as Curry [11]. In fact, there are several crosslinks to logic programming, for instance, embeddings of Prolog into Haskell [12,22] and fold-unfold systems for logic programs [23], which we plan to explore in the future.

Acknowledgements

I am grateful to the five anonymous referees, who went over and above the call of duty, providing numerous constructive comments for the revision of this paper. I am particularly indebted to Ernie Cohen for valuable suggestions regarding presentation and for spotting two errors in the derivation of *loop-to* and *loop-to'*.

References

1. Lex Augusteijn. An alternative derivation of a binary heap construction function. In R.S. Bird, C.C. Morgan, and J.C.P Woodcock, editors, *Second International Conference on the Mathematics of Program Construction, Oxford*, volume 669 of *Lecture Notes in Computer Science*, pages 368–374. Springer, 1992.
2. Roland Backhouse. Galois connections and fixed point calculus, 2001. Lecture Notes.
3. Richard Bird. *Introduction to Functional Programming using Haskell*. Prentice Hall Europe, London, 2nd edition, 1998.
4. Richard Bird and Oege de Moor. *Algebra of Programming*. Prentice Hall Europe, London, 1997.
5. Richard S. Bird. Lectures on constructive functional programming. In Manfred Broy, editor, *Constructive Methods in Computer Science*. Springer-Verlag, 1988.
6. R. Burstall and J. Darlington. A tranformation system for developing recursive programs. *Journal of the ACM*, 24(1):44–67, 1977.
7. Oege de Moor and Jeremy Gibbons. Pointwise relational programming. In T. Rus, editor, *Proceedings of Algebraic Methodology and Software Technology (AMAST 2000), Iowa*, volume 1816 of *Lecture Notes in Computer Science*, pages 371–390. Springer-Verlag, May 2000.
8. R.W. Floyd. Syntactic analysis and operator precedence. *Journal of the ACM*, 10(3):316–333, 1963.

9. H.N. Gabow, J.L. Bentley, and R.E. Tarjan. Scaling and related techniques for geometry problems. In *Proceedings of the 16th Annual ACM Symposium on Theory of Computing*, pages 135–143, 1984.

10. Cordelia V. Hall, Kevin Hammond, Simon L. Peyton Jones, and Philip L. Wadler. Type classes in Haskell. *ACM Transactions on Programming Languages and Systems*, 18(2):109–138, March 1996.

11. Michael Hanus, editor. *Curry—An Integrated Functional Logic Language (Version 0.7.1)*, June 2000.

12. Ralf Hinze. Prolog's control constructs in a functional setting — Axioms and implementation. *International Journal of Foundations of Computer Science*, 12(2):125–170, 2001.

13. Ralf Hinze and Ross Paterson. Derivation of a typed functional LR parser, 2002. in preparation.

14. B. Knaster. Un théorème sur les fonctions d'ensembles. *Annales de la Societé Polonaise de Mathematique*, 6:133–134, 1928.

15. Christos Levcopoulos and Ola Petersson. Heapsort—adapted for presorted files. In F. Dehne, J.-R. Sack, and N. Santoro, editors, *Algorithms and Data Structures*, volume 382 of *Lecture Notes in Computer Science*, pages 499–509. Springer, 1989.

16. Eugenio Moggi. An abstract view of programming languages. Technical Report ECS-LFCS-90-113, Department of Computer Science, Edinburgh University, 1990.

17. Eugenio Moggi. Notions of computation and monads. *Information and Computation*, 93(1):55–92, 1991.

18. Helmut A. Partsch. *Specification and Transformation of Programs—A Formal Approach to Software Development*. Texts and Monographs in Computer Science. Springer-Verlag, Berlin, 1990.

19. Simon Peyton Jones and John Hughes, editors. *Haskell 98 — A Non-strict, Purely Functional Language*, February 1999. Available from http://www.haskell.org/definition/.

20. Berry Schoenmakers. Inorder traversal of a binary heap and its inversion in optimal time and space. In R.S. Bird, C.C. Morgan, and J.C.P Woodcock, editors, *Second International Conference on the Mathematics of Program Construction, Oxford*, volume 669 of *Lecture Notes in Computer Science*, pages 291–301. Springer, 1992.

21. Michael Sperber and Peter Thiemann. Generation of LR parsers by partial evaluation. *ACM Transactions on Programming Languages and Systems*, 22(3):224–264, 2000.

22. J.M. Spivey and S. Seres. Embedding Prolog in Haskell. In Erik Meijer, editor, *Proceedings of the 3rd Haskell Workshop, Paris, France*, September 1999. The proceedings appeared as a technical report of Universiteit Utrecht, UU-CS-1999-28.

23. H. Tamaki and T. Sato. Unfold/fold transformations of logic programs. In *Second International Conference on Logic Programming*, pages 127–138, 1984.

24. A. Tarski. A lattice-theoretic fixpoint theorem and its applications. *Pacific Journal of Mathematics*, 5:285–309, 1955.

25. Paul Taylor. *Practical Foundations of Mathematics*. Number 59 in Cambridge Studies in Advanced Mathematics. Cambridge University Press, 1999.

26. Jean Vuillemin. A unifying look at data structures. *Communications of the ACM*, 23:229–239, 1980.

27. Philip Wadler. Comprehending monads. In *Proceedings of the 1990 ACM Conference on LISP and Functional Programming, Nice*, pages 61–78. ACM-Press, June 1990.

Type-Indexed Data Types

Ralf Hinze[1,2], Johan Jeuring[2,3], and Andres Löh[2]

[1] Institut für Informatik III, Universität Bonn
Römerstraße 164, 53117 Bonn, Germany
`ralf@informatik.uni-bonn.de`
`http://www.informatik.uni-bonn.de/~ralf/`
[2] Institute of Information and Computing Sciences, Utrecht University
P.O.Box 80.089, 3508 TB Utrecht, The Netherlands
`{ralf,johanj,andres}@cs.uu.nl`
`http://www.cs.uu.nl/~{ralf,johanj,andres}`
[3] Open University, Heerlen, The Netherlands

Abstract. A polytypic function is a function that can be instantiated on many data types to obtain data type specific functionality. Examples of polytypic functions are the functions that can be derived in Haskell, such as *show*, *read*, and '=='. More advanced examples are functions for digital searching, pattern matching, unification, rewriting, and structure editing. For each of these problems, we not only have to define polytypic functionality, but also a *type-indexed data type*: a data type that is constructed in a generic way from an argument data type. For example, in the case of digital searching we have to define a search tree type by induction on the structure of the type of search keys. This paper shows how to define type-indexed data types, discusses several examples of type-indexed data types, and shows how to specialize type-indexed data types. The approach has been implemented in *Generic Haskell*, a generic programming extension of the functional language Haskell.

1 Introduction

A polytypic (or generic, type-indexed) function is a function that can be instantiated on many data types to obtain data type specific functionality. Examples of polytypic functions are the functions that can be derived in Haskell [31], such as *show*, *read*, and '=='. See Backhouse et al [1] for an introduction to polytypic programming.

More advanced examples of polytypic functions are functions for digital searching [11], pattern matching [22], unification [19,4], and rewriting [20]. For each of these problems, we not only have to define polytypic functionality, but also a *type-indexed data type*: a data type that is constructed in a generic way from an argument data type. For instance, in the case of digital searching we have to define a search tree type by induction on the structure of the type of search keys. Since current programming languages do not support type-indexed data types, the examples that appear in the literature are either implemented in an ad-hoc fashion [19], or not implemented at all [11].

E.A. Boiten and B. Möller (Eds.): MPC 2002, LNCS 2386, pp. 148–174, 2002.
© Springer-Verlag Berlin Heidelberg 2002

This paper shows how to define type-indexed data types, discusses several examples of type-indexed data types, and shows how to specialize type-indexed data types. The specialisation is illustrated with example translations to Haskell. The approach has been implemented in *Generic Haskell*, a generic programming extension of the functional language Haskell. The current version of Generic Haskell can be obtained from http://www.generic-haskell.org/.

Example 1: Digital Searching. A digital search tree or trie is a search tree scheme that employs the structure of search keys to organize information. Searching is useful for various data types, so we would like to allow for keys and information of any data type. This means that we have to construct a new kind of trie for each key type. For example, consider the data type *String* defined by[1]

$$\textbf{data } String = nil \mid cons \ Char \ String.$$

We can represent string-indexed tries with associated values of type V as follows:

$$\textbf{data } FMap\_String \ V = trie\_String \ (Maybe \ V) \ (FMap\_Char \ (FMap\_String \ V)).$$

Such a trie for strings would typically be used for a concordance or another index on texts. The first component of the constructor *trie_String* contains the value associated with *nil*. The second component of *trie_String* is derived from the constructor $cons :: Char \rightarrow String \rightarrow String$. We assume that a suitable data structure, *FMap_Char*, and an associated look-up function $lookup\_Char :: \forall V . Char \rightarrow FMap\_Char \ V \rightarrow Maybe \ V$ for characters are predefined. Given these prerequisites we can define a look-up function for strings as follows:

$$
\begin{aligned}
&lookup\_String :: String \rightarrow FMap\_String \ V \rightarrow Maybe \ V \\
&lookup\_String \ nil \ (trie\_String \ tn \ tc) = tn \\
&lookup\_String \ (cons \ c \ s) \ (trie\_String \ tn \ tc) \\
&\quad = (lookup\_Char \ c \ \Diamond \ lookup\_String \ s) \ tc.
\end{aligned}
$$

To look up a non-empty string, $cons \ c \ s$, we look up c in the *FMap_Char* obtaining a trie, which is then recursively searched for s. Since the look-up functions have result type *Maybe V*, we use the monadic composition of the *Maybe* monad, called '$\Diamond$', to compose *lookup_String* and *lookup_Char*.

$$
\begin{aligned}
&(\Diamond) :: (A \rightarrow Maybe \ B) \rightarrow (B \rightarrow Maybe \ C) \rightarrow A \rightarrow Maybe \ C \\
&(f \ \Diamond \ g) \ a = \textbf{case } f \ a \textbf{ of } \{ nothing \rightarrow nothing; just \ b \rightarrow g \ b \}.
\end{aligned}
$$

In the following section we will show how to define a trie and an associated look-up function for an arbitrary data type. The material is taken from Hinze [11], and it is repeated here because it serves as a nice and simple example of a type-indexed data type.

---

[1] The examples are given in Haskell [31]. Deviating from Haskell we use identifiers starting with an upper case letter for types (this includes type variables), and identifiers starting with a lower case letter for values (this includes data constructors).

Example 2: Pattern Matching. The polytypic functions for the maximum segment sum problem [2] and pattern matching [22] use labelled data types. These labelled data types, introduced in [2], are used to store at each node the subtree rooted at that node, or a set of patterns (trees with variables) matching at a subtree, etc. For example, the data type of labelled bushes is defined by

$$\textbf{data } Lab\_Bush \ L = label\_Leaf \ Char \ L$$
$$| \ \ label\_Fork \ (Lab\_Bush \ L) \ (Lab\_Bush \ L) \ L.$$

In the following section we show how to define such a labelled data type generically.

Example 3: Zipper. The zipper [16] is a data structure that is used to represent a tree together with a subtree that is the focus of attention, where that focus may move left, right, up, or down the tree. For example, the data type *Bush* and its corresponding zipper, called *Loc_Bush*, are defined by

$$\textbf{data } Bush \qquad = leaf \ Char \ | \ fork \ Bush \ Bush$$
$$\textbf{type } Loc\_Bush \quad = (Bush, Context\_Bush)$$
$$\textbf{data } Context\_Bush = top$$
$$| \ \ forkL \ Context\_Bush \ Bush$$
$$| \ \ forkR \ Bush \ Context\_Bush.$$

Using the type of locations we can efficiently navigate through a tree. For example:

$$down\_Bush \qquad\qquad\quad :: \ Loc\_Bush \rightarrow Loc\_Bush$$
$$down\_Bush \ (leaf \ a, c) \qquad = (leaf \ a, c)$$
$$down\_Bush \ (fork \ tl \ tr, c) \ = (tl, forkL \ c \ tr)$$
$$right\_Bush \qquad\qquad\qquad :: \ Loc\_Bush \rightarrow Loc\_Bush$$
$$right\_Bush \ (tl, forkL \ c \ tr) = (tr, forkR \ tl \ c)$$
$$right\_Bush \ l \qquad\qquad\quad\ = l.$$

The navigator function *down_Bush* moves the focus of attention to the *leftmost* subtree of the current node; *right_Bush* moves the focus to its right sibling.

Huet [16] defines the zipper data structure for rose trees and for the data type *Bush*, and gives the generic construction in words. In Section 5 we describe the zipper in more detail and show how to define a zipper for an arbitrary data type.

Other Examples. Besides these three examples, a number of other examples of type-indexed data types have appeared in the literature [3,10,9,33]. We expect that type-indexed data types will also be useful for generic DTD transformations [24]. Generally, we believe that type-indexed data types are just as important as type-indexed functions.

Background and Related Work. There is little related work on type-indexed data types. Type-indexed functions [25,2,28,8,17] were introduced more than a decade ago. There are several other approaches to type-indexed functions, see Dubois et al [7], Jay et al [21] and Yang [36], but none of them mentions user-defined type-indexed data types (Yang does mention value-indexed types, usually called dependent types).

Type-indexed data types, however, appear in the work on intensional type analysis [10,6,5,32,34]. Intensional type analysis is used in typed intermediate languages in compilers for polymorphic languages, among others to be able to optimize code for polymorphic functions. This work differs from our work in several aspects:

- typed intermediate languages are expressive, but rather complex languages not intended for programmers but for compiler writers;
- since Generic Haskell is built on top of Haskell, there is the problem of how to combine user-defined functions and data types with type-indexed functions and data types. This problem does not appear in typed intermediate languages;
- typed intermediate languages interpret (a representation of a) type argument at run-time, whereas the specialisation technique described in this paper does not require passing around (representations of) type arguments;
- typed intermediate languages are restricted to data types of kind $\star$. There are many examples where we want to lift this restriction, and define type-indexed data types also on higher-order kinded types.

Organisation. The rest of this paper is organised as follows. We will show how to define type-indexed data types in Section 2 using Hinze's approach to polytypic programming [13,14]. Section 3 illustrates the process of specialisation by means of example. Section 4 shows that type-indexed data types possess kind-indexed kinds, and gives a theoretical background for the specialisation of type-indexed data types and functions with arguments of type-indexed data types. Section 5 provides the details of the zipper example. Finally, Section 6 summaries the main points and concludes.

2   Defining Type-Indexed Data Types

This section shows how to define type-indexed data types. Section 2.1 briefly reviews the concepts of polytypic programming necessary for defining type-indexed data types. The subsequent sections define type-indexed data types for the problems described in the introduction. We assume a basic familiarity with Haskell's type system and in particular with the concept of kinds [27]. For a more thorough treatment the reader is referred to Hinze's work [14,13].

2.1   Type-Indexed Definitions

The central idea of polytypic programming (or type-indexed programming) is to provide the programmer with the ability to define a function by induction on the structure of types. Since Haskell's type language is rather involved—we have mutually recursive types, parameterised types, nested types, and type constructors of higher-order kinds—this sounds like a hard nut to crack. Fortunately, one can show that a polytypic function is uniquely defined by giving cases for primitive types and type constructors. For concreteness, let us assume that 1, *Char*, '+', and '×' are primitive, that is, the language of types of kind $\star$ is defined by the following grammar:

$$T_\star ::= 1 \mid Char \mid T_\star + T_\star \mid T_\star \times T_\star.$$

The unit type, sum and product types are required for modelling Haskell's **data** construct that introduces a sum of products. We treat these type constructors as if they were given by the following **data** declarations:

$$\textbf{data } 1 \qquad = ()$$
$$\textbf{data } A + B = inl\ A \mid inr\ B$$
$$\textbf{data } A \times B = (A, B).$$

Now, a polytypic function is simply given by a definition that is inductive on the structure of $T_\star$. As an example, here is the polytypic equality function. For emphasis, the type index is enclosed in angle brackets.

$$
\begin{aligned}
equal\langle T :: \star \rangle && :: T \to T \to Bool \\
equal\langle 1 \rangle\ ()\ () && = true \\
equal\langle Char \rangle\ c_1\ c_2 && = equalChar\ c_1\ c_2 \\
equal\langle T_1 + T_2 \rangle\ (inl\ a_1)\ (inl\ a_2) && = equal\langle T_1 \rangle\ a_1\ a_2 \\
equal\langle T_1 + T_2 \rangle\ (inl\ a_1)\ (inr\ b_2) && = false \\
equal\langle T_1 + T_2 \rangle\ (inr\ b_1)\ (inl\ a_2) && = false \\
equal\langle T_1 + T_2 \rangle\ (inr\ b_1)\ (inr\ b_2) && = equal\langle T_2 \rangle\ b_1\ b_2 \\
equal\langle T_1 \times T_2 \rangle\ (a_1, b_1)\ (a_2, b_2) && = equal\langle T_1 \rangle\ a_1\ a_2 \wedge equal\langle T_2 \rangle\ b_1\ b_2.
\end{aligned}
$$

This simple definition contains all ingredients needed to specialise *equal* for arbitrary data types. Note that the type language $T_\star$ does not contain constructions for type abstraction, application, and fixed points. Instances of polytypic functions on types with these constructions are generated automatically, see Section 4.

The type language $T_\star$ does not contain a construction for referring to constructor names either. Since we sometimes want to be able to refer to the name of a constructor, for example in a polytypic show function, we add one extra case to the type language: c **of** T, where c is a value of type *String* or another appropriate abstract data type for constructors, and T is a value of $T_\star$. For example, the Haskell data type of natural numbers

$$\textbf{data } Nat = zero \mid succ\ Nat$$

is represented in $T_\star$ by

$$Nat = zero \textbf{ of } 1 + succ \textbf{ of } Nat.$$

We adopt the convention that if the 'c **of** T' case is omitted in the definition of a polytypic function $poly$, we assume that $poly\langle c$ **of** $T\rangle = poly\langle T\rangle$.

The function $equal$ is indexed by types of kind $\star$. A polytypic function may also be indexed by type constructors of kind $\star \rightarrow \star$ (and, of course, by type constructors of other kinds, but these are not needed in the sequel). The language of types of kind $\star \rightarrow \star$ is characterised by the following grammar:

$$F_{\star \rightarrow \star} ::= Id \mid K\ 1 \mid K\ Char \mid F_{\star \rightarrow \star} + F_{\star \rightarrow \star} \mid F_{\star \rightarrow \star} \times F_{\star \rightarrow \star} \mid c\ \textbf{of}\ F_{\star \rightarrow \star},$$

where Id, $K\ T$ ($T = 1$ or $Char$), '+', '$\times$', and **of** are given by (note that we overload the symbols '+', '$\times$', and **of**)

$$
\begin{aligned}
Id &= \Lambda A.\,A \\
K\ T &= \Lambda A.\,T \\
F_1 + F_2 &= \Lambda A.\,F_1\ A + F_2\ A \\
F_1 \times F_2 &= \Lambda A.\,F_1\ A \times F_2\ A \\
c\ \textbf{of}\ F &= \Lambda A.\,c\ \textbf{of}\ F\ A.
\end{aligned}
$$

Here, $\Lambda A.\,T$ denotes abstraction on the type level. For example, the type of lists parameterised by some type is defined by $List = K\ 1 + Id \times List$. Again, $F_{\star \rightarrow \star}$ is used to describe the language on which we define polytypic functions by induction, it is not a complete description of all types of kind $\star \rightarrow \star$.

A well-known example of a ($\star \rightarrow \star$)-indexed function is the mapping function, which applies a given function to each element of type A in a given structure of type $F\ A$.

$$
\begin{aligned}
map\langle F :: \star \rightarrow \star\rangle &\quad :: \quad \forall A\ B.\,(A \rightarrow B) \rightarrow (F\ A \rightarrow F\ B) \\
map\langle Id\rangle\ m\ a &\quad = \quad m\ a \\
map\langle K\ 1\rangle\ m\ c &\quad = \quad c \\
map\langle K\ Char\rangle\ m\ c &\quad = \quad c \\
map\langle F_1 + F_2\rangle\ m\ (inl\ f) &\quad = \quad inl\ (map\langle F_1\rangle\ m\ f) \\
map\langle F_1 + F_2\rangle\ m\ (inr\ g) &\quad = \quad inr\ (map\langle F_2\rangle\ m\ g) \\
map\langle F_1 \times F_2\rangle\ m\ (f, g) &\quad = \quad (map\langle F_1\rangle\ m\ f, map\langle F_2\rangle\ m\ g).
\end{aligned}
$$

Using map we can, for instance, define generic versions of cata- and anamorphisms [29]. To this end we assume that data types are given as fixed points of so-called pattern functors. In Haskell the fixed point combinator can be defined as follows.

$$\textbf{newtype}\ Fix\ F = in\{\,out :: F\ (Fix\ F)\,\}.$$

For example, the type of naturals might have been defined by $Nat = Fix\ (K\ 1 + Id)$. Cata- and anamorphisms are then given by

$$
\begin{aligned}
cata\langle F :: \star \rightarrow \star\rangle &\ :: \quad \forall A.\,(F\ A \rightarrow A) \rightarrow (Fix\ F \rightarrow A) \\
cata\langle F\rangle\ \varphi &\ = \quad \varphi \cdot map\langle F\rangle\ (cata\langle F\rangle\ \varphi) \cdot out \\
ana\langle F :: \star \rightarrow \star\rangle &\ :: \quad \forall A.\,(A \rightarrow F\ A) \rightarrow (A \rightarrow Fix\ F) \\
ana\langle F\rangle\ \psi &\ = \quad in \cdot map\langle F\rangle\ (ana\langle F\rangle\ \psi) \cdot \psi.
\end{aligned}
$$

Note that both functions are parameterised by the type functor F rather than by the fixed point $Fix\ F$.

2.2   Tries

Tries are based on the following isomorphisms, also known as the laws of exponentials.

$$1 \to_{\text{fin}} V \cong V$$
$$(T_1 + T_2) \to_{\text{fin}} V \cong (T_1 \to_{\text{fin}} V) \times (T_2 \to_{\text{fin}} V)$$
$$(T_1 \times T_2) \to_{\text{fin}} V \cong T_1 \to_{\text{fin}} (T_2 \to_{\text{fin}} V)$$

Here, $T \to_{\text{fin}} V$ denotes a finite map. As $FMap\langle T \rangle\ V$, the generalisation of $FMap\_String$ given in the introduction, represents the set of finite maps from T to V, the isomorphisms above can be rewritten as defining equations for $FMap\langle T \rangle$.

$$
\begin{aligned}
FMap\langle T :: \star \rangle &\ ::\quad \star \to \star \\
FMap\langle 1 \rangle &= \Lambda V . \, Maybe\ V \\
FMap\langle Char \rangle &= \Lambda V . \, FMapChar\ V \\
FMap\langle T_1 + T_2 \rangle &= \Lambda V . \, FMap\langle T_1 \rangle\ V \times FMap\langle T_2 \rangle\ V \\
FMap\langle T_1 \times T_2 \rangle &= \Lambda V . \, FMap\langle T_1 \rangle\ (FMap\langle T_2 \rangle\ V)
\end{aligned}
$$

Note that $FMap\langle 1 \rangle$ is $Maybe$ rather than Id since we use the $Maybe$ monad for exception handling. We assume that a suitable data structure, $FMapChar$, and an associated look-up function $lookupChar :: \forall V . \, Char \to FMapChar\ V \to Maybe\ V$ for characters are predefined. The generic look-up function is then given by the following definition.

$$
\begin{aligned}
lookup\langle T :: \star \rangle &\qquad\qquad\quad ::\ \forall V . \, T \to FMap\langle T \rangle\ V \to Maybe\ V \\
lookup\langle 1 \rangle\ ()\ t &= t \\
lookup\langle Char \rangle\ c\ t &= lookupChar\ c\ t \\
lookup\langle T_1 + T_2 \rangle\ (inl\ k_1)\ (t_1, t_2) &= lookup\langle T_1 \rangle\ k_1\ t_1 \\
lookup\langle T_1 + T_2 \rangle\ (inr\ k_2)\ (t_1, t_2) &= lookup\langle T_2 \rangle\ k_2\ t_2 \\
lookup\langle T_1 \times T_2 \rangle\ (k_1, k_2)\ t &= (lookup\langle T_1 \rangle\ k_1 \diamond lookup\langle T_2 \rangle\ k_2)\ t.
\end{aligned}
$$

On sums the look-up function selects the appropriate map; on products it 'composes' the look-up functions for the component keys.

2.3   Labelling

A labelled data type is used to store information at the nodes of a tree. The kind of information that is stored varies from application to application: in the case of the maximum segment sum it is the subtree rooted at that node, in the case of pattern matching it is the set of patterns matching at that node. We will show how to define such labelled data types in this section. The data type $Labelled$ labels a data type given by a so-called pattern functor:

$$
\begin{aligned}
Labelled\langle F :: \star \to \star \rangle &\ ::\quad \star \to \star \\
Labelled\langle F \rangle &= \Lambda L . \, Fix\ (\Lambda R . \, Label\langle F \rangle\ L\ R).
\end{aligned}
$$

The type-indexed data type *Label* distributes the label type over the sum, and adds a label type L to each other construct. Since each construct is guarded by a constructor (c **of** F), it suffices to add labels to constructors.

$$
\begin{aligned}
Label\langle F :: \star \to \star \rangle &:: \quad \star \to \star \to \star \\
Label\langle F_1 + F_2 \rangle &= \quad \Lambda L\ R\,.\,Label\langle F_1 \rangle\ L\ R + Label\langle F_2 \rangle\ L\ R \\
Label\langle c\ \textbf{of}\ F \rangle &= \quad \Lambda L\ R\,.\,F\ R \times L.
\end{aligned}
$$

The type-indexed function *suffixes* labels a value of a data type with the subtree rooted at each node. It uses a helper function *add*, which adds a label to a value of type $F\ T$, returning a value of type $Label\langle F \rangle\ L\ T$.

$$
\begin{aligned}
add\langle F :: \star \to \star \rangle &\qquad :: \quad \forall L\ T\,.\,L \to F\ T \to Label\langle F \rangle\ L\ T \\
add\langle F_1 + F_2 \rangle\ l\ (inl\ x) &= \quad inl\ (add\langle F_1 \rangle\ l\ x) \\
add\langle F_1 + F_2 \rangle\ l\ (inr\ y) &= \quad inr\ (add\langle F_2 \rangle\ l\ y) \\
add\langle c\ \textbf{of}\ F \rangle\ l\ x &= \quad (x, l).
\end{aligned}
$$

The function *suffixes* is then defined as a recursive function that adds the subtrees rooted at each level to the tree. It adds the argument tree to the top level, and applies *suffixes* to the children by means of function *map*.

$$
\begin{aligned}
suffixes\langle F :: \star \to \star \rangle &:: \quad Fix\ F \to Labelled\langle F \rangle\ (Fix\ F) \\
suffixes\langle F \rangle\ l@(in\ t) &= in\ (add\langle F \rangle\ l\ (map\langle F \rangle\ (suffixes\langle F \rangle)\ t)).
\end{aligned}
$$

3   Examples of Translations to Haskell

The semantics of type-indexed data types will be given by means of specialisation. This section gives some examples as an introduction to the formal rules provided in the following section.

We illustrate the main ideas by translating the digital search tree example to Haskell. This translation shows in particular how type-indexed data types are specialised in Generic Haskell: the Haskell code given here will be automatically generated by the Generic Haskell compiler. The example is structured into three sections: a translation of data types, a translation of type-indexed data types, and a translation of type-indexed functions that take type-indexed data types as arguments.

3.1   Translating Data Types

In general, a type-indexed function is translated to several functions: one for each user-defined data type on which it is used. These instances work on a slightly different, but isomorphic data type, that is close to the type language $T_\star$ and reveals the structure of the Haskell data type. This implies, of course, that values of user-defined data types have to be translated to these isomorphic data types. For example, the type *Nat* of natural numbers defined by

$$\textbf{data}\ Nat = zero\ |\ succ\ Nat,$$

is translated to the following type (in which *Nat* itself still appears), together with two conversion functions.

$$
\begin{aligned}
&\textbf{type } \mathit{Nat'} &&= 1 + \mathit{Nat} \\
&\mathit{from\_Nat} &&:: \mathit{Nat} \to \mathit{Nat'} \\
&\mathit{from\_Nat\ zero} &&= \mathit{inl}\ () \\
&\mathit{from\_Nat}\ (\mathit{succ}\ x) &&= \mathit{inr}\ x \\
\\
&\mathit{to\_Nat} &&:: \mathit{Nat'} \to \mathit{Nat} \\
&\mathit{to\_Nat}\ (\mathit{inl}\ ()) &&= \mathit{zero} \\
&\mathit{to\_Nat}\ (\mathit{inr}\ x) &&= \mathit{succ}\ x.
\end{aligned}
$$

This mapping avoids direct recursion by adding the extra layer of *Nat'*. [2]

For convenience, we collect the conversion functions together in an embedding-projection pair:

$$
\begin{aligned}
&\textbf{data } \mathit{EP}\ a\ b = \mathit{EP}\{\mathit{from} :: a \to b, \mathit{to} :: b \to a\} \\
&\mathit{ep\_Nat} &&:: \mathit{EP}\ \mathit{Nat}\ \mathit{Nat'} \\
&\mathit{ep\_Nat} &&= \mathit{EP}\ \mathit{from\_Nat}\ \mathit{to\_Nat}.
\end{aligned}
$$

3.2   Translating Type-Indexed Data Types

A type-indexed data type is translated to several **newtype**s in Haskell: one for each type case in its definition. The translation proceeds in a similar fashion as in Hinze [14], but now for types instead of values. For example, the product case $T_1 \times T_2$ takes two argument types for T_1 and T_2, and returns the type for the product. Recall the type-indexed data type *FMap* defined by

$$
\begin{aligned}
\mathit{FMap}\langle 1 \rangle &= \Lambda V.\mathit{Maybe}\ V \\
\mathit{FMap}\langle \mathit{Char} \rangle &= \Lambda V.\mathit{FMapChar}\ V \\
\mathit{FMap}\langle T_1 + T_2 \rangle &= \Lambda V.\mathit{FMap}\langle T_1 \rangle\ V \times \mathit{FMap}\langle T_2 \rangle\ V \\
\mathit{FMap}\langle T_1 \times T_2 \rangle &= \Lambda V.\mathit{FMap}\langle T_1 \rangle\ (\mathit{FMap}\langle T_2 \rangle\ V).
\end{aligned}
$$

These equations are translated to:

$$
\begin{aligned}
&\textbf{newtype } \mathit{FMap\_Unit}\ V &&= \mathit{fMap\_Unit}\ (\mathit{Maybe}\ V) \\
&\textbf{newtype } \mathit{FMap\_Char}\ V &&= \mathit{fMap\_Char}\ (\mathit{FMapChar}\ V) \\
&\textbf{newtype } \mathit{FMap\_Either}\ \mathit{FMA}\ \mathit{FMB}\ V &&= \mathit{fMap\_Either}\ (\mathit{FMA}\ V, \mathit{FMB}\ V) \\
&\textbf{newtype } \mathit{FMap\_Product}\ \mathit{FMA}\ \mathit{FMB}\ V &&= \mathit{fMap\_Product}\ (\mathit{FMA}\ (\mathit{FMB}\ V)).
\end{aligned}
$$

---

[2] Furthermore, the mapping translates n-ary products and sums to binary products and sums. This is revealed by looking at a more complex data type, for instance

$$\textbf{data } \mathit{Tree}\ A = \quad \mathit{empty} \mid \mathit{node}\ (\mathit{Tree}\ A)\ A\ (\mathit{Tree}\ A)$$

where the constructor *node* takes three arguments. The isomorphic type generated for *Tree* is

$$\textbf{data } \mathit{Tree'}\ a = \ 1 + \mathit{Tree}\ A \times (A \times \mathit{Tree}\ A).$$

Finally, for each data type on which we want to use a trie we generate a suitable instance.

type *FMap_Nat' V*   =   *fMap_Either FMap_Unit FMap_Nat V*
newtype *FMap_Nat V* =   *fMap_Nat{ unFMap_Nat :: FMap_Nat' V }.*

Note that we use **newtype** for *FMap_Nat* because it is not possible to define recursive **type**s in Haskell. The types *FMap_Nat* and *FMap_Nat'* can easily be converted into each other by means of the following embedding-projection pair:

$$ep\_FMap\_Nat \; :: \; EP \; (FMap\_Nat \; V) \; (FMap\_Nat' \; V)$$
$$ep\_FMap\_Nat = EP \; unFMap\_Nat \; fMap\_Nat.$$

3.3   Translating Type-Indexed Functions on Type-Indexed Data Types

The translation of a type-indexed function that takes a type-indexed data type as an argument is a generalisation of the translation of 'ordinary' type-indexed functions. The translation consists of two parts: a translation of the type-indexed function itself, and a specialisation on each data type on which the type-indexed function is used, together with a conversion function.

A type-indexed function is translated by generating a function, together with its type signature, for each line of its definition. For the type indices of kind $\star$ (i.e. 1 and *Char*) we generate types that are instances of the type of the generic function. The occurrences of the type index are replaced by the instance type, and occurrences of type-indexed data types are replaced by the translation of the type-indexed data type on the type index. As an example, for the generic function *lookup* of type:

$$lookup\langle T :: \star \rangle \; :: \; \forall V \,.\, T \to FMap\langle T \rangle \; V \to Maybe \; V,$$

the instances are obtained by replacing T by 1 or *Char*, and by replacing $FMap\langle T \rangle$ by *FMap_Unit* or *FMap_Char*, respectively. So, for the function *lookup* we have that the user-supplied equations

$$lookup\langle 1 \rangle \; () \; t \quad = \quad t$$
$$lookup\langle Char \rangle \; c \; t = \quad lookupChar \; c \; t,$$

are translated into

$lookup\_Unit$ $:: \; \forall V \,.\, 1 \to FMap\_Unit \; V \to Maybe \; V$
$lookup\_Unit \; () \; (fMapUnit \; t) = \; t$

$lookup\_Char$ $:: \; \forall V \,.\, Char \to FMap\_Char \; V \to Maybe \; V$
$lookup\_Char \; c \; (fMapChar \; t) = \; lookupChar \; c \; t.$

Note that we add the constructors for the tries to the trie arguments of the function.

For the type indices of kind $\star \to \star \to \star$ (i.e. '+' and '×') we generate types that take two functions as arguments, corresponding to the instances of the generic function on the arguments of '+' and '×', and return a function of the combined type, see Hinze [14]. For example, the following lines

$$
\begin{aligned}
lookup\langle T_1 + T_2\rangle \ (inl \ k_1) \ (t_1, t_2) &= \ lookup\langle T_1\rangle \ k_1 \ t_1 \\
lookup\langle T_1 + T_2\rangle \ (inr \ k_2) \ (t_1, t_2) &= \ lookup\langle T_2\rangle \ k_2 \ t_2 \\
lookup\langle T_1 \times T_2\rangle \ (k_1, k_2) \ t \quad &= \ (lookup\langle T_1\rangle \ k_1 \ \diamond \ lookup\langle T_2\rangle \ k_2) \ t
\end{aligned}
$$

are translated into the following functions

$$
\begin{aligned}
lookup\_Either :: \forall A \ FMA \ . \ \forall B \ FMB \ . \\
(\forall V \ . \ A \to FMA \ V \to Maybe \ V) \\
\to (\forall V \ . \ B \to FMB \ V \to Maybe \ V) \\
\to (\forall V \ . \ A + B \to FMap\_Either \ FMA \ FMB \ V \to Maybe \ V)
\end{aligned}
$$

$$
\begin{aligned}
lookup\_Either \ lua \ lub \ (inl \ a) \ (fMap\_Either \ (fma, fmb)) &= lua \ a \ fma \\
lookup\_Either \ lua \ lub \ (inr \ b) \ (fMap\_Either \ (fma, fmb)) &= lub \ b \ fmb
\end{aligned}
$$

$$
\begin{aligned}
lookup\_Product :: \forall A \ FMA \ . \ \forall B \ FMB \ . \\
(\forall V \ . \ A \to FMA \ V \to Maybe \ V) \\
\to (\forall V \ . \ B \to FMB \ V \to Maybe \ V) \\
\to (\forall V \ . \ A \times B \to FMap\_Product \ FMA \ FMB \ V \to Maybe \ V)
\end{aligned}
$$

$$
lookup\_Product \ lua \ lub \ (a, b) \ (fMap\_Product \ t) \qquad = (lua \ a \ \diamond \ lub \ b) \ t.
$$

These functions are obtained from the definition of *lookup* by replacing the occurrences of the *lookup* function in the right-hand sides by their corresponding arguments.

Finally, we generate a specialisation of the type-indexed function for each data type on which it is used. For example, on *Nat* we have

$$
\begin{aligned}
lookup\_Nat &:: \forall V \ . \ Nat \to FMap\_Nat \ V \to Maybe \ V \\
lookup\_Nat &= conv\_Lookup\_Nat \ (lookup\_Either \ lookup\_Unit \ lookup\_Nat).
\end{aligned}
$$

The argument of function *conv_Lookup_Nat* (defined below) is generated directly from the type *Nat'*. Finally, for each instance we have to generate a conversion function like *conv_Lookup_Nat*. In general, the conversion function converts a type-indexed function that works on the translated isomorphic data type to a function that works on the original data type. As an example, the function *conv_Lookup_Nat* converts a *lookup* function on the internal data type *Nat'* to a *lookup* function on the type of natural numbers itself.

$$
\begin{aligned}
conv\_Lookup\_Nat \quad &:: (\forall V \ . \ Nat' \to FMap\_Nat' \ V \to Maybe \ V) \\
&\to (\forall V \ . \ Nat \to FMap\_Nat \ V \to Maybe \ V) \\
conv\_Lookup\_Nat \ lu &= \lambda t \ fmt \to lu \ (from\_Nat \ t) \ (unFMap\_Nat \ fmt)
\end{aligned}
$$

Note that the functions *to_Nat* and *fMap_Nat* are not used on the right-hand side of the definition of *conv_Lookup_Nat*. This is because no values of type *Nat* or *FMap_Nat* are built for the result of the function. If the result of the type-indexed function consisted of values of the type index or of the type-indexed data type, these functions would be applied at the appropriate positions.

3.4   Implementing *FMap* in Haskell Directly

Alternatively, we can use multi-parameter type classes and functional dependencies [23] to implement a type-indexed data type such as *FMap* in Haskell. An example is given in Figure 1. However, to use this implementation we would have to marshal and unmarshal user-defined data types and values of user-defined data types by hand. Furthermore, this approach does not work for all types of all kinds.

```
class FMap fma a | a → fma where
    lookup                          :: a → fma v → Maybe v
instance FMap Maybe () where
    lookup () fm                    = fm
data Pair f g a                     = Pair (f a) (g a)
instance (FMap fma a, FMap fmb b) ⇒ FMap (Pair fma fmb) (Either a b) where
    lookup (Left a) (Pair fma fmb)  = lookup a fma
    lookup (Right b) (Pair fma fmb) = lookup b fmb
data Comp f g a                     = Comp (f (g a))
instance (FMap fma a, FMap fmb b) ⇒ FMap (Comp fma fmb) (a, b) where
    lookup (a, b) (Comp fma)        = (lookup a ◇ lookup b) fma
```

Fig. 1. Implementing *FMap* in Haskell directly

4   Specialising Type-Indexed Types and Values

This section gives a formal semantics of type-indexed data types by means of specialisation. Examples of this translation have been given in the previous section. The specialisation to concrete data type instances removes the type arguments of type-indexed data types and functions. In other words, type-indexed data types and functions can be used at no run-time cost, since all type arguments are removed at compile-time. The specialisation can be seen as partial evaluation of type-indexed functions where the type index is the static argument. The specialisation is obtained by lifting the semantic description of type-indexed functions given in Hinze [12] to the level of data types.

Type-indexed data types and type-indexed functions take types as arguments, and return types and functions. For the formal description of type-indexed data types and functions and for their semantics we use an extension of the polymorphic lambda calculus, described in Section 4.1. Section 4.2 briefly discusses the form of type-indexed definitions. The description of the specialisation is divided in two parts: Section 4.3 deals with the specialisation of type-indexed data types, and Section 4.4 deals with the specialisation of type-indexed functions that take type-indexed data types as arguments. Section 4.5 describes how the gap between the formal type language and Haskell's data types can be bridged.

4.1   The Polymorphic Lambda Calculus

This section briefly introduces kinds, types, type schemes, and terms.

Kind terms are formed by:

$$\mathfrak{T}, \mathfrak{U} \in \textit{Kind} ::= \star \qquad\qquad\quad \text{kind of types}$$
$$| \quad (\mathfrak{T} \to \mathfrak{U}) \qquad \text{function kind.}$$

We distinguish between type terms and type schemes: the language of type terms comprises the types that may appear as type indices; the language of type schemes comprises the constructs that are required for the translation of generic definitions (such as polymorphic types).

Type terms are built from type constants and type variables using type application and type abstraction.

$$
\begin{aligned}
T, U \in \textit{Type} ::= {}& C && \text{type constant} \\
| {}& A && \text{type variable} \\
| {}& (\varLambda A :: \mathfrak{U} . \, T) && \text{type abstraction} \\
| {}& (T \; U) && \text{type application}
\end{aligned}
$$

For typographic simplicity, we will often omit the kind annotation in $\varLambda A :: \mathfrak{U} . \, T$ (especially if $\mathfrak{U} = \star$) and we abbreviate nested abstractions $\varLambda A_1 . \ldots . \varLambda A_m . \, T$ by $\varLambda A_1 \ldots A_m . \, T$.

In order to be able to model Haskell's data types the set of type constants should include at least the types 1, *Char*, '+', '×', and '*c* **of**' for all known constructors in the program. Furthermore, it should include a family of fixed point operators indexed by kind: $\textit{Fix}_\mathfrak{T} :: (\mathfrak{T} \to \mathfrak{T}) \to \mathfrak{T}$. In the examples, we will often omit the kind annotation $\mathfrak{T}$ in $\textit{Fix}_\mathfrak{T}$. We may additionally add the function space constructor '$\to$' or universal quantifiers $\forall_\mathfrak{U} :: (\mathfrak{U} \to \star) \to \star$ to the set of type constants (see Section 4.5 for an example).

Note that both type languages we have introduced in Section 2.1, $T_\star$ and $F_{\star \to \star}$, are subsumed by this type language.

Type schemes are formed by:

$$
\begin{aligned}
R, S \in \textit{Scheme} ::= {}& T && \text{type term} \\
| {}& (R \to S) && \text{functional type} \\
| {}& (\forall A :: \mathfrak{U} . \, S) && \text{polymorphic type.}
\end{aligned}
$$

Terms are formed by:

$$
\begin{aligned}
t, u \in \textit{Term} ::= {}& c && \text{constant} \\
| {}& a && \text{variable} \\
| {}& (\lambda a :: S . \, t) && \text{abstraction} \\
| {}& (t \; u) && \text{application} \\
| {}& (\lambda A :: \mathfrak{U} . \, t) && \text{universal abstraction} \\
| {}& (t \; R) && \text{universal application.}
\end{aligned}
$$

Here, $\lambda A :: \mathfrak{U} . t$ denotes universal abstraction (forming a polymorphic value) and $t\ R$ denotes universal application (instantiating a polymorphic value). We use the same syntax for value abstraction $\lambda a :: S . t$ (here a is a value variable) and universal abstraction $\lambda A :: \mathfrak{U} . t$ (here A is a type variable). We assume that the set of value constants includes at least the polymorphic fixed point operator

$$fix :: \forall A . (A \rightarrow A) \rightarrow A$$

and suitable functions for each of the other type constants (such as () for '1', inl, inr, and **case** for '+', and $outl$, $outr$, and (,) for '×'). To improve readability we will usually omit the type argument of fix.

We omit the standard typing rules for the polymorphic lambda calculus.

4.2   On the Form of Type-Indexed Definitions

The type-indexed definitions given in Section 2 implicitly define a catamorphism on the language of types. For the specialisation we have to make these catamorphisms explicit. This section describes the different views on type-indexed definitions.

Almost all inductive definitions of type-indexed functions and data types given in Section 2 take the form of a catamorphism:

$$
\begin{aligned}
cata\langle 1 \rangle &= cata_1 \\
cata\langle Char \rangle &= cata_{Char} \\
cata\langle T_1 + T_2 \rangle &= cata_+ \ (cata\langle T_1 \rangle) \ (cata\langle T_2 \rangle) \\
cata\langle T_1 \times T_2 \rangle &= cata_\times \ (cata\langle T_1 \rangle) \ (cata\langle T_2 \rangle) \\
cata\langle c \ \mathbf{of} \ T_1 \rangle &= cata_{c \ \mathbf{of}} \ (cata\langle T_1 \rangle).
\end{aligned}
$$

These equations implicitly define the family of functions $cata_1$, $cata_{Char}$, $cata_+$, $cata_\times$, and $cata_{c \ \mathbf{of}}$. In the sequel, we will assume that type-indexed functions and data types are explicitly defined as a catamorphism. For example, for digital search trees we have

$$
\begin{aligned}
FMap_1 &= \Lambda V . Maybe \ V \\
FMap_{Char} &= \Lambda V . FMapChar \ V \\
FMap_+ &= \Lambda FMap_A \ FMap_B \ V . FMap_A \ V \times FMap_B \ V \\
FMap_\times &= \Lambda FMap_A \ FMap_B \ V . FMap_A \ (FMap_B \ V) \\
FMap_{c \ \mathbf{of}} &= \Lambda FMap_A \ V . FMap_A \ V .
\end{aligned}
$$

Some inductive definitions, such as the definition of $Label$, also use the argument types themselves in their right-hand sides. Such functions are called paramorphisms [28], and are characterized by:

$$
\begin{aligned}
para\langle 1 \rangle &= para_1 \\
para\langle Char \rangle &= para_{Char} \\
para\langle T_1 + T_2 \rangle &= para_+ \ T_1 \ T_2 \ (para\langle T_1 \rangle) \ (para\langle T_2 \rangle) \\
para\langle T_1 \times T_2 \rangle &= para_\times \ T_1 \ T_2 \ (para\langle T_1 \rangle) \ (para\langle T_2 \rangle) \\
para\langle c \ \mathbf{of} \ T_1 \rangle &= para_{c \ \mathbf{of}} \ T_1 \ (para\langle T_1 \rangle).
\end{aligned}
$$

Fortunately, every paramorphism can be transformed into a catamorphism by tupling it with the identity. Likewise, mutually recursive definitions can be transformed into simple catamorphisms using tupling.

Section 4.3 below describes how to specialise type-indexed data types with type indices that appear in the set C of type constants: 1, *Char*, '+', '×', and 'c **of**'. However, we have also used the type indices *Id*, *K* 1, *K Char*, and lifted versions of '+' and '×'. How are type-indexed data types with these type indices specialised? The specialisation of type-indexed data types with higher-order type indices proceeds in much the same fashion as in the following section. Essentially, the process only has to be lifted to higher-order type indices. For the details of of this lifting process see Hinze [12].

4.3   Specialising Type-Indexed Data Types

Rather amazingly, the process of specialisation can be phrased as an interpretation of the simply typed lambda calculus. The interpretation of the constants (1, *Char*, '+', '×', and 'c **of**') is obtained from the definition of the type-indexed data type as a catamorphism. The remaining constructs are interpreted generically: type application is interpreted as type application (albeit in a different domain), abstraction as abstraction, and fixed points as fixed points.

The first thing we have to do is to generalise the 'type' of a type-indexed data type. In the previous sections, the type-indexed data types had a fixed kind, for example, $FMap_{T::\star} :: \star \to \star$. However, when type application is interpreted as application, we have that $FMap_{List\ A} = FMap_{List}\ FMap_A$. Since *List* is of kind $\star \to \star$, we have to extend the domain of *FMap* by giving it a kind-indexed kind, in such a way that $FMap_{List} :: (\star \to \star) \to (\star \to \star)$.

Generalising the above example, we have that a type-indexed data type possesses a kind-indexed kind:

$$Data_{T::\mathfrak{T}} :: \mathfrak{Data}_{\mathfrak{T}},$$

where $\mathfrak{Data}_{\mathfrak{T}}$ has the following form:

$$\mathfrak{Data}_{\mathfrak{T}::\square} \quad :: \ \square$$
$$\mathfrak{Data}_{\star} \quad = \boxed{}$$
$$\mathfrak{Data}_{\mathfrak{A}\to\mathfrak{B}} = \mathfrak{Data}_{\mathfrak{A}} \to \mathfrak{Data}_{\mathfrak{B}}.$$

Here, '$\square$' is the superkind: the type of kinds. Note that only the definition of $\mathfrak{Data}_{\star}$, as indicated by the box, has to be given to complete the definition of the kind-indexed kind. The definition of $\mathfrak{Data}$ on functional kinds is dictated by the specialisation process. Since type application is interpreted by type application, the kind of a type with a functional kind is functional.

For example, the kind of the type-indexed data type $FMap_T$, where T is a type of kind $\star$ is:

$$\mathfrak{FMap}_{\star} = \star \to \star.$$

As noted above, the process of specialisation is phrased as an interpretation of the simply typed lambda calculus. The interpretation of the constants (1, *Char*,

'+', '×', and 'c **of**') is obtained from the definition of the type-indexed data type as a catamorphism, and the interpretation of application, abstraction, and fixed points is given via an environment model [30] for the type-indexed data type.

An environment model is an applicative structure (**M**, **app**, **const**), where **M** is the domain of the structure, **app** a mapping that interprets functions, and **const** maps constants to the domain of the structure. Furthermore, in order to qualify as an environment model, an applicative structure has to be extensional and must satisfy the so-called combinatory model condition. The precise definitions of these concepts can be found in Mitchell [30]. For an arbitrary type-indexed data type $Data_{T::\mathfrak{T}} :: \mathfrak{Data}_{\mathfrak{T}}$ we use the following applicative structure:

$$
\begin{aligned}
\mathbf{M}^{\mathfrak{T}} &= Type^{\mathfrak{Data}_{\mathfrak{T}}} / \mathcal{E} \\
\mathbf{app}_{\mathfrak{T},\mathfrak{U}}\,[\,T\,]\,[\,U\,] &= [\,T\ U\,] \\
\mathbf{const}(C) &= [\,Data_{C}\,].
\end{aligned}
$$

The domain of the applicative structure for a kind $\mathfrak{T}$ is the equivalence class of the set of types of kind $\mathfrak{Data}_{\mathfrak{T}}$, under an appropriate set of equations $\mathcal{E}$ between type terms (e.g. $F\ (Fix_{\mathfrak{T}}\ F) = Fix_{\mathfrak{T}}\ F$ for all kinds $\mathfrak{T}$ and type constructors F of kind $\mathfrak{T} \to \mathfrak{T}$). The application of two equivalence classes of types (denoted by $[\,T\,]$ and $[\,U\,]$) is the equivalence class of the application of the types. The definition of the constants is obtained from the definition as a catamorphism. It can be verified that the applicative structure defined thus is an environment model.

It remains to specify the interpretation of the fixed point operators, which is the same for all type-indexed data types:

$$
\mathbf{const}(Fix_{\mathfrak{T}}) - [\,Fix_{\mathfrak{Data}_{\mathfrak{T}}}\,].
$$

4.4   Specialising Type-Indexed Values

A type-indexed value possesses a kind-indexed type [14],

$$
poly_{T::\mathfrak{T}} :: Poly_{\mathfrak{T}}\ Data_{T}^{1}\ \ldots\ Data_{T}^{n}
$$

in which $Poly_{\mathfrak{T}}$ has the following general form

$$
\begin{aligned}
Poly_{\mathfrak{T}::\mathfrak{U}} &:: \mathfrak{Data}_{\mathfrak{T}}^{1} \ \cdots \to \mathfrak{Dulu}_{\mathfrak{T}}^{n} \to \star \\
Poly_{\star} &= \Lambda X_1 :: \mathfrak{Data}_{\star}^{1}.\ \ldots\ .\Lambda X_n :: \mathfrak{Data}_{\star}^{n}.\ \boxed{} \\
Poly_{\mathfrak{A}\to\mathfrak{B}} &= \Lambda X_1 :: \mathfrak{Data}_{\mathfrak{A}\to\mathfrak{B}}^{1}.\ \ldots\ .\Lambda X_n :: \mathfrak{Data}_{\mathfrak{A}\to\mathfrak{B}}^{n}. \\
&\quad \forall A_1 :: \mathfrak{Data}_{\mathfrak{A}}^{1}.\ \ldots\ .\forall A_n :: \mathfrak{Data}_{\mathfrak{A}}^{n}. \\
&\quad\quad Poly_{\mathfrak{A}}\ A_1\ \ldots\ A_n \to Poly_{\mathfrak{B}}\ (X_1\ A_1)\ \ldots\ (X_n\ A_n).
\end{aligned}
$$

Again, note that only an equation for $Poly_{\star}$ has to be given to complete the definition of the kind-indexed type. The definition of $Poly$ on functional kinds is dictated by the specialisation process. The presence of type-indexed data types slightly complicates the type of a type-indexed value. In Hinze [14] $Poly_{\mathfrak{T}}$ takes

n arguments of type $\mathfrak{T}$. Here $Poly_\mathfrak{T}$ takes n possibly different type arguments obtained from the type-indexed data type arguments. For example, for the look-up function we have:

$$Lookup_{\mathfrak{T}::\square} :: \mathfrak{Id}_\mathfrak{T} \to \mathfrak{FMap}_\mathfrak{T} \to \star$$
$$Lookup_\star = \Lambda K . \Lambda FMK . \forall V . K \to FMK \ V \to Maybe \ V,$$

where $\mathfrak{Id}$ is the identity function on kinds. From the definition of the generic look-up function we obtain the following equations:

$$lookup_{T::\mathfrak{T}} :: Lookup_\mathfrak{T} \ Id_T \ FMap_T$$
$$lookup_1 = \lambda V \ k \ fmk . fmk$$
$$lookup_{Char} = lookupChar$$
$$lookup_+ = \lambda A \ FMA \ lookup_A . \lambda B \ FMB \ lookup_B .$$
$$\lambda V \ k \ (fmkl, fmkr) . \mathbf{case} \ k \ \mathbf{of} \ \{ inl \ a \to lookup_A \ V \ a \ fmkl;$$
$$inr \ b \to lookup_B \ V \ b \ fmkr \}$$
$$lookup_\times = \lambda A \ FMA \ lookup_A . \lambda B \ FMB \ lookup_B .$$
$$\lambda V \ (kl, kr) \ fmk . (lookup_A \ V \ kl \diamond lookup_B \ V \ kr) \ fmk$$
$$lookup_{c \ \mathbf{of}} = \lambda A \ FMA \ lookup_A . \lambda V \ k \ fmk . lookup_A \ V \ k \ fmk.$$

Just as with type-indexed data types, type-indexed values on type-indexed data types are specialised by means of an interpretation of the simply typed lambda calculus. The environment model used for the specialisation is somewhat more involved than the one given in Section 4.3. The domain of the environment model is a dependent product: the type of the last component (the equivalence class of the terms of type $Poly_\mathfrak{T} \ D_1 \ ... \ D_n$) depends on the first n components (the equivalence classes of the type schemes $D_1 \ ... \ D_n$ of kind $\mathfrak{T}$). Note that the application operator applies the term component of its first argument to both the type and the term components of the second argument.

$$\mathbf{M}^\mathfrak{T} = ([D_1] \in Scheme^{\mathfrak{Data}^1_\mathfrak{T}} / \mathcal{E}, \ldots, [D_n] \in Scheme^{\mathfrak{Data}^n_\mathfrak{T}} / \mathcal{E};$$
$$Term^{Poly_\mathfrak{T} \ D_1 \ ... \ D_n} / \mathcal{E})$$
$$\mathbf{app}_{\mathfrak{T},\mathfrak{U}} ([R_1], \ldots, [R_n]; [t]) \ ([S_1], \ldots, [S_n]; [u])$$
$$= ([R_1 \ S_1], \ldots, [R_n \ S_n]; [t \ S_1 \ ... \ S_n \ u])$$
$$\mathbf{const}(C) = ([Data^1_C], \ldots, [Data^n_C]; [poly_C]).$$

Again, the interpretation of fixed points is the same for different type-indexed values:

$$\mathbf{const}(Fix_\mathfrak{T}) = ([Fix_{\mathfrak{Data}^1_\mathfrak{T}}], \ldots, [Fix_{\mathfrak{Data}^n_\mathfrak{T}}]; [poly_{Fix_\mathfrak{T}}]),$$

where $poly_{Fix_\mathfrak{T}}$ is given by

$$poly_{Fix_\mathfrak{T}} = \lambda F_1 \ ... \ F_n . \lambda poly_F :: Poly_{\mathfrak{T}\to\mathfrak{T}} \ F_1 \ ... \ F_n .$$
$$fix \ poly_F \ (Fix_{\mathfrak{Data}^1_\mathfrak{T}} \ F_1) \ ... \ (Fix_{\mathfrak{Data}^n_\mathfrak{T}} \ F_n).$$

4.5   Conversion Functions

As can be seen in the example of Section 3, we do not interpret type-indexed functions and data types on Haskell data types directly, but rather on slightly different, yet isomorphic types. Furthermore, since Haskell does not allow recursive type synonyms, we must introduce a **newtype** for each specialisation of a type-indexed data type, thereby again creating a different, but isomorphic type from the one we are interested in. As a consequence, we have to generate conversion functions between these isomorphic types.

These conversion functions are easily generated, both for type-indexed values and data types, and can be stored in embedding-projection pairs. The only difficult task is to plug them in at the right positions. This problem is solved by lifting the conversion functions to the type of the specialised generic function. This again is a generic program [12], which makes use of the $bimap$ function displayed in Figure 2.

$$
\begin{aligned}
&Bimap_{\mathfrak{T}::\Box} \;::\; \mathfrak{Iso}_\mathfrak{T} \to \mathfrak{Iso}_\mathfrak{T} \to \star \\
&Bimap_\star \;\;\;= \Lambda T_1 . \Lambda T_2 . EP \; T_1 \; T_2 \\[4pt]
&bimap_{T::\mathfrak{T}} \;::\; Bimap_\mathfrak{T} \; Id_T \; Id_T \\
&bimap_1 \;\;\;= EP \; id \; id \\
&bimap_{Char} = EP \; id \; id \\
&bimap_+ \;\;\;= \lambda A_1 \; A_2 \; bimap_A . \lambda B_1 \; B_2 \; bimap_B . \\
&\qquad\qquad EP \; (\lambda ab \to \textbf{case } ab \textbf{ of } \{\, inl \; a \to (inl . from \; bimap_A) \; a; \\
&\qquad\qquad\qquad\qquad\qquad\qquad\qquad\quad inr \; b \to (inr . from \; bimap_B) \; b\,\}) \\
&\qquad\qquad\quad (\lambda ab \to \textbf{case } ab \textbf{ of } \{\, inl \; a \to (inl . to \; bimap_A) \; a; \\
&\qquad\qquad\qquad\qquad\qquad\qquad\qquad\quad inr \; b \to (inr . to \; bimap_B) \; b\,\}) \\
&bimap_\times \;\;\;= \lambda A_1 \; A_2 \; bimap_A . \lambda B_1 \; B_2 \; bimap_B . \\
&\qquad\qquad EP \; (\lambda(a, b) \to (from \; bimap_A \; a, from \; bimap_B \; b)) \\
&\qquad\qquad\quad (\lambda(a, b) \to (to \; bimap_A \; a, to \; bimap_B \; b)) \\
&bimap_\to \;\;\;= \lambda A_1 \; A_2 \; bimap_A . \lambda B_1 \; B_2 \; bimap_B . \\
&\qquad\qquad EP \; (\lambda ab \to from \; bimap_B . ab . to \; bimap_A) \\
&\qquad\qquad\quad (\lambda ab \to to \; bimap_B . ab . from \; bimap_A) \\
&bimap_{\forall_\star} \;\;\;- \lambda F_1 \; F_2 \; bimap_F . \\
&\qquad\qquad EP \; (\lambda f \; V . from \; (bimap_F \; V \; V \; (EP \; id \; id)) \; (f \; V)) \\
&\qquad\qquad\quad (\lambda f \; V . to \; (bimap_F \; V \; V \; (EP \; id \; id)) \; (f \; V)) \\
&bimap_{c \textbf{ of}} = \lambda A_1 \; A_2 \; bimap_A . bimap_A
\end{aligned}
$$

Fig. 2. Lifting isomorphisms with a generic function

Consider the generic function

$$ poly_{T::\mathfrak{T}} \;::\; Poly_\mathfrak{T} \; Data_T^1 \; \dots \; Data_T^n . $$

Let ep_{Data_T} denote ep_T if $Data_T = Id_T$, and ep_Data_T otherwise. The conversion function can now be derived as

$$ conv\_poly\_T = to \; (bimap_{Poly_\star} \; ep_{Data_T^1} \; \dots \; ep_{Data_T^n}). $$

For example, the conversion function for the specialisation of *lookup* to *Nat* is given by

$$conv\_lookup\_Nat = to\ (bimap_{Lookup_\star}\ ep\_Nat\ ep\_FMap\_Nat),$$

which is extensionally the same as the function given in Section 3.

Note that the definition of *bimap* must include a case for the quantifier $\forall_\star :: (\star \rightarrow \star) \rightarrow \star$ since $Lookup_\star$ is a polymorphic type. In this specific case, however, polymorphic type indices can be easily handled, see Figure 2. The further details are exactly the same as for type-indexed values [15,12], and are omitted here.

5   An Advanced Example: The Zipper

This section shows how to define a zipper for an arbitrary data type. This is a more complex example demonstrating the full power of a type-indexed data structure together with a number of type-indexed functions working on it.

The zipper is a data structure that is used to represent a tree together with a subtree that is the focus of attention, where that focus may move left, right, up or down in the tree. The zipper is used in tools where a user interactively manipulates trees, for instance, in editors for structured documents such as proofs and programs. For the following it is important to note that the focus of the zipper may only move to recursive components. Consider as an example the data type *Tree*:

data *Tree A* = *empty* | *node* (*Tree A*) *A* (*Tree A*).

If the left subtree of a *node* constructor is selected, moving right means moving to the right tree, not to the *A*-label. This implies that recursive positions in trees play an important rôle in the definition of a generic zipper data structure. To obtain access to these recursive positions, we have to be explicit about the fixed points in data type definitions. The zipper data structure is then defined by induction on the so-called pattern functor of a data type.

The tools in which the zipper is used, allow the user to repeatedly apply navigation or edit commands, and to update the focus accordingly. In this section we define a type-indexed data type for locations, which consist of a subtree (the focus) together with a context, and we define several navigation functions on locations.

5.1   Locations

A location is a subtree, together with a context, which encodes the path from the top of the original tree to the selected subtree. The type-indexed data type *Loc* returns a type for locations given an argument pattern functor.

$$Loc\langle F :: \star \rightarrow \star\rangle \qquad :: \star$$
$$Loc\langle F\rangle \qquad = (Fix\ F, Context\langle F\rangle\ (Fix\ F))$$
$$Context\langle F :: \star \rightarrow \star\rangle :: \star \rightarrow \star$$
$$Context\langle F\rangle \qquad = \Lambda R\,.\,Fix\ (\Lambda C\,.\,1 + Ctx\langle F\rangle\ C\ R).$$

The type *Loc* is defined in terms *Context*, which constructs the context parameterised by the original tree type. The *Context* of a value is either empty (represented by 1 in the pattern functor for *Context*), or it is a path from the root down into the tree. Such a path is constructed by means of the second component of the pattern functor for *Context*: the type-indexed data type *Ctx*. The type-indexed data type *Ctx* is defined by induction on the pattern functor of the original data type.

$$
\begin{aligned}
Ctx\langle F :: \star \to \star \rangle &:: \star \to \star \to \star \\
Ctx\langle Id \rangle &= \Lambda C\ R.\ C \\
Ctx\langle K\ 1 \rangle &= \Lambda C\ R.\ 0 \\
Ctx\langle K\ Char \rangle &= \Lambda C\ R.\ 0 \\
Ctx\langle F_1 + F_2 \rangle &= \Lambda C\ R.\ Ctx\langle F_1 \rangle\ C\ R + Ctx\langle F_2 \rangle\ C\ R \\
Ctx\langle F_1 \times F_2 \rangle &= \Lambda C\ R.\ (Ctx\langle F_1 \rangle\ C\ R \times F_2\ R) + (F_1\ R \times Ctx\langle F_2 \rangle\ C\ R)
\end{aligned}
$$

This definition can be understood as follows. Since it is not possible to descend into a constant, the constant cases do not contribute to the result type, which is denoted by the 'empty type' 0. Note that although 0 does not appear in the grammars for types introduced in Section 2.1, it may appear as the result of a type-indexed data type. The *Id* case denotes a recursive component, in which it is possible to descend. Hence it may occur in a context. Descending in a value of a sum type follows the structure of the input value. Finally, there are two ways to descend in a product: descending left, adding the contents to the right of the node to the context, or descending right, adding the contents to the left of the node to the context.

For example, for natural numbers with pattern functor $K\ 1 + Id$ or, equivalently, $\Lambda N.\ 1 + N$, and for trees of type *Bush* whose pattern functor is $K\ Char + Id \times Id$ or, equivalently, $\Lambda T.\ Char + (T \times T)$ we obtain

$$
\begin{aligned}
Context\langle K\ 1 + Id \rangle &= \Lambda R.\ Fix\ (\Lambda C.\ 1 + (0 + C)) \\
Context\langle K\ Char + Id \times Id \rangle &= \Lambda R.\ Fix\ (\Lambda C.\ 1 + (0 + (C \times R + R \times C))),
\end{aligned}
$$

Note that the context of a natural number is isomorphic to a natural number (the context of m in n is $n - m$), and the context of a *Bush* applied to the data type *Bush* itself is isomorphic to the type *Ctx_Bush* introduced in Section 1.

We recently found that McBride [26] also defines a type-indexed zipper data type. His zipper slightly deviates from Huet's and our zipper: the navigation functions on McBride's zipper are not constant time anymore. Interestingly, he observes that the *Context* of a data type is its derivative (as in calculus).

5.2   Navigation Functions

We define type-indexed functions on the type-indexed data types *Loc*, *Context*, and *Ctx* for navigating through a tree. All of these functions act on locations. These are the basic functions for the zipper.

Function down. The function *down* is a type-indexed function that moves down to the leftmost recursive child of the current node, if such a child exists. Otherwise, if the current node is a leaf node, then *down* returns the location unchanged. The instantiation of *down* to the data type *Bush* has been given in Section 1. The function *down* satisfies the following property:

$$\forall l \, . \, down\langle F \rangle \, l \neq l \implies (up\langle F \rangle \cdot down\langle F \rangle) \, l = l,$$

where function *up* goes up in a tree. So first going down the tree and then up again is the identity function on locations in which it is possible to go down.

Since *down* moves down to the leftmost recursive child of the current node, the inverse equality $down\langle F \rangle \cdot up\langle F \rangle = id$ also does not hold in general. However, there does exist a natural number n such that

$$\forall l \, . \, up\langle F \rangle \, l \neq l \implies (right\langle F \rangle^n \cdot down\langle F \rangle \cdot up\langle F \rangle) \, l = l.$$

The function *down* is defined as follows.

$$
\begin{aligned}
&down\langle F :: \star \to \star \rangle :: Loc\langle F \rangle \to Loc\langle F \rangle \\
&down\langle F \rangle \, (t, c) \quad = \textbf{case } first\langle F \rangle \, (out \, t) \, c \textbf{ of} \\
&\qquad\qquad\qquad\qquad just \, (t', c') \to (t', in \, (inr \, c')) \\
&\qquad\qquad\qquad\qquad nothing \to (t, c).
\end{aligned}
$$

To find the leftmost recursive child, we have to pattern match on the pattern functor F, and find the first occurrence of *Id*. The helper function *first* is a type-indexed function that possibly returns the leftmost recursive child of a node, together with the context (a value of type $Ctx\langle F \rangle \, C \, T$) of the selected child. The function *down* then turns this context into a value of type *Context* by inserting it in the right ('non-top') component of a sum by means of *inr*, and applying the fixed point constructor *in* to it.

$$
\begin{aligned}
&first\langle F :: \star \to \star \rangle \qquad\quad :: \forall C \, T \, . \, F \, T \to C \to Maybe \, (T, Ctx\langle F \rangle \, C \, T) \\
&first\langle Id \rangle \, t \, c \qquad\qquad\quad = return \, (t, c) \\
&first\langle K \, 1 \rangle \, t \, c \qquad\qquad\quad = fail \\
&first\langle K \, Char \rangle \, t \, c \qquad\quad = fail \\
&first\langle F_1 + F_2 \rangle \, (inl \, x) \, c = \textbf{do } \{ (t, cx) \leftarrow first\langle F_1 \rangle \, x \, c; return \, (t, inl \, cx) \} \\
&first\langle F_1 + F_2 \rangle \, (inr \, y) \, c = \textbf{do } \{ (t, cy) \leftarrow first\langle F_2 \rangle \, y \, c; return \, (t, inr \, cy) \} \\
&first\langle F_1 \times F_2 \rangle \, (x, y) \, c = \textbf{do } \{ (t, cx) \leftarrow first\langle F_1 \rangle \, x \, c; return \, (t, inl \, (cx, y)) \} \\
&\qquad\qquad\qquad\qquad\quad +\!\!+\textbf{do } \{ (t, cy) \leftarrow first\langle F_2 \rangle \, y \, c; return \, (t, inr \, (x, cy)) \}
\end{aligned}
$$

Here, $(+\!\!+)$ is the standard monadic plus, called *mplus* in Haskell, given by

$$
\begin{aligned}
&(+\!\!+) \qquad\qquad :: Maybe \, A \to Maybe \, A \to Maybe \, A \\
&nothing +\!\!+ m = m \\
&just \, a +\!\!+ m \quad = just \, a.
\end{aligned}
$$

The function *first* returns the value and the context at the leftmost *Id* position. So in the product case, it first tries the left component, and only if it fails, it tries the right component.

The definitions of functions *up*, *right* and *left* are not as simple as the definition of *down*, since they are defined by pattern matching on the context instead of on the tree itself. We will just define functions *up* and *right*, and leave function *left* to the reader.

Function up. The function *up* moves up to the parent of the current node, if the current node is not the top node.

$$
\begin{aligned}
&up\langle F :: \star \to \star \rangle :: Loc\langle F \rangle \to Loc\langle F \rangle \\
&up\langle F \rangle \ (t, c) \quad = \mathbf{case} \ out \ c \ \mathbf{of} \\
&\qquad\qquad\qquad inl \ () \to (t, c) \\
&\qquad\qquad\qquad inr \ c' \to \mathbf{do} \ \{ ft \leftarrow insert\langle F \rangle \ c' \ t; \\
&\qquad\qquad\qquad\qquad\qquad\qquad c'' \leftarrow extract\langle F \rangle \ c'; \\
&\qquad\qquad\qquad\qquad\qquad\qquad return \ (in \ ft, c'') \}.
\end{aligned}
$$

Remember that *inl* () denotes the empty top context. The navigation function *up* uses two helper functions: *insert* and *extract*. The latter returns the context of the parent of the current node. Note that each element of type $Ctx\langle F \rangle \ C \ T$ has at most one C component (by an easy inductive argument), which marks the context of the parent of the current node. The polytypic function *extract* extracts this context.

$$
\begin{aligned}
extract\langle F :: \star \to \star \rangle &\qquad\qquad :: \forall C \ T . \ Ctx\langle F \rangle \ C \ T \to Maybe \ C \\
extract\langle Id \rangle \ c &\qquad\qquad = return \ c \\
extract\langle K \ 1 \rangle \ c &\qquad\qquad = fail \\
extract\langle K \ Char \rangle \ c &\qquad\qquad = fail \\
extract\langle F_1 + F_2 \rangle \ (inl \ cx) &\qquad\qquad = extract\langle F_1 \rangle \ cx \\
extract\langle F_1 + F_2 \rangle \ (inr \ cy) &\qquad\qquad = extract\langle F_2 \rangle \ cy \\
extract\langle F_1 \times F_2 \rangle \ (inl \ (cx, y)) &= extract\langle F_1 \rangle \ cx \\
extract\langle F_1 \times F_2 \rangle \ (inr \ (x, cy)) &= extract\langle F_2 \rangle \ cy
\end{aligned}
$$

Here, *return* is obtained from the *Maybe* monad and *fail* is shorthand for *nothing*. Note that *extract* is polymorphic in C and in T.

Function *insert* takes a context and a tree, and inserts the tree in the current focus of the context, effectively turning a context into a tree.

$$
\begin{aligned}
insert\langle F :: \star \to \star \rangle &\qquad\qquad :: \forall C \ T . \ Ctx\langle F \rangle \ C \ T \to T \to Maybe \ (F \ T) \\
insert\langle Id \rangle \ c \ t &\qquad\qquad = return \ t \\
insert\langle K \ 1 \rangle \ c \ t &\qquad\qquad = fail \\
insert\langle K \ Char \rangle \ c \ t &\qquad\qquad = fail \\
insert\langle F_1 + F_2 \rangle \ (inl \ cx) \ t &\qquad\qquad = \mathbf{do} \ \{ x \leftarrow insert\langle F_1 \rangle \ cx \ t; return \ (inl \ x) \} \\
insert\langle F_1 + F_2 \rangle \ (inr \ cy) \ t &\qquad\qquad = \mathbf{do} \ \{ y \leftarrow insert\langle F_2 \rangle \ cy \ t; return \ (inr \ y) \} \\
insert\langle F_1 \times F_2 \rangle \ (inl \ (cx, y)) \ t &= \mathbf{do} \ \{ x \leftarrow insert\langle F_1 \rangle \ cx \ t; return \ (x, y) \} \\
insert\langle F_1 \times F_2 \rangle \ (inr \ (x, cy)) \ t &= \mathbf{do} \ \{ y \leftarrow insert\langle F_2 \rangle \ cy \ t; return \ (x, y) \}.
\end{aligned}
$$

Note that the extraction and insertion is happening in the identity case *Id*; the other cases only pass on the results.

Since $up\langle F \rangle \cdot down\langle F \rangle = id$ on locations in which it is possible to go down, we expect similar equalities for the functions *first*, *extract*, and *insert*. We have that the following computation

$$
\begin{aligned}
\mathbf{do}\; \{\, (t, c') &\leftarrow first\langle F \rangle\; ft\; c; \\
c'' &\leftarrow extract\langle F \rangle\; c'; \\
ft' &\leftarrow insert\langle F \rangle\; c'\; t; \\
return\; (c &== c'' \wedge ft == ft'\,)\; \}
\end{aligned}
$$

returns *true* on locations in which it is possible to go down.

Function right. The function *right* moves the focus to the next sibling to the right in a tree, if it exists. The context is moved accordingly. The instance of *right* on the data type *Bush* has been given in Section 1. The function *right* satisfies the following property:

$$
\forall l \,.\, right\langle F \rangle\; l \neq l \implies (left\langle F \rangle \cdot right\langle F \rangle)\; l = l,
$$

that is, first going right in the tree and then left again is the identity function on locations in which it is possible to go to the right. Of course, the dual equality holds on locations in which it is possible to go to the left.

Function *right* is defined by pattern matching on the context. It is impossible to go to the right at the top of a value. Otherwise, we try to find the right sibling of the current focus.

$$
\begin{aligned}
right\langle F :: \star \to \star \rangle &:: \; Loc\langle F \rangle \to Loc\langle F \rangle \\
right\langle F \rangle\; (t, c) &= \; \mathbf{case}\; out\; c\; \mathbf{of} \\
&\qquad inl\; () \to (t, c) \\
&\qquad inr\; c' \to \mathbf{case}\; next\langle F \rangle\; t\; c'\; \mathbf{of} \\
&\qquad\qquad\qquad just\; (t', c'') \to (t', in\; (inr\; c'')) \\
&\qquad\qquad\qquad nothing \to (t, c).
\end{aligned}
$$

The helper function *next* is a type-indexed function that returns the first location that has the recursive value to the right of the selected value as its focus. Just as there exists a function *left* such that $left\langle F \rangle \cdot right\langle F \rangle = id$ (on locations in which it is possible to go to the right), there exists a function *previous*, such that

$$
\begin{aligned}
\mathbf{do}\; \{\, (t', c') &\leftarrow next\langle F \rangle\; t\; c; \\
(t'', c'') &\leftarrow previous\langle F \rangle\; t'\; c'; \\
return\; (c &== c'' \wedge t == t'') \}
\end{aligned}
$$

returns *true* (on locations in which it is possible to go to the right). We will define function *next*, and omit the definition of function *previous*.

$$next\langle F :: \star \to \star \rangle :: \forall C\ T\ .\ T \to Ctx\langle F \rangle\ C\ T \to Maybe\ (T, Ctx\langle F \rangle\ C\ T)$$
$$next\langle Id \rangle\ t\ c \qquad\qquad = fail$$
$$next\langle K\ 1 \rangle\ t\ c \qquad\qquad = fail$$
$$next\langle K\ Char \rangle\ t\ c \qquad = fail$$
$$next\langle F_1 + F_2 \rangle\ t\ (inl\ cx) = \mathbf{do}\ \{(t', cx') \leftarrow next\langle F_1 \rangle\ t\ cx; return\ (t', inl\ cx')\}$$
$$next\langle F_1 + F_2 \rangle\ t\ (inr\ cy) = \mathbf{do}\ \{(t', cy') \leftarrow next\langle F_2 \rangle\ t\ cy; return\ (t', inr\ cy')\}$$
$$next\langle F_1 \times F_2 \rangle\ t\ (inl\ (cx, y))$$
$$= \mathbf{do}\ \{(t', cx') \leftarrow next\langle F_1 \rangle\ t\ cx; return\ (t', inl\ (cx', y))\}$$
$$+\!\!\!+\ \mathbf{do}\ \{c \leftarrow extract\langle F_1 \rangle\ cx;$$
$$x \leftarrow insert\langle F_1 \rangle\ cx\ t;$$
$$(t', cy) \leftarrow first\langle F_2 \rangle\ y\ c;$$
$$return\ (t', inr\ (x, cy))\}$$
$$next\langle F_1 \times F_2 \rangle\ t\ (inr\ (x, cy))$$
$$= \mathbf{do}\ \{(t', cy') \leftarrow next\langle F_2 \rangle\ t\ cy; return\ (t', inr\ (x, cy'))\}.$$

The first three lines in this definition show that it is impossible to go to the right in an identity or constant context. If the context argument is a value of a sum, we select the next element in the appropriate component of the sum. The product case is the most interesting one. If the context is in the right component of a pair, *next* returns the next value of that context, properly combined with the left component of the tuple. On the other hand, if the context is in the left component of a pair, the next value may be either in that left component (the context), or it may be in the right component (the value). If the next value is in the left component, it is returned by the first line in the definition of the product case. If it is not, *next* extracts the context c (the context of the parent) from the left context cx, it inserts the given value in the context cx giving a 'tree' value x, and selects the first component in the right component of the pair, using the extracted context c for the new context. The new context that is thus obtained is combined with x into a context for the selected tree.

6   Conclusion

We have shown how to define type-indexed data types, and we have given several examples of type-indexed data types: digital search trees, the zipper, and labelling a data type. Furthermore, we have shown how to specialise type-indexed data types and type-indexed functions that take values of type-indexed data types as arguments. The treatment generalises the specialisation of type-indexed functions given in Hinze [14], and is used in the implementation of Generic Haskell, a generic programming extension of the functional language Haskell. The first release of Generic Haskell was published on 1st November 2001, see http://www.generic-haskell.org/. A technical overview of the compiler can be found in De Wit's thesis [35]. The next release will contain an experimental implementation of type-indexed data types. Check the webpage or contact the authors for a preliminary version.

A type-indexed data type is defined in a similar way as a type-indexed function. The only difference is that the 'type' of a type-indexed data type is a kind instead of a type. Note that a type-indexed data type may also be a type constructor, it need not necessarily be a type of kind $\star$. For instance, *Label* is indexed by types of kind $\star \to \star$ and yields types of kind $\star \to \star \to \star$.

There are several things that remain to be done. We want to test our framework on the type-indexed data types appearing in the literature [3,9,33], and we want to create a library of recurring examples. Furthermore, we have to investigate how we can deal with sets of mutually recursive type-indexed data types (this extension requires tuples on the kind level).

Acknowledgements

Thanks are due to Dave Clarke, Ralf Lämmel, Doaitse Swierstra, and the anonymous referees for comments on previous versions of the paper. Jan de Wit suggested an improvement in the labelling functions.

References

1. R. Backhouse, P. Jansson, J. Jeuring, and L. Meertens. Generic programming: An introduction. In S. Doaitse Swierstra, Pedro R. Henriques, and José N. Oliveira, editors, *Advanced Functional Programming*, volume 1608 of *LNCS*, pages 28–115. Springer-Verlag, 1999.
2. Richard Bird, Oege de Moor, and Paul Hoogendijk. Generic functional programming with types and relations. *Journal of Functional Programming*, 6(1):1–28, 1996.
3. Manuel M.T. Chakravarty and Gabriele Keller. More types for nested data parallel programming. In *Proceedings ICFP 2000: International Conference on Functional Programming*, pages 94–105. ACM Press, 2000.
4. Koen Claessen and Peter Ljunglöf. Typed logical variables in Haskell. In *Proceedings Haskell Workshop 2000*, 2000.
5. Karl Crary and Stephanie Weirich. Flexible type analysis. In *Proceedings ICFP 1999: International Conference on Functional Programming*, pages 233–248. ACM Press, 1999.
6. Karl Crary, Stephanie Weirich, and J. Gregory Morrisett. Intensional polymorphism in type-erasure semantics. In *Proceedings ICFP 1998: International Conference on Functional Programming*, pages 301–312. ACM Press, 1998.
7. C. Dubois, F. Rouaix, and P. Weis. Extensional polymorphism. In *22nd Symposium on Principles of Programming Languages, POPL '95*, pages 118–129, 1995.
8. M.M. Fokkinga. *Law and Order in Algorithmics*. PhD thesis, University of Twente, Dept INF, Enschede, The Netherlands, 1992.
9. Jeremy Gibbons. Polytypic downwards accumulations. In *Proceedings of Mathematics of Program Construction*, volume 1422 of *LNCS*. Springer-Verlag, June 1998.

10. Robert Harper and Greg Morrisett. Compiling polymorphism using intensional type analysis. In *22nd Symposium on Principles of Programming Languages, POPL '95*, pages 130–141, 1995.
11. Ralf Hinze. Generalizing generalized tries. *Journal of Functional Programming*, 10(4):327–351, 2000.
12. Ralf Hinze. *Generic Programs and Proofs*. 2000. Habilitationsschrift, Bonn University.
13. Ralf Hinze. A new approach to generic functional programming. In *Conference Record of POPL '00: The 27th ACM SIGPLAN-SIGACT Symposium on Principles of Programming Languages*, pages 119–132. ACM Press, 2000.
14. Ralf Hinze. Polytypic values possess polykinded types. In Roland Backhouse and José Nuno Oliveira, editors, *Mathematics of Program Construction*, volume 1837 of *LNCS*, pages 2–27. Springer-Verlag, 2000.
15. Ralf Hinze and Simon Peyton Jones. Derivable type classes. In Graham Hutton, editor, *Proceedings of the 2000 ACM SIGPLAN Haskell Workshop*, volume 41.1 of Electronic Notes in Theoretical Computer Science. Elsevier Science, August 2001. The preliminary proceedings appeared as a University of Nottingham technical report.
16. Gérard Huet. The zipper. *Journal of Functional Programming*, 7(5):549–554, 1997.
17. P. Jansson and J. Jeuring. PolyP — a polytypic programming language extension. In *Conference Record of POPL '97: The 24th ACM SIGPLAN-SIGACT Symposium on Principles of Programming Languages*, pages 470–482. ACM Press, 1997.
18. Patrik Jansson. The WWW home page for polytypic programming. Available from http://www.cs.chalmers.se/~patrikj/poly/, 2001.
19. Patrik Jansson and Johan Jeuring. Functional pearl: Polytypic unification. *Journal of Functional Programming*, 8(5):527–536, September 1998.
20. Patrik Jansson and Johan Jeuring. A framework for polytypic programming on terms, with an application to rewriting. In J. Jeuring, editor, *Workshop on Generic Programming 2000, Ponte de Lima, Portugal, July 2000*, pages 33–45, 2000. Utrecht Technical Report UU-CS-2000-19.
21. C.B. Jay, G. Bellè, and E. Moggi. Functorial ML. *Journal of Functional Programming*, 8(6):573 619, 1998.
22. J. Jeuring. Polytypic pattern matching. In *Conference Record of FPCA'95, SIGPLAN-SIGARCH-WG2.8 Conference on Functional Programming Languages and Computer Architecture*, pages 238–248. ACM Press, 1995.
23. Mark P. Jones. Type classes with functional dependencies. In G. Smolka, editor, *Proceedings of the 9th European Symposium on Programming, ESOP 2000, Berlin, Germany*, volume 1782 of *LNCS*, pages 230–244. Springer-Verlag, March 2000.
24. Ralf Lämmel and Wolfgang Lohmann. Format Evolution. In J. Kouloumdjian, H.C. Mayr, and A. Erkollar, editors, *Proc. 7th International Conference on Reverse Engineering for Information Systems (RETIS 2001)*, volume 155 of *books@ocg.at*, pages 113–134. OCG, 2001.
25. G. Malcolm. Data structures and program transformation. *Science of Computer Programming*, 14:255–279, 1990.
26. Connor McBride. The derivative of a regular type is its type of one-hole contexts. Unpublished manuscript, 2001.
27. Nancy J. McCracken. *An investigation of a programming language with a polymorphic type structure*. PhD thesis, Syracuse University, June 1979.
28. L. Meertens. Paramorphisms. *Formal Aspects of Computing*, 4(5):413–425, 1992.

29. E. Meijer, M.M. Fokkinga, and R. Paterson. Functional programming with bananas, lenses, envelopes, and barbed wire. In J. Hughes, editor, *FPCA'91: Functional Programming Languages and Computer Architecture*, volume 523 of *LNCS*, pages 124–144. Springer-Verlag, 1991.
30. John C. Mitchell. *Foundations for Programming Languages*. The MIT Press, 1996.
31. Simon Peyton Jones [editor], John Hughes [editor], Lennart Augustsson, Dave Barton, Brian Boutel, Warren Burton, Simon Fraser, Joseph Fasel, Kevin Hammond, Ralf Hinze, Paul Hudak, Thomas Johnsson, Mark Jones, John Launchbury, Erik Meijer, John Peterson, Alastair Reid, Colin Runciman, and Philip Wadler. Haskell 98 — A non-strict, purely functional language. Available from `http://www.haskell.org/definition/`, February 1999.
32. Valery Trifonov, Bratin Saha, and Zhong Shao. Fully reflexive intensional type analysis. In *Proceedings ICFP 2000: International Conference on Functional Programming*, pages 82–93. ACM Press, 2000.
33. Måns Vestin. Genetic algorithms in Haskell with polytypic programming. Examensarbeten 1997:36, Göteborg University, Gothenburg, Sweden, 1997. Available from the Polytypic programming WWW page [18].
34. Stephanie Weirich. Encoding intensional type analysis. In *European Symposium on Programming*, volume 2028 of *LNCS*, pages 92–106. Springer-Verlag, 2001.
35. Jan de Wit. A technical overview of Generic Haskell. Master's thesis, Department of Information and Computing Sciences, Utrecht University, 2002.
36. Zhe Yang. Encoding types in ML-like languages. In *Proceedings ICFP 1998: International Conference on Functional Programming*, pages 289–300. ACM Press, 1998.

Verification of Java's AbstractCollection Class: A Case Study

Marieke Huisman

INRIA Sophia-Antipolis, France
Marieke.Huisman@sophia.inria.fr

Abstract. This paper presents the specification and (modular) verification of Java's AbstractCollection class. This work is done as a case study within the LOOP project (at the university of Nijmegen). It is the first major verification within the project using the theorem prover Isabelle. The class AbstractCollection is automatically translated into a series of Isabelle theories. The specifications, written in the Java Modeling Language (JML), give rise to appropriate proof obligations. The paper explains how the specifications are constructed and verified. When working on this case study, it became clear that there is a problem that is not documented in the informal documentation: when a collection contains a reference to itself it has unexpected behaviour. It is discussed how the specifications are adapted to overcome this problem.

1 Introduction

One of the reasons for the popularity of Java [2] is that it comes with a large collection of ready-made, general-purpose classes, a so-called Application Program Interface (API) [19]. These classes provide general data structures (like lists, sets and hash tables) and utility functions (*e.g.* input-output or graphical user interface operations). An API enables an application developer to focus on the special aspects of the application at hand, while using the already defined classes for the underlying data structures.

However, to be able to use such pre-defined classes correctly, the application developer has to understand their behaviour. To achieve this, one can look at the informal documentation and study the implementation, but there are some drawbacks to this. The informal documentation might be ambiguous or unclear at some points, and one never can be completely sure that it describes the correct behaviour. Studying the implementation is often cumbersome, as it requires understanding all the details of the actual implementation – while the application developer is only interested in the visible behaviour of the method.

A different approach is to annotate a class with a formal specification, describing its behaviour, but abstracting away from implementation details. Together with the informal documentation this gives the application developer the necessary information. Naturally, to be usable, such a formal specification should be correct and easy to understand. JML, the Java Modeling Language [20], provides a way to write specifications that are easy to understand for a Java programmer.

E.A. Boiten and B. Möller (Eds.): MPC 2002, LNCS 2386, pp. 175–194, 2002.

By providing a semantics for Java and JML, it can actually be verified whether the source code satisfies the specification (and in the case of a mismatch, one of the two can be adapted).

This case study is done in the context of the LOOP project [24], which aims at reasoning about Java programs with the use of modern, powerful tools. A semantics for Java has been developed, based on coalgebras. The so-called LOOP compiler [4] translates Java programs into a series of logical theories, capturing their semantics. These theories are written in the input language of a theorem prover (a compiler switch decides whether output is generated for PVS [27] or Isabelle [28]). The verifications in this case study are done using Isabelle, in contrast to the case studies done earlier in the LOOP project.

The desired properties of the Java program can be specified in JML. The current version of the LOOP compiler translates JML specifications into PVS proof obligations. In order to use Isabelle for the verifications, the JML specifications have to be translated by hand into Isabelle proof obligations. More information on the LOOP project and the formalisation of Java can be found in [24]. Within the LOOP project, several other classes from the Java API or the JavaCard API have been specified and verified (in PVS), see *e.g.* [16,5,6,10]. We are not aware of similar case studies in the context of other projects on Java verification.

The verifications in this case study are typical examples of modular verifications [21]. Every method is verified in isolation, assuming that all methods and classes used are correctly implemented, *i.e.* satisfy their specification. Thus, if some method implementation is modified later (possibly in a subclass), it only has to be shown that the new implementation still satisfies its specification, and the correctness of all other parts follows immediately. In the literature, many different aspects of modular verification are described, and this case study rigorously applies this to a realistic example.

This case study describes the JML specification and verification of two Java API classes, namely `Collection` and `AbstractCollection`[1]. These two classes were chosen because they provide a good example of how to deal with inheritance and abstract methods in the context of verification. We give a specification for the interface `Collection` and show that the class `AbstractCollection` is a correct implementation of `Collection`. The specifications that we have verified are non-trivial: besides showing termination of a method, we also show how the state of the object has changed.

During verification we found non-trivial omissions in our initial versions of the specifications – that are tightly based on the informal documentation of these classes – thus confirming that it was important to actually do the verifications ([5] reports similar experiences). In particular, at first we were not aware of the problems that occur when a collection contains a reference to itself, or when a method argument contains a reference to the receiving collection. These subtle problems – that cause collections to have unexpected behaviour – only became apparent during the verification, and also were not revealed from the informal

---

[1] We use version number 1.25, written by Josh Bloch, under Sun Microsystems copyright from the JDK1.2 distribution.

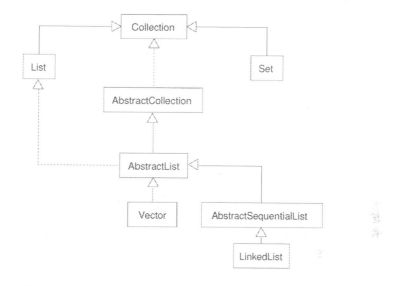

Fig. 1. Part of the Collection hierarchy

documentation. This example demonstrates that only with formal verification, one can completely rely on a specification. Below, in Sect. 4.4, we discuss this point in more detail.

Almost all the methods that we have verified contain loops, therefore we could not rely on tools as the Extended Static Checker (ESC/Java) [22] to check the specifications. The current implementation of ESC/Java only checks loops by unfolding one iteration[2] and this is an important source of unsoundness of ESC/Java. Therefore, ESC/Java is useful to check specifications of methods without loops and recursion [8], but to go beyond this, one needs full verification as is done in the LOOP project.

This paper is organised as follows. First, Sect. 2 gives more information on the interface `Collection` and its descendants. Then, Sect. 3 discusses modular specification and verification techniques. Sect. 4 discusses the specification of the interface `Collection` (and the strongly related `Iterator` interface), and finally Sect. 5 describes how Isabelle proof obligations are produced from the specification, and gives more details about the verification. We end with conclusions.

2   The Collection Hierarchy

The Java API contains several container classes, like `Set` and `List` that can be used to store objects. These classes form a hierarchy – a part of which is displayed as a UML diagram in Fig. 1 – with the interface `Collection` as root. A Java interface only contains method declarations, thus providing some means of

---

[2] The number of iterations can be changed by a parameter.

abstraction: several classes can provide different implementations of the same interface, but the user of an interface does not have to be aware of these differences in implementation.

There are several sub-interfaces, *e.g.* List and Set. At the bottom of the hierarchy there are complete implementations of collection structures, like Vector and LinkedList. These classes can immediately be used by application programmers. The classes in the middle of the hierarchy, such as AbstractCollection and AbstractList, give an incomplete implementation of the interfaces. They contain several methods without an implementation, so-called abstract methods, while their other methods are implemented in terms of these abstract methods. This gives users of the Java API the possibility to program specific container classes with little effort, by implementing only the abstract methods and inheriting the other implementations.

The Collection interface declares all the basic operations on collections, such as add, remove, size *etc.*[3]

― JAVA ────────────────────────────────────

```
public interface Collection {
    int size();
    boolean isEmpty();
    boolean contains(Object o);
    Iterator iterator();
    Object[] toArray();
    boolean add(Object o);
    boolean remove(Object o);
    boolean containsAll(Collection c);
    boolean addAll(Collection c);
    boolean removeAll(Collection c);
    boolean retainAll(Collection c);
    void clear();                }
```

The boolean result of methods as add and remove is intended to denote success or failure of the operation. The method iterator declared in Collection returns an object implementing the Iterator interface. Iterators provide a way to enumerate all the elements in a collection.

― JAVA ────────────────────────────────────

```
public interface Iterator {
    boolean hasNext();
    Object next();
    void remove();        }
```

From the method declarations in the Iterator interface it seems like Iterator is independent of Collection, but the informal documentation [19] reveals that a mutually recursive dependency is intended: the remove method in the iterator removes an element from the underlying collection.

───────

[3] We do not discuss equals and hashCode in this case study, because AbstractCollection simply inherits the implementations from Object.

Since Java-1.2, the abstract collection in the API classes also provide so-called *optional methods*. Such a method is implemented by throwing an `Unsupported-OperationException`. The programmer of a class that inherits such a method, has the possibility to decide whether this operation is supported. In that case, the programmer has to give a new implementation for the method, overriding the implementation throwing the `UnsupportedOperationException`. There has been some objection to the introduction of these optional methods in the library classes [7] because users of the library have to be aware of the possibility that a method may be unimplemented. The advantage of a formal specification is that it makes not only explicit that a method is optional, but also on what it depends whether the method is supported. For example, in Fig. 4 below, it can be seen that `addAll` is only supported when the `add` operation is defined. This information cannot be deduced only from the fact that the method can throw an `UnsupportedOperationException`. The class `AbstractCollection` that implements the `Collection` interface has abstract methods `size` and `iterator`, and an optional method `add`[4]. The other methods that are declared in `Collection` are implemented in `AbstractCollection`, in terms of the methods `size`, `add`, `iterator` and the methods declared in `Iterator`.

3   Modular Specification and Verification Techniques

The verification that is described in this case study is a typical example of a modular verification, where each method is verified in isolation in such a way that the correctness of the whole class can be established from the individual verifications. When verifying a method `m`, it is assumed that all components (instance variables, parameters and local variables with reference types *etc.*) satisfy their class specification, which is the combination of all method specifications and class invariants. In particular, it is assumed that the object `this` itself satisfies its class specification.

Thus, given a variable `c` in class `C`, for each method call `c.n()` it is assumed that this call satisfies the specification of `n` in `C`[5]. This verification approach ensures that if the implementation of a part of the system is changed, only the correctness of that part has to be re-established, all other parts remain correct.

3.1   JML: A Language for Writing Specifications

To write the specifications, the Java Modeling Language (JML) [20] is used. JML allows one to write class specifications as comments to Java programs. The JML annotations use a Java-like syntax, thus making the specifications easier to understand for somebody familiar with Java. In JML, method specifications are written as pre-post-condition pairs. A formal semantics for JML is currently

---

[4] As `add` is an optional method instead of an abstract method, it is possible to implement unmodifiable collections.

[5] In the case of (mutual) recursive method calls, some extra care has to be taken. This is not relevant for this case study.

under development, translating the specifications into Hoare logic sentences, tailored to Java [18].

As an example of a JML specification, we look at a specification of `equals` in `Object`. For more information about JML, the reader is referred to [20].

```
- JML ────────────────────────────────────────────────────
  /*@ normal_behavior
    @    requires true;
    @    ensures (this == obj ==> \result) &&
    @            (obj == null ==> !\result);
    @*/
  public boolean equals(Object obj)
```

This `normal_behavior` specification is translated into a total correctness sentence, asserting that if the method is called in a state satisfying `true`[6], the method will terminate normally (*i.e.* without throwing an exception) in a state satisfying the postcondition (denoted by the keyword `ensures`). The special keyword `\result` denotes the result value of the method. The post-condition states that if the argument is the same reference as the receiving object, the result of the method will be true, while if the argument is a null-reference, the result will always be false.

In good object-oriented programming, fields should be declared private, so that they are not visible from outside the object. But in that case, fields also cannot be used in class specifications (as they are intended to give public information about the class). To solve this problem, so-called model (or abstract or specification-only) variables can be declared in JML [21,20]. The value of a model variable is defined as a function of the concrete variables, *i.e.* it represents these concrete variables. The use of model variables is an extension of Hoare's data abstraction technique [12].

3.2   The Behavioural Subtype Approach

Using specifications to reason about method calls only makes sense if the actual implementations that can be called at run-time satisfy this specification. If `o` is declared to be in class `C`, then at run-time `o` is always an instance of `C` or a subclass of `C`, because of Java's type-safety [9,29,26]. Therefore, to ensure that all method implementations that can be called satisfy the specification, one has to show that all method implementations in subclasses also satisfy the specifications of the superclass. This ensures that subclasses behave as their superclass, *i.e.* that they are behavioural subtypes [25,1,23].

Behavioural Subtype: Class D is a behavioural subtype of its superclass C if:

1. the class invariant of class D implies the class invariant of class C

$$\forall x\colon \mathsf{State}.\,\mathsf{invariant}_D\, x \Rightarrow \mathsf{invariant}_C\, x$$

---
[6] This trivial precondition could have been left implicit.

2. subtype methods preserve the behaviour of supertype methods, *i.e* for all methods m_C that are overridden by m_D, the following holds.

$$\forall x\colon \text{State. pre}_{m_C}\, x \Rightarrow \text{pre}_{m_D}\, x \;\wedge\; \forall x\colon \text{State. post}_{m_D}\, x \Rightarrow \text{post}_{m_C}\, x$$

In fact, to avoid that inheritance breaks encapsulation (this is also known as the fragile base class problem) one also has to show *e.g.* that the inherited methods preserve the invariant of the subclass (that can be stronger than the invariant of the superclass) [17]. Finally, all instance variables of objects should be private, so that it is not possible to break the class invariants by directly changing the variables.

Notice for example that the specification of `equals` above does not completely specify the outcome of this method, thus allowing it to be redefined in such a way that it takes structural equivalence of objects into account.

3.3   The Frame Problem: Changing the State

Using only functional specifications of methods usually is not sufficient to reason about arbitrary method calls. Suppose that we verify the method m in the following class.

```
- JML

  class C {
    int [] a;

    /*@ normal_behavior
      @    ensures   a.length >= 4;
      @*/
    void m () { a = new int [5]; n (); }

    /*@ normal_behavior
      @    ensures   true;
      @*/
    void n () { }
  }
```

In the verification of method m the specification of n is used. However, to establish the postcondition of m we need to know that n does not change the length of the array a, and using only the functional behaviour of n this cannot be established. Therefore, so-called modifies clauses [11,21] are introduced, using the keyword `modifiable` in JML. A modifies clause in a method specification states which variables may be changed by a method; all other variables must remain unchanged.

If a modifies clause contains a model variable, it means that all variables on which this model variable depends may change.

4   The Specification of Collection and Iterator

The most difficult step in this case study is to write appropriate specifications for `Collection` and `Iterator`. To start with, we used the informal documentation [19] as a basis to write the class specifications. In this way, we identified the appropriate model variables and we constructed method specifications[7]. Below we discuss first the model variables that we use in the specifications of `Collection` and `Iterator`, then we discuss the method specifications for `Iterator`, and finally we discuss some of the method specifications of `Collection`, together with the particular issues involved in formulating them.

4.1   The Model Variables of Collection

To determine which model variables are needed to specify `Collection`, we start by looking at some fragments of the informal documentation of `Collection`. The first fragment gives a general description of the interface.

```
/* A collection represents a group of objects, known as its elements.
 * Some collections allow duplicate elements and others do not. [...]
 * Bags or multisets (unordered collections that may contain
 * duplicate elements) should implement this interface directly. [...]
 */
public interface Collection {
```

Thus, we need a model variable of type "bag of objects"[8], representing the contents of the collection, and another model variable of type boolean that denotes whether duplicate elements are allowed in the collection. Reading further we find the following remark in the documentation of the method add.

```
/* Ensures that this collection contains the specified element
 * (optional operation). [...]
 * Collections that support this operation may place limitations
 * on what elements may be added to this collection. In particular,
 * some collections will refuse to add null elements, and others will
 * impose restrictions on the type of elements that may be added. [...]
 */
boolean add(Object o);
```

As the **add** method is an optional method, we need a boolean model variable that states whether the operation is supported. Every method that uses the **add** method will only be supported if **add** is defined. Further, we need a predicate that determines whether an element can be stored in the collection.

In a similar way, we find from the documentation of **remove** that we need a boolean variable, telling whether this optional method is supported[9]. Fig. 2

---

[7] As explained below, during the verification we realised that the initial specifications for the methods in `Collection` were not sufficient, and that because of some subtle problems, improvements were required.

[8] Objects are formalised as arbitrary references, see [3].

[9] The **remove** operation can only be supported if `Iterator` also supports its **remove** operation.

name	type	represents
`contents`	`Object multiset`	contents of collection
`addDefined`	`boolean`	true iff `add` operation supported
`removeDefined`	`boolean`	true iff `remove` operation supported
`storable`	`Object => boolean`	true iff argument may be added to collection
`allowDoubles`	`boolean`	true iff collection can contain duplicate elements

Fig. 2. Model variables used in the specification of interface `Collection`

summarises the model variables for the interface `Collection`. Strictly speaking, we should specify a model class for bags in JML, and translate this model class into a series of Isabelle theories as well. While reasoning about the model variable `contents` we should use the method specifications of this model class. However, as we do the translation from JML annotation to Isabelle theory by hand, we can use multisets as defined in the Isabelle library directly. This has the advantage that we immediately have access to the whole theory developed about multisets in Isabelle, and we do not have to develop this theory ourselves, based on the JML specifications. This simplifies our verification, but does not affect its validity.

Further, we use a so-called dependency constraint on the model variables, stating when they are unchanged. We assume that the value of `contents` is preserved if the heap is not changed at the memory location where the fields of the collection are stored. In other words: `contents` only changes if the internal state of the collection changes. The variables `addDefined`, `removeDefined`, `allowDoubles` and `storable` are constants. As an invariant of `Collection` we specify the following:

- `contents` is a finite bag; and
- if `allowDoubles` is false, every element occurs at most once in the collection (*w.r.t.* the `equals` operation on objects).

Notice that the implementation of `AbstractCollection` is such that this invariant is always preserved, even in states which are internal to a method. Thus when a method in `AbstractCollection` calls back another method declared in `Collection` the invariant will always hold. This might not be the case for arbitrary programs: when verifying methods that potentially can make *call backs* to the current object, one has to be careful and for example show explicitly that the invariant is re-established at the moment this call back can be made. However, this falls out of the scope of this case study.

4.2 The Model Variables of Iterator

The purpose of the `Iterator` interface (see Sect. 2) is to provide means to walk through all the elements of a collection, and possibly remove selected elements from the underlying collection. Again, the interface does not declare any variables, but we need several model variables to write the specification. First of all, we need a model variable `contents` that initially contains all the elements of

name	type	represents
contents	Object multiset	the elements through which is iterated
removeDefined	boolean	true iff remove operation supported
underlyingCollection	Collection	reference to underlying collection
lastElement	Object	reference to element most recently returned by next
removeAllowed	boolean	true iff remove is preceded by next

Fig. 3. Model variables used in the specification of interface Iterator

the collection that is iterated through. During iteration, every visited element is removed from contents, thus ensuring that each element is visited exactly once.

The motivation for the other model variables of Iterator can be found in the documentation of the method remove.

```
/* Removes from the underlying collection the last element returned by
 * the iterator (optional operation). This method can be called only once
 * per call to next. [...]
 */
void remove();
```

The boolean removeDefined states whether the remove operation is supported. To be able to remove an element from the underlying collection, the model variable underlyingCollection maintains a reference to this collection. Every remove operation has to be preceded by one or more next operations (possibly with a number of hasNext operations in between), and the object that was returned by the last next operation, remembered in the variable lastElement, is removed from the underlying collection. + Whether a remove is allowed is denoted by the variable removeAllowed.

Fig. 3 gives an overview of the model variables used in the specification of Iterator. The model variables underlyingCollection and removeDefined are constant, the values of removeAllowed, lastElement and contents are preserved as long as the heap is not changed at the position of the iterator object (thus they depend on the internal state of the iterator). As an invariant of Iterator we specify that contents is a finite bag.

4.3   The Specification of the Methods in Iterator

Next, we write specifications for the methods declared in the interface Iterator: hasNext(), next() and remove(). For each method we briefly state an informal description of its behaviour, followed by the formal JML specification. The verifications did not reveal any problems in these specifications. In the specifications, we use Isabelle notation for multisets, *e.g.* {#} denotes the empty bag, and {#v#} denotes a bag with the single element v.

hasNext() checks whether there are still elements that have not been visited yet. It always terminates normally and does not have side-effects.

```
— JML ————————————————————————————————————————
  /*@ normal_behavior
   @    ensures \result == (contents != {#});
   @*/
  public boolean hasNext();
```

`next()` returns an element from `contents` of `Iterator`. Every element should be visited only once, therefore the returned element is removed from the `contents` of the iterator (but of course, not from the contents of the collection). The `next` operation terminates normally only if `contents` is not empty. Besides changing the value of `contents`, this method also sets the values of `lastElement` and `removeAllowed` appropriately.

```
— JML ————————————————————————————————————————
  /*@ normal_behavior
   @     requires contents != {#};
   @  modifiable contents, lastElement, removeAllowed;
   @     ensures contents == \old(contents) - {#\result#} &&
   @             \old(contents.elem(\result)) &&
   @             removeAllowed && lastElement == \result;
   @*/
  public Object next();
```

The special JML-keyword `\old()` is used to refer to the value of expressions in the pre-state of a method.

`remove()` terminates normally only if the `remove` operation is supported and if there has been a call to `next` before (denoted by `removeAllowed`). If so, it removes one occurrence of the element that was returned by the last call to `next` from the collection underlying the `Iterator` (stored in `lastElement`).

```
— JML ————————————————————————————————————————
  /*@ normal_behavior
   @    requires removeDefined && removeAllowed;
   @ modifiable underlyingCollection.contents, removeAllowed;
   @    ensures !removeAllowed &&
   @            underlyingCollection.contents ==
   @            \old(underlyingCollection.contents) - {#lastElement#};
   @*/
  public void remove();
```

4.4   The Specification of the Methods in Collection

The next step is to write the specifications of the methods in `Collection`. There are two important points that we encountered while formulating and verifying these specifications: (1) how to express membership of a collection, and

(2) how to handle self-referential collections, *i.e.* collections containing references to themselves. The second point only became clear during verification,
and forced us to improve our specifications. Below we describe this in more detail, and we give relevant example specifications, as we finally have verified. The
complete specification of `Collection` is available at [13].

Membership of a Collection. The first specification problem is how to state
that an element occurs in a collection. A first approach is to use the membership
test on multisets, as provided by Isabelle, but it is easily seen that this is not
sufficient. For example, every collection has a method `contains` that can be used
to test whether a certain element occurs in a collection. However, according to the
informal documentation (and as confirmed by the implementation of `contains`
in `AbstractCollection`) a call `contains(Object o)` returns true if and only if
the collection contains an element x, such that

$$o == null ? x == null : o.equals(x)$$

Notice that while verifying we do not know which implementation of `equals` will
be used, this depends on the dynamic type of the object o. In class `Object` the
definition of equality coincides with pointer equality[10], but typically this method
will be overridden in subclasses to deal with structural equivalences.

Thus, in the specifications we state membership of the variable `contents`
w.r.t. the `equals` operation on (non-null) objects. To keep the specifications
readable, by avoiding the explicit use of the conditional expression as above, the
abbreviation `occurs` is introduced[11]. In the JML framework, such an abbreviation is introduced by defining a so-called model method, *i.e.* a method that is
part of the specification.

```
— JML
  /*@ model boolean occurs(Object o) {
   @   return (o == null ? elem(null) :
   @                       (\exists (Object x) elem(x) && o.equals(x)));
   @ }
   @*/
```

Using this abbreviation, we can write for example a specification for the method
`containsAll`. This method takes as argument a collection c and it tests whether
every element in c occurs in this collection.

```
— JML
  /*@ normal_behavior
   @   requires c instanceof Collection;
   @   ensures \result == (\forall (Object x) (c.contents).elem(x) ==>
   @                                          contents.occurs(x));
   @*/
  boolean containsAll(Collection c);
```

---

[10] See `java/lang/Object.html#equals(java.lang.Object)` of [19].
[11] However, in the verifications we still need to make this case-distinction at several
places.

The precondition of `containsAll` requires that c is a non-null reference, satisfying the specification of `Collection`. The postcondition quantifies over all elements in `c.contents` and tests whether they occur in the `contents` of this collection (*w.r.t.* `equals`).

In a similar way, a model method `count_occurs` is defined, which counts the occurrences of an object o *w.r.t.* the `equals` operation.

Self-Referential Collections. The other problem deals with self-referential collections. This problem was only encountered during verification, because this required us to consider *all* possible parameters of the operations. To overcome the problem we had to improve our specifications and exclude certain method arguments.

If a collection contains a reference to itself (direct or indirect), its behaviour becomes unpredictable. Consider for example the following Java program.

— JAVA ————————————————————————————

```
class RemoveCollectionFromCollection {
  Vector w;

  boolean remove_one_element () {
    Vector v = new Vector (); Object o = new Object ();
    v.add(o); v.add(v);                 // v contains itself
    w = (Vector)v.clone();
    boolean first_time = v.contains(w);  // first_time == true
    v.remove(o);
    boolean second_time = v.contains(w); // second_time == false
    return (first_time == second_time);  // \result == false
  }
}
```

The method `remove_one_element()` returns false, as the variable `first_time` is true, while `second_time` is false. Thus, by removing an element o from the collection, suddenly other objects are not contained in it anymore either.

Careful analysis shows that in general it is not possible to specify modifications to a self-referential collection[12]. Therefore, in these method specifications we require the following:

− the collection does not contain itself;
− the method arguments are not equal to the collection itself; and
− if the method argument is a collection, it does not contain the receiving collection.

---

[12] Many similar examples can be constructed, by changing the fields of an object that is stored in a collection. What is special about this example is that it is an operation on the collection itself that changes the contents of the collection. These examples show how important it is to reason carefully about aliases.

```
— JML
 /*@ normal_behavior
   @    requires addDefined && c instanceof Collection && c != this &&
   @              (\forall (Object o)
   @                (c.contents).elem(o) ==> o != this &&
   @                                    storable(o)) &&
   @              (\forall (Object o) contents.elem(o) ==>
   @                                    \reach(o).has(this));
   @  modifiable contents;
   @      ensures \result == (contents != \old(contents)) &&
   @              allowDoubles?
   @                contents == \old(contents) + c.contents :
   @                (\forall (Object o) o != this ==>
   @                    (contents.occurs(o) ==
   @                    (c.contents + \old(contents)).occurs(o)) &&
   @                    contents.count_occurs(o) <= 1);
   @*/
 boolean addAll(Collection c);
```

Fig. 4. JML specification for method `addAll`

The last condition is necessary to ensure that we can prove that the contents of the argument collection is unchanged. Notice that these restrictions are not visible from the informal documentation, they only became apparent during formal verification.

An example of a method where these restrictions are needed is `addAll`. Fig. 4 contains its specification. This specification states that this method terminates normally in a state satisfying the postcondition if the following conditions are satisfied:

– the collection supports the `add` operation;
– the argument collection c is a non-null reference, satisfying the specification of `Collection`;
– the argument collection and all its elements should be different from `this` (which is the receiving collection);
– all the elements in the argument collection can be stored in the collection (otherwise a `StorableException` will be thrown); and
– the receiving collection is not self-referential, *i.e.* `this` should not be reachable from any element in the collection.

The postcondition states that the argument collection is added to the collection. If duplicate elements are allowed, the method `addAll` corresponds to multiset union. If the collection does not allow duplicate elements, then elements are added only if they did not already occur (thus explicitly ensuring that the second clause of the class invariant is preserved).

— ISABELLE

```
next'spec` :: [OM' => OM' Iterator'IFace, MemLoc'] => bool
"next'spec c p ==
 let next = java_util_IteratorInterface.next' c in
 (ALL z.
  total'expr_correctness
  (%x. x = z & p < heap'top x & it_contents c x ~= {#})
  next
  (%x v.(case v of
         Null' => True
        |Reference' r => SubClass' (get'type r x) ''Object'' &
                         r < heap'top x &
                         equals'spec (Object'clg (get'type r x) r) r) &
   it_contents c x + {#v#}= it_contents c z &
   elem (it_contents c z) v &
   removeAllowed c x &
   lastElement c x = v &
   heap'top z <= heap'top x &
   get'type p x = get'type p z & get'dimlen p x = get'dimlen p z &
   stack_equality z x & static_equality z x))"
```

Fig. 5. Translated specification of next

5   Proof Obligations and Verification

Given the JML specifications for Collection and Iterator, the next step is to
translate this into proof obligations in Isabelle and to verify that the implementations in AbstractCollection (translated into Isabelle theories by the LOOP
compiler) satisfy these specifications.

5.1   From Specification to Proof Obligation

All specifications in this case study are so called normal_behavior specifications, describing the functional behaviour of the methods. As explained above,
normal_behavior specifications give rise to total correctness sentences as proof
obligations. Comparing the proof obligations in Isabelle with the corresponding
JML specifications reveals several differences.

– Each variable declaration (e.g. method parameters and the variables over
  which a \forall expression ranges in the specification) implicitly implies
  that this variable satisfies the class specification of its static type. In the
  Isabelle translation this becomes explicit.

- Modifies clauses are translated into postconditions, stating which variables should be left unchanged[13]. If a method specification does not contain a `modifiable` clause, the postcondition states that heap, stack and static memory (which together form the whole memory) are unchanged.
- To be able to translate `\old()` expressions, the pre-state of a method is remembered explicitly, by using a special logical variable.
- Aspects dealing with the memory model underlying the Java formalisation [3] are stated explicitly, *e.g.* it is stated explicitly that the collection is in allocated memory, *i.e.* below the heaptop.

To illustrate these differences, Fig. 5 contains the translated specification of the method `next()`. We do not expect the reader to understand all the details of this specification, but hopefully the structure of the original JML specification can be recognised.

5.2   Verification of AbstractCollection

Once we have formulated suitable specifications, the verifications are relatively easy. We try to use as much automation as possible. Almost all methods that we verify contain loops, therefore we make extensive use of the Hoare logic that has been developed for Java [15]. Resolution is used to let Isabelle select the appropriate proof rule. Of course, loop invariants and variants still have to be given explicitly. However, for most methods these are very similar.

Roughly, all (translated) method bodies have the following structure[14].

```
body = { set parameters and local variables;
         Iterator e = iterator();
         while (e.hasNext()) {something with next();}
         return something;
       }
```

Typically, verification proceeds as follows. First it is shown that at the moment that the loop is entered, the precondition of the method still holds and the values of the parameters and local variables are properly assigned. In particular, it is shown that the iterator is appropriately initialised. This subproof is more or less the same for every method. It uses automatic rewriting to deal with the first assignments, and instantiates the method specification of `iterator` to deal with the initialisation of e. Next, an appropriate Hoare logic rule instantiated with a suitable loop invariant is applied to the loop body (which rule is used depends on how the loop is expected to terminate: normally, or abnormally – because of a return). In all cases, the variant is the number of elements left in the `contents`

---

[13] To reduce the size of the proof obligations, we only state this condition for variables which we do not assume to be constant.

[14] Except for the method `isEmpty()` that only consists of one line of code. In some cases, the `return` statement already occurs in the loop body, or there is no `return` statement.

of the iterator. Application of the proof rule gives 1 or 3 Hoare triples over the loop body as subgoals[15]. The loop body always consists of the `hasNext()` test (evaluated for its side-effect), followed by some statements containing `next()`. For all subgoals, it first is shown that `hasNext()` preserves the precondition of the loop body (which is a conjunction of the loop invariant and the fact that the condition is true) as it does not have any side-effects. This is shown by using the specification of `hasNext()`. Then, the most difficult part in the verifications is to show that the postcondition of the Hoare triple – either the loop invariant or the exit condition of the loop – is ensured by the statements containing `next()` (and possibly some other operation). This is in particular difficult for methods that change the collection, like `remove` and `addAll`, because they involve both reasoning with the `occurs` abbreviation, and restrictions on self-referential collections. The specifications of the methods used in the fragment are appropriately instantiated and manipulated to construct the proof. Finally, it has to be shown that after the loop has been exited, the postcondition is ensured by the last `return` statement. Basically, this is done by automatic rewriting.

To conclude, some statistics. In total, the correctness of 9 methods has been shown. For each method, 1 to 4 different lemmas are proven. The proof of such a lemma takes on average approximately 400 proof steps. Memory usage can be problematic: sometimes Isabelle uses over 1000 MB[16]. We started this case study on a Pentium II with 300MB memory, which clearly was not enough. Therefore we shifted to a Sun Enterprise 10000, with 24 UltraSPARC processors of 333MHz and 12GB memory. Overall, the whole case study took us approximately 2 man-month, after solving the initial hardware problems.

6 Conclusions

This paper presents the specification and verification of the interface `Collection` and the (abstract) class `AbstractCollection`, both from Java's API. It describes how the specifications have been constructed, identifying the model variables and method specifications from the informal documentation. Two problems occurred in the specifications, dealing with equality of objects and membership of a collection and with self-referential collections. It is discussed how the specifications take these problems into account.

The verification of the class `AbstractCollection` is done in a modular way, following the behavioural subtype approach, reasoning with specifications of method calls. This has the advantage that every method implementation can be replaced by a different application without breaking the correctness of the complete class, as long as the new implementation still satisfies the specification.

The verifications itself are labour-intensive and basically all proceed along the same lines. However, the most interesting aspect of this paper is the construction of the correct specifications. The problems that we encountered are not specific

---

[15] If the loop is shown to terminate normally, the appropriate rule gives 1 subgoal, in the case of abnormal termination the appropriate rule results in 3 subgoals, see [15].

[16] We used SML to run Isabelle, Poly/ML should give better statistics.

for this case study, they are more general and will appear in the specification of many other Java classes as well.

Useful future work would be to develop a collection of standard results on equality of objects, which would facilitate specifying and reasoning about this. Now we found that the case-distinctions on whether an object is a null reference or not were often cluttering our proofs, without providing any new insights. A collection of standard results could help to avoid this.

The problem with the self-referential collections is more subtle, and could not be identified from the informal documentation: it only became apparent during verification, because this required us to consider *all* cases. However, once we had found one problematic example, it was easy to identify which methods had similar problems and to adapt the specifications of these methods. When writing a specification for a different class, we will probably be more aware of this problem and identify it earlier.

Tool support should still be improved. As mentioned above, in this case study the proof obligations are translated by hand from JML into Isabelle. This has the advantage that we could leave out unnecessary details, but the big disadvantage that it is error-prone. The current extension of the LOOP compiler to do this translation looks very promising, but unfortunately is only available for PVS at the moment.

This case study is the first big case study in the LOOP project in Isabelle. In the verification we usually make extensive use of automatic rewriting, but as Isabelle has a different rewrite strategy than PVS, we found that the collection of standard rewrite rules was not sufficient. During the verification, we extended the collection of rewrite rules, but it is still not optimal. A complicating factor is that rewriting strategies of theorem provers are not very clearly documented (see also [14]). Despite the fact that probably an even higher degree of automation could have been achieved in the proofs, we still think that this case study is a good and impressive example, showing that it has become feasible to construct complete and fully verified specifications of classes from Java's standard library, revealing subtle omissions in the informal documentation.

Acknowledgements

Thanks to Néstor Cataño and the anonymous referees, whose comments greatly helped to improve this paper.

References

1. P. America. Designing an object-oriented programming language with behavioural subtyping. In J.W. de Bakker, W.P. de Roever, and G.Rozenberg, editors, *Foundations of Object-Oriented Languages*, number 489 in LNCS, pages 60–90. Springer, 1990.
2. K. Arnold, J. Gosling, and D. Holmes. *The Java Programming Language*. Addison-Wesley, 3rd edition, 2000.

3. J. van den Berg, M. Huisman, B. Jacobs, and E. Poll. A type-theoretic memory model for verification of sequential Java programs. In D. Bert, C. Choppy, and P.D. Mosses, editors, *Recent Trends in Algebraic Development Techniques*, number 1827 in LNCS, pages 1–21. Springer, 2000.
4. J. van den Berg and B. Jacobs. The LOOP compiler for Java and JML. In T. Margaria and W. Yi, editors, *Tools and Algorithms for the Construction and Analysis of Systems (TACAS 2001)*, number 2031 in LNCS, pages 299–312. Springer, 2001.
5. J. van den Berg, B. Jacobs, and E. Poll. Formal Specification and Verification of JavaCard's Application Identifier Class. In *Java on Smart Cards: Programming and Security*, number 2041 in LNCS, pages 137–150. Springer, 2001.
6. C. Breunesse, B. Jacobs, and J. van den Berg. Specifying and Verifying an Example: a decimal representation in Java for smartcards , 2002. Manuscript.
7. T. Budd. *Understanding Object-oriented programming with Java – updated edition*. Addison-Wesley, 2000.
8. N. Cataño and M. Huisman. Formal specification of Gemplus' electronic purse case study. In *Formal Methods Europe (FME'02)*, LNCS. Springer, 2002. To appear.
9. S. Drossopoulou and S. Eisenbach. Java is type safe–probably. In M. Aksit, editor, *European Conference on Object-Oriented Programming*, number 1241 in LNCS, pages 389–418. Springer, 1997.
10. ESC/Java specifications for the JavaCard API.
   `http://www.cs.kun.nl/~erikpoll/publications/jc211_specs.html`.
11. J. Guttag, J. Horning, and J. Wing. The Larch family of specification languages. *IEEE Software*, 2(5):24–36, 1985.
12. C.A.R. Hoare. Proof of correctness of data representations. *Acta Informatica*, 1:271–281, 1972.
13. M. Huisman. Specifications of Java's Collection class.
   `http://www-sop.inria.fr/lemme/Marieke.Huisman/collection.html`
14. M. Huisman. *Reasoning about Java programs in higher order logic using PVS and Isabelle*. PhD thesis, Computing Science Institute, University of Nijmegen, 2001.
15. M. Huisman and B. Jacobs. Java program verification via a Hoare logic with abrupt termination. In T. Maibaum, editor, *Fundamental Approaches to Software Engineering (FASE 2000)*, number 1783 in LNCS, pages 284–303. Springer, 2000.
16. M. Huisman, B. Jacobs, and J. van den Berg. A Case Study in Class Library Verification: Java's Vector Class. *Software Tools for Technology Transfer*, 3/3:332–352, 2001.
17. K. Huizing and R. Kuiper. Reinforcing fragile base classes. In *Proceedings of Workshop on Formal Techniques for Java Programs (FTfJP)*, 2001.
18. B. Jacobs and E. Poll. A logic for the Java Modeling Language JML. In H. Hussmann, editor, *Fundamental Approaches to Software Engineering (FASE 2001)*, number 2029 in LNCS, pages 284–299. Springer, 2001.
19. JavaTM 2 platform, standard edition, version 1.3 API specification.
   `http://www.java.sun.com/j2se/1.3/docs/api/index.html`.
20. G.T. Leavens, A.L. Baker, and C. Ruby. Preliminary design of JML: A behavioral interface specification language for Java. Technical Report 98-06, Iowa State University, Department of Computer Science, 1998.
21. K.R.M. Leino. *Toward Reliable Modular Programs*. PhD thesis, California Inst. of Techn., 1995.
22. K.R.M. Leino, G. Nelson, and J. B. Saxe. ESC/Java User's Manual. Technical Report SRC 2000-002, Compaq System Research Center, 2000.
23. B.H. Liskov and J.M. Wing. A behavioral notion of subtyping. *ACM Trans. on Progr. Lang. and Systems*, 16(1):1811–1841, 1994.

24. *The LOOP project.* http://www.cs.kun.nl/~bart/LOOP/index.html.
25. B. Meyer. *Object-Oriented Software Construction.* Prentice Hall, 2nd rev. edition, 1997.
26. D. von Oheimb and T. Nipkow. Machine-checking the Java specification: Proving type-safety. In J. Alves-Foss, editor, *Formal Syntax and Semantics of Java*, number 1523 in LNCS, pages 119–156. Springer, 1999.
27. S. Owre, J. Rushby, N. Shankar, and F von Henke. Formal verification for fault-tolerant architectures: Prolegomena to the design of PVS. *IEEE Transactions on Software Engineering*, 21(2):107–125, 1995.
28. L.C. Paulson. *Isabelle - a generic theorem prover.* Number 828 in LNCS. Springer, 1994. With contributions by Tobias Nipkow.
29. D. Syme. Proving Java type soundness. In J. Alves-Foss, editor, *Formal Syntax and Semantics of Java*, number 1523 in LNCS, pages 83–118. Springer, 1999.

Solving Regular Path Queries*

Yanhong A. Liu and Fuxiang Yu

Computer Science Dept., State University of New York, Stony Brook, NY 11794
{liu,fuxiang}@cs.sunysb.edu

Abstract. Regular path queries are a way of declaratively specifying program analyses as a kind of regular expressions that are matched against paths in graph representations of programs. These and similar queries are useful for other path analysis problems as well. This paper describes the precise specification, derivation, and analysis of a complete algorithm and data structures for solving regular path queries. We first show two ways of specifying the problem and deriving a high-level algorithmic solution, using predicate logic and language inclusion, respectively. Both lead to a set-based fixed-point specification. We then derive a complete implementation from this specification using Paige's methods that consist of dominated convergence, finite differencing, and real-time simulation. This formal derivation allows us to analyse the time and space complexity of the implementation precisely in terms of size parameters of the graph and the deterministic finite automaton that corresponds to the regular expression. In particular, the time and space complexity is linear in the size of the graph. We also note that the problem is PSPACE-complete in terms of the size of the regular expression. In applications such as program analysis, the size of the graph may be very large, but the size of the regular expression is small and can be considered a constant.

1 Introduction

Regular path queries are a way of declaratively specifying program analyses as a kind of regular expressions that are matched against paths in graph representations of programs [5]. Related queries are also used in model checking [9]. Program analysis and model checking are important for many applications. For example, program analysis is critical for program optimisation, and model checking is important for formal verification. In fact, regular expressions provide a general framework for capturing many path problems [18,17]. Program analysis and model checking are just two of many applications.

This paper describes the precise specification, derivation, and analysis of a complete algorithm and data structures for solving regular path queries. The specification and derivation consist of two parts. First, specify the problem and derive a high-level algorithm that can be expressed using a set-based language with fixed-point operations. Then, start with a set-based fixed-point specification and derive a complete implementation with precise data structures and

---

* This work was supported in part by ONR under grants N00014-01-1-0109 and N00014-99-1-0132.

E.A. Boiten and B. Möller (Eds.): MPC 2002, LNCS 2386, pp. 195–208, 2002.
© Springer-Verlag Berlin Heidelberg 2002

operations on them. This formal derivation allows us to analyse the time and space complexity of the implementation precisely in terms of size parameters of the graph and the deterministic finite automaton that corresponds to the regular expression. In particular, the time and space complexity is linear in the size of the graph. We also note that the problem is PSPACE-complete in terms of the size of the regular expression. In applications such as program analysis and model checking, the size of the graph may be very large, but the size of the regular expression is small and can be considered a constant [5].

The derivation from a set-based fixed-point specification to a complete implementation uses Paige's methods that are centered around finite differencing [10,14,11], i.e., computing expensive set expressions incrementally. We first use dominated convergence [3] at the higher level to transform fixed-point operations into loops. We then apply finite differencing [14,11] to transform expensive set expressions in loops into incremental operations. Finally, we use real-time simulation [12,2] at the lower level to implement sets and set operations using efficient data structures. The derivation is completely systematic, and the resulting algorithm and data structures can be analysed precisely and map to physical implementations directly.

In contrast, starting at some initial specification of the problem and arriving at a set-based fixed-point specification have not been as systematic. A fixed-point specification often corresponds to some high-level algorithm already. How should one obtain it? In a most recent work by de Moor et al. [5], specification and derivation that arrive at such a high-level algorithm are given, using calculus of relations and universal algebra. This paper shows two other ways of specifying the problem and deriving a high-level algorithmic solution, using predicate logic and language inclusion, respectively. Both derivations are extremely succinct, and both results lead easily to a set-based fixed-point specification. The initial specification using predicate logic corresponds rather directly to the given English description of the problem.

The rest of the paper is organised as follows. Section 2 describes the problem specification and two ways of arriving at a high-level algorithmic solution. Section 3 expresses the high-level solution using a set-based language with fixed-point operations, and introduces Paige's approach for computing fixed points iteratively. Sections 4 and 5 derive the precise incremental computation steps and data structures, respectively. Section 6 discusses related issues. Section 7 compares with related work and concludes.

2   Problem Specification and High-Level Algorithmic Solution

We describe how the problem can be specified and how a high-level algorithm for solving it can be derived succinctly in two ways, using predicate logic and language inclusion, respectively.

The Regular Path Query Problem. Consider an edge-labelled directed graph G and a regular-expression pattern P. We say that a path in G matches

P if the sequence of edge labels on the path is in the regular language generated by P. The regular path query problem is:

> Given an edge-labelled directed graph G with a special vertex $v0$, and a regular expression P, compute all vertices v in G such that all paths from $v0$ to v match P.

Precisely, we regard the given graph as a set G of labelled edges of the form $\langle v1, a, v2 \rangle$, with source and target vertices $v1$ and $v2$ respectively and edge label a, where $v0$ is a special vertex in the graph. We consider a deterministic finite automaton (DFA) corresponding to the given regular expression, where P is a set of labelled transitions of the form $\langle s1, a, s2 \rangle$, with source and target states (vertices) $s1$ and $s2$ respectively and transition (edge) label a, and where $s0$ is the start state, and F is the set of final states. We assume that for each state there is an outgoing edge for each label; a trap state can be added to achieve this if needed. The initial specifications (1) and (4) below are correct even if P is nondeterministic. We discuss why we use a DFA instead of the regular expression or its corresponding nondeterministic finite automaton (NFA) in Section 6.

Using Predicate Logic. The problem as described above can be written directly as: Given G, $v0$, P, $s0$, and F, compute the set

$$\{v \in vertices(G) \mid \forall p \, (p \in path(v0, v, G) \Rightarrow \exists s \, (p \in path(s0, s, P) \land s \in F))\} \quad (1)$$

where $vertices(G)$ is the set of all vertices in G, $path(v0, v, G)$ is the set of all sequences of edge labels on paths from $v0$ to v in G, and $path(s0, s, P)$ is similar.

Since P is a DFA, i.e., it is deterministic, the right side of $\Rightarrow$ in (1) equals

$$\neg \exists s \, (p \in path(s0, s, P) \land s \notin F)$$

which equals

$$\forall s \, (\neg p \in path(s0, s, P) \lor s \in F).$$

Now, move $\forall s$ above out of $\Rightarrow$, and move negated left operand of $\lor$ to left of $\Rightarrow$. We have that (1) equals

$$\{v \in vertices(G) \mid \forall p \, \forall s \, (p \in path(v0, v, G) \land p \in path(s0, s, P) \Rightarrow s \in F)\}$$

which, letting $G \times P = \{\langle \langle v1, s1 \rangle, a, \langle v2, s2 \rangle \rangle \mid \langle v1, a, v2 \rangle \in G \land \langle s1, a, s2 \rangle \in P\}$ be the product of P and Q, equals

$$\{v \in vertices(G) \mid \forall p \, \forall s \, (p \in path(\langle v0, s0 \rangle, \langle v, s \rangle, G \times P) \Rightarrow s \in F)\} \quad (2)$$

We can see that (2) computes the set of vertices v in G such that, if there is a path from $\langle v0, s0 \rangle$ to $\langle v, s \rangle$ in $G \times P$, i.e., if $\langle v, s \rangle$ is reachable from $\langle v0, s0 \rangle$, then s is in F. Precisely, moving $\forall p$ inside yields $\exists p \, (p \in path(\langle v0, s0 \rangle, \langle v, s \rangle, G \times P))$ on the left side of $\Rightarrow$. If we let $reach(G \times P, \langle v0, s0 \rangle)$ be the set of nodes reachable from $\langle v0, s0 \rangle$ in $G \times P$, then $\exists p \, (p \in path(\langle v0, s0 \rangle, \langle v, s \rangle, G \times P))$ equals $\langle v, s \rangle \in reach(G \times P, \langle v0, s0 \rangle)$, and (2) equals

$$\{v \in vertices(G) \mid \forall s \, (\langle v, s \rangle \in reach(G \times P, \langle v0, s0 \rangle) \Rightarrow s \in F)\} \quad (3)$$

Either (2) or (3) expresses the same high-level algorithm derived earlier [5].

Using Language Inclusion. We can regard the given graph G as a labelled transition system, or an NFA, with start state $v0$ and the set of final states not yet defined. Then the problem is to compute a subset U of the vertices in G, such that if $v0$ is the start state and U is the set of final states, then the language $L_{(G,v0,U)}$ generated by the NFA $(G, v0, U)$ is a subset of the language $L_{(P,s0,F)}$ generated by the DFA $(P, s0, F)$, and U is the largest such set. That is, given G, $v0$, P, $s0$, and F, the problem is to compute

$$\max\{U \subseteq vertices(G) \mid L_{(G,v0,U)} \subseteq L_{(P,s0,F)}\} \tag{4}$$

where max follows the partial order of set inclusion $\subseteq$.

Since P is a DFA, if S^c denotes the complement of set S, we have

$$L_{(P,s0,F)} = (L_{(P,s0,F^c)})^c$$

Thus, the language inclusion in (4), with the new right side $(L_{(P,s0,F^c)})^c$, equals

$$L_{(G,v0,U)} \cap L_{(P,s0,F^c)} = \emptyset$$

which equals

$$L_{(G \times P,\langle v0,s0 \rangle, U \times F^c)} = \emptyset \tag{5}$$

where the second $\times$ is a simple Cartesian product.

Using the *reach* notation in (3), (5) equals

$$reach(G \times P, \langle v0, s0 \rangle) \cap (U \times F^c) = \emptyset$$

which equals

$$\forall \langle v, s \rangle \; (\langle v, s \rangle \in reach(G \times P, \langle v0, s0 \rangle) \wedge s \in F^c \Rightarrow v \notin U)$$

Thus, (4) equals

$$\max\{U \subseteq vertices(G) \mid \forall \langle v, s \rangle \; (\langle v, s \rangle \in reach(G \times P, \langle v0, s0 \rangle) \wedge s \in F^c \Rightarrow v \notin U)\}$$

which equals

$$vertices(G) - \{v \mid \exists s \; (\langle v, s \rangle \in reach(G \times P, \langle v0, s0 \rangle) \wedge s \in F^c)\} \tag{6}$$

Note that (6) equals (3) except for the double negation based on the rule

$$\{x \in S \mid predicate(x)\} = S - \{x \in S \mid \neg \, predicate(x)\}.$$

Starting with either (6) or (3) will lead to not only the same complete algorithm but also the same derivation except for the initial appearance of set difference. We will use (6) for no particular reason.

3   Approach for Deriving a Complete Implementation

Notation. We use a set-based language for deriving a complete implementation. The language is based on SETL [15,16] extended with a fixed-point operation [3]. Primitive data types are sets, pairs, and maps, i.e., binary relations represented as sets of pairs. Their syntax and operations on them are summarised below:

$\{X_1, ..., X_n\}$	a set with elements $X_1, ..., X_n$
$[X_1, X_2]$	a pair with elements X_1 and X_2
$\{[X_1, Y_1], ..., [X_n, Y_n]\}$	a map that maps X_1 to Y_1, ..., X_n to Y_n
$\{\}$	empty set
$S + T$, $S - T$	union and difference, respectively, of sets S and T
S **with** X, S **less** X	$S + \{X\}$ and $S - \{X\}$, respectively
$S \subseteq T$	whether S is a subset of T
$X \in S$, $X \notin S$	whether or not, respectively, X is an element of S
dom(M)	domain of map M, i.e., $\{X : [X, Y] \in M\}$
ran(M)	range of map M, i.e., $\{Y : [X, Y] \in M\}$
$M\{Z\}$	image set of Z under map M, i.e., $\{Y : [X, Y] \in M \mid X = Z\}$
$M[S]$	image set union of S under M, i.e., $\{Y : [X, Y] \in M \mid X \in S\}$

We use the notation below for set comprehension. Y_i's enumerate elements of all S_i's; for each combination of $Y_1, ..., Y_n$, if the Boolean value of expression Z is true, then the value of expression X forms an element of the resulting set.

$$\{X : Y_1 \in S_1, ..., Y_n \in S_n \mid Z\} \quad \text{set former}$$

$\mathbf{LFP}_{\subseteq, S_0}(F(S), S)$ denotes the minimum element S, with respect to partial ordering $\subseteq$, that satisfies the condition $S_0 \subseteq S$ and $F(S) = S$. We use standard control constructs **while**, **for**, and **if**, and we use indentation to indicate scoping. We abbreviate $X := X$ **op** Y as X **op** $:= Y$.

A Set-Based Fixed-Point Specification. We represent a set of labelled edges of the form $\langle x1, a, x2 \rangle$ using a set of pairs of the form $[x1, [a, x2]]$, which can be built straightforwardly in the same loop that reads in the 3-tuple form. Thus, if $[x1, [a, x2]]$ is a labelled edge in G, then $x1$ is in **dom**(G), a is in **dom**(**ran**(G)), and $x2$ is in **ran**(**ran**(G)). So $vertices(G) = \mathbf{dom}(G) + \mathbf{ran}(\mathbf{ran}(G))$, and (6) can be expressed directly using set and fixed-point notation as

$$\mathbf{dom}(G) + \mathbf{ran}(\mathbf{ran}(G)) - \{v : [v, s] \in \mathbf{LFP}_{\subseteq, \{[v0, s0]\}}((G \times P)[R], R) \mid s \notin F\} \quad (7)$$

where $G \times P = \{[[v1, s1], [a, [v2, s2]]] : [v1, [a, v2]] \in G \wedge [s1, [b, s2]] \in P \mid a = b\}$.

Approach. The method has three steps: (1) dominated convergence, (2) finite differencing, and (3) real-time simulation.

Dominated convergence [3] transforms a set-based fixed-point specification into a **while**-loop. The idea is to perform a small update operation in each iteration. The fixed-point expression $\mathbf{LFP}_{\subseteq, \{[v0, s0]\}}((G \times P)[R], R)$ in (7) is transformed into the following **while**-loop, making use of $\lambda R.F(R) \cup R$ being monotone and inflationary at $[v0, s0]$:

$$R := \{[v0, s0]\};$$
$$\mathbf{while\ exists}\ [v, s] \in (G \times P)[R] - R \quad (8)$$
$$R\ \mathbf{with} := [v, s];$$

This code is followed by

$$O := \mathbf{dom}(G) + \mathbf{ran}(\mathbf{ran}(G)) - \{v : [v, s] \in R \mid s \notin F\};$$

When the loop in (8) terminates, R is the set of nodes in $G \times P$ reachable from $[v0, s0]$. O is the output set.

To simplify the initialisation code, we can move initialisation of R into the loop body, yielding:

$$
\begin{aligned}
&R := \{\}; \\
&\textbf{while exists } [v, s] \in \{[v0, s0]\} + (G \times P)[R] - R \\
&\quad R \textbf{ with } := [v, s]; \\
&O := \mathbf{dom}(G) + \mathbf{ran}(\mathbf{ran}(G)) - \{v : [v, s] \in R \mid s \notin F\};
\end{aligned}
\tag{9}
$$

Finite differencing [14,11] transforms expensive set operations in a loop into incremental operations. The idea is to replace expensive expressions exp_1, ..., exp_n in a loop $LOOP$ with fresh variables E_1, ..., E_n, respectively, and maintain the invariants $E_1 = exp_1$, ..., $E_n = exp_n$ by inserting appropriate initialisations or updates to E_1, ..., E_n at each assignment in $LOOP$. We denote the transformed loop as

$$\Delta\, E_1, ..., E_n \langle LOOP \rangle$$

For our program (9), expensive expressions, i.e., non-constant-time expressions here, are the one that computes O and others that are needed for computing $\{[v0, s0]\} + (G \times P)[R] - R$. We use fresh variables to hold their values. These variables are initialised together with the assignment $R := \{\}$ and are updated incrementally as R is augmented by $[v, s]$ in each iteration. Liu [7] gives references to much work that exploits similar ideas.

Real-time simulation [12,2] selects appropriate data structures for representing sets so that operations on them can be implemented efficiently. The idea is to design sophisticated linked structures based on how sets and set elements are accessed, so that each operation can be performed in worst-case constant time and with at most a constant (a small fraction) factor of overall space overhead.

4   Finite Differencing

This section transforms (9) to compute expensive set operations incrementally.

Identifying Expensive Subexpressions. The expensive subcomputations in (9) are named as follows,

$$
\begin{aligned}
I &= G \times P & &\text{// product graph} \\
S &= I[R] & &\text{// successors in product graph} \\
W &= \{[v0, s0]\} + S - R & &\text{// workset} \\
O &= \mathbf{dom}(G) + \mathbf{ran}(\mathbf{ran}(G)) - \{v : [v, s] \in R \mid s \notin F\} & &\text{// output set}
\end{aligned}
\tag{10}
$$

We want to compute these computations incrementally using finite differencing. That is, we want to update the sets I, S, W, and O whenever we update R. Thus, the overall computation in (9) becomes

$$
\begin{aligned}
\Delta\, I, S, W, O \,\langle\, &R := \{\}; \\
&\textbf{while exists } [v, s] \in W \\
&\quad R \textbf{ with } := [v, s]; \rangle
\end{aligned}
\tag{11}
$$

Initialisation and Incremental Maintenance. First, sets I, S, W, and O need to be initialised together with $R := \{\}$ before the loop in (11). That is, they need to be set to values that correspond to $R = \{\}$ based on their definitions in (10). This yields

$$
\begin{aligned}
I &:= G \times P; \\
S &:= \{\}; \\
W &:= \{[v0, s0]\}; \\
O &:= \mathbf{dom}(G) + \mathbf{ran}(\mathbf{ran}(G)).
\end{aligned}
$$

Then, sets I, S, W, and O also need to be maintained incrementally together with R **with** $:= [v, s]$ in the loop body in (11). That is, we need to update their values corresponding to the update R **with** $:= [v, s]$ based on their definitions in (10). Clearly, set I remain unchanged, and the other sets can be updated as follows, where the two updates to W are with respects to the update to S and R, respectively.

$S + := \{[v2, s2] : [v, [a, v2]] \in G, [s, [b, s2]] \in P \mid a = b \wedge [v2, s2] \notin S\};$
$W + := \{[v2, s2] : [v, [a, v2]] \in G, [s, [b, s2]] \in P \mid a = b \wedge [v2, s2] \notin W \wedge [v2, s2] \notin R\};$
W **less** $:= [v, s];$
if $s \notin F \wedge v \in O$ **then**
  O **less** $:= v;$

Adding these initialisation and incremental updates to the initialisation and the body of the loop in (11), we obtain the following complete program:

$I := G \times P;$
$S := \{\};$
$W := \{[v0, s0]\};$
$O := \mathbf{dom}(G) + \mathbf{ran}(\mathbf{ran}(G));$
$R := \{\};$
while exists $[v, s] \in W$
  $S + := \{[v2, s2] : [v, [a, v2]] \in G, [s, [b, s2]] \in P \mid a = b \wedge [v2, s2] \notin S\};$
  $W + := \{[v2, s2] : [v, [a, v2]] \in G, [s, [b, s2]] \in P \mid a = b \wedge [v2, s2] \notin W \wedge [v2, s2] \notin R\};$
  W **less** $:= [v, s];$
  if $s \notin F \wedge v \in O$ **then**
    O **less** $:= v;$
  R **with** $:= [v, s];$

$$(12)$$

Eliminating Dead Code. It is easy to see that sets I and S can be eliminated, and (12) becomes

$W := \{[v0, s0]\};$ // initialize W
$O := \mathbf{dom}(G) + \mathbf{ran}(\mathbf{ran}(G));$ // initialize O
$R := \{\};$ // initialize R
while exists $[v, s] \in W$
  $W + := \{[v2, s2] : [v, [a, v2]] \in G, [s, [b, s2]] \in P \mid a = b \wedge [v2, s2] \notin W \wedge [v2, s2] \notin R\};$
     // add to W
  W **less** $:= [v, s];$ // delete from W
  if $s \notin F \wedge v \in O$ **then**
    O **less** $:= v;$ // update O
  R **with** $:= [v, s];$ // update R

$$(13)$$

Finally, transform all aggregate set operations into explicit loops that process set elements one at a time. We obtain the following complete algorithm after finite differencing; for completeness, we also show the input and output explicitly.

$$
\begin{aligned}
&\mathbf{input}(G, P, v0, s0, F); \\
&W := \{[v0, s0]\}; && // \text{ initialize } W \\
&O := \{\}; && // \text{ initialize } O \\
&\mathbf{for}\ v1 \in \mathbf{dom}(G) && // \quad \text{using } \mathbf{for}\text{-loops} \\
&\quad \mathbf{if}\ v1 \notin O\ \mathbf{then} \\
&\quad\quad O\ \mathbf{with} := v1; \\
&\quad\quad \mathbf{for}\ a \in \mathbf{dom}(G\{v1\}) \\
&\quad\quad\quad \mathbf{for}\ v2 \in (G\{v1\})\{a\} \\
&\quad\quad\quad\quad \mathbf{if}\ v2 \notin O\ \mathbf{then} \\
&\quad\quad\quad\quad\quad O\ \mathbf{with} := v2; \\
&R := \{\}; && // \text{ initialize } R \\
\\
&\mathbf{while\ exists}\ v \in \mathbf{dom}(W) && // \text{ iterate through } W \\
&\quad \mathbf{while\ exists}\ s \in W\{v\} && // \quad \text{using } \mathbf{while}\text{-loops} \\
&\quad\quad \mathbf{for}\ a \in \mathbf{dom}(G\{v\}) && // \text{ iterate through } (G \times P)\{[v, s]\} \\
&\quad\quad\quad \mathbf{for}\ v2 \in (G\{v\})\{a\} && // \quad \text{using } \mathbf{for}\text{-loops} \\
&\quad\quad\quad\quad \mathbf{for}\ s2 \in (P\{s\})\{a\} && // \quad \text{to add to } W \\
&\quad\quad\quad\quad\quad \mathbf{if}\ s2 \notin W\{v2\} \wedge s2 \notin R\{v2\}\ \mathbf{then} \\
&\quad\quad\quad\quad\quad\quad W\{v2\}\ \mathbf{with} := s2; && // \text{ add to } W \\
&\quad\quad W\{v\}\ \mathbf{less} := s; && // \text{ delete from } W \\
&\quad\quad \mathbf{if}\ s \notin F \wedge v \in O\ \mathbf{then} \\
&\quad\quad\quad O\ \mathbf{less} := v; && // \text{ update } O \\
&\quad\quad\quad R\{v\}\ \mathbf{with} := s; && // \text{ update } R \\
&\mathbf{output}(O);
\end{aligned}
$$

$$(14)$$

Analysis of Time Complexity. Assume each primitive operation in the above algorithm takes $\mathcal{O}(1)$ time, which will be achieved using data structures in the next section. The algorithm considers each edge in $G \times P$ at most twice, once for adding to and once for deleting from W. Therefore, the time complexity of the above algorithm is $\mathcal{O}(|G| * |P|)$.

5   Data Structure Selection

We describe how to guarantee that each set operation in algorithm (14) takes worst-case $\mathcal{O}(1)$ time.

All set operations in (14) are of the following primitive forms: set initialisation $S := \{\}$, computing domain set $\mathbf{dom}(M)$, computing image set $M\{x\}$, element retrieval $\mathbf{for}\ X \in S$ and $\mathbf{while\ exists}\ X \in S$, membership test $X \in S$ and $X \notin S$, and element addition $S\ \mathbf{with}\ X$ and deletion $S\ \mathbf{less}\ X$.

We use *associative access* to refer to membership test ($X \in S$ and $X \notin S$) and computing image set ($M\{X\}$). Such an operation requires one to be able to locate an element (X) in a set (S or $\mathbf{dom}(M)$).

Based Representations. Consider using a singly linked list for a set and for each of the domain and image sets of a map, and letting each element in a domain linked list contain a pointer to its image linked list. That is, represent a set as a linked list, and represent a map as a linked list of linked lists. It is easy to see that, if associative access can be done in worst-case $\mathcal{O}(1)$ time, so can all other primitive operations. To see this, note that computing a domain set or an image set needs to return only a pointer to the set; retrieving an element from a set needs to locate only any element in the set; and adding or deleting an element from a set can be done in constant time after doing an associate access. An associative access would take linear time if a linked list is naively traversed to locate an element. A classical approach to solve this problem is to use hash tables [1] instead of linked lists. However, this gives average, rather than worst-case, $\mathcal{O}(1)$ time for each operation, and has an overhead of computing hashing related functions for each operation.

Page et al. [12,2] describe a technique for designing linked structures that support associative access in worst-case $\mathcal{O}(1)$ time with little space overhead for a general class of set-based programs. Consider

> **for** $X \in W$ or **while exists** $X \in W$
> ...$X \in S$... or ...$X \notin S$... or ...$M\{X\}$... where the domain of M is S

We want to locate value X in S after it has been located in W. The idea is to use a finite universal set B, called a base, to store values for both W and S, so that retrieval from W also locates the value in S. B is represented as a set (this set is only conceptual) of records, with a K field storing the key (i.e., value). Set S is represented using a S field of B: records of B whose keys belong to S are connected by a linked list where the links are stored in the S field; records of B whose keys are not in S store a special value for undefined in the S field. Set W is represented as a separate linked list of pointers to records of B whose keys belong to W. Thus, an element of S is represented as *a field in* the record, and S is said to be *strongly based* on B; and element of W is represented as *a pointer to* the record, and W is said to be *weakly based* on B. This representation allows an arbitrary number of weakly based sets but only a constant number of strongly based sets. Essentially, base B provides a kind of indexing.

It is easy to see the S field can be a single bit if S is not traversed; otherwise, if there is no deletion from S, then elements in S only need to be linked using a singly linked list. Only when S is traversed and there is any deletion operation from S do we need a doubly linked list.

Data Structures. Consider the **while**-loops in (14). The outer **while**-loop retrieves elements (named v) from the domain of W and locates it in the domain of G (by $G\{v\}$), in set O (by $v \in O$), and in the domain of R (by $R\{v\}$). The inner **while**-loop retrieves elements (named s) from a image set of W and locates it in the domain of P (by $P\{s\}$) and in set F (by $s \notin F$). There are also associative accesses into the domain of the range of G (by $(G\{v\})\{a\}$) and the domain of the range of P (by $(P\{v\})\{a\}$). Finally, there are associative accesses into both the domains and ranges of both W (by $s2 \notin W\{v2\}$) and R (by $s2 \notin R\{v2\}$).

Note that the kinds of accesses in the **while**-loops include also those needed for initialisation before the **while**-loops.

We use a base $B1$ for the set of vertices in G and a base $B2$ for the set of states in P. The domain of G and set O are strongly based on $B1$, and the domain of P and set F are strongly based on $B2$. The domains of W and R are also strongly based on $B1$. However, due to associative accesses into the image sets of G, P, W, and R, there are more than a constant number of sets that also need to be strongly based. Therefore, the based-representation method does not completely apply. Nevertheless, we may use arrays for the image sets of G, P, W, and R. This still guarantees the worst-case constant running time for each primitive operation in (14).

The precise data structures are as follows. First, we have a set of records for vertices in G, and each record has the following fields:

1. a key representing the vertex;
2. an array for the image set of this vertex under G, indexed by labels (for outgoing edges), and where each element includes the head of a singly linked list of vertices (for target vertices following an edge with the indexing label) in G and includes a link that links elements in the image set in a singly linked list; plus a header for the linked list of elements in the image set;
3. a bit for whether the vertex is in O;
4. an array for the image set of this vertex under W, indexed by the states in P, and where each element includes a bit for whether the state is in the image set and includes a link that links elements in the image set in a singly linked list; plus a header for the linked list of elements in the image set;
5. an array for the image set of this vertex under R, indexed by the states in P, and where each element includes a bit for whether the state is in the image set.

We also have a set of records for states in P, and each record has the following fields:

1. a key representing the state;
2. an array for the image set of this state under P, indexed by labels (for outgoing transitions), and where each element includes the pointer to a state (target state following an edge with the indexing label) in P;
3. a bit for whether the state is in F.

We also link vertices in G in a singly linked list for traversal in the initialisation of W and O. Finally, we use a singly linked list to link elements in $\mathbf{dom}(W)$ for traversal by the outer **while**-loop. Any other variable in the program is just a pointer to one of these two kinds of records.

Items 2 to 5 in the first set of records are for representing G, O, W, and R, respectively, and items 2 to 3 in the second set of records are for representing P and F, respectively. Note that the first three items in the two sets of records are similar, except that item 2 for P is simpler than item 2 for G, because P is deterministic, and because elements in the image sets for P do not need to be traversed. Also, item 5 is similar to item 4 but is simpler, because elements in the image sets for R do not need to be traversed.

It is easy to see that, with the above data structures, each primitive operation can be done in $\mathcal{O}(1)$ time. For example, to remove a vertex v from O, we only need to change the bit field for O in the record for v from 1 to 0.

Analysis of Space Complexity. Let N be the number of nodes in G; let S be the number of states in P, and let A be the number of distinct labels (i.e., the alphabet) in G and P. For the first set of records, item 2 together takes $\mathcal{O}(|G| + N * A)$ space, for edges in input graph G plus for each vertex the array indexed by labels; items 4 and 5 both take $\mathcal{O}(N * S)$ space. For the second set of records, item 2 together takes $\mathcal{O}(|P| + S * A)$ space, for transitions in the DFA P plus for each state the array indexed by labels. Others take space associated with parts of the above data structures. Therefore, the space complexity is

$$\mathcal{O}(|G| + |P| + N * A + S * A + N * S).$$

Note that the input size is $\Theta(|G| + |P|)$, and $reach(G \times P, [v0, s0])$ is of size $\mathcal{O}(N * S)$.

6   Discussion

This section discusses related issues about special cases in the input graph, about the computational complexity of the problem with respect to the regular-expression pattern, and about variables in regular-expression patterns.

Unreachable Vertices and Epsilon Edges in Input Graph. There may be vertices in G that are not reachable from vertex $v0$. Since there is no path from $v0$ to these vertices, they satisfy any property about paths. Therefore, according to the specification of the problem, these vertices belong to the output set. Our algorithm computes exactly as specified and includes these vertices in the output. If, in some applications, we are not interested in those unreachable vertices. Starting from a slightly revised specification, we can easily obtain a slightly revised algorithm, using exactly the same derivation method.

There might be epsilon edges in G in general. In this case, one has to compute the product of G and P slightly differently. The idea is to add an epsilon edge from each state to itself in P before computing the product graph. After this addition, our method works as shown. Note that, in either case, our algorithm does not actually build the product of G and P. Building it would incur a substantial space and time overhead which is unacceptable for analysing large graphs.

PSPACE-Completeness with Respect to Input Regular Expression. We have used a DFA instead of the regular expression or its corresponding NFA to solve this problem. However, there is yet no polynomial time algorithm to convert a regular expression to a DFA. Is it possible to use the regular expression or its corresponding NFA directly and obtain an efficient overall algorithm?

We have proved that the regular path query problem is PSPACE-complete and thus NP-hard with respect to the regular expression. Basically, we can reduce the regular path query problem to the totality of regular expression problem [6], and vice versa, both in polynomial time. Since the totality of regular expression problem is PSPACE-complete [6], so is the regular path query problem. Therefore we consider using a DFA the best we can do for now.

In practice, typical in program analysis and model checking, the size of the input graph may be very large, but the size of the regular expression is small and is considered a constant [5]. Therefore, we can just convert the regular expression to a DFA and then use our derived algorithm.

We have skipped the step that converts a regular expression to a DFA, since there are standard algorithms. Those who are interested in this may find an algorithm by Chang and Paige [4], also derived using Paige's methods, that improves over previous algorithms for this.

Variables in Regular-Expression Patterns. For applications in program analysis and model checking, it is often desirable to include variables in regular-expression patterns. Such a variable can match any labels in the program graph. To handle such variables, two extensions are needed.

First, the mapping between a pattern variable and the label it is instantiated to must be maintained so that multiple occurrences of the same variable are instantiated to the same label in the query result. Such a mapping is established when a variable is matched against a label for the first time; afterwards, all occurrences of the variable are treated as the instantiated label.

Second, all possible instantiations of all variables must be explored. One way of implementing this is to use backtracking; if coded in Prolog, this is achieved automatically by the Prolog engine. Another way is to maintain all possible instantiations at the same time, by incrementally adding new possible instantiations and removing failed instantiations. This achieves a kind of bottom-up computation.

A complete formal derivation that arrives at precise algorithmic steps and data structures, together with precise time and space complexity analysis, is yet to be studied. Based on our experience with derivation that exploits finite differencing in particular and incrementalization [7] in general, we believe that the derived algorithm would not be a backtracking algorithm; instead it would perform a bottom-up computation that exploits and maintains all instantiations incrementally at the same time.

7   Related Work and Conclusion

Tarjan showed, over two decades ago, that regular expressions provide a general approach for path analysis problems [18], and he gave efficient algorithms for constructing regular-expression patterns for various path problems [17]. The regular path query problem considered in this paper is a kind of inverse to the single-source path expression problem [17] Tarjan studied.

The regular path query problem was studied by de Moor et al. recently for program analysis and compiler optimisation [5], where the problem was specified, and a high-level algorithm for solving it was derived, formally using calculus of relations and universal algebra. They analyse this high-level algorithm and conclude that the time complexity is linear in the size of the input graph. They also describe an implementation using a tabled Prolog system.

In contrast, we show how a high-level algorithm can be derived formally and easily using tools such as predicate logic. The initial specification using predicate logic corresponds rather directly to the given English description of the problem. We further derive a complete algorithm and data structures with precise analysis of both time and space complexity. We also describe related issues explicitly including the PSPACE-completeness of the problem with respect to the input regular expression.

The derivation of the complete algorithm and data structures uses Paige's methods [10,14,11,3,12,2] with no invention, except that arrays have to be used since based representations [12,2] do not apply to this problem completely. Even though Paige's method for data structure selection advocates the use of no arrays but pointers for low-level implementation, we found through our experience that arrays are necessary for many applications not only to achieve better asymptotic complexity but also to reduce significant constant factors. Systematic methods for the use of arrays in place of pointers, with precise analysis of time and space trade offs, is an important subject that needs further study.

Another important issue is how to find an appropriate high-level specification to start a derivation. Paige's methods are completely systematic for derivations starting with set-based fixed-point specifications. While such specifications can be obtained straightforwardly for many program analysis problems, it is not true in general, which is the case for the problem considered in this paper. The fact that obtaining a high-level algorithmic solution for this problem requires substantial exposition in [5] confirms that this is not a trivial issue. We make this step easier for this problem using tools such as predicate logic which captures the English description of the problem more directly.

Much previous work has studied specification and derivation starting with predicate logic, e.g., deductive synthesis [8]. However existing techniques are not systematic or automatable, unlike Paige's methods (when they apply of course) and system [13]. How to make these methods and techniques more systematic is a subject for future research.

Acknowledgements

We would like to thank Ernie Cohen for initially suggesting the use of predicate logic for the high-level specification and derivation. We are grateful to Ker-I Ko for his advice on how to explain and prove PSPACE-complete problems precisely. We thank Eerke Boiten and anonymous referees whose detailed comments helped improve the paper.

References

1. A. V. Aho, J. E. Hopcroft, and J. D. Ullman. *Data Structures and Algorithms.* Addison-Wesley, Reading, Mass., 1983.
2. J. Cai, P. Facon, F. Henglein, R. Paige, and E. Schonberg. Type analysis and data structure selection. In B. Möller, editor, *Constructing Programs from Specifications,* pages 126–164. North-Holland, Amsterdam, 1991.
3. J. Cai and R. Paige. Program derivation by fixed point computation. *Sci. Comput. Program.,* 11:197–261, Sept. 1988/89.
4. C.-H. Chang and R. Paige. From regular expressions to DFA's using compressed NFA's. *Theoret. Comput. Sci.,* 178(1-2):1–36, May 1997.
5. O. de Moor, D. Lacey, and E. V. Wyk. Universal regular path queires, Nov. 2001. Revised and being reviewed for *Special Issue of Higher-Order and Symbolic Computation* dedicated to Bob Paige.
6. D.-Z. Du and K.-I. Ko. *Theory of Computational Complexity.* John Wiley & Sons, 2000.
7. Y. A. Liu. Efficiency by incrementalization: An introduction. *Higher-Order and Symbolic Computation,* 13(4):289–313, Dec. 2000.
8. Z. Manna and R. Waldinger. *The Deductive Foundations of Computer Programming.* Addison-Wesley, Reading, Mass., 1993.
9. M. Müller-Olm, D. Schmidt, and B. Steffen. Model-checking: A tutorial introduction. In *Proceedings of the 6th International Static Analysis Symposium,* volume 1694 of *Lecture Notes in Computer Science,* pages 331–354. Springer-Verlag, Berlin, Sept. 1999.
10. R. Paige. *Formal Differentiation: A Program Synthesis Technique,* volume 6 of *Computer Science and Artificial Intelligence.* UMI Research Press, Ann Arbor, Michigan, 1981. Revision of Ph.D. dissertation, New York University, 1979.
11. R. Paige. Programming with invariants. *IEEE Software,* 3(1):56–69, Jan. 1986.
12. R. Paige. Real-time simulation of a set machine on a RAM. In *Computing and Information, Vol. II,* pages 69–73. Canadian Scholars Press, 1989. Proceedings of ICCI '89: The International Conference on Computing and Information, Toronto, Canada, May 23-27, 1989.
13. R. Paige. Viewing a program transformation system at work. In M. Hermenegildo and J. Penjam, editors, *Proceedings of Joint 6th International Conference on Programming Languages: Implementations, Logics and Programs and 4th International Conference on Algebraic and Logic Programming,* volume 844 of *Lecture Notes in Computer Science,* pages 5–24. Springer-Verlag, Berlin, Sept. 1994.
14. R. Paige and S. Koenig. Finite differencing of computable expressions. *ACM Trans. Program. Lang. Syst.,* 4(3):402–454, July 1982.
15. J. T. Schwartz, R. B. K. Dewar, E. Dubinsky, and E. Schonberg. *Programming with Sets: An Introduction to SETL.* Springer-Verlag, Berlin, New York, 1986.
16. W. K. Snyder. The SETL2 Programming Language. Technical report 490, Courant Institute of Mathematical Sciences, New York University, Sept. 1990.
17. R. E. Tarjan. Fast algorithms for solving path problems. *J. ACM,* 28(3):594–614, July 1981.
18. R. E. Tarjan. A unified approach to path problems. *J. ACM,* 28(3):577–593, July 1981.

Inverting Functions as Folds

Shin-Cheng Mu and Richard Bird

Programming Research Group, Oxford University
Wolfson Building, Parks Road, OX1 3QD, UK

Abstract. This paper is devoted to the proof and applications of a theorem giving conditions under which the inverse of a partial function can be expressed as a relational hylomorphism. The theorem is a generalisation of a previous result, due to Bird and de Moor, that gave conditions under which a total function can be expressed a relational fold. The theorem is illustrated with three problems, all dealing with constructing trees with various properties.

1 Introduction

Many problems in computation can be specified in terms of computing the inverse of an easily constructed function. The purpose of this paper is to describe one technique for inverting functions and to illustrate it with three examples. We will begin by describing the three problems. First, consider the following datatype *Tree A* of tip-valued binary trees:

data *Tree A* = *Tip A* | *Bin* (*Tree A*) (*Tree A*)

Suppose we are given two lists, one representing the depths of the tips of a tree in left-to-right order, and the other the tip values themselves. How can we reconstruct the tree from the two lists? This particular problem arises, for instance, in the final phase of the Hu-Tucker algorithm [18]. For simplicity, we will identify tip values with their depths, as in Figure 1. Of course, not every list of numbers corresponds to the depths of the tips of a tree.

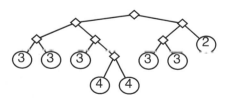

Fig. 1. A tree whose tips have depths $[3, 3, 3, 4, 4, 3, 3, 2]$

In the second problem, we are given a list of trees. The task is to combine them into a single tree, retaining the left-to-right order of the subtrees. How can

E.A. Boiten and B. Möller (Eds.): MPC 2002, LNCS 2386, pp. 209–232, 2002.
© Springer-Verlag Berlin Heidelberg 2002

we do this to make the height of the resulting tree as small as possible? Figure 2 illustrates one such tree, of height 11, for given subtrees of heights $[2, 9, 8, 3, 6, 9]$. As the actual content of the subtrees isn't important, we can think of them simply as numbers representing the heights. The problem is therefore also one of turning a list of numbers to a tree.

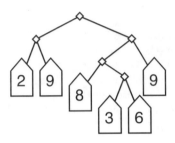

Fig. 2. A tree with height 11 built from trees with heights $[2, 9, 8, 3, 6, 9]$

The third problem is that of breadth-first labelling. Consider the following definition of internally and externally labelled binary trees:

data *Tree A* = *Tip A* | *Bin A* (*Tree A*) (*Tree A*)

A breadth-first labelling of a tree with respect to a given list is the problem of augmenting the nodes of the tree with values in the list in breadth-first order. Figure 3 shows the result of breadth-first labelling a tree with 13 nodes with the infinite list $[1 \cdot \cdot]$. While everybody knows how to do breadth-first traversal, the closely related problem of efficient breadth-first labelling is not so widely understood.

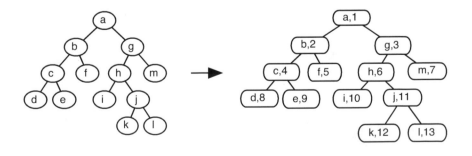

Fig. 3. Breadth-first labelling a tree on the left with $[1 \cdot \cdot]$.

All three problems involve building (or rebuilding) a tree of some kind, and all can be specified in terms of the converse operation of flattening a tree into a list of its values. Functional programmers are aware that flattening a structure is usually performed by a fold operation. Consequently, building a structure is usually performed by the converse operation, unfold. However, there is no reason why the converse operation should necessarily involve an unfold. The converse-of-a-function theorem, to which this paper is devoted, gives us conditions under which the inverse of a function can be written as a fold.

In the following sections we will show how this theorem can be applied to derive solutions to the above problems. We claim that the converse-of-a-function theorem is useful because many problems can be specified in terms of an inverse of a known function. Functional programmers make use of a handful of laws and theorems to transform specifications to optimising code. The converse-of-a-function theorem is another useful tool worth adding to the functional programmer's arsenal. Its joint use with the fold fusion theorem turns out to be a recurring pattern in program derivation. Finally, we will present and prove a generalised theorem allowing one to write the inverse of a partial function as a hylomorphism.

2   Theory

The converse of a function is a relation, so our framework is of necessity a calculus of relational programs [3,5]. In this section we will present enough notation to describe the main ideas. Further concepts are introduced in Section 7.

2.1   Relations

Set-theoretically speaking, a relation $R :: A \rightsquigarrow B$ is a set of pairs (a, b) where a has type A and b type B. The *converse* of a relation is defined by flipping the pairs, that is,

$$(b, a) \in R^\circ \equiv (a, b) \in R$$

For $R :: B \rightsquigarrow A$ and $S :: C \rightsquigarrow B$, the composition $R \cdot S :: C \rightsquigarrow A$ is defined by

$$(c, a) \in R \cdot S \equiv (\exists b ; b \in B : (c, b) \in S \land (b, a) \in R)$$

Converse is contravariant with respect to composition, so $(R \cdot S)^\circ = S^\circ \cdot R^\circ$.

For each type A, a relation id_A is defined by $id_A = \{(a, a) | a \in A\}$. We will omit the subscript when it is clear from the context. A relation $R :: A \rightsquigarrow B$ is called *simple* if $R \cdot R^\circ \subseteq id$. That is, every value in A is mapped to at most one value in B. In other words, R is a partial function. A relation R is called *entire* if $id \subseteq R^\circ \cdot R$, that is, every value in A is mapped to at least one value in B. A relation is a (total) function if it is both simple and entire.

In this paper we write the type of a function as $A \rightarrow B$, that of a partial function as $A \nrightarrow B$, and that of a relation as $A \rightsquigarrow B$.

A relation is called a *coreflexive* if it is a subset of *id*. We use coreflexives to model predicates. The ? operator converts a boolean-valued function to a coreflexive:

$$(a, a) \in p? \equiv p\, a$$

For convenience, we let $(a, a) \notin p?$ both when $p\, a$ yields *False* and when a is not in the domain of p. If we perform two consecutive tests, one of them being stronger than the other, the stronger one can absorb the weaker one:

$$(p\, a \Rightarrow q\, a) \Rightarrow p? \cdot q? = p? \tag{1}$$

Given a relation $R :: A \rightsquigarrow B$, the coreflexive $dom\, R :: A \nrightarrow A$ determines the domain of R and is defined by

$$(a, a) \in dom\, R \equiv (\exists b : b \in B : (a, b) \in R)$$

Alternatively, $dom\, R = R^\circ \cdot R \cap id$, where $\cap$ denotes set intersection. It follows that

$$dom\, R \subseteq R^\circ \cdot R \tag{2}$$

The coreflexive $ran\, R$ determines the range of a relation and is defined by $ran\, R = dom\, R^\circ$.

When writing in a pointwise style, relations can be introduced by the choice operator $\square$. The expression $x \square y$ non-deterministically yields either x or y. For example, the following relation *prefix* maps a list to one of its prefixes:

$$\begin{aligned}
&prefix :: List\, A \rightsquigarrow List\, A \\
&prefix = foldr\, step\, [\,] \\
&\quad\textbf{where}\ step \qquad :: A \to List\, A \rightsquigarrow List\, A \\
&\qquad\qquad\ step\, a\, x = (a : x)\ \square\ [\,]
\end{aligned}$$

In each step of the fold we can choose either to cons the current item to some prefix of the sublist, or just return the empty sequence $[\,]$, which is a prefix of every list. For a more rigorous semantics of $\square$, the reader is referred to [9].

2.2   Folds

Datatypes come with fold functions. For lists, the Haskell Prelude function $foldr :: (A \to B \to B) \to B \to List\, A \to B$ is well known. A slight variation for non-empty lists can be defined by

$$\begin{aligned}
&foldrn \qquad\qquad :: (A \to B \to B) \to (A \to B) \to List^+ A \to B \\
&foldrn\, f\, g\, [a] \quad\ = g\, a \\
&foldrn\, f\, g\, (a : x) = f\, a\, (foldrn\, f\, g\, x)
\end{aligned}$$

Here $List^+ A$ denotes the type of non-empty lists. Recall the *Tree* datatype defined in the introduction; its fold function can be defined as:

$$\begin{aligned}
&foldtree \qquad\qquad\ :: (B \to B \to B) \to (A \to B) \to Tree\, A \to B \\
&foldtree\, f\, g\, (Tip\, a) \quad = g\, a \\
&foldtree\, f\, g\, (Bin\, x\, y) = f\, (foldtree\, f\, g\, x)\, (foldtree\, f\, g\, y)
\end{aligned}$$

All of these folds are instances of a more general definition. A regular datatype T can be defined as the fixed-point of a *base functor* F. That is to say, there is an isomorphism

$$\alpha_F :: FT \to T$$

Datatypes are often parameterised. In that case α_F has type $F_A(TA) \to TA$. For example, cons-lists over an arbitrary is the fixed-point of $F_A X = 1 + (A \times X)$. When denoting types, we will write $F(A, X)$ instead of $F_A X$, thinking of F as a bifunctor. For more example, the base functor for non-empty lists is $F(A, X) = A + (A \times X)$, and that for *Tree* is $F(A, X) = A + (X \times X)$.

Given a base functor F for a datatype TA and a function f of type $F(A, B) \to B$ for some B, the *catamorphism* $(\![f]\!)_F :: TA \to B$ is the unique function satisfying

$$(\![f]\!)_F \cdot \alpha_F = f \cdot F(\![f]\!)_F$$

The different folds are special cases of $(\![f]\!)_F$ instantiated to different base functors, except that in Haskell, we usually divide f into several functions or constants, each of which corresponds to the operation on a particular operand of the coproduct in the base functor.

A functor on relations that takes functions to functions and is monotonic under relational inclusion is called a *relator*. By switching from functors to relators, the above theory extends to relations as well. A catamorphism $(\![R]\!)_F$, where R is a relation of type $F(A, B) \rightsquigarrow B$, now has type $TA \rightsquigarrow B$. For a fuller account of relator theory and relational catamorphisms, the reader is referred to [2,3].

3   The Converse-of-a-Function Theorem

The converse-of-a-function theorem, introduced in [5,9], tells us how we can write the inverse of a function as a fold. It reads:

Theorem 1 (Converse of a Function). Let $f :: B \to TA$ be a function and F the base functor for T. If $R :: F(A, B) \rightsquigarrow B$ is surjective and $f \cdot R \subseteq \alpha_F \cdot Ff$, then $f^\circ = (\![R]\!)_F$.

The specialisation of this theorem to functions over lists reads as follows: let $f :: B \to List\,A$ be given. If $base :: B$ and $step :: A \to B \rightsquigarrow B$ are jointly surjective (meaning that $\{base\} \cup \{b' \mid \exists\, a, b : (b', b) \in step\,a\} - B$) and satisfy

$$f\,base \quad\; = [\,]$$
$$f(step\,a\,x) = a : f\,x$$

then $f^\circ = foldr\,step\,base$.

Similarly, to invert a total function f on non-empty lists, Theorem 1 states that if $base :: A \rightsquigarrow B$ and $step :: A \to B \rightsquigarrow B$ are jointly surjective (that is, $ran\,base \cup ran\,step = id_B$) and satisfy

$$f\,(base\,a) \;\; = [a]$$
$$f(step\,a\,x) = a : f\,x$$

then $f° = foldrn \ step \ base$.

We will postpone the proof of Theorem 1 to Sect. 7, where in fact a more general result is proved. For now, let us see some of its applications.

4   Building a Tree from Its Depths

We will start with a formal specification of the problem of a building a tree given the depths of its tips. First of all, the familiar function *flatten*, which takes a tree and returns its tips in left-to-right order, can be written as a fold:

$$flatten :: Tree \ A \to List^+ \ A$$
$$flatten = foldtree \ (+\!\!+) \ wrap$$

Here *wrap* $x = [x]$ wraps an item into a singleton list.

A tree of integers is *well-formed* if one can assign to it a *level*, where the level of a tip is the number at the tip, and the level of a non-tip is defined only if its two subtrees have the same level, in which case it is one less than the levels. The partial function *level* can be defined by:

$$level :: Tree \ Int \longmapsto Int$$
$$level = foldtree \ up \ id$$
$$\mathbf{where} \ up \ a \ b = \mathbf{if} \ \ a \ \text{==} \ b \ \mathbf{then} \ a - 1$$

Note that the **if** clause in the definition of *up* has only one branch. Therefore, *level* is a partial function which only returns a value for a tree when its left and right subtrees have been assigned the same level.

We call a tree *well-formed* if it is in the domain of *level*. Our problem can thus be specified by

$$build = dom \ level \cdot flatten°$$

We have generalised the problem a little, allowing the level number of the resulting tree to be other than zero.

The relation *flatten°* maps a list to an arbitrary tree that flattens to the list. For a given list, there will be many such trees. The coreflexive *dom level* acts as a filter picking those that are well-formed. Our specification is therefore an instance of the "generator – filter" paradigm that recurs frequently in functional programming.

Now we have got the problem specification, we are left with two problems: how to compute *flatten°*, and how to fuse *dom level* into the computation.

4.1   Building a Tree with a Fold

Our aim is to apply the converse-of-a-function theorem to invert *flatten*. We need a pair of relations *one* :: $A \rightsquigarrow Tree \ A$ and *add* :: $A \to Tree \ A \rightsquigarrow Tree \ A$ that are jointly surjective and satisfy

$$flatten \ (one \ a) \ \ = [a]$$
$$flatten \ (add \ a \ x) = a : flatten \ x$$

Look at the second equation. It says that if we have a tree x which flattens to some list as, the relation add must be able to create a new tree y out of a and x such that y flattens to $a : as$. One way to do that is illustrated in Fig. 4. We divide the left spine of x in two parts, move down the lower part for one level, and attach a to the end.

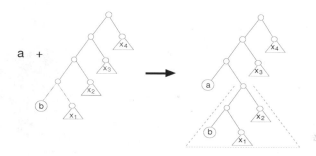

Fig. 4. Adding a new node to a tree

To facilitate this operation, we introduce an alternative *spine representation*. A tree is represented by the list of subtrees along the left spine, plus the left-most tip. The function *roll* converts a spine back into a single tree, and is in fact an isomorphism between *Spine A* and *Tree A*.

type $Spine\ A = A \times List(Tree\ A)$

$$
\begin{aligned}
roll \qquad &:: Spine\ A \to Tree\ A \\
roll(a, x) \quad &= foldl\ Bin\ (Tip\ a)\ x
\end{aligned}
$$

The advantage of this representation is that we can trace the spine upward from the left-most leaf, rather than downwards from the root. As we will see in the end of the next section, this is necessary for an efficient algorithm.

The function *flatten* · *roll* flattens a spine tree. Our task now is to invert it as a fold. We need a pair of relations $one :: A \rightsquigarrow Spine\ A$ and $add :: A \to Spine\ A \rightsquigarrow Spine\ A$ satisfying

$$flatten\,(roll\,(one\ a)) = \lfloor a \rfloor \tag{3}$$

$$flatten\,(roll\,(add\ a\,(b, xs))) = a : flatten\,(roll\,(b, xs)) \tag{4}$$

We claim that the following definition for *one* and *add* does the job:

$$
\begin{aligned}
one\ a \qquad &= (a, [\,]) \\
add\ a\,(b, xs) &= (a, roll\,(b, ys) : zs) \\
&\quad \textbf{where}\ ys \mathbin{+\!\!+} zs = xs
\end{aligned}
$$

The non-deterministic pattern in the definition of *add*, dividing the list xs into two parts, indicates that *add* is a relation. The relations *one* and *add* are jointly surjective because *roll*, being an isomorphism, is surjective; thus, given any spine tree (a, ws), either ws is empty, in which case it is covered by *one a*, or there always exists a pair of (b, ys) such that they roll into the head of ws, in which case (a, ws) would be one of the results of $add\ a\ (b, ys + tail\ ws)$.

It is clear that the function *one* satisfies (3). To show that *add* satisfies (4), we will need the following fact, whose proof is left to the diligent reader:

$$flatten(roll\ (a, xs)) = a : concat(map\ flatten\ xs) \tag{5}$$

Now we will show that *add* satisfies (4):

$$a : flatten(roll\ (b, ys + zs))$$
$$= \quad \{(5)\}$$
$$a : b : concat(map\ flatten\ (ys + zs))$$
$$= \quad \{concat\ \text{and}\ map\ \text{distributes over}\ + \}$$
$$a : b : concat(map\ flatten\ ys) + concat(map\ flatten\ zs)$$
$$= \quad \{(5)\}$$
$$a : flatten(roll\ (b, ys)) + concat(map\ flatten\ zs)$$
$$= \quad \{\text{definition of}\ concat\ \text{and}\ map\}$$
$$a : concat(map\ flatten\ (roll(b, ys) : zs))$$
$$= \quad \{(5)\}$$
$$flatten\ (roll\ (a, roll(b, ys) : zs))$$
$$= \quad \{\text{definition of}\ add\}$$
$$flatten\ (roll\ (add\ a\ (b, ys + zs)))$$

Thus $(flatten \cdot roll)^{\circ} = foldrn\ add\ one$ by Theorem 1.

4.2   The Derivation

Having inverted $flatten \cdot roll$, we can start the derivation:

$$build$$
$$= \quad \{\text{definition}\}$$
$$dom\ level \cdot flatten^{\circ}$$
$$= \quad \{roll\ \text{is an isomorphism}\}$$
$$dom\ level \cdot (flatten \cdot roll \cdot roll^{\circ})^{\circ}$$
$$= \quad \{\text{converse is contravariant}\}$$
$$dom\ level \cdot roll \cdot (flatten \cdot roll)^{\circ}$$
$$= \quad \{\text{inverting}\ flatten \cdot roll\ \text{as in the last section}\}$$
$$dom\ level \cdot roll \cdot foldrn\ add\ one$$
$$= \quad \{\text{since}\ dom\ R \cdot f = f \cdot dom\ (R \cdot f),\ \text{let}\ wellform = dom\ (level \cdot roll)\}$$
$$roll \cdot wellform \cdot foldrn\ add\ one$$

Except for the introduction of *roll*, the derivation so far is mostly mechanical. Whereas *dom level* checks whether a tree is well-formed, *wellform* is its counterpart defined on spine trees. Intuitively, a spine tree (b, xs) is well-formed if and only if all the trees in xs are well-formed, and the first tree in xs has a level number b, the second tree has a level number $b - 1$, and so on.

As *roll·wellform* is a partial function, it can be easily implemented in Haskell. However, *add* is still a relation. If we can fuse *wellform* into the fold and thereby refine *add* to a partial function, the whole expression will be implementable.

However, *wellform* is a rather strong condition to enforce. It is not possible to maintain this invariant within the fold before and after each application of *add*. It is time to take the second inventive step: to invent a weaker condition. The predicate *decform* holds for a spine tree (b, xs) if the level number of the first tree in xs is at most b and the trees in xs have strictly decreasing level numbers:

$$decform\,(b, xs) = leading\ b\ xs \wedge decreasing\,(map\ level\ xs)$$
$$leading\ b\ xs \quad = null\ xs \vee level(head\ xs) \leq b$$

Note that the application of *level* to all the trees in xs implicitly states the requirement that all the trees are well-formed.

The predicate *decform* is weaker than *wellform*. We can thus derive:

$$roll \cdot wellform \cdot foldrn\ add\ one$$
$$= \quad \{(1)\}$$
$$roll \cdot wellform \cdot decform? \cdot foldrn\ add\ one$$
$$= \quad \{\text{fold fusion, see below}\}$$
$$roll \cdot wellform \cdot foldrn\ add'\ one$$

The equality established by fold fusion in the last step ensures that no result is lost from the refinement. Fortunately, it can be shown that the following fusion condition is valid:

$$decform? \cdot add\ a = add'\ a \cdot decform?$$

where *add'* is defined by rolling the given spine tree up to the point when the two left-most trees do not have the same level number:

$$add'\ a\,(b, xs) \quad = leading?\,(a, decRoll\,(Tip\ b)\ xs)$$
$$decRoll\ x\,[] \quad = [x]$$
$$decRoll\ x\,(y : zs) \mid (level\ x == level\ y) = decRoll\,(Bin\ x\ y)\ zs$$
$$\mid otherwise \quad = x : y : zs$$

The code is shown in Fig. 5. We refine the data structure to avoid recomputing *level* by defining type *SpineI* and maintain the invariant that $level\ x = n$ for all pairs (x, n) along the spine. Constructors *Tip* and *Bin* are lifted accordingly. The function *rollwf* implements *roll·wellform*. The check is performed implicitly by *bin* each time two trees are joined. This algorithm is linear in the number of nodes in the tree, as each call to *join* either stops or builds a new node.

```
data Tree a = Tip a | Bin (Tree a) (Tree a) deriving Show
type SpineI = (Int, [(Tree Int, Int)])

build :: [Int] -> Tree Int
build = rollwf . foldrn add' one

one a = (a,[])

add' a (b,xs) | leading (a,zs) = (a,zs)
                where zs = decRoll (tip b) xs
decRoll x [] = [x]
decRoll x (y:zs) | level x == level y = decRoll (bin x y) zs
                 | otherwise          = x:y:zs
leading (a,xs) = level (head xs) <= a

tip a = (Tip a, a)
bin (x,m) (y,n) | m == n = (Bin x y, m-1)
level = snd

rollwf :: SpineI -> Tree Int
rollwf (b,xs) = fst (foldl bin (tip b) xs)

foldrn f g [x] = g x
foldrn f g (a:x) = f a (foldrn f g x)
```

Fig. 5. Code for rebuilding a tree from the depths of its tips

5   Building Trees with Minimum Height

Next we consider the second problem of building a tree with minimum height.
A linear-time algorithm to this problem has been proposed in [4], but here we
will demonstrate how a similar algorithm can be derived.

Given a tip-valued binary tree whose tip values represent the heights of trees,
the function computing the height of the combined tree can be defined as a fold
in the obvious way:

$$height :: Tree\ Int \rightarrow Int$$
$$height = foldtree\ ht\ id$$
$$\textbf{where}\ ht\ a\ b = (a \sqcup b) + 1$$

where $\sqcup$ returns the larger of its two arguments. The problem is thus to find,
among all the trees which flatten to the given list, one for which $height$ yields
the minimal value. The specification needs to consider all possible results. For
that we need the power transpose operator Λ, also called the $breadth$ function.

The power transpose operator Λ converts a relation $R :: A \rightsquigarrow B$ to a function
$\Lambda R :: A \rightarrow Set\ B$. For $a \in A$, the set $(\Lambda R)a$ contains all values in B to which a
is mapped:

$$(\Lambda R)a = \{b\ |\ (a, b) \in R\}$$

To extract a value from a set we need the relation $min\ (\preceq) :: Set\ A \rightsquigarrow A$, defined by

$$(xs, x) \in min\ (\preceq) \equiv x \in xs \land (\forall y : y \in xs : x \preceq y)$$

For this definition to be of any use, $(\preceq)$ has to be a *connected preorder*, meaning an ordering which is reflexive, transitive, and compares everything of the correct type. The relation $min\ (\preceq)$ will not in general be a function because a preorder is not necessarily anti-symmetric.

For our problem, define $(\preceq)$ to be a comparison between the heights of two trees:

$$x \preceq y \equiv height\ x \leq height\ y$$

Our problem can then be specified as:

$$bmh = min\ (\preceq) \cdot \Lambda(flatten^\circ)$$

The reasoning in Sect. 4.1 can be reused: we introduce the spine representation and invert *flatten* to *roll · foldrn add one*. Furthermore, *roll* can be factored out of Λ, and we get:

$$bmh = roll \cdot min\ (\preceq') \cdot \Lambda(foldrn\ add\ one)$$

where $xs \preceq' ys \equiv roll\ xs \preceq roll\ ys$, i.e., $(\preceq')$ is the counterpart of $(\preceq)$ defined on spine trees.

Since the relation *add* has $n + 1$ choices when given a spine tree of length n, the above specification generates an exponential number of trees. To eliminate the non-determinism in *add* and thereby improve the efficiency, we make use of the following *greedy theorem*. Presented below is a special case of the more general version proved in [5].

Theorem 2 (The Greedy Theorem (For Non-empty Lists)). Let *base* :: $A \rightsquigarrow A$ and *step* :: $A \rightarrow B \rightsquigarrow B$ be two relations. If *step* is monotonic on a connected preorder $(\trianglelefteq)$, that is,

$$(x \trianglelefteq y \land (y, y') \in step\ a) \Rightarrow (\exists x' : (x, x') \in step\ a : x' \trianglelefteq y') \tag{6}$$

then we have

$$foldrn\ (min\ (\trianglelefteq) \cdot \Lambda step)\ (min\ (\trianglelefteq) \cdot \Lambda base) \subseteq min\ (\trianglelefteq) \cdot \Lambda(foldrn\ step\ base)$$

Informally, the monotonicity condition means that a worse partial solution in some stage of the fold always gives a worse result. If this condition holds, then at each stage of the fold we need only retain one of the best results computed so far. Thus $min\ (\trianglelefteq)$ gets promoted into *foldrn*.

Had *add* satisfied the monotonicity condition (6) with respect to $(\preceq')$, we could apply the greedy theorem. However, that is not true: a tree with the smallest height does not always remain the smallest after being extended by *add*.

This is where human ingenuity gets involved. Fortunately, *add* is monotonic on a stronger ordering. We define:

$$heights\,(a, xs) = (reverse \cdot map\,height \cdot scanl\,Bin\,(Tip\,a))\,xs$$

In words, *heights* returns a list of heights along the left spine, starting from the root. The relation *add* is then monotonic on $\ll$, defined by:

$$x \ll y \equiv heights\,x \trianglelefteq heights\,y$$

where $(\trianglelefteq)$ is the lexicographic ordering on sequences. This choice does make sense: to ensure monotonicity, we need to optimise not only the whole tree, but also all the subtrees on the left spine. The proof that *add* is monotonic on $(\ll)$, however, is quite involved and will not be presented here. The reader is referred to [6] for more detailed discussion.

Applying the greedy theorem, we get:

$$bmh = roll \cdot foldrn\,(min\,(\trianglelefteq) \cdot \Lambda add)\,(min\,(\trianglelefteq) \cdot \Lambda one)$$

Since *one* is a function, $min\,(\ll)\cdot\Lambda one = one$. With some analysis, we can further optimise $min\,(\ll) \cdot \Lambda add$. Let $(b, [x_1, x_2, \cdots, x_n])$ be the spine tree to which we are about to insert a value a. It can be shown that in order to construct the best tree under the ordering $(\ll)$, we do not need to actually check through all the $n + 1$ possibilities. We can always break the list between x_i and x_{i+1} such that i is the smallest index such that $a < height\,x_{i+1}$ and $height\,(roll\,(b, [x_1, x_2, \cdots, x_i])) < height\,x_{i+1}$. We will also omit the details and refer the interested readers to [6].

The code is shown in Fig. 6. As in the first problem, we annotate each tree with its height to avoid re-computation. By the same argument as that in the end of Sect. 4.2, this algorithm is also linear in the number of nodes in the tree.

6   Breadth-First Labelling

To breadth-first label a tree with respect to a given list is to label the nodes in the tree in breadth-first order, using the values in the list. Jones and Gibbons [13] proposed a neat solution to this problem, based on a clever use of cyclic data structures. The problem was recently revisited by Okasaki [22]. We are going to show how Okasaki's algorithm can be derived using the converse-of-a-function theorem.

Recall the data structure for binary trees:

data *Tree A* = *Tip A* | *Bin A* (*Tree A*) (*Tree A*)

The queue-based algorithm for breadth-first traversal is well-known:

```
bft   :: Tree A → List A
bft x = bftF [x]
```

type *Forest A* = *List* (*Tree A*)

```
bmh :: [Int] -> (Tree Int, Int)
bmh = roll . foldrn minadd one

one a = (a,[])

minadd :: Int -> SpineI -> SpineI
minadd a (b,xs) = (a, minsplit (tip b) xs)
  where minsplit x [] = [x]
        minsplit x (y:xs) | a < height y
                            && height x < height y = x:y:xs
                          | otherwise = minsplit (bin x y) xs

tip a = (Tip a, a)
bin (x,a) (y,b) = (Bin x y, ht a b)
height = snd

ht a b = (a 'max' b) + 1

roll :: SpineI -> (Tree Int, Int)
roll (a,x) = foldl bin (tip a) x
```

Fig. 6. Code for building trees with minimum height

$$
\begin{aligned}
&bftF && :: Forest\ A \to List\ A \\
&bftF\ [] && -\ [] \\
&bftF\ (Tip\ a : xs) && = a : bftF\ xs \\
&bftF\ (Bin\ a\ x\ y : xs) && = a : bftF\ (xs \mathbin{+\!\!+} [x, y])
\end{aligned}
$$

To perform the labelling, we use the following partial function $zipTree$:

$$
\begin{aligned}
&zipTree && :: Tree\ A \to Tree\ B \rightarrowtail Tree\ (A \times B) \\
&zipTree\ (Tip\ a)\ (Tip\ b) && = Tip\ (a, b) \\
&zipTree\ (Bin\ a\ x\ y)\ (Bin\ b\ u\ v) && = Bin\ (a, b)\ (zipTree\ x\ u)\ (zipTree\ y\ v)
\end{aligned}
$$

Breadth-first labelling of a tree x can then be seen as zipping x with another tree y, in which the breadth-first traversal of y is a prefix of the given list as:

$$
\begin{aligned}
&bfl && :: List\ A \to Tree\ B \rightarrowtail Tree\ (A \times B) \\
&bfl\ as\ x = zipTree\ y\ x \\
&\qquad \textbf{where}\ (bft\ y) \mathbin{+\!\!+} bs = as
\end{aligned}
$$

Equivalently,

$$
\begin{aligned}
bfl\ as\ x &= zipTree\ ((bft^\circ \cdot prefix)\ as)\ x \\
&= (zipTree \cdot bft^\circ \cdot prefix)\ as\ x
\end{aligned}
$$

This completes the specification. The relation $prefix$ non-deterministically maps a list to one of its finite prefixes. The prefix is then passed to bft°, yet again being non-deterministically mapped to a tree whose breadth-first traversal equals the chosen prefix. It is important that *zipTree* is a partial function which yields a value only when the given two trees are of exactly the same shape. Therefore, the tree composed by $bft^{\circ} \cdot prefix$ can be zipped with the input tree only if it is of the correct size and shape. The partial function *zipTree* plays the role of the filter.

Since breadth-first traversal is an algorithm more naturally defined in terms of queues of trees (or forests) rather than of a single tree, it is reasonable to try to invert *bftF* rather than *bft*. The problem can be rephrased in terms of *bftF*:

$$bfl \ as \ x = wrap^{\circ} \left((zipForest \cdot bftF^{\circ} \cdot prefix) \ as \ [x] \right)$$

Here $zipForest :: Forest \ A \to Forest \ B \nrightarrow Forest \ (A, B)$ is a simple extension of *zipTree* to forests, which, like *zipTree*, is a partial function:

$$
\begin{aligned}
&zipForest \ [] \ [] &&= [] \\
&zipForest \ (x : xs) \ (y : ys) &&= zipTree \ x \ y : zipForest \ xs \ ys
\end{aligned}
$$

Once the decision to focus on *bftF* is made, the rest is mechanical. To invert *bftF*, we are to find *base* and *step* such that

$$
\begin{aligned}
&bftF \ base &&= [] \\
&bftF \ (step \ a \ xs) &&= a : bftF \ xs
\end{aligned}
$$

The value of *base* can only be $[]$. The derivation for *step* is not too difficult either. We start with the general case which does not assume any structure in *xs*:

$$
\begin{aligned}
&\quad a : bftF \ xs \\
&= \quad \{\text{definition of } bftF\} \\
&\quad bftF \ (Tip \ a : xs)
\end{aligned}
$$

Therefore *step a xs* might contain $(Tip \ a : xs)$ as one of the possible values. But this choice alone does not make *step* jointly surjective with $[]$, since it cannot generate a forest with a non-tip tree as its head. We therefore consider the case when *xs* contains contains more than two trees:

$$
\begin{aligned}
&\quad a : bftF (xs \mathbin{+\mkern-8mu+} [x, y]) \\
&= \quad \{\text{definition of } bftF\} \\
&\quad bftF \ (Bin \ a \ x \ y : xs)
\end{aligned}
$$

Therefore we define *step* to be:

$$
\begin{aligned}
&step &&:: A \to Forest \ A \rightsquigarrow Forest \ A \\
&step \ a \ xs = (Tip \ a : xs) \ \Box \ (Bin \ a \ x \ y : xs') \\
&\qquad\qquad \textbf{where} \ (xs' \mathbin{+\mkern-8mu+} [x, y]) = xs
\end{aligned}
$$

Since a forest either begins with a tip tree, begins with a non-tip tree, or is empty, *step* is jointly surjective with $[]$. The converse of *bftF* is thus constructed as $bftF^{\circ} = foldr \ step \ []$.

Knowing that $bftF^\circ :: List\ A \rightsquigarrow Forest\ A$ is a fold, we can fuse $zipForest$ and $bftF^\circ$ as a fold :

$$zipForest \cdot bftF^\circ = foldr\ revZip\ stop$$
$$\textbf{where}\ \ stop\,[\,] \qquad\qquad\qquad = [\,]$$
$$revZip\ a\ f\ (\,Tip\ b : ts) \qquad = Tip\ (a, b) : f\ ts$$
$$revZip\ a\ f\ (Bin\ b\ u\ v : ts) = Bin\ (a, b)\ x\ y : ys$$
$$\textbf{where}\ \ ys + [x, y] = f\ (ts + [u, v])$$

The expression $zipForest \cdot bftF^\circ$ has type $List\ A \to Forest\ B \rightsquigarrow Forest\ (A \times B)$. Consider $(zipForest \cdot bftF^\circ)\,x$ where x is a list of labels. Constructors building x are replaced by $revZip$ and $stop$, yielding a relation mapping an unlabelled forest to a labelled forest. A pattern matching error will be invoked by $stop$ if x is too short, and by $revZip$ if x is too long. Applying fold fusion again to fuse $zipForest \cdot bftF^\circ$ with $prefix$ in effect adds another case for $revZip$, that is, $revZip\ a\ f\,[\,] = [\,]$, which cuts the list of labels when the forest is consumed earlier than the list. Still, the list of labels cannot be too short.

The resulting code is shown in Fig. 7. It can be made linear if we use an implementation of deques supporting constant-time addition and deletion [8,21] for both the input and output of $revzip$. For clarity, we will just leave it as it is. It is nothing more than an adaption of Okasaki's algorithm in [22] to lists. In his paper, Okasaki raised the question why most people did not come up with this algorithm but instead appealed to more complicated approaches. Our answer is because they did not know the converse-of-a-function theorem.

```
data Tree a = Tip a | Bin a (Tree a) (Tree a) deriving Show

bfl :: [a] -> Tree b -> Tree (a,b)
bfl xs = unwrap . foldr revzip stop xs . wrap
 where stop [] = []
       revzip a f [] = []
       revzip a f (Tip b:ts) = Tip (a,b) : f ts
       revzip a f (Bin b u v :ts) = Bin (a,b) x y : ys'
          where ys = f (ts ++ [u,v])
                (ys',x,y) = (init (init ys), last (init ys), last ys)

wrap a = [a]
unwrap [a] = a
```

Fig. 7. Code for breadth-first labelling

7   The Hylomorphism Theorem

By definition, a *hylomorphism* is the composition of a fold with the converse of a fold. The hylomorphism $(\!|R|\!)_\mathsf{F} \cdot (\!|S|\!)_\mathsf{F}^\circ$ can be characterised as the least solution for X of the inequation $R \cdot \mathsf{F}X \cdot S^\circ \subseteq X$. In other words, we have:

$$([R])_\mathsf{F} \cdot ([S])_\mathsf{F}^{\ \circ} \subseteq X \Leftarrow R \cdot \mathsf{F}X \cdot S^\circ \subseteq X \tag{7}$$

The aim of this section is to prove the following generalisation of Theorem 1:

Theorem 3 (Hylomorphism Theorem). Let $S :: A \rightsquigarrow B$ be a simple relation. If relation $R :: \mathsf{F}(C, A) \rightsquigarrow A$ and function $f :: \mathsf{F}(C, B) \to B$ are such that (i) $dom\ S = ran\ R$; (ii) $S \cdot R \subseteq f \cdot \mathsf{F}S$; and (iii) $\delta_\mathsf{F} \cdot R^\circ$ is inductive, then

$$S = ([f])_\mathsf{F} \cdot ([R])_\mathsf{F}^{\ \circ}$$

In words, Theorem 3 gives conditions under which a simple relation can be expressed as a hylomorphism. The new ingredients in Theorem 3 are the *membership* relation δ_F of a relator F, and the notion of an *inductive* relation. Both are described below in Sect. 7.1. The main proof is given in Sect. 7.2.

Theorem 1 follows as a special instance of Theorem 3 by taking $f = \alpha$ and S to be an entire relation as well as a simple one, that is, a function. An entire relation S is one for which $dom\ S = id$, so condition (i) translates to the requirement that R be a surjective relation. In Sect. 7.2, we will prove that condition (iii) holds if both (i) and (ii) do and if $\delta_\mathsf{F} \cdot f^\circ$ is inductive. Fact 1 below gives us that $\delta_\mathsf{F} \cdot \alpha_\mathsf{F}^\circ$ is inductive. Since $([\alpha_\mathsf{F}])_\mathsf{F} = id$, we then obtain the result $S = ([R])_\mathsf{F}^{\ \circ}$. Taking converses, this is the conclusion of Theorem 1.

7.1 Inductivity and Membership

We say that a relation admits induction, or is inductive, if we can use it to perform induction[11]. Formally, inductivity is defined by:

Definition 1 (Inductivity). A relation $R :: A \rightsquigarrow A$ is inductive if for all $X :: B \rightsquigarrow A$,

$$R \backslash X \subseteq X \Rightarrow \Pi \subseteq X$$

Here Π denotes the largest relation of its type, and the left division operator $(\backslash)$ is defined by the Galois connection:

$$S \subseteq R \backslash T \equiv R \cdot S \subseteq T$$

The definition can be translated to the point level to aid understanding. It says that R is inductive if the property

$$(\forall c :: (c, a) \in R \Rightarrow (c, b) \in X) \Rightarrow (a, b) \in X$$

where a and b are arbitrary, implies X contains all the pairs of its type. As an example, take R to be $<$, the ordering on natural numbers, and $P\ a = (a, b) \in X$ to be some property we want to prove for all a and some fixed b. The definition specialises to the claim that if

$$(\forall c :: c < a \Rightarrow P\ c) \Rightarrow P\ a$$

then $P\ a$ holds for all natural numbers a. Thus we can see that inductivity captures the principle of induction.

Three facts we will need are the following:

Fact 1 The relation $\delta_{\mathsf{F}} \cdot \alpha_{\mathsf{F}}{}^\circ$ is inductive.

Fact 2 If R is inductive and $S \subseteq R$, then S is inductive.

Fact 3 If R is inductive, so is $S^\circ \cdot R \cdot S$ for any simple relation S.

The other concept we need, due to Hoogendijk and de Moor [17], is the membership relation of a datatype. For example, a membership relation δ_{List} for lists can be specified informally by:

$$(a, [a_0, a_1, \ldots a_n]) \in \delta_{List} \equiv (\exists i :: a = a_i)$$

The formal definition of membership is not at all intuitive, and we refer the reader to [17] for more discussion. A fact about membership we will use is that it is a lax natural transformation, which is to say,

$$\delta_{\mathsf{F}} \cdot \mathsf{F} R \subseteq R \cdot \delta_{\mathsf{F}} \tag{8}$$

for all R.

7.2 The Proof

We begin by reciting some basic facts about a simple relation S. First, for any X and Y,

$$S \cdot X \subseteq Y \Leftarrow X \subseteq S^\circ \cdot Y \tag{9}$$

The proof is immediate from the fact that $S \cdot S^\circ \subseteq id$. More generally,

$$S \cdot X \subseteq Y \equiv dom\, S \cdot X \subseteq S^\circ \cdot Y \tag{10}$$

When S is also entire, i.e., $dom\, S = id$, this reduces to the usual shunting rule for functions. The following shunting lemma will be used a number of times:

Lemma 1. Let S be simple and suppose R satisfies (i) $ran\, R \subseteq dom\, S$, and (ii) $S \cdot R \subseteq f \cdot \mathsf{F} S$. Then $R \subseteq S^\circ \cdot f \cdot \mathsf{F} S$.

Proof.

$$\begin{aligned}
&\quad R \subseteq S^\circ \cdot f \cdot \mathsf{F} S \\
&\equiv \quad \{\text{using } R = ran\, R \cdot R\} \\
&\quad ran\, R \cdot R \subseteq S^\circ \cdot f \cdot \mathsf{F} S \\
&\Leftarrow \quad \{\text{assumption (i)}\} \\
&\quad dom\, S \cdot R \subseteq S^\circ \cdot f \cdot \mathsf{F} S \\
&\equiv \quad \{\text{shunting (10)}\} \\
&\quad S \cdot R \subseteq f \cdot \mathsf{F} S
\end{aligned}$$

$\square$

Now comes the main proof of Theorem 3. In one direction, the proof is relatively easy:

$$(\! [f] \!) \cdot (\! [R] \!)^\circ \subseteq S$$
$$\Leftarrow \quad \{(7)\}$$
$$f \cdot \mathsf{F}S \cdot R^\circ \subseteq S$$
$$\Leftarrow \quad \{\text{shunting (9), since } f \cdot \mathsf{F}S \text{ simple if } S \text{ is}\}$$
$$R^\circ \subseteq (f \cdot \mathsf{F}S)^\circ \cdot S$$
$$\equiv \quad \{\text{converses; Lemma 1}\}$$
$$true$$

For the other direction, we reason:

$$S \subseteq (\! [f] \!) \cdot (\! [R] \!)^\circ$$
$$\equiv \quad \{\text{shunting (10)}\}$$
$$dom\, S \subseteq S^\circ \cdot (\! [f] \!) \cdot (\! [R] \!)^\circ$$
$$\equiv \quad \{\text{assumption (i): } dom\, S = ran\, R\}$$
$$ran\, R \subseteq S^\circ \cdot (\! [f] \!) \cdot (\! [R] \!)^\circ$$
$$\Leftarrow \quad \{\text{claim : } ran\, R \subseteq ran\, (\! [R] \!)\}$$
$$ran\, (\! [R] \!) \subseteq S^\circ \cdot (\! [f] \!) \cdot (\! [R] \!)^\circ$$
$$\Leftarrow \quad \{(2)\colon ran\, X \subseteq X \cdot X^\circ\}$$
$$(\! [R] \!) \cdot (\! [R] \!)^\circ \subseteq S^\circ \cdot (\! [f] \!) \cdot (\! [R] \!)^\circ$$
$$\Leftarrow \quad \{\text{monotonicity}\}$$
$$(\! [R] \!) \subseteq S^\circ \cdot (\! [f] \!)$$
$$\equiv \quad \{\text{converses and shunting, since } (\! [f] \!) \text{ is a function if } f \text{ is}\}$$
$$(\! [R] \!) \cdot (\! [f] \!)^\circ \subseteq S$$
$$\equiv \quad \{\text{proved above}\}$$
$$true$$

We still need to prove the claim that $ran\, R \subseteq ran\, (\! [R] \!)$ under the given conditions. We will appeal to the following lemma[1], whose proof is postponed to the appendix.

Lemma 2. If $\delta_\mathsf{F} \cdot R^\circ$ is inductive and $dom\, R \subseteq \mathsf{F}(ran\, R)$, then

$$ran\, (R \cdot \mathsf{F}C) \subseteq C \Rightarrow ran\, R \subseteq C \qquad (11)$$

for coreflexives C.

To check that $dom\, R \subseteq \mathsf{F}(ran\, R)$, we reason:

$$dom\, R$$
$$\subseteq \quad \{\text{Lemma 1} : R \subseteq S^\circ \cdot f \cdot \mathsf{F}S\}$$

---

[1] Property (11) is called F-inductivity in [11].

$$dom\,(S^\circ \cdot f \cdot \mathsf{F}S)$$

$\subseteq$ {since $dom\,(X \cdot Y) \subseteq dom\,Y$}

$$dom\,(\mathsf{F}S)$$

$\subseteq$ {relators preserve domains: $dom\,(\mathsf{F}S) = \mathsf{F}(dom\,S)$}

$$\mathsf{F}(dom\,S)$$

$=$ {by assumption (i): $dom\,S = ran\,R$}

$$\mathsf{F}(ran\,R)$$

That relators preserve domains is given in [5] as an exercise on tabulation.

Finally, the left-hand side of property (11), namely $ran\,(R{\cdot}\mathsf{F}C) \subseteq C$, actually holds for all R when C is $ran\,([R])$.

$$ran\,([R])$$

$=$ {definition of $([R])$}

$$ran\,(R \cdot \mathsf{F}([R]) \cdot \alpha^\circ)$$

$=$ {since $ran\,(X \cdot Y) = ran\,(X \cdot ran\,Y)$}

$$ran\,(R \cdot ran\,(\mathsf{F}([R]) \cdot ran\,(\alpha^\circ)))$$

$=$ {since $ran\,(\alpha^\circ) = id$}

$$ran\,(R \cdot ran\,(\mathsf{F}([R])))$$

$=$ {relators preserve domains}

$$ran\,(R \cdot \mathsf{F}(ran\,([R])))$$

We therefore conclude that $ran\,R \subseteq ran\,([R])$ under the given assumptions.

We will now prove a lemma which shows that condition (iii) of Theorem 3 holds if conditions (i) and (ii) do and if $\delta_\mathsf{F} \cdot f^\circ$ is inductive. It is this lemma that establishes the connection between Theorem 1 and Theorem 3.

Lemma 3. The relation $\delta_\mathsf{F} \cdot R^\circ$ is inductive if (i) $ran\,R \subseteq dom\,S$; (ii) $S \cdot R \subseteq f \cdot \mathsf{F}S$; and (iii) $\delta_\mathsf{F} \cdot f^\circ$ is inductive.

Proof. We reason:

$$\delta_\mathsf{F} \cdot R^\circ$$

$\subseteq$ {Lemma 1, converse}

$$\delta_\mathsf{F} \cdot \mathsf{F}S^\circ \cdot f^\circ \cdot S$$

$\subseteq$ {(8)}

$$S^\circ \cdot \delta_\mathsf{F} \cdot f^\circ \cdot S$$

Since $\delta_\mathsf{F} \cdot f^\circ$ is inductive, so is $S^\circ \cdot \delta_\mathsf{F} \cdot f^\circ \cdot S$ by Fact 3. We then obtain that $\delta_\mathsf{F} \cdot R^\circ$ is inductive by Fact 2.

$\square$

8   Conclusions and Related Work

The idea of program inversion can be traced back to Dijkstra [10]. However, given the importance of inversion as a specification technique, relatively few papers have been devoted to the topic, and of those that have, most deal with program inversion in an imperative setting. A program is inverted by running it "backwards" and the challenging part is when we encounter a branch or a loop [24]. The classic example was to construct a binary tree given its inorder and preorder traversal [14,15,7,26,25]. Inversion of functional programs has received even less attention. Most published results (e.g. [20,16]) are based on a "compositional" approach, which is essentially the same as its imperative counterpart: if h is defined by $f \cdot g$, then $h^\circ = g^\circ \cdot f^\circ$. The inverse of f and g are then recursively constructed until we reach primitives whose inverses are pre-defined. Efforts have also been made to automate the process, such as in [1]. This paper also contains a detailed bibliography.

The converse-of-a-function theorem, however, takes a non-compositional approach to invert a function. To invert a function, what matters is not how it is defined but what properties it satisfies. This technique is not new. Similar techniques have been adopted in, for example, [19] and [23]. However, to the best our knowledge, it was de Moor [5,9] who first presented the technique as a theorem, suggesting a wider range of application. The problem dealt with in [9] was precedence parsing, leading to a derivation of Floyd's algorithm.

We have applied the converse-of-a-function theorem to three examples. The inverted function is usually a non-deterministic fold. To make it useful, it is often composed before some other function which acts as a filter. The fold fusion theorem is then applied to fuse the filter into the fold to remove the non-determinism, refining the specification to an implementable function. This pattern of derivation turned out to be useful in solving many problems.

One natural question is how widely the theorem can be applied. In other words, how to determine whether the converse-of-a-function theorem can be applied a particular function. Part of the answer is given in [12]: if the converse of a function can be written as a fold, the function itself must be an unfold. The necessary and sufficient conditions for a function to be an unfold given in [12] can thus be used as a test before applying the converse-of-a function theorem.

We have not fully exploited the generality of Theorem 3. It can potentially be very useful since it allows the functor F, which determines the pattern of recursion, to be independent from the input and output types. A much wider class of algorithms can thus be covered. However, the theorem itself offers no clue how F and f could be chosen. It is therefore less useful for program derivation and probably more helpful in proving the correctness of known algorithms. We have applied the theorem to some simple cases, such as letting $F(A, X) = A + X$ to verify some loop-based algorithms. The authors are enthusiastic to see more examples for which the more general theorem is necessary.

Acknowledgements

Thanks are due to members of the Algebra of Programming group in Oxford University Computing Laboratory, to Oege de Moor, for his interest, encouragement and comments throughout the development of this paper, and to Roland Backhouse, who filled in a key step in an earlier proof of the theorem based on F-reductivity and F-inductivity. The authors would also like to thank the anonymous referees for detailed and useful advices.

References

1. S. M. Abramov and R. Glück. The universal resolving algorithm: inverse computation in a functional language. In R. C. Backhouse and J. N. F. d. Oliveira, editors, *Mathematics of Program Construction 2000*, number 1837 in Lecture Notes in Computer Science, pages 187–212. Springer-Verlag, 2000.
2. R. C. Backhouse, P. de Bruin, G. Malcolm, T. S. Voermans, and J. van der Woude. Relational catamorphisms. In B. Moller, editor, *Proceedings of the IFIP TC2/WG2.1 Working Conference on Constructing Programs*, pages 287–318. Elsevier Science Publishers B.V., 1991.
3. R. C. Backhouse and P. F. Hoogendijk. Elements of a relational theory of datatypes. In B. Moller, H. Partsch, and S. A. Schuman, editors, *Formal Program Development. Proc. IFIP TC2/WG 2.1 State of the Art Seminar.*, number 755 in Lecture Notes in Computer Science, pages 7–42. Springer-Verlag, January 1992.
4. R. S. Bird. On building trees with minimum height. *Journal of Functional Programming*, 7(4):441–445, 1997.
5. R. S. Bird and O. de Moor. *Algebra of Programming*. International Series in Computer Science. Prentice Hall, 1997.
6. R. S. Bird, J. Gibbons, and S.-C. Mu. Algebraic methods for optimization problems. In R. C. Backhouse, R. Crole, and J. Gibbons, editors, *Algebraic and Coalgebraic Methods in the Mathematics of Program Construction*, number 2297 in Lecture Notes in Computer Science, pages 281–307. Springer-Verlag, January 2002.
7. W. Chen and J. T. Udding. Program inversion: more than fun! *Science of Computer Programming*, 15:1–13, 1990.
8. T.-R. Chuang and B. Goldberg. Real-time deques, multihead Turing machines, and purely functional programming. In *Conference on Functional Programming Languages and Computer Architecture*, Copenhagen, Denmark, June 1993. ACM Press.
9. O. de Moor and J. Gibbons. Pointwise relational programming. In *Proceedings of Algebraic Methodology and Software Technology 2000*, number 1816 in Lecture Notes in Computer Science, pages 371–390. Springer-Verlag, May 2000.
10. E. W. Dijkstra. Program inversion. Technical Report EWD671, Eindhoven University of Technology, 1978.
11. H. Doornbos and R. C. Backhouse. Induction and recursion on datatypes. In B. Moller, editor, *Mathematics of Program Construction, 3rd International Conference*, number 947 in Lecture Notes in Computer Science, pages 242–256. Springer-Verlag, July 1995.
12. J. Gibbons, G. Hutton, and T. Altenkirch. When is a function a fold or an unfold? In A. Corradini, M. Lenisa, and U. Montanari, editors, *Coalgebraic Methods*

230 Shin-Cheng Mu and Richard Bird

in *Computer Science*, number 44.1 in Electronic Notes in Theoretical Computer Science, April 2001.

13. J. Gibbons and G. Jones. Linear-time breadth-first tree algorithms: an exercise in the arithmetic of folds and zips. Technical report, University of Auckland, 1993. University of Auckland Computer Science Report No. 71, and IFIP Working Group 2.1 working paper 705 WIN-2.
14. D. Gries. *The Science of Programming*. Springer Verlag, 1981.
15. D. Gries and J. L. van de Snepscheut. Inorder traversal of a binary tree and its inversion. In E. W. Dijkstra, editor, *Formal Development of Programs and Proofs*, pages 37–42. Addison Wesley, 1990.
16. P. G. Harrison and H. Khoshnevisan. On the synthesis of function inverses. *Acta Informatica*, 29:211–239, 1992.
17. P. F. Hoogendijk and O. de Moor. Container types categorically. *Journal of Functional Programming*, 10(2):191–225, March 2000.
18. T. C. Hu and A. C. Tucker. Optimal computer search trees and variable-length alphabetical codes. *SIAM Journal on Applied Mathematics*, 21(4):514–532, 1971.
19. E. Knapen. Relational Programming, Program Inversion, and the Derivation of Parsing Algorithms. Master's thesis, Eindhoven University of Technology, 23 November 1993.
20. R. E. Korf. Inversion of applicative programs. In *Proceedings of the Seventh Intern. Joint Conference on Artificial Intelligence (IJCAI-81)*, pages 1007–1009. William Kaufmann, Inc., 1981.
21. C. Okasaki. Simple and efficient purely functional queues and deques. *Journal of Functional Programming*, 5(4):583–592, 1995.
22. C. Okasaki. Breadth-first numbering: lessons from a small exercise in algorithm design. In *Proceedings of the 2000 ACM SIGPLAN International Conference on Functional Programming*, pages 131–136. ACM Press, September 2000.
23. C. Pareja-Flores and J. Á. Velázquez-Iturbide. Synthesis of functions by transformations and constraints. In *Proceedings of the 1997 ACM SIGPLAN International Conference on Functional Programming*, page 317, Amsterdam, The Netherlands, June 1997. ACM Press.
24. B. J. Ross. Running programs backwards: the logical inversion of imperative computation. *Formal Aspects of Computing Journal*, 9:331–348, 1997.
25. B. Schoenmakers. Inorder traversal of a binary heap and its inversion in optimal time and space. In *Mathematics of Program Construction 1992*, number 669 in Lecture Notes in Computer Science, pages 291–301. Springer-Verlag, 1993.
26. J. L. van de Snepscheut. Inversion of a recursive tree traversal. Technical Report JAN 171a, California Institute of Technology, May 1991. Available online at `ftp://ftp.cs.caltech.edu/tr/cs-tr-91-07.ps.Z`.

A Proof of Lemma 2

For completeness we will record the proof of Lemma 2, namely that if $\delta_\mathsf{F} \cdot R^\circ$ is inductive and $dom\, R \subseteq \mathsf{F}(ran\, R)$, then

$$ran\, (R \cdot \mathsf{F}C) \subseteq C \Rightarrow ran\, R \subseteq C$$

for coreflexives C.

To carry out the proof, we need to appeal to some properties left out earlier in the paper. Firstly, there is yet another definition of *ran* via a Galois connection:

$$ran\, R \subseteq S \equiv R \subseteq S \cdot \Pi$$

Once a Galois connection (f, g) is established, many properties follows. Since any coreflexive can be a result of a *ran*, we have

$$C \subseteq D \equiv C \cdot \Pi \subseteq D \cdot \Pi \tag{12}$$

for coreflexives C and D. Secondly, from the definition of left division it follows that

$$(S \cdot R)\backslash T = R\backslash(S\backslash T) \tag{13}$$

It also follows that division is anti-monotonic, that is

$$S \subseteq R \Rightarrow R\backslash T \subseteq S\backslash T$$

Finally, the equality below is proved in [17].

$$\delta_{\mathsf{F}}\backslash(R \cdot S) = \mathsf{F}R \cdot \delta_{\mathsf{F}}\backslash S \tag{14}$$

The proof of Lemma 2 proceeds by proving $ran\, R \subseteq C$, given $ran\,(R \cdot \mathsf{F}C)$, $dom\, R \subseteq \mathsf{F}(ran\, R)$ and $\delta_{\mathsf{F}} \cdot R^{\circ}$ inductive.

Proof.

$$ran\, R \subseteq C$$
$$\equiv \quad \{(12)\}$$
$$ran\, R \cdot \Pi \subseteq C \cdot \Pi$$
$$\equiv \quad \{\text{division}\}$$
$$\Pi \subseteq ran\, R\backslash(C \cdot \Pi)$$
$$\Leftarrow \quad \{\text{since } \delta_{\mathsf{F}} \cdot R^{\circ} \text{ inductive}\}$$
$$(\delta_{\mathsf{F}} \cdot R^{\circ})\backslash(ran\, R\backslash(C \cdot \Pi)) \subseteq ran\, R\backslash(C \cdot \Pi)$$
$$\Leftarrow \quad \{\text{claim 1: } (\delta_{\mathsf{F}} \cdot R^{\circ})\backslash(ran\, R\backslash(C \cdot \Pi)) \subseteq R^{\circ}\backslash \mathsf{F}C \cdot \Pi\}$$
$$R^{\circ}\backslash \mathsf{F}C \cdot \Pi \subseteq ran\, R\backslash(C \cdot \Pi)$$
$$\equiv \quad \{\text{division}\}$$
$$ran\, R \cdot R^{\circ}\backslash(\mathsf{F}C \cdot \Pi) \subseteq C \cdot \Pi$$
$$\Leftarrow \quad \{\text{claim 2: } ran\, R \cdot R^{\circ}\backslash(\mathsf{F}C \cdot \Pi) \subseteq R \cdot \mathsf{F}C \cdot \Pi\}$$
$$R \cdot \mathsf{F}C \cdot \Pi \subseteq C \cdot \Pi$$
$$\equiv \quad \{\text{range}\}$$
$$ran\,(R \cdot \mathsf{F}C \cdot \Pi) \subseteq C$$
$$\equiv \quad \{\text{since } ran\,(X \cdot Y) = ran\,(X \cdot ran\, Y) \text{ and } ran\, \Pi = id\}$$
$$ran\,(R \cdot \mathsf{F}C) \subseteq C$$

To prove claim 1, we reason:

$$(\delta_{\mathsf{F}} \cdot R^{\circ}) \backslash (ran\,R \backslash (C \cdot \Pi))$$
$$= \quad \{(13)\}$$
$$(ran\,R \cdot \delta_{\mathsf{F}} \cdot R^{\circ}) \backslash (C \cdot \Pi)$$
$$\subseteq \quad \{(8), \text{ division is anti-monotonic}\}$$
$$(\delta_{\mathsf{F}} \cdot \mathsf{F}(ran\,R) \cdot R^{\circ}) \backslash (C \cdot \Pi)$$
$$\subseteq \quad \{\text{by assumption: } dom\,R \subseteq \mathsf{F}(ran\,R), \text{ division is anti-monotonic}\}$$
$$(\delta_{\mathsf{F}} \cdot dom\,R \cdot R^{\circ}) \backslash (C \cdot \Pi)$$
$$= \quad \{dom\,R \cdot R^{\circ} = R^{\circ}\}$$
$$(\delta_{\mathsf{F}} \cdot R^{\circ}) \backslash (C \cdot \Pi)$$
$$= \quad \{(13)\}$$
$$R^{\circ} \backslash (\delta_{\mathsf{F}} \backslash (C \cdot \Pi))$$
$$= \quad \{(14)\}$$
$$R^{\circ} \backslash (\mathsf{F}C \cdot \delta_{\mathsf{F}} \backslash \Pi)$$
$$= \quad \{\text{since } \delta_{\mathsf{F}} \backslash \Pi = \Pi \text{ by division}\}$$
$$R^{\circ} \backslash (\mathsf{F}C \cdot \Pi)$$

The proof for claim 2 goes:

$$ran\,R \cdot R^{\circ} \backslash (\mathsf{F}C \cdot \Pi)$$
$$\subseteq \quad \{\text{since } ran\,R = (R \cdot R^{\circ}) \cap id\}$$
$$R \cdot R^{\circ} \cdot R^{\circ} \backslash (\mathsf{F}C \cdot \Pi)$$
$$\subseteq \quad \{\text{division}\}$$
$$R \cdot \mathsf{F}C \cdot \Pi$$

$\square$

From Kleene Algebra to Refinement Algebra

Joakim von Wright

Åbo Akademi University and Turku Centre for Computer Science (TUCS)
Lemminkäisenkatu 14, FIN-20520 Turku, Finland
jockum.wright@abo.fi

Abstract. Kleene Algebra with Tests (KAT) has proved to be useful for reasoning about programs in a partial correctness framework. We describe Demonic Refinement Algebra (DRA), a variation of KAT for total correctness and illustrate its modeling and reasoning power with a number of applications and examples.

1 Introduction

A good programming theory should have an algebra that allows transparent and powerful reasoning about programs but at the same time is close enough to the programming intuition to make expressions and derivations easy to interpret intuitively. Kleene Algebra (the algebra of regular languages) has a simple and beautiful equational theory, and its extension Kleene Algebra with Tests (KAT) has proved suitable for reasoning about programs in a partial correctness framework [17].

The Refinement Calculus [3,6,21] is a calculus for program development in a total correctness framework, based on predicate transformers. In this paper we explore a variation of KAT, called Demonic Refinement Algebra (DRA), which is similar to KAT, but allows axiomatic reasoning within the predicate transformer framework. Thus, we take earlier algebraic approaches to weakest precondition reasoning [6,7,22] one step further, and as a result we can give succinct and elegant formulations of many results that have previously required much more complicated descriptions and longer proofs.

Our refinement algebra is in many ways similar to Cohen's extension of KAT, Omega Algebra [12]. However, Omega Algebra has no notion of nontermination, and models total correctness by reasoning separately about finite and infinite executions. On the other hand, we drop the axiom that prevents a proper treatment of nontermination ($x0 = 0$), and model total correctness (i.e., a notion of correctness which includes termination) directly. Thus, Omega Algebra is a conservative extension of KAT, while DRA is not. Most basic results of KA/KAT also hold in DRA, but the single notion of (partial) correctness in KAT gives rise to two different notions of correctness in DRA. Similarly, to the tests (predicates) of KAT correspond two dual notions in DRA: guards and assertions.

The focus of this paper is to show how the same kind of reasoning about correctness and program transformation that is possible for partial correctness and equivalence in KAT [8,12,17] can be done for total correctness and refinement

E.A. Boiten and B. Möller (Eds.): MPC 2002, LNCS 2386, pp. 233–262, 2002.
© Springer-Verlag Berlin Heidelberg 2002

in DRA, but also to show some new applications. We do not investigate abstract properties of the algebra and its axiomatisation, such as complexity, decidability, or completeness with respect to the predicate transformer model.

Some of the results for total correctness and refinement that we prove have also been derived previously in the predicate transformer model [7,20,22], but typically with much more complicated proofs. For many of our theorems, there is also a similar result in Omega Algebra, and in those cases Cohen's proofs [12] can be reused with minor changes.

The paper is organised as follows. The refinement algebra is described in Section 2, and Sections 3–7 contains a sequence of applications and examples that illustrate modeling and reasoning in DRA. These include both extensions of traditional KAT-applications to a total correctness framework (correctness reasoning, program transformation, distributed systems), and new applications (program inversion, data refinement). Finally, Section 8 contains some concluding remarks. Only the most interesting proofs are included in the paper. Some additional proofs can be found in Appendix B. We write derivations in a calculational format and we use ≡ (equivalence), ∧, ⇒, ⇐ and true as metalogical symbols in rules and derivations, i.e., they build inferences rather than formulas.

2   A Demonic Refinement Algebra

2.1   Basic Definitions

A Kleene Algebra (KA) is a structure $(+, \cdot, *, 0, 1)$ over some carrier set where $(+, \cdot, 0, 1)$ is an idempotent semiring and $*$ (written postfix) satisfies unfolding and induction (for a standard axiomatisation, see Appendix A). In a Kleene Algebra with Tests (KAT) there is a Boolean subalgebra $(+, \cdot, ^-, 0, 1)$ of elements called *tests* [17] or *predicates* [12].

Models for KA include regular languages, relations and universally conjunctive predicate transformers. In a programming intuition, $\cdot$ models composition (sequence), $+$ models choice and $*$ models (finite) iteration.

In order to get a structure that can handle potentially nonterminating computations in a way that is consistent with the total correctness approach of the Refinement Calculus [6], we introduce a *strong iteration* operator (ω), which stands for a finite or infinite repetition (the reader should note that this is not a standard meaning for the symbol ω). Furthermore, we replace the standard notation with one that better fits the intended interpretation (program refinement) and the extensions we are going to introduce. We write $\top$ instead of 0, $\sqcap$ instead of $+$, and $\sqsupseteq$ instead of $\leq$ (we also write ; instead of $\cdot$, but since this operator is always left implicit, that does not really matter). Thus, a *demonic refinement algebra* (DRA) is a structure $(\sqcap, ;, *, \omega, \top, 1)$ satisfying the following axioms:

$$
\begin{array}{lll}
x(yz) = (xy)z & & (\textit{associativity}) \\
1x = x & x1 = x & (\textit{unit}) \\
x \sqcap (y \sqcap z) = (x \sqcap y) \sqcap z & & (\textit{associativity}) \\
\top \sqcap x = x & & (\textit{unit}) \\
x \sqcap y = y \sqcap x & & (\textit{commutativity}) \\
x \sqcap x = x & & (\textit{idempotence}) \\
x(y \sqcap z) = xy \sqcap xz & (x \sqcap y)z = xz \sqcap yz & (\textit{distributivity}) \\
\top x = \top & & (\textit{preemption}) \\
x^* = xx^* \sqcap 1 & x^\omega = xx^\omega \sqcap 1 & (\textit{unfolding}) \\
x^\omega = x^* \sqcap x^\omega \top & & (\textit{isolation})
\end{array}
$$

and the following rules:

$$
\begin{array}{lll}
z \sqsubseteq xz \sqcap y \Rightarrow z \sqsubseteq x^*y & z \sqsubseteq zx \sqcap y \Rightarrow z \sqsubseteq yx^* & (\ast\textit{-induction}) \\
xz \sqcap y \sqsubseteq z \Rightarrow x^\omega y \sqsubseteq z & & (\omega\textit{-induction})
\end{array}
$$

where the ordering $x \sqsubseteq y$ is defined to hold if and only if $x \sqcap y = x$.

Note that compared with KA, we have no right-hand preemption axiom ($x\top = \top$) and we have added three axioms for ω. Omitting right-hand preemption means that we cannot assume that all basic theorems of KA are true in DRA. Apart from this, we have reused the traditional axioms of KA. The added axioms (unfolding, isolation, ω-induction) are intended to show how ω and $\ast$ are related, and justified by the intended model (see below).

The following list explains the intuition behind DRA:

- xy is *sequential composition*, x being executed before y
- $x \sqcap y$ is *demonic choice*, a choice over which we have no influence
- 1 is *skip*, leaving the state unchanged
- $\top$ is *magic*, immediately establishing any postcondition desired, even false (so $\top$ is the top element wrt $\sqsubseteq$)
- x^* is *weak iteration*, x being executed some finite number of times
- x^ω is *strong iteration*, x being executed some finite or infinite number of times (where infinite execution is equivalent to nontermination)
- $x \sqsubseteq y$ is *refinement*, meaning that y accomplishes whatever x does (so x can be replaced by y in all contexts)

The intended model for DRA is the set of *conjunctive predicate transformers over a fixed state space*, i.e., the functions $(\Sigma \rightarrow \mathsf{Bool}) \rightarrow (\Sigma \rightarrow \mathsf{Bool})$ that distribute over arbitrary conjunctions of predicates (Σ is the underlying state space). These model demonically nondeterministic programs according to a *weakest precondition semantics* [13], i.e., if S is a conjunctive predicate transformer and $q : \Sigma \rightarrow \mathsf{Bool}$ is a predicate, then the predicate $S.q$ (S applied to q) is true exactly for those initial states from which execution of S is guaranteed to terminate in a state where q holds.

In the predicate transformer model, ; is function composition, 1 is the identity function, $\sqcap$ is lattice meet, $\top$ is the top element and $\sqsubseteq$ is the twice pointwise extended implication ordering on Bool. Finally, S^* and S^ω correspond to the greatest and least fixpoints $(\nu X \bullet S ; X \sqcap 1)$ and $(\mu X \bullet S ; X \sqcap 1)$, respectively. It is easily proved that these satisfy the axioms.

Note that we have only one induction rule for strong iteration. In fact, in the predicate transformer model, a counterexample (with $\top$ for y and with 1 for x and z) shows we cannot have a rule such as $zx \sqcap y \sqsubseteq z \Rightarrow yx^\omega \sqsubseteq z$.

2.2 Some Basic Theorems

The most interesting theorems of classical Kleene Algebra all have to do with iterations. Many interesting properties of KA also hold in DRA, and there are corresponding results for the strong iteration (since we focus on strong iteration in this paper, we do not state results for weak iteration, unless they have independent interest or are used in later arguments):

$$x^\omega = x^\omega x \sqcap 1 \tag{1}$$
$$x(yx)^\omega = (xy)^\omega x \tag{2}$$
$$(x \sqcap y)^\omega = x^\omega (yx^\omega)^\omega \tag{3}$$

We use the name *dual unfolding* for property (1), *leapfrog* for (2) and *decomposition* for (3) (Kozen uses *sliding* and *denesting* for the latter two [17]).

We also need the following stronger versions of unfolding and of decomposition, taken from corresponding lemmas in [12]:

$$(x \sqcap y)^\omega = y^*x(x \sqcap y)^\omega \sqcap y^\omega \tag{4}$$
$$(x \sqcap y)^\omega = (y^*x)^\omega y^\omega \tag{5}$$

The following important property will be used in proofs and arguments implicitly or possibly with a reference to "monotonicity": *the operators* ;, $\sqcap$, $*$ *and* ω *are monotonic in all their arguments with respect to the ordering* $\sqsubseteq$ (this is easily proved from the axioms).

2.3 Guards

We call an element p of DRA a *guard* if it has a *complement* p^- satisfying the following conditions:

$$pp^- = p^-p = \top \qquad \text{and} \qquad p \sqcap p^- = 1 \qquad (guard)$$

Obviously, if p is a guard, then p^- is also a guard with complement p. Furthermore $\top$ is the complement of 1. In fact, *the guards form a boolean algebra* $(\sqcap, ;, ^-, \top, 1)$. This fact is noted by Cohen [12], and we will use it freely in proofs involving guards.

Intuitively, guards model conditions, exactly like tests in KAT; if p is a guard then px behaves like x if the condition is satisfied and like $\top$ otherwise. As a guard, $\top$ corresponds to "everywhere false" and 1 to "everywhere true". However, in a total correctness framework there is also a dual notion of *assertions* that model conditions in a different way (see Section 2.6 below).

Using guards, we can do case analyses in proofs. This follows from the following basic rules, which are easily verified:

$$x \sqsubseteq y \;\equiv\; x \sqsubseteq py \,\wedge\, x \sqsubseteq p^- y \tag{6}$$

$$px \sqcap p^- y \sqsubseteq z \;\equiv\; px \sqsubseteq pz \,\wedge\, p^- y \sqsubseteq p^- z \tag{7}$$

Note that the implication ordering on predicates is modelled by the reverse order $\sqsupseteq$. Also note that the property $1 \sqsubseteq p$ can be interpreted as saying that p has no effect on the state (since it refines 1 which is interpreted as a skip).[1]

2.4   Nontermination

Intuitively, the difference between the two iteration operators is that x^ω permits infinite (nonterminating) behaviour. To make this more explicit, we define a new constant which stands for an always nonterminating computation:

$$\bot \stackrel{\wedge}{=} 1^\omega \qquad\qquad\qquad (abort)$$

Then $\bot$ is a bottom element,

$$\bot \sqsubseteq x \qquad\qquad \bot \sqcap x = \bot \tag{8}$$

and it has a preemption property similar to that of $\top$:

$$\bot x = \bot \tag{9}$$

The preemption property (9) shows where a conflict with the classical axiom $x\top = \top$ would arise in DRA.

2.5   Modeling Programs

We want to use the refinement algebra to reason about loop programs in the style of Dijkstra's *guarded commands* [13] and also about parallel programs and distributed systems that have the form of *action systems* [5,7], in the same way as KAT is used to reason about while-programs in a partial correctness framework [17].

Using DRA, conditionals and guarded loops are modeled as follows:

$$\text{if } p \text{ then } x \text{ else } y \text{ fi } = px \sqcap p^- y$$

$$\text{do } p \to x \,[\!]\, q \to y \text{ od } = (px \sqcap qy)^\omega p^- \, q^-$$

---

[1] We use the same definition for guards as Cohen's predicates [12]. Thus our notion of guards is slightly more restricted than Kozen's tests, since Kozen allows *any* boolean subalgebra to be considered as tests [17]. It is also possible to take $1 \sqsubseteq p$ as the defining property of guards (as done in [11]), but this easily interferes with extensions to the algebra.

(here the guarded loop has two alternatives, but the same idea can be used for any finite number of alternatives). Furthermore, an action system is modeled by an expression of the form

$$s(a_1 \sqcap \ldots \sqcap a_n)^\omega e$$

where s is an initialisation, a_i are the *actions* and e is a *finalisation*. We assume that an *enabling guard* is part of each action a_i, and only if there is a need to refer to the guard do we write the action as a composition $p_i x_i$. This will keep the expressions and the proofs simpler, and it will help show in what situations it is actually essential to consider the guard as a separate entity – if needed, we may without loss of generality assume that $x_i \bot = \bot$. The intuition is that actions are repeatedly executed, the choice of an enabled action being demonic, and termination can be chosen whenever e is enabled. In practice, e often has the form qe', where q is an *exit guard*.

Our action system notion is slightly more general than the traditional one. In traditional presentations, the exit guard is of the form q^-, where q is the disjunction of the action guards, which means that no miracles can occur and that termination is deterministic. An ordinary while-loop is then a traditional action system with only a single action. What was treated as two separate cases (action systems and loops) in [7] is here captured with a single slightly more abstract framework.

2.6   Assertions (Dual Guards)

Our guards correspond to *guard statements* (also known as naked guards, assumptions or coercions) that have been used in weakest precondition reasoning to represent context information and to link correctness to refinement [9,21]. The dual notion of *assertion statements* was introduced independently [3] for the same purpose. The equivalence of the two approaches is due to the fact that assertions and guards are linked by two Galois connections, and we shall now describe this in our algebra.

We define the assertion corresponding to the guard p as follows:

$$p^\circ \overset{\wedge}{=} p^- \bot \sqcap 1 \qquad\qquad\qquad (assertion)$$

Intuitively, p° aborts where p is miraculous and skips where p skips. In particular, $1^\circ = 1$ and $\top^\circ = \bot$ and the ordering $\sqsubseteq$ on assertions matches the implication ordering of the corresponding predicates.

We find that for any guards p and q,

$$p^\circ q^\circ \ = \ p^\circ \sqcap q^\circ \ = \ (pq)^\circ$$

i.e., choice and composition of assertions give the same result. Thus, assertions have a slightly weaker expressive power than guards. For example, guards cannot be defined in terms of assertions, although the opposite is possible.

Assertions also inherit many of the properties of guards, e.g., $p°p° = p°$ and $p°q° = q°p°$. The basic duality between guards and assertions is described by the following Galois connections:

$$p°x \sqsubseteq y \equiv x \sqsubseteq py \qquad \text{and} \qquad xp \sqsubseteq y \equiv x \sqsubseteq yp° \qquad (10)$$

for any guard p, and for arbitrary x and y.

In particular, we see that the equivalence between the traditional ways of transporting context information using guards or assertions[2] is mirrored by the following equivalence which follows directly from (10):

$$p°x \sqsubseteq xq° \equiv xq \sqsubseteq px \qquad (11)$$

The interpretation of either refinement is approximately "if p holds before x is executed and the execution terminates, then q is guaranteed to hold afterwards" (i.e., something close to a partial correctness assertion).

Using assertions we can model Dijkstra's guarded conditional in the well-known way:

$$\text{if } p \to x \;[\!]\; q \to y \text{ fi} = p°q°(px \sqcap qy)$$

and similarly for more than two alternatives.

3   Correctness Reasoning

In KAT, a (partial) correctness assertion of the form $\{P\}S\{Q\}$ corresponds to the following equivalent formulations [18]:

$$pxq^- = \top \qquad\qquad px = pxq \qquad\qquad xq \sqsubseteq px \qquad (12)$$

where p models the precondition, x the program and q the postcondition.

3.1   Two Notions of Correctness

In the proof that the three formulations of correctness in (12) are equivalent, the axiom of KAT that we have now dropped ($x\top = \top$) is used. In DRA, it turns out that the same conditions still model correctness, but in two different ways, for which we make the following definitions:

$$p \,(\!|x|\!)\, q \;\overset{\wedge}{=}\; px = pxq \quad (\equiv\;\; xq \sqsubseteq px\;) \qquad (\textit{weak correctness})$$
$$p \,\{\!|x|\!\}\, q \;\overset{\wedge}{=}\; pxq^- = \top \quad (\equiv\;\; p^-\bot \sqsubseteq xq^-\;) \quad (\textit{total correctness})$$

The alternative characterisations in terms of refinement given in parentheses are easily shown to be equivalent to the definitions, which are given in terms of equality (see Appendix B).

Weak correctness can be characterised as "partial correctness in a total correctness framework". In the predicate transformer model, let guard p correspond

---

[2] Using the syntax of [6,21] this corresponds to $\{P\}\,;S \sqsubseteq S\,;\{Q\} \;\equiv\; S\,;[Q] \sqsubseteq [P]\,;S$.

to a predicate transformer $(\lambda R \bullet \neg P \cup R)$ and x to a predicate transformer S. Then the conditions for weak correctness correspond to a condition of the form

$$S.\mathsf{true} \cap P \;\subseteq\; S.Q$$

while the conditions for total correctness correspond to

$$P \;\subseteq\; S.Q$$

The latter is the classical definition of total correctness while the former is a slightly weaker notion, often used in connection with invariants, where termination is not required.[3]

Obviously, total correctness implies weak correctness. Also note that total correctness is monotonic (if $x \sqsubseteq y$, then $p\,\{\!|x|\!\}\,q$ implies $p\,\{\!|y|\!\}\,q$) while weak correctness is not. Weak correctness can by (11) also be expressed with assertions:

$$p\,(\!|x|\!)\,q \;\equiv\; p^\circ x \sqsubseteq xq^\circ$$

but total correctness cannot.

For weak correctness, we can prove all the rules that Kozen proves for partial correctness in KAT, plus the following *invariant rule* for strong iteration:

$$p\,(\!|x|\!)\,p \;\Rightarrow\; p\,(\!|x^\omega|\!)\,p \tag{13}$$

3.2   Total Correctness

The essential difference between the two notions of correctness is that total correctness includes termination. Thus, the rules for total correctness are essentially the same as for weak correctness, except for strong iteration, which requires something corresponding to a variant (a termination argument) in addition to the invariant. To describe this, we first introduce a dual induction rule for strong iteration.

The induction rule for strong iteration gives a conclusion of the form $x^\omega y \sqsubseteq z$, but that is not helpful when verifying total correctness. However, a rule with a conclusion of the form $z \sqsubseteq x^\omega y$ can be derived in much the same way as the corresponding rule in complete lattices, using *ranked* collections of objects (i.e., objects indexed by some well-founded set).[4]

We do not have general join or limit operators available in DRA, but we can still prove a weaker version of dual induction, where $\{z_n \mid n \in W\}$ is a ranked collection of elements:

$$(\forall n \bullet (z_n \sqsubseteq x \bot \sqcap y) \vee (\exists m < n \bullet z_n \sqsubseteq xz_m \sqcap y)) \Rightarrow (\forall n \bullet z_n \sqsubseteq x^\omega y) \tag{14}$$

---

[3] In the original style of working with weakest preconditions, these would be written $wp(S, \mathsf{true}) \wedge P \Rightarrow wp(S, Q)$ and $P \Rightarrow wp(S, Q)$, respectively.

[4] For complete lattices, the rule can be written

$$\frac{x_n \sqsubseteq f.(\sqcup m < n \bullet x_m)}{(\sqcup n \bullet x_n) \sqsubseteq \mu f}$$

where m and n range over some well-founded set.

where the indices n and m range over W.

Because W is assumed to be well-founded, we can use the principle of well-founded induction when proving (14):

$$(\forall n \bullet (\forall m < n \bullet P(m)) \Rightarrow P(n)) \Rightarrow (\forall n \bullet P(n))$$

With $z_n \sqsubseteq x^\omega y$ for $P(n)$, we have

$$(\forall n \bullet (\forall m < n \bullet z_m \sqsubseteq x^\omega y) \Rightarrow z_n \sqsubseteq x^\omega y) \Rightarrow (\forall n \bullet z_n \sqsubseteq x^\omega y)$$

and so we want to prove the antecedent of this implication, assuming

$$(\forall n \bullet (z_n \sqsubseteq x \bot \sqcap y) \vee (\exists m < n \bullet z_n \sqsubseteq xz_m \sqcap y))$$

Thus we let n be arbitrary and assume $(\forall m < n \bullet z_m \sqsubseteq x^\omega y)$. Regardless of which disjunct of the assumption above holds, it is now straightforward to prove $z_n \sqsubseteq x^\omega y$, and the proof is finished (a more detailed proof is given in Appendix B).

Note that if the well-founded set W has a smallest element 0, then we get the following variation of the rule in (14):

$$(z_0 \sqsubseteq x \bot \sqcap y) \wedge (\forall n > 0 \bullet \exists m < n \bullet z_n \sqsubseteq xz_m \sqcap y)) \Rightarrow (\forall n \bullet z_n \sqsubseteq x^\omega y)$$

Now the rule for total correctness of strong iterations can be formulated: If $\{p_n\}$ is a collection of guards indexed by $\mathsf{Nat} \cup \{\infty\}$ satisfying the following conditions:

(i) $p_0 = \top$,
(ii) $(\forall m\, n \bullet m \leq n \Rightarrow p_m \sqsupseteq p_n)$, and
(iii) $(\forall n > 0 \bullet \exists m < n \bullet p_n \{|x|\} p_m)$,

then

$$p_\infty \{|x^\omega|\} p_\infty \tag{15}$$

To prove this rule, we first have

$p_\infty \{|x^\omega|\} p_\infty$
$\equiv \{\text{definition of correctness, assumption (ii)}\}$
   $(\forall n \bullet p_n^- \bot \sqsubseteq x^\omega p_\infty^-)$
$\Leftarrow \{\text{dual induction (14)}\}$
   $(\forall n \bullet (p_n^- \bot \sqsubseteq x \bot \sqcap p_\infty^-) \vee (\exists m < n \bullet p_n^- \bot \sqsubseteq xp_m^- \sqcap p_\infty^-))$

If $n = 0$, then by assumption (i), $p_0^- \bot = 1 \bot \sqsubseteq x \bot \sqcap p_\infty^-$. On the other hand, if $n > 0$, then by assumption (iii) there is $m < n$ such that

$$p_n^- \bot = p_n^- \bot \bot \sqcap p_n^- \bot \sqsubseteq p_n^- \bot \bot \sqcap p_n^- \sqsubseteq xp_m^- \sqcap p_\infty^-$$

where we have used assumption (ii) to deduce $p_n^- \sqsubseteq p_\infty^-$. Thus the proof is finished.

3.3   Loop Correctness

In practice, the rule in (15) is used when proving loop correctness with a variant and an invariant. In order to prove correctness of a while-loop using invariant I and variant t ranging over the natural numbers, we let p_n stand for $I \wedge (t < n)$. Then p_∞ stands for I and conditions (i) and (ii) of (15) are satisfied. Thus, with the while-loop modelled as $(bx)^\omega b^-$,

$$p_\infty \, \{|(bx)^\omega b^-|\} \, b^- p_\infty$$
$$\equiv \{\text{definition of correctness}\}$$
$$p_\infty (bx)^\omega b^- (b \sqcap p_\infty^-) = \top$$
$$\equiv \{\text{properties of guards: } b^- b = \top\}$$
$$p_\infty (bx)^\omega b^- p_\infty^- = \top$$
$$\Leftarrow \{\text{properties of guards: } 1 \sqsubseteq b^-\}$$
$$p_\infty (bx)^\omega p_\infty^- = \top$$
$$\equiv \{\text{definition of correctness}\}$$
$$p_\infty \, \{|(bx)^\omega|\} \, p_\infty$$
$$\Leftarrow \{\text{correctness of iteration (15)}\}$$
$$(\forall n > 0 \bullet \exists m < n \bullet p_n \, \{|bx|\} \, p_m)$$
$$\equiv \{\text{definition of correctness}\}$$
$$(\forall n > 0 \bullet \exists m < n \bullet p_n bx p_m^- = \top)$$
$$\equiv \{\text{definition of correctness}\}$$
$$(\forall n > 0 \bullet \exists m < n \bullet b p_n \, \{|x|\} \, p_m)$$

This corresponds the classical rule for loop correctness: if we want to prove

$$P \, \{|\text{do } B \to S \text{ od}|\} \, \neg B \wedge P$$

it is sufficient to show that when the loop guard B is true, the body S maintains the invariant P and decreases a variant.

It should be noted that this rule is sufficient for loops with bounded nondeterminism. Replacing the natural numbers by a general well-founded set does not help; since the algebra does not have a limit (join) operator, we cannot formulate the more general rule that could also handle loop bodies with unbounded nondeterminism.

4   Program Transformation

Program transformation is one of the main applications of Kleene Algebra [8,12,17], and we will here only show by two small examples that our Refinement Algebra is also suited for deriving program transformations that preserve total correctness. Both examples have appeared in [7], but the strictly axiomatic framework makes the proofs below much shorter.

First we show how a *decomposition rule* for loops can be derived in a short calculation. From a methodological point of view, the challenge is to do the transformation step by step and to identify conditions as they are needed in individual derivation steps:

$$(px \sqcap qy)^\omega p^- q^-$$
$$= \{\text{decomposition (3)}\}$$
$$(px)^\omega (qy(px)^\omega)^\omega p^- q^-$$
$$= \{\textbf{assume } q = p^- q\}$$
$$(px)^\omega (p^- qy(px)^\omega)^\omega p^- q^-$$
$$= \{\text{leapfrog (2)}\}$$
$$(px)^\omega p^- (qy(px)^\omega p^-)^\omega q^-$$

Written in traditional syntax, what we have proved here is the rule

$$\text{do } P \to S \;\|\; Q \to S' \text{ od } = \text{ do } P \to S \text{ od} \,;\, \text{do } Q \to S' \,;\, (\text{do } P \to S \text{ od}) \text{ od}$$

under the assumption that P and Q are disjoint (since $q = p^- q$ is equivalent to $q \sqsupseteq p^-$). Earlier proofs of this rule have been long and involved [20,22].

Our second example shows how a redundant loop can be removed in a refinement step:

$$(pqx)^\omega (pq)^- (px)^\omega p^- \sqsubseteq (px)^\omega p^-$$
$$\Leftarrow \{\text{induction}\}$$
$$pqx(px)^\omega p^- \sqcap (pq)^- (px)^\omega p^- \sqsubseteq (px)^\omega p$$
$$\equiv \{\text{case split (7)}\}$$
$$pqx(px)^\omega p^- \sqsubseteq pq(px)^\omega p^- \;\wedge\; (pq)^- (px)^\omega p^- \sqsubseteq (pq)^- (px)^\omega p^-$$
$$\equiv \{\text{second conjunct holds by reflexivity}\}$$
$$pqx(px)^\omega p^- \sqsubseteq pq(px)^\omega p$$
$$\equiv \{\text{unfolding on rhs, distributivity}\}$$
$$pqx(px)^\omega p^- \sqsubseteq pqpx(px)^\omega p^- \sqcap pqp^-$$
$$\equiv \{\text{guard properties } pqp = pq \text{ and } pqp^- = \top\}$$
$$\text{true}$$

In traditional syntax, the rule is

$$\text{do } g \wedge h \to S \text{ od} \,;\, \text{do } g \to S \text{ od} \sqsubseteq \text{do } g \to S \text{ od}$$

which is intuitively obvious but not easily proved using traditional methods.

5   Program Inversion

Inverting a program S means finding a program S' such that when the sequence $S \,;\, S'$ is executed (under some given precondition P), then the final state is the same as the initial state.

Gries [15] described basic rules for inverting programs in Dijkstra's guarded commands language, and Chen and Udding later formalised the same notion of program inversion [10]. We have earlier shown how angelic constructs in the Refinement Calculus can be used to give a more general theory of program inversion [23].

We get a simple formulation of the classical notion of program inversion if we assume that the precondition is included as part of the program S under consideration: S' inverts S if and only if $\{S.\,\text{true}\} \sqsubseteq S\,;\,S'$.

It is easily verified in the refinement calculus that $\{S.\,\text{true}\} = S\,;\,\text{magic} \sqcap \text{skip}$, and so we can define program inversion in DRA:

$$z \text{ inv } x \overset{\wedge}{=} x\top \sqcap 1 \sqsubseteq xz \tag{16}$$

where z inv x is to be read "z inverts x".

It now turns out that the inversion rules that have appeared in the literature can be verified with straightforward derivations in DRA. For the basic constants, we have

$$z \text{ inv } 1 \equiv 1 \sqsubseteq z \qquad\qquad z \text{ inv } \top \equiv \text{true} \qquad\qquad z \text{ inv } \bot \equiv \text{true} \tag{17}$$

and for guards and assertions:

$$z \text{ inv } p \equiv z \text{ inv } p^\circ \equiv p^\circ \sqsubseteq z \tag{18}$$

(so p° inverts both p and p°). For composition, choice and iterations, the rules become more interesting:

$$y'x' \text{ inv } xy \Leftarrow x' \text{ inv } x \wedge y' \text{ inv } y \tag{19}$$
$$px' \sqcap p^- y' \text{ inv } x \sqcap y \Leftarrow x' \text{ inv } x \wedge y' \text{ inv } y \wedge x = xp \wedge y = yp^- \tag{20}$$
$$(px')^\omega p^- \text{ inv } p^- x^\omega \Leftarrow x' \text{ inv } x \wedge x = xp \tag{21}$$

The proof of the rule for loop inversion (21) is quite tricky. The main proof is for weak rather than strong iteration. Our first derivation establishes a "strengthened invariant":

$$p^- ((px')^\omega p^- \sqcap x^* \top)$$
$$= \{\text{distributivity}\}$$
$$p^- (px')^\omega p^- \sqcap p^- x^* \top)$$
$$= \{\text{general rule } p^- (px)^\omega = p^-\}$$
$$p^- \sqcap p^- x^* \top$$
$$\sqsupseteq \{\text{general rule } 1 \sqsubseteq p\}$$
$$p^- x^* \top \sqcap 1$$

Assuming x' inv x and $x = xp$ we then use this to do the induction:

$$p^- x^* \top \sqcap 1 \sqsubseteq p^- x^* (px')^\omega p^-$$
$$\Leftarrow \{\text{preceding derivation}\}$$

$$p^-((px')^\omega p^- \sqcap x^* \top) \sqsubseteq p^- x^*(px')^\omega p^-$$
$\Leftarrow \{\text{monotonicity}\}$
$$(px')^\omega p^- \sqcap x^* \top \sqsubseteq x^*(px')^\omega p^-$$
$\Leftarrow \{\text{induction, distributivity}\}$
$$(px')^\omega p^- \sqcap x^* \top \sqsubseteq x(px')^\omega p^- \sqcap xx^* \top \sqcap (px')^\omega p^-$$
$\equiv \{\text{simplify, general rule } x^* \sqsubseteq xx^*\}$
$$(px')^\omega p^- \sqcap x^* \top \sqsubseteq x(px')^\omega p^-$$
$\equiv \{\text{unfold, distributivity}\}$
$$(px')^\omega p^- \sqcap x^* \top \sqsubseteq xpx'(px')^\omega p^- \sqcap xp^-$$
$\equiv \{\text{assumption } x = xp\}$
$$(px')^\omega p^- \sqcap x^* \top \sqsubseteq xx'(px')^\omega p^- \sqcap xpp^-$$
$\equiv \{\text{guard property, distributivity, } \top \text{ is top}\}$
$$(px')^\omega p^- \sqcap x^* \top \sqsubseteq xx'(px')^\omega p^-$$
$\Leftarrow \{\text{assumption } x' \text{ inv } x, \text{ distributivity}\}$
$$(px')^\omega p^- \sqcap x^* \top \sqsubseteq x \top (px')^\omega p^- \sqcap (px')^\omega p^-$$
$\Leftarrow \{\text{monotonicity, preemption}\}$
$$x^* \top \sqsubseteq x \top$$
$\equiv \{\text{general rule } x^* \sqsubseteq x, \text{ monotonicity}\}$
true

and we have shown $(px')^\omega p^-$ inv $p^- x^*$. Now (21) follows from the fact (which is straightforward to prove, using the isolation axiom) that z inv yx^* implies z inv yx^ω.

Gries's inversion rule for loops can be stated as follows:

$$\{\neg P\} \,; \text{do } Q \to S' \,; \{P\} \text{ od} \quad \text{inverts} \quad \{\neg Q\} \,; \text{do } P \to S \,; \{Q\} \text{ od}$$

if S' inverts S. Intuitively, since the first execution of S changes Q from false to true, we get the inverse of the loop by repeating the inverse of S until Q is no longer true. In DRA, the rule is easily derived from the rules given above, as follows. Using the rules for iteration (with pxq° for x and $q^\circ x'p^\circ$ for x'), composition, guards and assertions, we first get

$$p^{-\circ}(qq^\circ x'p^\circ)^\omega q^- q^{-\circ} \text{ inv } q^{-\circ} q^-(pxq^\circ)^\omega p^- \Leftarrow q^\circ x'p^\circ \text{ inv } pxq^\circ \wedge pxq^\circ = pxq^\circ q$$

and (using the general rules $pp^\circ = p$ and $p^\circ p = p^\circ$) this simplifies to

$$p^{-\circ}(qx'p^\circ)^\omega q^- \text{ inv } q^{-\circ}(pxq^\circ)^\omega p^- \Leftarrow x' \text{ inv } x \tag{22}$$

which is exactly Gries' rule.

A similar argument can be used to derive the rule for conditionals from the rule for choice: we get

$$qx'p^\circ \sqcap q^- y'p^{-\circ} \text{ inv } pxq^\circ \sqcap p^- yq^{-\circ} \Leftarrow x' \text{ inv } x \wedge y' \text{ inv } y \tag{23}$$

which corresponds to the rule that

if Q then S_1' ; $\{P\}$ else S_2' ; $\{\neg P\}$ fi inverts if P then S ; $\{Q\}$ else S_2 ; $\{\neg Q\}$ fi

if S_1' inverts S_1 and S_2' inverts S_2.

6   Commutativity and Data Refinement

Data refinement can on an abstract level be described as commutativity of the form $xz \sqsubseteq zy$, where x is the abstract program, y is the concrete program and z is an *encoding*. This models forward data refinement; backward data refinement is modeled as $zx \sqsubseteq yz$ where z is a *decoding* [2].

The interesting cases of data refinement involve iterations and the proofs are based on rules that describe how iterations inherit commutativity:

$$\text{if } \ xz \sqsubseteq zy \ \text{ then } \ x^*z \sqsubseteq zy^* \ \text{ and } \ x^\omega z \sqsubseteq zy^\omega \tag{24}$$

$$\text{if } \ zx \sqsubseteq yz \ \text{ then } \ zx^* \sqsubseteq y^*z \tag{25}$$

Note the missing case here: to deduce $zx^\omega \sqsubseteq y^\omega z$ from $zx \sqsubseteq yz$ we would need something corresponding to a continuity requirement on z [2].

From the commutativity lemmas we then get the following rule for data refinement of action systems: Assume that

(i) $sz \sqsubseteq s'$ and $e \sqsubseteq ze'$,
(ii) $az \sqsubseteq za'$ and $z \sqsubseteq zb$, and
(iii) $b^\omega = b^*$

Then

$$sa^\omega e \sqsubseteq s'(a' \sqcap b)^\omega e' \tag{26}$$

Intuitively, condition (i) expresses data refinement of initialisations and finalisations, condition (ii) expresses that a is data refined by a' and 1 by b (so b is a *stuttering action*), and condition (iii) expresses that b cannot loop infinitely (i.e., b eventually disables itself).

To prove (26), first from $1z \sqsubseteq zb$ and $1^* = 1$ we get

$$z \sqsubseteq zb^*$$

by (24). From this and the assumption $az \sqsubseteq za'$ we then get

$$a^\omega z \sqsubseteq z(a'b^*)^\omega$$

also by (24). Then

$$
\begin{aligned}
&s'(a' \sqcap b)^\omega e' \\
={} &\{\text{decomposition (3), assumption } b^\omega = b^*\} \\
&s'b^*(a'b^*)^\omega e' \\
\sqsupseteq{} &\{\text{assumption } sz \sqsubseteq s'\}
\end{aligned}
$$

$$szb^*(a'b^*)^\omega e'$$

$\sqsupseteq$ {first fact above}

$$sz(a'b^*)^\omega e'$$

$\sqsupseteq$ {second fact above}

$$sa^\omega ze'$$

$\sqsupseteq$ {assumption $e \sqsubseteq ze'$}

$$sa^\omega e$$

and the proof is finished.

The classical rule for data refinement of action systems is now only a slight variation of (26), with explicitly guarded actions and the standard exit guard.

7   Reasoning about Distributed Systems

A distributed system can be modeled in Kleene Algebra as an iteration of a choice $(x \sqcap y \sqcap \ldots)^*$. One of the most important features of a distributed system is what units can be thought of as executed as an atomic unit, even though this is not directly visible from the form of the system. The following basic *separation theorem* illustrates the basics of this kind of reasoning:

$$\text{if } xy \sqsubseteq yx \text{ then } (x \sqcap y)^* = x^* y^* \text{ and } (x \sqcap y)^\omega = x^\omega y^\omega \tag{27}$$

Cohen [12] investigates a number of more elaborate separation theorems in KAT, most of which can also be proved to hold in DRA (in some cases with slight variations to account for the fact that $x\top = \top$ is not an axiom of DRA). Two useful examples are the following:

$$xy^* \sqsubseteq yx \;\Rightarrow\; (x \sqcap y)^\omega = x^\omega y^\omega \tag{28}$$
$$x(x \sqcap y) \sqsubseteq yx \;\Rightarrow\; (x \sqcap y)^\omega = x^\omega y^\omega \tag{29}$$

as well as the following more involved one:

$$y\top = \top \;\wedge\; zx = \top \;\wedge\; (x \sqcap z)y^* \sqsubseteq yx \;\Rightarrow\; (x \sqcap y \sqcap z)^\omega = x^\omega (y \sqcap z)^\omega \tag{30}$$

(here we need the condition $y\top = \top$ which in Cohen's version is an axiom).

Back's *atomicity refinement theorem* for action systems [4] was originally proved using tedious reasoning over state sequences and later using more algebraic predicate transformer reasoning [7]. It is an interesting challenge to formulate and prove the same theorem in our purely algebraic framework. Assume that

(i) $s = sq$, $a = qa$ and $qb = \top$,
(ii) $br \sqsubseteq rb$, $lr \sqsubseteq rl$ and $qr \sqsubseteq rq$,
(iii) $la \sqsubseteq al$, $lb \sqsubseteq bl$ and $lq \sqsubseteq ql$,
(iv) $b^\omega = b^*$ and $l^\omega = l^*$.

Then

$$s(ab^\omega q \sqcap r \sqcap l)^\omega \sqsubseteq s(a \sqcap b \sqcap r \sqcap l)^\omega q \qquad (31)$$

Here the main adjustment that we have had to make is that we require that the action l cannot be repeated indefinitely ($l^\omega = l^*$) while the original formulation assumed that l was continuous.

An outline of the proof is as follows (a detailed proof can be found in Appendix B):

$$s(a \sqcap b \sqcap l \sqcap r)^\omega q$$
$$= \{\text{separation}\}$$
$$sl^\omega(a \sqcap b \sqcap r)^\omega q$$
$$= \{\text{separation and decomposition}\}$$
$$sl^\omega b^\omega r^\omega (ab^\omega r^\omega)^\omega q$$
$$= \{\text{assumption } a = qa, \text{ leapfrog}\}$$
$$sl^\omega b^\omega r^\omega q(ab^\omega r^\omega q)^\omega$$
$$\sqsupseteq \{\text{commutativity}\}$$
$$sl^\omega r^\omega (ab^\omega qr^\omega)^\omega$$
$$= \{\text{decomposition and separation}\}$$
$$s(ab^\omega q \sqcap l \sqcap r)^\omega$$

Cohen describes a variation of this theorem and verifies it in his Omega Algebra [12]. In DRA, his theorem can be approximated as follows: Assume that

(i) $yr \sqsubseteq rpy$, $ly \sqsubseteq ypl$ and $lr \sqsubseteq rpl$
(ii) $prp^- = \top$ and $plp^- = \top$
(iii) $y\top = \top$ and $r\top = \top$

Then

$$(y \sqcap r \sqcap l)^\omega = (pl)^\omega(y \sqcap p^-l \sqcap rp^-)^\omega(rp)^\omega \qquad (32)$$

Here it is in particular worth noting that the conditions $y\top = \top$ and $r\top = \top$ (which are true in all Kleene Algebras) must be stated explicitly in DRA. The fact that we have two notions of correctness also highlights a difference between the correctness assumptions in Back's original theorem (weak correctness) and Cohen's version (total correctness).

8   Conclusion

We have described an algebra for reasoning about demonically nondeterministic programs in a total correctness and refinement framework. This algebra, DRA, is similar to Kleene Algebra with Tests, which is suitable for reasoning about partial correctness and equivalence.

Although our approach is similar to Cohen's Omega Algebra [12], there are important differences. Cohen introduces an iteration operator similar to our ω but he keeps all KA axioms, which means that his framework is really for partial correctness. Also, Cohen explicitly avoids guarded loops while we think they provide the best link between KA-style algebra and reasoning about realistic programs.

The applications and examples given here are all on the level of program structures. However, it is also possible to combine the kind of reasoning illustrated here with detailed reasoning about concrete programs, with assignments and other basic statements, as shown for KAT by Kozen and Patron [19]. For such reasoning, we have made a small experimental tool based on the HOL theorem prover (in fact, the soundness of all the axioms of DRA with respect to the conjunctive predicate transformers was also verified in full detail using HOL).

This paper was inspired by joint work with R.J.R. Back [7] where some of the results presented here were derived within the predicate transformer model. There, the iteration operators were defined using least and greatest fixpoints. The same kind of reasoning is possible within other calculi with explicit fixpoint operators [1,14], but we think our more abstract and algebraic investigation is worthwhile, without explicit assumptions about the underlying mathematical structure.

Many variations and extensions of DRA are possible. Initial experiments indicate that a slight variation of DRA, with infinite iteration x^∞ (our $x^\omega\top$) as primitive, would be suitable for reasoning in Hayes's Real-Time Refinement Calculus [16]. We could also extend our algebra to include monotonic predicate transformers (the domain of the full Refinement Calculus, with angelic as well as demonic nondeterminism) by dropping right distributivity, as well as isolation and right $*$-induction. Then many of the basic properties of KAT and DRA no longer hold and the duality between guards and assertions breaks down (and consequently the duality between correctness and context information). One step even further would be to introduce angelic choice $\sqcup$ as a separate operator. Then we would have a lattice structure with full duality and guards and assertions would have equal status (be definable in terms of the other).

References

1. C. Aarts et al. Fixpoint calculus. *Information Processing Letters*, 53(3), February 1995.
2. R. J. Back and J. von Wright. Encoding, decoding, and data refinement. *Formal Aspects of Computing*, 12(5):313–349, 2000.
3. R.J. Back. *Correctness Preserving Program Refinements: Proof Theory and Applications*, volume 131 of *Mathematical Centre Tracts*. Mathematical Centre, Amsterdam, 1980.
4. R.J. Back. Refining atomicity in parallel algorithms. In *PARLE Conference on Parallel Architectures and Languages Europe*, Eindhoven, the Netherlands, June 1989. Springer-Verlag.
5. R.J. Back and K. Sere. Stepwise refinement of action systems. *Structured Programming*, 12:17–30, 1991.

6. R.J. Back and J. von Wright. *Refinement Calculus: A Systematic Introduction.* Springer-Verlag, 1998.
7. R.J. Back and J. von Wright. Reasoning algebraically about loops. *Acta Informatica*, 36:295–334, 1999.
8. R.C. Backhouse and B.A. Carré. Regular algebra applied to path finding problems. *Journal Inst. Math. Appl.*, 15:161–186, 1975.
9. J.W. de Bakker. *Mathematical Theory of Program Correctness.* Prentice-Hall, 1980.
10. W. Chen and J.T. Udding. Program inversion: more than fun! Report CS 8903, Department of Mathematics and Computer Science, University of Groningen, 1988.
11. E. Cohen. Hypotheses in Kleene Algebra. Unpublished manuscript, Telcordia, 1994.
12. E. Cohen. Separation and reduction. In *Mathematics of Program Construction*, volume 1837 of *Lecture Notes in Computer Science*, Portugal, July 2000. Springer-Verlag.
13. E.W. Dijkstra. *A Discipline of Programming.* Prentice-Hall International, 1976.
14. R.M. Dijkstra. Computation calculus bridging a formalization gap. *Science of Computer Programming*, 37:3–36, 20000.
15. D. Gries. *The Science of Programming.* Springer-Verlag, New York, 1981.
16. I.J. Hayes. Reasoning about real-time repetitions: Terminating and nonterminating. Techn. Rep. 01-04, Software Verification Research Centre, The University of Queensland, February 2001.
17. D. Kozen. Kleene algebra with tests. *ACM Transactions on Programming Languages and Systems*, 19(3):427–443, 1999.
18. D. Kozen. On Hoare logic and Kleene algebra with tests. *ACM Transactions on Computational Logic*, 1(1):60–76, 2000.
19. D. Kozen and M-C. Patron. Certification of compiler optimizations using Kleene Algebra with tests. In *1st International Conference on Computational logic,* volume 1861 of *Lecture Notes in Artificial Intelligence*, pages 568–582, London, July 2000. Springer-Verlag.
20. M.S. Manasse and C.G. Nelson. Correct compilation of control structures. Techn. Memo. 11271-840909-09TM, AT&T Bell Laboratories, September 1984.
21. C.C. Morgan. *Programming from Specifications.* Prentice-Hall, 1990.
22. J.L.A. van de Snepscheut. On lattice theory and program semantics. Technical Report CS-TR-93-19, Caltech, Pasadena, California, USA, 1993.
23. J. von Wright. Program inversion in the refinement calculus. *Information Processing Letters*, 37(2):95–100, January 1991.

A   Axioms of Kleene Algebra

The axioms of Kleene Algebra are the following:

$$x(yz) = (xy)z \qquad\qquad\qquad\qquad (associativity)$$
$$1x = x \qquad\qquad x1 = x \qquad\qquad (unit)$$
$$x + (y + z) = (x + y) + z \qquad\qquad\qquad (associativity)$$
$$0 + x = x \qquad\qquad\qquad\qquad (unit)$$
$$x + y = y + x \qquad\qquad\qquad\qquad (commutativity)$$
$$x + x = x \qquad\qquad\qquad\qquad (idempotence)$$
$$x(y + z) = xy + xz \qquad (x + y)z = xz + yz \qquad (distributivity)$$
$$0x = 0 \qquad\qquad x0 = 0 \qquad\qquad (preemption)$$
$$x^* = xx^* + 1 \qquad\qquad\qquad\qquad (unfolding)$$

plus the following rules:

$$xz + y \le z \Rightarrow x^*y \le z \qquad zx + y \le z \Rightarrow yx^* \le z \qquad (induction)$$

where the ordering $\le$ is defined by $x \le y \equiv x + y = y$.

Traditionally, the $x^* = x^*x + 1$ (dual unfolding) is also given as an axiom, but it can be derived from those given above.

B   Proofs

Proof of Dual Unfolding (1)

We first have

$$x^\omega \sqsubseteq x^\omega x \sqcap 1$$
$$\Leftarrow \{\text{induction}\}$$
$$x(x^\omega x \sqcap 1) \sqcap 1 \sqsubseteq x^\omega x \sqcap 1$$
$$\equiv \{\text{unfolding on rhs}\}$$
$$x(x^\omega x \sqcap 1) \sqcap 1 \sqsubseteq (xx^\omega \sqcap 1)x \sqcap 1$$
$$\equiv \{\text{distributivity}\}$$
$$\text{true}$$

and then

$$x^\omega x \sqcap 1 \sqsubseteq x^\omega$$
$$\equiv \{\text{unfolding on rhs}\}$$
$$x^\omega x \sqcap 1 \sqsubseteq xx^\omega \sqcap 1$$
$$\Leftarrow \{\text{monotonicity}\}$$
$$x^\omega x \sqsubseteq xx^\omega$$
$$\Leftarrow \{\text{induction}\}$$

$$xxx^\omega \sqcap x \sqsubseteq xx^\omega$$
$= \{\text{unfolding on rhs}\}$
$$xxx^\omega \sqcap x \sqsubseteq x(xx^\omega \sqcap 1)$$
$\equiv \{\text{distributivity}\}$
   true

Proof of Leapfrog (2)

First,

$$(xy)^\omega x \sqsubseteq x(yx)^\omega$$
$\Leftarrow \{\text{induction}\}$
$$xyx(yx)^\omega \sqcap x \sqsubseteq x(yx)^\omega$$
$\equiv \{\text{unfolding on rhs}\}$
$$xyx(yx)^\omega \sqcap x \sqsubseteq x(yx(yx)^\omega \sqcap 1)$$
$\equiv \{\text{distributivity}\}$
   true

and then

$$x(yx)^\omega \sqsubseteq (xy)^\omega x$$
$\equiv \{\text{unfolding on rhs, distributivity}\}$
$$x(yx)^\omega \sqsubseteq xy(xy)^\omega x \sqcap x$$
$\Leftarrow \{\text{distributivity, monotonicity}\}$
$$(yx)^\omega \sqsubseteq y(xy)^\omega x \sqcap 1$$
$\Leftarrow \{\text{first half of this proof}\}$
$$(yx)^\omega \sqsubseteq (yx)^\omega yx \sqcap 1$$
$= \{\text{dual unfolding (1)}\}$
   true

Proof of Decomposition (3)

First,

$$(x \sqcap y)^\omega \sqsubseteq x^\omega(yx^\omega)^\omega$$
$\Leftarrow \{\text{induction, distributivity}\}$
$$xx^\omega(yx^\omega)^\omega \sqcap yx^\omega(yx^\omega)^\omega \sqcap 1 \sqsubseteq x^\omega(yx^\omega)^\omega$$
$\equiv \{\text{folding on lhs}\}$
$$xx^\omega(yx^\omega)^\omega \sqcap (yx^\omega)^\omega \sqsubseteq x^\omega(yx^\omega)^\omega$$
$\equiv \{\text{distributivity, folding on lhs}\}$
   true

For the reverse direction we first note

$$(x \sqcap y)^\omega$$
$$= \{\text{unfolding, distributivity}\}$$
$$x(x \sqcap y)^\omega \sqcap y(x \sqcap y)^\omega \sqcap 1$$

from which we get

$$x^\omega(y(x \sqcap y)^\omega \sqcap 1) \sqsubseteq (x \sqcap y)^\omega$$

by induction (with $y(x \sqcap y)^\omega \sqcap 1$ for y and $(x \sqcap y)^\omega$ for z). Now,

$$x^\omega(yx^\omega)^\omega \sqsubseteq (x \sqcap y)^\omega$$
$$\Leftarrow \{\text{preceding derivation}\}$$
$$x^\omega(yx^\omega)^\omega \sqsubseteq x^\omega(y(x \sqcap y)^\omega \sqcap 1)$$
$$\Leftarrow \{\text{monotonicity}\}$$
$$(yx^\omega)^\omega \sqsubseteq y(x \sqcap y)^\omega \sqcap 1$$
$$\Leftarrow \{\text{induction}\}$$
$$yx^\omega(y(x \sqcap y)^\omega \sqcap 1) \sqcap 1 \sqsubseteq y(x \sqcap y)^\omega \sqcap 1$$
$$\Leftarrow \{\text{monotonicity}\}$$
$$x^\omega(y(x \sqcap y)^\omega \sqcap 1) \sqsubseteq (x \sqcap y)^\omega$$
$$\Leftarrow \{\text{induction}\}$$
$$x(x \sqcap y)^\omega \sqcap y(x \sqcap y)^\omega \sqcap 1 \sqsubseteq (x \sqcap y)^\omega$$
$$\equiv \{\text{unfolding, distributivity}\}$$
$$\text{true}$$

Proof of (4)

$$(x \sqcap y)^\omega$$
$$= \{\text{decomposition (3)}\}$$
$$(y^\omega x)^\omega y^\omega$$
$$= \{\text{unfold, distributivity}\}$$
$$y^\omega x(y^\omega x)^\omega y^\omega \sqcap y^\omega$$
$$= \{\text{isolation, distributivity, preemption}\}$$
$$y^* x(y^\omega x)^\omega y^\omega \sqcap y^\omega \top \sqcap y^\omega$$
$$= \{\text{distributivity}, \top \text{ is unit for } \sqcap\}$$
$$y^* x(y^\omega x)^\omega y^\omega \sqcap y^\omega$$
$$= \{\text{decomposition (3)}\}$$
$$y^* x(x \sqcap y)^\omega \sqcap y^\omega$$

Proof of (5)

We have $y^*x(x \sqcap y)^\omega \sqcap y^\omega \sqsubseteq (x \sqcap y)^\omega$ by (4), and from this $(y^*x)^\omega y^\omega \sqsubseteq (x \sqcap y)^\omega$ follows by induction. The reverse refinement follows by

$$(x \sqcap y)^\omega$$
$$= \{\text{decomposition (3)}\}$$
$$y^\omega (xy^\omega)^\omega$$
$$= \{\text{leapfrog (2)}\}$$
$$(y^\omega x)^\omega y^\omega$$
$$\sqsubseteq \{\text{general rule } y^\omega \sqsubseteq y^*\}$$
$$(y^*x)^\omega y^\omega$$

Proof of (8)

First,

$$\perp \sqsubseteq x$$
$$\Leftarrow \{\text{definition } \perp = 1^\omega, \text{ induction}\}$$
$$1x \sqcap 1 \sqsubseteq x$$
$$\equiv \{1 \text{ is unit, definition of } \sqsubseteq\}$$
$$\text{true}$$

and $\perp \sqcap x = \perp$ follows immediately by the definition of the ordering $\sqsubseteq$.

Proof of (9)

We have

$$\perp x \sqsubseteq \perp$$
$$\Leftarrow \{\text{definition } \perp = 1^\omega, \text{ induction}\}$$
$$1\perp \sqcap x \sqsubseteq 1$$
$$\Leftarrow \{1 \text{ is unit, } \perp \text{ is bottom (8)}\}$$
$$\text{true}$$

and the reverse refinement $\perp \sqsubseteq \perp x$ follows directly from (8).

Proof of (10)

If $p^\circ x \sqsubseteq y$, then

$$py \sqsupseteq pp^\circ x = pp^- \perp x \sqcap px \sqsupseteq px \sqsupseteq x$$

and if $x \sqsubseteq py$, then

$$p^\circ x \sqsubseteq p^\circ py = p^- \perp py \sqcap py \sqsubseteq p^- y \sqcap py = y$$

The proof of the other connection is similar.

Proof of Correctness Characterisations (Section 3.1)

First, if $px = pxq$ then

$$px \;=\; pxq \;\sqsupseteq\; 1xq \;=\; xq$$

and if $xq \sqsubseteq px$ then

$$px \;=\; px1 \;\sqsubseteq\; pxq$$

and

$$pxq \;\sqsubseteq\; ppx \;=\; px$$

which shows that the two characterisations of weak correctness are equivalent.

Next, if $pxq^- = \top$, then

$$xq^- \;=\; pxq^- \sqcap p^-xq^- \;=\; p^-xq^- \;\sqsupseteq\; p^-\bot$$

and if $p^-\bot \sqsubseteq xq^-$, then

$$pxq^- \;\sqsupseteq\; pp^-\bot \;=\; \top$$

so the two characterisations of total correctness are equivalent.

Now, if $pxq^- = \top$, then

$$px \;=\; pxq \sqcap pxq^- \;=\; pxq$$

so total correctness implies weak correctness. On the other hand, choosing $x = \bot$ and $p = q = 1$, we have $px = pxq$ but $pxq^- \neq \top$, so the two notions of correctness are not equivalent.

Proof of (13)

We have

$$x^\omega p \sqsubseteq px^\omega$$
$\Leftarrow \{\text{induction}\}$
$$xpx^\omega \sqcap p \sqsubseteq px^\omega$$
$\equiv \{\text{unfolding on right-hand side, distributivity}\}$
$$xpx^\omega \sqcap p \sqsubseteq pxx^\omega \sqcap p$$
$\Leftarrow \{\text{monotonicity}\}$
$$xp \sqsubseteq px$$

Detailed Proof of (14)

Because W is assumed to be well-founded, we can use the principle of well-founded induction.

$$(\forall n \bullet (\forall m < n \bullet P(m)) \Rightarrow P(n)) \Rightarrow (\forall n \bullet P(n))$$

With $z_n \sqsubseteq x^\omega y$ for $P(n)$, we have

$$(\forall n \bullet (\forall m < n \bullet z_m \sqsubseteq x^\omega y) \Rightarrow z_n \sqsubseteq x^\omega y) \Rightarrow (\forall n \bullet z_n \sqsubseteq x^\omega y)$$

and so we want to prove the antecedent of this implication, assuming

$$(\forall n \bullet (z_n \sqsubseteq x \bot \sqcap y) \vee (\exists m < n \bullet z_n \sqsubseteq x z_m \sqcap y))$$

Thus we let n be arbitrary and assume $(\forall m < n \bullet z_m \sqsubseteq x^\omega y)$. If the first disjunct of the assumption above holds, then we get

$$z_n$$
$$\sqsubseteq \{\text{assumption}\}$$
$$x \bot \sqcap y$$
$$\sqsubseteq \{\text{monotonicity}, \bot \text{ is bottom}\}$$
$$x x^\omega y \sqcap y$$
$$= \{\text{distributivity, unfolding}\}$$
$$x^\omega y$$

If on the other hand the second disjunct of holds, then we know there is an $m < n$ such that

$$z_n$$
$$\sqsubseteq \{\text{assumption}\}$$
$$x z_m \sqcap y$$
$$\sqsubseteq \{\text{assumption}\}$$
$$x x^\omega y \sqcap y$$
$$= \{\text{distributivity, unfolding}\}$$
$$x^\omega y$$

and the proof is finished.

Proof of (19)

Assuming x' inv x and y' inv y we have

$$x y y' x'$$
$$\sqsupseteq \{\text{assumption } y' \text{ inv } y, \text{ distributivity}\}$$
$$x y \top x' \sqcap x x'$$
$$\sqsupseteq \{\text{assumption } x' \text{ inv } x, \text{ preemption}\}$$
$$x y \top \sqcap x \top \sqcap 1$$
$$= \{\text{distributivity}, \top \text{ is top}\}$$
$$x y \top \sqcap 1$$

Proof of (20)

Assuming x' inv x and y' inv y and $x = xp$ and $y = yp^-$ we have

$$(x \sqcap y)(px' \sqcap p^- y')$$
$= \{\text{distributivity}\}$
$$xpx' \sqcap xp^- y' \sqcap ypx' \sqcap yp^- y'$$
$= \{\text{assumptions}\}$
$$xx' \sqcap xpp^- y' \sqcap yp^- px' \sqcap yy'$$
$\sqsupseteq \{\text{assumptions, guard properties, preemption}\}$
$$x\top \sqcap 1 \sqcap x\top \sqcap y\top \sqcap y\top \sqcap 1$$
$\sqsupseteq \{\text{simplify, distributivity}\}$
$$(x \sqcap y)\top \sqcap 1$$

Proof of (24)

For strong iteration we have

$$x^\omega z \sqsubseteq z y^\omega$$
$\Leftarrow \{\text{induction}\}$
$$xzy^\omega \sqcap z \sqsubseteq z y^\omega$$
$\equiv \{\text{unfolding on rhs, distributivity}\}$
$$xzy^\omega \sqcap z \sqsubseteq zyy^\omega \sqcap z$$
$\Leftarrow \{\text{monotonicity}\}$
$$xz \sqsubseteq zy$$

and the proof for weak iteration is similar.

Proof of (25)

We have

$$zx^* \sqsubseteq y^* z$$
$\Leftarrow \{\text{induction}\}$
$$zx^* \sqsubseteq yzx^* \sqcap z$$
$\equiv \{\text{unfolding on lhs, distributivity}\}$
$$zxx^* \sqcap z \sqsubseteq yzx^* \sqcap z$$
$\Leftarrow \{\text{monotonicity}\}$
$$zx \sqsubseteq yz$$

Proof of (27)

For strong iteration, we first have

$$(x \sqcap y)^\omega$$
$$= \{\text{general rule } x^\omega = x^\omega x^\omega\}$$
$$(x \sqcap y)^\omega (x \sqcap y)^\omega$$
$$\sqsubseteq \{\text{general rule } x \sqcap y \sqsubseteq x\}$$
$$x^\omega y^\omega$$

Now

$$x^\omega y^\omega \sqsubseteq (x \sqcap y)^\omega$$
$$\Leftarrow \{\text{induction}\}$$
$$x(x \sqcap y)^\omega \sqcap y^\omega \sqsubseteq (x \sqcap y)^\omega$$
$$\equiv \{\text{special unfolding (4)}\}$$
$$x(x \sqcap y)^\omega \sqcap y^\omega \sqsubseteq y^* x(x \sqcap y)^\omega \sqcap y^\omega$$
$$\Leftarrow \{\text{monotonicity}\}$$
$$x(x \sqcap y)^\omega \sqsubseteq y^* x(x \sqcap y)^\omega$$
$$\equiv \{\text{general rule } x^\omega = x^* x^\omega\}$$
$$x(x \sqcap y)^* (x \sqcap y)^\omega \sqsubseteq y^* x(x \sqcap y)^\omega$$
$$\Leftarrow \{\text{monotonicity, basic fact } x \sqcap y \sqsubseteq y\}$$
$$xy^* \sqsubseteq y^* x$$
$$\Leftarrow \{\text{commutativity (25)}\}$$
$$xy \sqsubseteq yx$$

The proof for weak iteration is similar (but simpler).

Proof of (28)

$$(x \sqcap y)^\omega$$
$$= \{\text{decomposition (5)}\}$$
$$(y^* x)^\omega y^\omega$$
$$\sqsupseteq \{\text{general rule } 1 \sqsubseteq y^*\}$$
$$y^* (y^* x)^\omega y^\omega$$
$$\sqsupseteq \{xy^* = x(y^*)^* \sqsubseteq y^* x = y^* y^* x \text{ by (25), then use (24)}\}$$
$$x^\omega y^* y^\omega$$
$$\sqsupseteq \{\text{general rule } y^* y^\omega = y^\omega\}$$
$$x^\omega y^\omega$$

Proof of (29)

We have

$$x^\omega y^\omega \sqsubseteq (x \sqcap y)^\omega$$
$\Leftarrow \{\text{induction}\}$
$$x(x \sqcap y)^\omega \sqcap y^\omega \sqsubseteq (x \sqcap y)^\omega$$
$\equiv \{\text{general rule } z^\omega = z^* z^\omega \text{ use (4) on rhs}\}$
$$x(x \sqcap y)^*(x \sqcap y)^\omega \sqcap y^\omega \sqsubseteq y^* x(x \sqcap y)^\omega \sqcap y^\omega$$
$\Leftarrow \{\text{monotonicity}\}$
$$x(x \sqcap y)^* \sqsubseteq y^* x$$
$\Leftarrow \{\text{commutativity (25)}\}$
$$x(x \sqcap y) \sqsubseteq yx$$

and so $x^\omega y^\omega \sqsubseteq (x \sqcap y)^\omega$ follows by induction, while the reverse refinement always holds (see the proof of (27)).

Proof of (30)

First,

$$y(x \sqcap y^* z)$$
$= \{\text{distributivity}\}$
$$yx \sqcap yy^* z$$
$\sqsupseteq \{\text{assumption } (x \sqcap z)y^* \sqsubseteq yx\}$
$$(x \sqcap z)y^* \sqcap yy^* z$$
$\sqsupseteq \{\text{general rule } y^* \sqsubseteq 1\}$
$$(x \sqcap y^* z)y^* \sqcap yy^* z$$
$\sqsupseteq \{y^* z y^* \sqsubseteq y^* z = yy^* z \sqcap 1 \sqsubseteq yy^* z\}$
$$(x \sqcap y^* z)y^* \sqcap y^* z y^*$$
$= \{\text{distributivity, idempotence}\}$
$$(x \sqcap y^* z)y^*$$

and so

$$(x \sqcap y \sqcap z)^\omega$$
$\sqsupseteq \{\text{general rule } y^* \sqsubseteq 1\}$
$$(x \sqcap y \sqcap y^* z)^\omega$$
$= \{\text{separation (28), preceding derivation}\}$
$$(x \sqcap y^* z)^\omega y^\omega$$
$= \{\text{separation (27), } xy^* z \sqsubseteq \top = = y^* zx \text{ using } y\top = \top \text{ and } zx = \top\}$
$$x^\omega (y^* z)^\omega y^\omega$$

$= \{\text{decomposition (5)}\}$

$x^{\omega}(y \sqcap z)^{\omega}$

Detailed Proof of (31)

The main proof is as follows (the hints are expanded below):

$s(a \sqcap b \sqcap l \sqcap r)^{\omega}q$

$= \{\text{step 1: separation}\}$

$sl^{\omega}(a \sqcap b \sqcap r)^{\omega}q$

$= \{\text{step 2: separation and decomposition}\}$

$sl^{\omega}b^{\omega}r^{\omega}(ab^{\omega}r^{\omega})^{\omega}q$

$= \{\text{step 3: assumption } a = qa, \text{ leapfrog}\}$

$sl^{\omega}b^{\omega}r^{\omega}q(ab^{\omega}r^{\omega}q)^{\omega}$

$\sqsupseteq \{\text{step 4: commutativity}\}$

$sl^{\omega}r^{\omega}(ab^{\omega}qr^{\omega})^{\omega}$

$= \{\text{step 5: decomposition and separation}\}$

$s(ab^{\omega}q \sqcap l \sqcap r)^{\omega}$

The individual steps are justified as follows:

Step 1. From $la \sqsubseteq al$, $lb \sqsubseteq bl$ and $lr \sqsubseteq rl$ we get $l(a \sqcap b \sqcap r) \sqsubseteq (a \sqcap b \sqcap r)l$ and so separation (27) can be used.

Step 2.

$(a \sqcap b \sqcap r)^{\omega}$

$= \{\text{decomposition (3)}\}$

$(b \sqcap r)^{\omega}(a(b \sqcap r)^{\omega})^{\omega}$

$= \{\text{separation (27) using } br \sqsubseteq rb\}$

$b^{\omega}r^{\omega}(ab^{\omega}r^{\omega})^{\omega}$

Step 3.

$(ab^{\omega}r^{\omega})^{\omega}q$

$= \{\text{assumption } a = qa\}$

$(qab^{\omega}r^{\omega})^{\omega}q$

$= \{\text{leapfrog (2)}\}$

$q(ab^{\omega}r^{\omega}q)^{\omega}$

Step 4.

$$sl^\omega b^\omega r^\omega q(ab^\omega r^\omega q)^\omega$$

$= \{$assumptions $qr \sqsubseteq rq$ and $r^\omega = r^*$, (25)$\}$

$$sl^\omega b^\omega r^\omega q(ab^\omega qr^\omega)^\omega$$

$= \{$general rule $q \sqsupseteq 1$, assumption $s = sq\}$

$$sql^\omega b^\omega r^\omega (ab^\omega qr^\omega)^\omega$$

$\sqsupseteq \{$assumption $lq \sqsubseteq ql$, (25)$\}$

$$sl^\omega qb^\omega r^\omega (ab^\omega qr^\omega)^\omega$$

$= \{$assumption $qb = \top$ implies $qb^\omega = q$, general rule $q \sqsupseteq 1\}$

$$sl^\omega r^\omega (ab^\omega qr^\omega)^\omega$$

Step 5.

$$l^\omega r^\omega (ab^\omega qr^\omega)^\omega$$

$= \{$decomposition (3)$\}$

$$l^\omega (ab^\omega q \sqcap r)^\omega$$

$= \{$separation (27); see argument below$\}$

$$(ab^\omega q \sqcap l \sqcap r)^\omega$$

Here the second step requires $l(ab^\omega q \sqcap r) \sqsubseteq (ab^\omega q \sqcap r)l$ which follows from the assumption $lr \sqsubseteq rl$ and

$$l(ab^\omega q \sqcap r)$$

$\sqsubseteq \{$distributivity, assumptions $la \sqsubseteq al$ and $lr \sqsubseteq rl\}$

$$alb^\omega q \sqcap rl$$

$\sqsubseteq \{$assumptions $lb \sqsubseteq bl$ and $b^\omega = b^*$, commutativity (25)$\}$

$$ab^\omega lq \sqcap rl$$

$\sqsubseteq \{$assumption $lq \sqsubseteq ql$, distributivity$\}$

$$(ab^\omega q \sqcap r)l$$

Proof of (32)

The main proof is as follows:

$$(y \sqcap r \sqcap l)^\omega$$

$= \{$guard properties$\}$

$$(pl \sqcap p^- l \sqcap y \sqcap r)^\omega$$

$= \{$step A: separation$\}$

$$(pl)^\omega (p^- l \sqcap y \sqcap r)^\omega$$

$= \{$guard properties$\}$

$$(pl)^\omega (p^- l \sqcap y \sqcap pr \sqcap p^- r)^\omega$$
$$= \{\text{step B: separation}\}$$
$$(pl)^\omega (p^- l \sqcap y \sqcap rp^-)^\omega (rp)^\omega$$

The details of the two big steps in this proof are as follows.

Step A. Here (30) can be used since we assumed $y\top = \top$ and $r\top = \top$ and $p^- lpl = \top l = \top$, and

$$(pl \sqcap p^- l)(y \sqcap r)^*$$
$$\sqsubseteq \{\text{general rule } x^* \sqsubseteq x, \text{ guard properties, distributivity}\}$$
$$ly \sqcap lr$$
$$\sqsubseteq \{\text{assumptions (i), distributivity}\}$$
$$(y \sqcap r)pl$$

Step B. Here (29) can be used since

$$rp(y \sqcap rp^- \sqcap p^- l)$$
$$= \{\text{general rule } x^* \sqsubseteq x, \text{ guard properties, distributivity}\}$$
$$rpy \sqcap rprp^- \sqcap rpp^- l$$
$$= \{\text{guard properties, assumptions (ii) and } r\top = \top\}$$
$$rpy$$
$$\sqsupseteq \{\text{assumption (i), general guard property } p \sqcap p^- = 1, \text{ distributivity}\}$$
$$y(rp \sqcap rp^-)$$
$$\sqsupseteq \{\text{general strengthening}\}$$
$$(y \sqcap rp^- \sqcap p^- l)(rp \sqcap (y \sqcap rp^- \sqcap p^- l))$$

Author Index

Lecture Notes in Computer Science

For information about Vols. 1–2287
please contact your bookseller or Springer-Verlag

Vol. 2323: À. Frohner (Ed.), Object-Oriented Technology. Proceedings, 2001. IX, 225 pages. 2002.

Vol. 2324: T. Field, P.G. Harrison, J. Bradley, U. Harder (Eds.), Computer Performance Evaluation. Proceedings, 2002. XI, 349 pages. 2002.

Vol 2326: D. Grigoras, A. Nicolau. B. Toursel, B. Folliot (Eds.), Advanced Environments, Tools, and Applications for Cluster Computing. Proceedings. 2001. XIII, 321 pages. 2002.

Vol. 2327: H.P. Zima, K. Joe, M. Sato, Y. Seo, M. Shimasaki (Eds.), High Performance Computing. Proceedings, 2002. XV, 564 pages. 2002.

Vol. 2328: R. Wyrzykowski, J. Dongarra, M. Paprzycki, J. Waśniewski (Eds.), Parallel Processing and Applied Mathematics. Proceedings, 2001. XIX, 915 pages. 2002.

Vol. 2329: P.M.A. Sloot, C.J.K. Tan, J.J. Dongarra, A.G. Hoekstra (Eds.), Computational Science – ICCS 2002. Proceedings, Part I. XLI, 1095 pages. 2002.

Vol. 2330: P.M.A. Sloot, C.J.K. Tan, J.J. Dongarra, A.G. Hoekstra (Eds.), Computational Science – ICCS 2002. Proceedings, Part II. XLI, 1115 pages. 2002.

Vol. 2331: P.M.A. Sloot, C.J.K. Tan, J.J. Dongarra, A.G. Hoekstra (Eds.), Computational Science – ICCS 2002. Proceedings, Part III. XLI, 1227 pages. 2002.

Vol. 2332: L. Knudsen (Ed.), Advances in Cryptology – EUROCRYPT 2002. Proceedings, 2002. XII, 547 pages. 2002.

Vol. 2334: G. Carle. M. Zitterbart (Eds.). Protocols for High Speed Networks. Proceedings, 2002. X, 267 pages. 2002.

Vol. 2335: M. Butler, L. Petre, K. Sere (Eds.), Integrated Formal Methods. Proceedings, 2002. X, 401 pages. 2002.

Vol. 2336: M.-S. Chen, P.S. Yu, B. Liu (Eds.), Advances in Knowledge Discovery and Data Mining. Proceedings, 2002. XIII, 568 pages. 2002. (Subseries LNAI).

Vol. 2337: W.J. Cook, A.S. Schulz (Eds.), Integer Programming and Combinatorial Optimization. Proceedings, 2002. XI, 487 pages. 2002.

Vol. 2338: R. Cohen, B. Spencer (Eds.), Advances in Artificial Intelligence. Proceedings, 2002. X, 197 pages. 2002. (Subseries LNAI).

Vol. 2340: N. Jonoska, N.C. Seeman (Eds.), DNA Computing. Proceedings, 2001. XI, 392 pages. 2002.

Vol. 2342: I. Horrocks, J. Hendler (Eds.), The Semantic Web – ISCW 2002. Proceedings, 2002. XVI, 476 pages. 2002.

Vol. 2345: E. Gregori, M. Conti, A.T. Campbell, G. Omidyar, M. Zukerman (Eds.). NETWORKING 2002. Proceedings, 2002. XXVI, 1256 pages. 2002.

Vol. 2346: H. Unger, T. Böhme, A. Mikler (Eds.), Innovative Internet Computing Systems. Proceedings, 2002. VIII, 251 pages. 2002.

Vol. 2347: P. De Bra, P. Brusilovsky, R. Conejo (Eds.), Adaptive Hypermedia and Adaptive Web-Based Systems. Proceedings, 2002. XV. 615 pages. 2002.

Vol. 2348: A. Banks Pidduck, J. Mylopoulos, C.C. Woo, M. Tamer Ozsu (Eds.). Advanced Information Systems Engineering. Proceedings, 2002. XIV, 799 pages. 2002.

Vol. 2349: J. Kontio, R. Conradi (Eds.), Software Quality – ECSQ 2002. Proceedings, 2002. XIV, 363 pages. 2002.

Vol. 2350: A. Heyden, G. Sparr, M. Nielsen, P. Johansen (Eds.), Computer Vision – ECCV 2002. Proceedings, Part I. XXVIII, 817 pages. 2002.

Vol. 2351: A. Heyden, G. Sparr, M. Nielsen, P. Johansen (Eds.), Computer Vision – ECCV 2002. Proceedings, Part II. XXVIII, 903 pages. 2002.

Vol. 2352: A. Heyden, G. Sparr, M. Nielsen, P. Johansen (Eds.), Computer Vision – ECCV 2002. Proceedings, Part III. XXVIII, 919 pages. 2002.

Vol. 2353: A. Heyden, G. Sparr, M. Nielsen, P. Johansen (Eds.), Computer Vision – ECCV 2002. Proceedings, Part IV. XXVIII, 841 pages. 2002.

Vol. 2358: T. Hendtlass, M. Ali (Eds.), Developments in Applied Artificial Intelligence. Proceedings, 2002 XIII, 833 pages. 2002. (Subseries LNAI).

Vol. 2359: M. Tistarelli, J. Bigun, A.K. Jain (Eds.), Biometric Authentication. Proceedings, 2002. XII, 373 pages. 2002.

Vol. 2360: J. Esparza, C. Lakos (Eds.), Application and Theory of Petri Nets 2002. Proceedings, 2002. X, 445 pages. 2002.

Vol. 2361: J. Blieberger, A. Strohmeier (Eds.), Reliable Software Technologies – Ada-Europe 2002. Proceedings, 2002 XIII, 367 pages. 2002.

Vol. 2363: S.A. Cerri, G. Gouardères, F. Paraguaçu (Eds.), Intelligent Tutoring Systems. Proceedings, 2002. XXVIII, 1016 pages. 2002.

Vol. 2364: F. Roli, J. Kittler (Eds.), Multiple Classifier Systems. Proceedings, 2002. XI, 337 pages. 2002.

Vol. 2366: M.-S. Hacid, Z.W. Raś, D.A. Zighed, Y. Kodratoff (Eds.), Foundations of Intelligent Systems. Proceedings, 2002. XII, 614 pages. 2002. (Subseries LNAI).

Vol. 2367: J. Fagerholm. J. Haataja, J. Järvinen, M. Lyly. P. Råback, V. Savolainen (Eds.), Applied Parallel Computing. Proceedings, 2002. XIV, 612 pages. 2002.

Vol. 2368: M. Penttonen, E. Meineche Schmidt (Eds.), Algorithm Theory – SWAT 2002. Proceedings, 2002. XIV, 450 pages. 2002.

Vol. 2370: J. Bishop (Ed.), Component Deployment. Proceedings, 2002. XII, 269 pages. 2002.

Vol. 2374: B. Magnusson (Ed.), ECOOP 2002 – Object-Oriented Programming. XI, 637 pages. 2002.

Vol. 2382: A. Halevy, A. Gal (Eds.), Next Generation Information Technologies and Systems. Proceedings, 2002. VIII, 169 pages. 2002.

Vol. 2385: J. Calmet, B. Benhamou, O. Caprotti, L. Henocque, V. Sorge (Eds.), Artificial Intelligence, Automated Reasoning, and Symbolic Computation. Proceedings, 2002. XI, 343 pages. 2002. (Subseries LNAI).

Vol. 2386: E.A. Boiten, B. Möller (Eds.), Mathematics of Program Construction. Proceedings, 2002. X, 263 pages. 2002.

Vol. 2389: E. Ranchhod, N.J. Mamede (Eds.), Advances in Natural Language Processing. Proceedings, 2002. XII, 275 pages. 2002. (Subseries LNAI).